HANDBOOK ON RESPONSIBLE LEADERSHIP AND GOVERNANCE IN GLOBAL BUSINESS

Handbook on Responsible Leadership and Governance in Global Business

Edited by

Jonathan P. Doh and Stephen A. Stumpf

Villanova University, USA

Edward Elgar

Cheltenham, UK • Northampton, MA, USA

Published by
Edward Elgar Publishing Limited
Glensanda House
Montpellier Parade
Cheltenham
Glos GL50 1UA
UK

Edward Elgar Publishing, Inc.
136 West Street
Suite 202
Northampton
Massachusetts 01060
USA

A catalogue record for this book
is available from the British Library

ISBN   1 84376 636 1 (cased)

Printed and bound in Great Britain by MPG Books Ltd, Bodmin, Cornwall

Contents

Preface

Ethics, social responsibility, leadership, governance: these are terms that are heard increasingly often in the classroom and in the boardroom, and viewed on the front page of newspapers and magazines. Yet serious attention to the relationships among these important concepts is lacking. This volume was born from a recognition of the need to bring together varying perspectives on leadership, corporate responsibility, professional ethics and governance so as to integrate them in a way that would be of use to managers, educators and researchers.

Paradoxically many companies that have had serious ethical breaches also had leaders who were lauded by the popular press and management consultants, and many had well-developed ethical codes and programs. During their reign, Bernie Ebbers of Worldcom and Kenneth Lay of Enron were among the top-ranked corporate leaders. Enron was frequently cited for its 'innovative' financial practices. During Dennis Kozlowski's tenure as Tyco chairman and chief executive officer (CEO), Tyco was an active member of the Ethics Forum, a group devoted to advancing strong ethical commitments in business. Enron had a strong commitment to philanthropy, having contributed to education, health and other charities. Arthur Andersen provided ethics training for its own employees as well as marketing an ethics practice to other organizations, including business schools. Clearly there was something missing between these commitments and the practices of many individuals within these organizations.

In our view, the missing element was a broad-based and integrated approach to responsible leadership and governance. Although individual commitments to leadership, ethics and social responsibility are evident in most corporations, many companies appear to fall short in combining these duties into an integrated set of policies and culture that guides behavior and decisions. Similarly management research streams in ethics, leadership, social responsibility and governance have examined these issues from many theoretical and practical vantages, but absent in the literature is an integrated contribution that links these disparate perspectives into one, unified approach.

This volume is intended to provide a state-of-the-art presentation of leading thinking on these important issues and include both a review of what we know and a discussion of emerging areas that will require future attention. In assembling these contributions, we sought to provide theoretically grounded insights from the leading scholars in ethics, social responsibility, leadership and governance, and to offer guidance for what constructs and frameworks might help executives and managers to put these perspectives to work. Although authors have drawn on their past research and scholarship, each contribution is fresh, original and prepared exclusively for this outlet. Contributors have sought to integrate one or more of these concepts in order to respond to the overall theme. They all contribute to our emerging understanding of what constitutes responsible leadership and governance, and how it can be made to work in modern organizations.

Many of the contributions summarize the 'state of the literature' within those fields, identify complementary insights and perspectives, discuss areas of conflict and disagreement and include a provocative and stimulating agenda for future investigation. They also point up practical consequences or applications of these perspectives, especially in light of recent developments that have exposed the shortcomings in leadership and governance as it is currently practiced. Several contributions focus specifically on the challenges faced by global companies in developing and maintaining leadership and governance practices that are responsive to different national, institutional and cultural settings.

Effective responsible leadership and governance is essential to the success of any global business. Clearly organizations, their officers and boards, have come under criticism for focusing on a narrow set of financial goals that involve a limited number of stakeholder groups, and for featuring governance structures that are dominated by insider members, lack independence and neglect vital fiduciary and ethical responsibilities. This volume explores the concepts of responsible leadership and governance and their application in the modern global business environment. We hope that it provides a valuable contribution to scholars, researchers and managers around the world.

J.P.D.
S.A.S.

Contributors

John Alexander, Ph.D. is President of the Center for Creative Leadership.

Kim Cameron, Ph.D. is Professor, Organizational Behavior, School of Business, and Professor, Higher Education, School of Education, University of Michigan.

Arran Caza, Management and Organizations, Ross School of Business and Department of Psychology, University of Michigan.

Joanne B. Ciulla, Ph.D. is Professor and Coston Family Chair in Leadership and Ethics, Jepson School of Leadership Studies, University of Richmond.

Kevin D. Clark, Ph.D. is Assistant Professor of Strategic Management, College of Commerce and Finance, Villanova University.

Mary Sully de Luque, Ph.D. is Assistant Professor of Management and Research Fellow in the Garvin Center for Cultures and Languages, Thunderbird, The Garvin School of International Management.

Jonathan P. Doh, Ph.D. is Assistant Professor of Management, Director, Center for Responsible Leadership and Governance, College of Commerce and Finance, Villanova University.

Charles J. Fombrun, Ph.D. is Executive Director of the Reputation Institute.

Robert M. Fulmer, Ph.D. is Distinguished Professor of Strategy, Pepperdine University and Academic Director, Duke Corporate Education.

Mary C. Gentile, Ph.D. is Senior Advisor on the Aspen Institute Business and Society Program.

Michael A. Hitt, Ph.D. is Distinguished Professor, Joe B. Foster Chair in Business Leadership, C.W. and Dorothy Conn Chair in New Ventures, Mays Business School, Texas A&M University.

Robert J. House, Ph.D. is Professor of Management and Joseph Frank Bernstein Professor of Organizational Studies, The Wharton School, University of Pennsylvania.

Shawn D. Howton, Ph.D. is Associate Professor of Finance, College of Commerce and Finance, Villanova University.

Shelly W. Howton, Ph.D. is Associate Professor of Finance, College of Commerce and Finance, Villanova University.

R. Duane Ireland, Ph.D. is Foreman R. and Ruby S. Chair in Business Administration, Professor of Management, Mays Business School, Texas A&M University.

Rakesh Khurana, Ph.D. is Associate Professor of Organizational Behavior, Harvard Business School, Harvard University.

Christine Mallin, Ph.D. is Professor of Corporate Governance and Finance, Director, Centre for Corporate Governance Research, The Birmingham Business School, University of Birmingham, UK.

Victoria B. McWilliams, Ph.D. is Professor of Finance, College of Commerce and Finance, Villanova University.

Andre A. Pekerti, Ph.D. is a Lecturer at the University of Queensland Business School.

Narda R. Quigley, Ph.D. is Assistant Professor of Management, College of Commerce and Finance, Villanova University.

Glenn W. Rowe, Ph.D. is Paul MacPherson Chair in Strategic leadership, Assistant Professor of Strategic Management, Richard Ivey School of Business, University of Western Ontario.

Sonja A. Sackmann, Ph.D. is Director, Institute of Human Resources and Organization Research, and Professor, Department of Economics, Management and Organization Sciences, University Bundeswehr Munich.

Ernest J. Scalberg, Ph.D. is Associate Vice President for External Programs and Dean, Fisher Graduate School of International Business, Monterey Institute of International Studies.

Donald Siegel, Ph.D. is Professor of Economics and Chair, Department of Economics, Rensselaer Polytechnic Institute.

Stephen A. Stumpf, Ph.D. is Fred J. Springer Chair in Business Leadership and Professor of Management, College of Commerce and Finance, Villanova University.

Michael Useem, Ph.D. is William and Jacalyn Egan Professor of Management and Director, Wharton Center for Leadership and Change Management, The Wharton School, University of Pennsylvania.

David A. Waldman, Ph.D. is Professor and Chair of the Department of Management, School of Global Management and Leadership, Arizona State University.

Sandra Waddock, Ph.D. is Professor of Management, Carroll School of Management and Senior Research Fellow, Center for Corporate Citizenship, Boston College.

Meena Wilson, Ph.D. is Enterprise Associate, Design and Evaluation Center for Creative Leadership.

PART I

RESPONSIBLE LEADERSHIP AND GOVERNANCE: CONCEPTUAL FOUNDATIONS AND PRACTICAL REALITIES

1 Towards a framework of responsible leadership and governance

Jonathan P. Doh and Stephen A. Stumpf

Introduction

The American Heritage Dictionary (2000) defines responsibility as follows:

1. Liable to be required to give account, as of one's actions or of the discharge of a duty or trust.
2. Involving personal accountability or ability to act without guidance or superior authority: *a responsible position within the firm.*
3. Able to make moral or rational decisions on one's own and therefore answerable for one's behavior.
4. Able to be trusted or depended upon; reliable.

Governance has been variously defined as follows:

1. The act, process, or power of governing; government: 'Regaining a sense of the state is thus an absolute priority, not only for an effective policy against ... terrorism, but also for governance itself' (Moorhead Kennedy, as cited in the *American Heritage Dictionary of English*).
2. The state of being governed (*The American Heritage Dictionary*, 2000).
3. Exercise of authority; control; government; arrangement (*Webster's Revised Unabridged Dictionary*, 1996, 1998).

Management research in leadership, ethics and in corporate social responsibility (CSR) has evolved somewhat independently. Despite the proliferation of literature on effective leadership, surprisingly little research attention has been devoted to the interaction among leadership traits, ethical behavior and corporate social responsibility, at least within the mainstream leadership literature. Although business ethicists and those studying or advocating corporate social responsibility have advanced perspectives that integrate tenets from leadership research and ethics/social responsibility, these efforts have not, to date, produced an alternative to the standard leadership classifications summarized by Conger and others (charismatic, transformational, transactional and so on). In this chapter, we develop the concept of responsible leadership as a construct that may offer an effective integration of theories of corporate social responsibility, ethics and leadership.

We begin by reviewing literature on leadership that has included a moral or values-based dimension. We then explore literature that has attempted to integrate theories, paradigms and constructs from leadership and ethics. We summarize a selection of research in CSR and in corporate social performance (CSP) that could inform leadership theory and practice. Drawing from the practical definitions listed above, we identify common and complementary themes from the existing theoretical perspectives in leadership theory, ethics and CSR to build a construct of responsible leadership and governance. Such a construct integrates both the personal antecedents of leadership and ethics and organizational characteristics demonstrated in corporate social responsibility, and manifests in specific personal and organizational behaviors of values-based leadership, ethical decision making and quality stakeholder relationships. We believe this conceptualization provides both an integrative and additive contribution to the existing literature base and can guide future scholarship in these areas.

Individual antecedents: leadership and ethics
Leadership has long occupied a prominent place in management research and theory development. The evolution of literature describing leadership has come a long way since Chester Barnard's classic contribution, *The Functions of the Executive* (1938), one of the first management volumes to address leadership issues. Since that time, leadership researchers have offered a range of theories and approaches to understanding the traits, behaviors and influence of leaders.

Early leadership research: traits and situations
Early investigations of leadership focused on individual possession of specific personality traits that define leadership abilities. These include intelligence, birth order, socioeconomic status and child-rearing practices (Bird, 1940; Stogdill, 1948, 1974). Stogdill (1948) identified six groups of individual factors associated with leadership: capacity, achievement, responsibility, participation, status and situation. However he also argued that these characteristics were, by themselves, not sufficient for defining leadership behavior (Stogdill, 1948, p. 64).

Other researchers have maintained that leadership is situational; the environment in which the behavior is taking place is a determinant of the ability of leadership characteristics to flourish. Hoy and Miskel (1987, p. 273) attempted to identify 'distinctive characteristics of the setting to which the leader's success could be attributed'. Hencley (1973, p. 38) argued, 'the situation approach maintains that leadership is determined not so much by the characters of the individuals as by the requirements of social situation'. Hence, if the situational context or environment can be better understood and classified, the likelihood of the exhibition of effective leadership can be better predicted. Hoy and Miskel (1987) identified four areas of leadership that were driven by situational circumstance: structural properties of the organization, organizational climate, role characteristics and subordinate characteristics.

Contemporary leadership research: charismatic and transformational
More recent leadership research has focused on questions surrounding CEO and top management team leadership (House *et al.*, 1991; Klein and House, 1995; Pawar and Eastman, 1997), strategic leadership at the corporate level (Hambrick and Mason, 1984; Hitt and Tyler, 1991; Ireland and Hitt, 1999) and so-called 'transformational' leadership, that is, leadership that prompts a fundamental shift in organizational paradigm (Bass, 1985; Bryman, 1992; Sashkin, 1988; Tichy and Devanna, 1986; Westley and Mintzberg, 1989).

In response to the attention given to leadership in both management research and the popular business press, researchers have addressed various issues associated with the emergence and implications of leadership. The predominant focus has been on the processes of organizational and individual transformation that are associated with leadership. In addressing these issues, researchers have studied leadership's behavioral aspects and the impact of these characteristics on employees and organizations (Bass, 1985; Conger, 1989, 1990; Kanungo, 1988). In the present-day environment, many researchers, practitioners and even broader observers have become fascinated with 'charismatic' leaders (Bryman, 1992; Conger, 1989; Kanungo, 1988), although recent studies have called into question the value of these characteristics to firm success (Khurana, 2002; see also Khurana, Chapter 7 of the present volume).

One traditional definition of a leader is 'someone who occupies a position in a group, influences others in accordance with the role expectation of the position and co-ordinates and directs the group in maintaining itself and reaching its goal' (Ravin and Rubin, 1976, p. 37). Leadership may therefore be defined as a 'process of influence between a leader and his followers to attain group, organizational and societal goals' (Avery and Baker, 1990, p. 453). Such goals would certainly include maintaining an ethical and socially responsible organizational environment and strategy, and both leadership and scholars in the philosophical foundation of management sought to integrate leadership and ethics theory and practice.

Leadership ethics and ethical leadership

Although investigations of the attributes of what makes a leader ethical have occupied academic research and publication for over 30 years (Rost, 1995), over the past decade there have been a number of efforts to integrate these research streams more systematically. Among the characteristics thought to be important in ethical leadership are clarity of vision, strategic insight, relationship management and adaptability (ibid.). Of special importance, many researchers have recognized the need for a coherent ethical foundation which would make legitimate the goals of the organization and justify its actions as it interacts with internal and external stakeholders.

Normative perspectives on ethical leadership

Ciulla (1995) uses normative leadership theories to explore the relationship between ethics and leadership and suggests that one of the most important questions is what criteria should be used to evaluate whether a leader is ethical. She suggests that effective leadership involves both ethics and competence, and that 'ethics is located within the heart of leadership studies' (Ciulla, 1995, p. 6). According to Ciulla, transformational leadership studies should serve as the basis for further research on this topic since empirical data are accumulated in such research.

Following Ciulla's suggestions, researchers have addressed the relationship between perceived leader integrity and transformational leadership, finding a positive relationship between these two variables (Parry and Proctor-Thomson, 2002). A similar relationship was observed between perceived integrity and the demonstration of transformational leadership behaviors. Perceived integrity was also found to have a positive correlation with leader and organizational effectiveness.

Confucianism may be an effective managerial ethic because it is compatible with accepted management practices, it suggests that individuals and organizations are required to make a positive contribution to society, and it recognizes the structure of hierarchy as an important organizational principle and demands moral leadership from managers (Romar, 2002). Confucian morality demands giving respect and dignity to each member of an organization, regardless of status. While these principles reflect the importance of structured leadership, Confucian teachings promote empowerment and trust. The basic premise is that 'an individual's humanity is defined through relationships and interactions with others' (ibid., p. 120). Confucian ethics is based on the concepts of ritual and etiquette, virtue and the Golden Rule. 'Individuals should be held morally responsible for their behavior' and 'the way individuals contribute to the business process, rituals and etiquette, determines how moral the organization is' (ibid., p. 127).

Instrumental perspectives on ethical leadership

A number of researchers have developed typologies, frameworks and instrumental tools to guide classification, assessment and evaluation of ethical leadership. An important dimension of these studies is that the ethical evaluation of leadership requires standards of assessment that are independent of the definition of the leader. A practical approach to resolving this dilemma is the creation of a system in which stakeholders can resolve conflicting rights claims through a method that determines what responsibilities corporate management might have to employees. McCall (2002, p. 133) defines leading as an act 'taken to require some level of buy-in by followers to the leader's goals and methods, strategies and tactics'. If leaders' ethics and values are corrupt, the organization's moral climate will also be contaminated. A method for distinguishing between the rights claimed by both owner and non-owner stakeholders would move us 'toward the range of, and the process for, morally adequate corporate accountability' (ibid., p. 135).

The 'Four Umpires' model examines how four leadership types view reality and perception, and provides a useful example of an effective steward leader (Caldwell *et al.*, 2002). Umpire One (Objective Neutral) is a leader who sees the world characterized by 'clear differences, defined values and precise distinction' (ibid., p. 155). Umpire Two (Unbiased Realist) is much like Umpire One but acknowledges the possibility of random error and distortion. Umpire Three (Subjective Controller) believes that he or she holds the correct moral view. Umpire Three's inherent weakness 'lies in the fundamental assumption of his/her superiority over others' (ibid., 2002, p. 156). Umpire Four, the Facilitating Idealist, strives to oversee the welfare of all stakeholders. This person recognizes the complexity in decision making and values others' point of view and empowers subordinates and seeks solutions that are in the best interests of all concerned parties.

The relationships between leaders and organizations, and the ability of leaders to convey ethical principles throughout an organization, have been another subject of study. One study developed a model of the way active leadership affects conformity in members' ethical decision frameworks using formalism and utilitarianism, studying 36 work groups over a 12-week period (Schminke *et al.*, 2002). Their goal was to determine 'leadership influences on individual ethics, and in particular the decision frameworks individuals employ when facing an ethical dilemma' (ibid., p. 273). They concluded that more active leadership led to conformity in team members' ethical frameworks, both formalist and utilitarian. Group leaders must be careful to see that group members do not automatically conform to ethical standards just for the sake of doing so. Conformity may limit participation if members feel as if their point of view is not aligned with those of the group leader. Results supported the argument that groups may either enhance or reduce the strength of ethical frameworks because of these particular elements.

Waldman and Siegel (in Chapter 11 of this volume) specifically link transformational leadership to social responsibility actions. Building on upper-echelons theory, they contend that charismatic leadership and intellectual stimulation are positively correlated with the tendency of leaders and their organizations to engage in corporate social responsibility. This result is based on two characteristics: charismatic leaders tend to have strong moral beliefs and do not hesitate to extend those beliefs to their organizations, and charismatic leaders attempt to balance interests of all stakeholders (Bass and Steidlemeid, 1999). They find, however, that intellectual stimulation contributes to strategic CSR but not social CSR, but charismatic leadership contributes to neither, challenging the notion that charismatic leaders are also oriented toward greater CSR commitments.

Organizational antecedents: corporate social responsibility, governance and accountability

Organizational moral development is necessarily more complex than the moral development of individuals (Logsdon and Yuthas, 1997). Managerial expectations are influenced by the level of moral development and personal characteristics of the persons holding top management positions in the firm. They are conveyed to other members of the firm through the organizational processes of strategic formulation, and thus eventually embodied in organizational moral norms. Many forces influence both organizational and individual moral development, particularly the 'set of ethical expectations held by top management' (ibid., p. 1218).

Researchers in organizational culture have explored the relationship between individual attitudes and organizational climate. An ethical culture emphasizes 'broad patterns of underlying values, beliefs, and assumptions, [and] the uniqueness of individual social settings' (Trevino *et al.*, p. 451). Ethical culture may be viewed as a subset of organizational culture, a behavioral system controlling ethical or unethical behavior. Ethical climate represents 'an organization's social environment that is consciously perceived by organizational members' (ibid.). While climates may vary in different departments, work climates influence a number of organizational outcomes, including performance and satisfaction. A strong ethical climate is one that aligns organizational and personal interests.

Corporate social responsibility
Study of corporate social responsibility (CSR) offers a complementary perspective on the ethical dimensions of organizations. CSR has been

described using several different definitions. Clarkson (1995) suggested that it is the notion that companies are responsible, not just to their shareholders, but also to other stakeholders (workers, suppliers, environmentalists, communities and so on). McWilliams and Siegel (2001) proposed that CSR is actions taken by the firm intended to further social goods beyond the direct interests of the firm and that which is required by law. CSR has now been internalized and institutionalized in many organizations and national legal settings. It is now a given that executives actively pursue CSR, albeit for a range of motivations, such as self-interest, altruism, strategic advantage and political gain.

There is an extensive managerial literature dedicated to developing and testing models of corporate social performance (CSP), corporate social responsibility (CSR1), and corporate social responsiveness (CSR2). Although this literature has made some progress in terms of theoretical development, Clarkson's (1995) concern that the business and society field has been hampered by the absence of widely accepted definitions of these concepts remains a valid criticism. This lack of definition, among other problems, has inhibited empirical testing of the theories (see Wood, 1991, for a review and critique of the evolution of CSP; see Griffin and Mahon, 1997, Margolis and Walsh, 2001; Orlitzky, Schmidt and Rynes, 2003, for reviews of the impact of corporate social responsibility on economic performance).

Clarkson (1995) believed that the social issues concept was foreign to managers, while the notion of stakeholders was sensible and integral to their orientation. Under Clarkson's leadership, a range of stakeholder studies were conducted to test stakeholder theory and its relationship to other economic and organizational variables. The stakeholder model is an appropriate and intuitively attractive theoretical lens through which to view individual and organizational commitments to social responsibility, and is particularly apt in efforts to understand differences in conceptions about and implementation of CSR in various national contexts.

Global responsibility and accountability
Dunning (2003) argues that modern capitalism has failed on at least three basic dimensions: failure of markets, failure of institutions and failure of moral virtues. Criticisms have been especially sharp in relation to the activities of multinational companies – such as Nike, Levi's, United Fruit and others – whose sourcing practices in developing countries have been alleged to exploit low-wage workers, take advantage of lax environmental and workplace standards and otherwise contribute to social and economic degradation. Many governments, international organizations and both local and multinational non-governmental organizations (NGOs) have criticized

the low-cost labor-seeking behavior of MNEs in developing countries, suggesting such firms scan the globe for the cheapest, least regulated and most exploitive situations in which to source raw materials and semi-finished products (Singer, 2002).

There are a number of serious challenges to maintenance of globally standardized ethical practices in a range of different cultures and institutional settings around the world. Many have argued that valid moral principles are relative to culture or individual choice (Shomali, 2001). Ethical relativism has been defined as a 'cluster of doctrines arising from reflection on differences in ethical belief across time and between individuals, groups and societies' (ibid., p. 25). In the modern economic environment, ethical differences among countries and communities may be more subtle but no less vexing. Multinational corporations, for example, face expectations to participate in bribery, a practice considered unethical and illegal in some jurisdictions, but perfectly acceptable in others. Wong's view of ethical relativism is that there is no 'single true morality' because it is used to solve specific conflicts between people where situational differences disenable one complete morality (ibid., p. 176).

Weaver argues that, even if there were substantial agreement across cultures on the normative issues of business ethics, corporate ethics management programs would nonetheless fail to mesh in different cultural settings (Weaver, 2001). By adopting American ethical parameters for corporate management, multinational businesses risk failing to achieve the goals of their corporate ethics initiatives. Moreover pursuing 'shared' multinational ethical goals will undermine the effectiveness of ethics management efforts. Weaver recommends the development and application of a culture structure contingency analysis for the task of encouraging ethical behavior in global business.

There are a number of scholars who have criticized any approach to ethical relativism across cultures. Midgley (1981) equates relativism with 'isolationism' and argues that relativism is an inappropriate rationalization for what might otherwise be viewed as amoral behavior. Indeed she notes that it would require a ban on all moral reasoning simply because one lacks full understanding of foreign cultures. This means that one could not criticize or commend any foreign practice, which really amounts to an abnegation of human rationality and judgment. But no one, even avowed relativists, will accept this eventuality; they often want to make absolute judgments, for example that tolerance is universally valuable or that no value set is better or worse than any other. The underlying mistake of the relativist approach, she notes insightfully, is that it overlooks the fact that, in all but the most isolated societies, cultures are being mixed and fertilized such that both moral and physical isolationism are no longer an accurate way to describe the human condition (ibid.).

In an effort to resolve this theoretical and practical divide through development of a social contracts perspective on international business ethics, Donaldson and Dunfee (1999) defend the existence of 'hypernorms' that transcend individual cultural differences. Such norms address fundamental human rights or basic prescriptions common to most religions which, by definition, are acceptable to all cultures and all organizations. These hypernorms (for example, that one should keep promises and respect human dignity or that society should encourage voice and permit exit) give rise to 'universally binding moral precepts' on the basis of which one can judge the morality of a particular culture to be invalid. They note that almost no respected philosophers subscribe to relativism, for such a belief 'is equivalent to believing child rapists are as worthy as child educators' (ibid., pp. 22–3).

The challenges of organizational governance
Within individual organizations, the challenges associated with how best to oversee, govern and constrain potential individual opportunism have been especially prominent in recent years. Inherent to the notion of governance is accountability and oversight. From a theoretical standpoint, governance is the system by which managers are constrained from tendencies to engage in opportunistic exploitation of their position.

The literature on governance in organizations is extensive. As Clark, Doh and Stumpf report (Chapter 15 of the present volume), this research has emanated from agency theory and the desire to solve 'the agency problem' (Alchian and Demsetz, 1972; Eisenhardt, 1989; Fama and Jensen, 1983; Jensen and Meckling, 1976). As they note, governance mechanisms typically take three principal forms: (1) establishment of an independent board of directors that oversees the activities of top management; (2) the presence of large block shareholders who take an active interest in the activities of top management; and (3) a market for corporate control that serves to discipline managers for poor performance.

Although the agency issue (and responses to it) continue to present a core challenge to organizational governance, here we are concerned with a broader challenge: the ability of executives and managers to hear and receive input from a range of voices, and the ability of a range of stakeholders important to the firm to provide appropriate feedback. This feedback could be via traditional boards and take the form of specific initiatives to encourage accountability and responsibility, or it could take place via nontraditional channels, including structured or unstructured stakeholder dialogue, focus groups, surveys or other interactions. An effective governance system is one that allows for access and oversight by a range of constituencies, internal and external to the focal organizations, at multiple levels and via regular and continuing channels.

A practical example is the steps companies may take to improve their standing with the growing socially responsible investment (SRI) movement. Such actions would involve interactions with NGOs, customers, pension funds, analysts, suppliers and other stakeholders in order to receive input as to the aspects of the business that are meeting expectations for social responsibility. This type of governance involves oversight by and accountability to many entities, all directed to making the firm more responsive and responsible to these diverse constituencies.

Toward a conceptualization of 'responsible leadership and governance'
Both individual and organizational antecedents contribute to responsible leadership and governance. An instrumental interpretation of the stakeholder model provides an initial frame for developing our responsible leadership and governance concept.

Jones (1995) developed an instrumental theory of stakeholder management, arguing that a subset of ethical principles (trust, trustworthiness and cooperativeness) can result in significant competitive advantage. He argued that honest, trusting and ethical relationships result in positive reputation effects and minimize opportunism, as contracting parties interact and grow to depend on the reliable behavior of their business partners. This voluntary but genuine trust building further reinforces positive responses and serves as a constraint to opportunism. People who are honest, demonstrate personal integrity and honor their commitments are clearly moral in nature and are desirable partners for a large range of economic relationships. As applied to global corporate responsibility, Jones (ibid., p. 435) suggests that 'certain types of corporate social performance are manifestations of attempts to establish trusting, cooperative firm/stakeholder relationships and should be positively linked to a company's financial performance'.

Building on Jones's perspectives, and the individual and organizational antecedents described above, we suggest that the concept of responsible leadership and governance has three important dimensions, each of which can be observed through specific individual or organizational behaviors: (1) values-based leadership; (2) ethical decision making and (3) quality stakeholder relationships.

Values-based leadership
To be successful, leadership must be based on core values and credos that reflect principled business and leadership practices, high levels of ethical and moral behavior and a set of shared ideals that advance organizational and

societal wellbeing. Trevino *et al.* (2000) argue that a reputation for executive ethical leadership ultimately resides in two critical areas: the manager's visibility as a moral person and her visibility as a moral manager. Possessing a strong ethical reputation reduces legal problems, increases employee satisfaction and promotes ethical conduct throughout the organization. While strong ethical principles are important, a manager must 'focus the organization's attention on ethics and values that will guide the actions of all employees', emphasizing the importance of ethical leadership to an overall organizational success (ibid., p. 128).

Ethical decision making
The importance of ethical decision making in corporations, governments, not-for-profit organizations and professional services firms is omnipresent. Temptations for unethical behavior are great and practicing sound ethical principles requires great discipline. Executives must make decisions based on core values and shared ideals that enhance both organizations and society. More specifically employees and other stakeholders must have faith in their leaders and trust that they incorporate ethics in their everyday decisions. In many large organizations, employees have infrequent interactions with executive management. Corporate culture – the accepted behavioral norms of the organization – becomes the avenue for the dissemination of a company's commitment to ethical decision making. Leaders must voice and act on ethical positions or employees will make their own determinations through gossip and cluster chains. 'People are going to judge you not by what you say but what you do' (Trevino *et al.*, 2000, p. 131). While executives know their own ethical values, consistent action is needed to convey their beliefs to the entire organization. In the end, ethical decision making is one of an organization's most important intangible assets.

Quality stakeholder relationships
The quality of relationships with internal and external stakeholders is increasingly critical to organizational success, especially to governance processes, herein defined. Relationships involving mutual trust and respect are important within organizations, between organizations and the range of constituencies that they affect, and among the extended networks of individuals and their organizational affiliates. Through a more responsible, expansive and inclusive governance structure, firms can increase performance and provide mechanisms to pre-empt problems that arise from narrow board structures. Particular attention must be directed toward systems that can provide for effective functioning of independent boards representative of the widest range of stakeholders, and other mechanisms that allow for unimpeded and unconstrained access to information from

community groups, NGOs and others who have been underrepresented in governance.

Petrick and Quinn (2001, p. 332) suggest that 'Business leaders and organizations with high integrity capacity are more likely than competitors to be aware of and more rapidly respond to stakeholder moral concerns, arrive at balanced decisions that form sound policies, and build supportive systems that sustain excellence.' Long-term competitive advantage is the result of internal management skills and assets, both tangible and intangible. Integrity capacity, an intangible asset, is easy to overlook in today's fast-paced global environment. 'Enhancing integrity capacity can contribute to the global sustainable competitive advantage of firms, whereas its current neglect has dysfunctional consequences' (ibid., p. 340). Providing business education that supports the development of responsible leaders and expanding the scope of governance accountability will result in more balanced, organizational decision making.

Figure 1.1 presents a graphic depiction of the relationship among leadership, ethics, corporate social responsibility and responsible leadership behaviors. Although stylized, this depiction helps to clarify the relationships among these constructs that have heretofore emerged somewhat independently into a conceptual map of responsible leadership and governance.

Conclusions and implications for research and practice
Research and theory linking leadership, ethics and social responsibility are in their infancy. This volume is designed to encourage and help frame future scholarship in this area. The concept of responsible leadership and governance is yet to be fully specified, and further theoretical development and research can provide more rigorous definitions and delimitations.

Future scholarship, some of which is reflected in this volume, could extend theory building in the areas of ethics and leadership (Ciulla, Chapter 9 and Fombrun, Chapter 4), begin to link different styles of leadership, ethics and social responsibility (Hitt, Ireland and Rowe, Chapter 2 and Waldman and Siegel, Chapter 11) and provide practical recommendations on how to develop ethical leaders in modern organizations (Fulmer, Chapter 3; Gentile, Chapter 12; Useem, Chapter 5 and Waddock, Chapter 10).

Much more needs to be done to understand some of the theoretical issues around governance, including where traditional theory must be modified or respecified (Clark, Doh, and Stumpf, Chapter 15; Howton, Howton and McWilliams, Chapter 13). The relationship between leadership, emotion and personality is also an important area for future inquiry (Useem, Chapter 5).

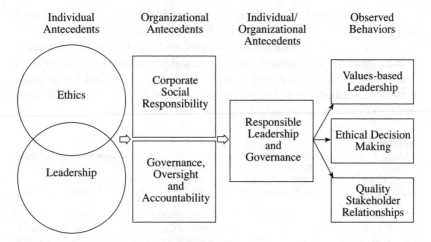

*Figure 1.1   A framework of responsible leadership and governance:
antecedents, construct and behaviors*

The global and cross-cultural challenges of responsible leadership
and governance pose especially interesting opportunities for scholarship.
Questions related to whether leadership concepts are universal or
idiosyncratic around the world (Sackman, Chapter 16; Pekerti, Chapter
17 and Quigley, deLuque and House, Chapter 18) and how governance
regimes are both converging and diverging in response to pressures for
change (Mallin, Chapter 14) are among these exciting questions. Finally
the practical implications of pressure for change and the responsibilities
of educational and other training institutions are a relevant area for future
inquiry (Alexander and Wilson, Chapter 8 and Scalberg, Chapter 19).

This is not a theoretical discussion. Many companies are pursuing a
mission of responsible leadership and governance. AES corporation has
added a strong ethical element to its workplace environment, as reflected
in its commitment to its 'shared' principles: to act with integrity, to be fair,
to have fun and to be socially responsible. These principles are goals and
aspirations to guide the efforts of the people of AES as it carries out the
mission of the company. At Johnson & Johnson, a credo that prioritizes
medical professionals, customers and the community before stockholders
is embraced by employees and advanced by a team of training specialists
to ensure that it is understood and employed in J&J facilities around the
world. At Vanguard, clear expectations for employees and companies in
which it owns shares regarding ethics and governance have set a standard
for a mutual fund industry rocked by scandal and alleged conflicts.

We see clear and compelling arguments for development of sound responsible leadership for both moral and practical reasons. Responsible leadership and governance are morally preferable to alternative approaches to management and oversight and economically beneficial to the companies and organizations that adopt it, and they provide a system for decision making, administration and organizational development that will serve multiple constituencies and advance organizational goals.

References

Alchian, A. and H. Demetz (1972), 'Production, information costs, and economic organization', *American Economic Review*, **62**, 777–95.

Avery, G. and E. Baker (1990*), Psychology at Work*, New York: Prentice-Hall.

Barnard, C.I. (1938), *The Functions of the Executive*, Cambridge, MA: Harvard University Press.

Bass, B.M. (1981), *Stogdill's Handbook of Leadership*, New York: The Free Press.

Bass, B.M. (1985), *Leadership and Performance beyond Expectation*, New York: Free Press.

Bass, B.M. and P. Steidlmeier (1999), 'Ethics, character and authentic transformational leadership behavior', *Leadership Quarterly*, **10**, 187–217.

Bird, C. (1940), *Social Psychology*. New York: D. Appleton-Century Company.

Bryman, A. (1992), *Charisma and Leadership in Organizations*. Newbury Park, CA: Sage.

Caldwell, C., S.J. Bischoff and R. Karri (2002), 'The four umpires: a paradigm for ethical leadership', *Journal of Business Ethics*, **36** (1), 153–63.

Ciulla, J. (1995), 'Leadership ethics: mapping the territory', *Business Ethics Quarterly*, **5** (1), 5–28.

Clarkson, M.B.E. (1995), 'A stakeholder framework for analyzing and evaluating corporate social performance', *Academy of Management Review*, **20** (1), 92–106.

Collier, J. and R. Esteban (2000), 'Systemic leadership: ethical and effective', *Leadership & Organizational Development Journal*, **21** (4), 207–15.

Conger, J.A. (1989), *The Charismatic Leader*, San Francisco: Jossey-Bass.

Conger, J.A. (1990), 'The dark side of leadership', *Organizational Dynamics*, **19** (2), 44–55.

Donaldson, T. and T. Dunfee (1999), *Ties That Bind,* Boston: Harvard Press.

Dunning, J. (2003), 'The moral imperatives of global capitalism: an overview', in J. Dunning, (ed.), *Making Globalization Good: The Moral Challenges of Global Capitalism*, London: Oxford University Press, pp. 11–40.

Eisenhardt, K. (1989), 'Agency theory: an assessment and review', *Academy of Management Review*, **14**, 57–74.

Fama, E.F. and M.C. Jensen, (1983), 'Separation of ownership and control', *Journal of Law and Economics*, **26**, 301–25.

Griffin, J.J. and J.F. Mahon (1997), 'The corporate social performance and corporate financial performance debate: twenty-five years of incomparable research', *Business and Society*, **36** (1), 5–15.

Hambrick, D.C. and P.A. Mason (1984), 'Upper echelons: the organization as a reflection of its top managers', *Academy of Management Review*, **9**, 193–206.

Hencley, S.P. (1973), 'Situational behavioral approach to the study of educational leadership', in L.C. Cunningham and W.J. Gephart (eds), *Leadership: the Science and Art Today*, Itaska, IL: FE Peacock Publishers, pp. 139–64.

Hitt, M.A. and B.B. Tyler (1991), 'Strategic decision models: integrating different perspectives', *Strategic Management Journal*, **12**, 327–51.

House, R.J., W.D. Spangler and J. Woycke (1991), 'Personality and charisma in the U.S. presidency: a psychological theory of leader effectiveness', *Administrative Science Quarterly*, **36**, 364–96.

Hoy, W.K. and C.G. Miskel (1987), *Educational Administration: Theory, Research and Practice*, 3rd edn, New York: Random House.

Ireland, D.R. and M. Hitt (1999), 'Achieving and maintaining strategic competitiveness in the 21st century: the role of strategic leadership', *The Academy of Management Executive*, **13** (1), 43–7.

Jensen, M.C. and W.H. Meckling (1976), 'Theory of the firm: managerial behavior, agency costs and ownership structure', *Journal of Financial Economics*, **3**, 305–60.

Jones, T.M. (1995), 'Instrumental stakeholder theory: a synthesis of ethics and economics', *Academy of Management Review*, **20** (2), 404–37.

Kanungo, R.N. (1988), 'Problems and prospects in understanding charismatic leadership', in J.A. Conger and R.N. Kanungo (eds), *Charismatic Leadership*, San Francisco: Jossey-Bass, pp. 1–11.

Khurana, R. (2002), *Searching for a Corporate Savior: The Irrational Quest for Charismatic CEOs*, Princeton: Princeton University Press.

Klein, J.K. and R.J. House (1995), 'On fire: charismatic leadership and levels of analysis', *Leadership Quarterly*, **6**, 183–98.

Logsdon, J. and K. Yuthas (1997), 'Corporate social performance stakeholder orientation and organizational moral development', *Journal of Business Ethics*, **16** (12), 1213–26.

Margolis, J.D. and J.P. Walsh (2001), *People & Profits: The Search for a Link Between a Company's Social and Financial Performance*, Mahwah, NJ: Lawrence Erlbaum Associates.

McCall, J.J. (2002), 'Leadership and ethics: corporate accountability to whom, for what and by what means', *Journal of Business Ethics*, **38** (1), 133–9.

McWilliams, A. and D. Siegel (2001), 'Corporate social responsibility: a theory of the firm perspective', *Academy of Management Review*, **26** (1), 117–27.

Midgley, M. (1981), *Heart and Mind: The Varieties of Moral Expertise*, London: Palgrave.

Orlitzky, M., F.L. Schmidt and S.L. Rynes (2003), 'Corporate social and financial performance: a meta-analysis', *Organization Studies*, **24** (3), 403–42.

Parry, K. and S. Proctor-Thomson (2002), 'Perceived integrity of transformational leaders in organizational settings', *Journal of Business Ethics*, **35** (2), 75–96.

Pawar, B.S. and K.K. Eastman (1997), 'The nature and implications of contextual influences on transformational leadership: a conceptual examination', *Academy of Management Review*, **22**, 80–109.

Petrick, J. and J. Quinn (2000), 'The integrity capacity construct and moral progress in business', *Journal of Business Ethics*, **23** (1), 3–19.

Petrick, J. and J. Quinn (2001), 'The challenge of leadership accountability for integrity as a strategic asset', *Journal of Business Ethics*, **34** (3), 331–43.

Petrick, J., P. Scherer, J.D. Brodzinsli and J. Quinn (1999), 'Global leadership skills and reputational capital: intangible resources for sustainable competitive advantage', *The Academy of Management Executive*, **13** (1), 58–69.

Raven, B.H. and J.E. Rubin (1976), *Social Psychology: People in Groups*, New York: John Wiley & Sons.

Romar, E.J. (2002), 'Virtue is good business: Confucianism as a practical business ethic', *Journal of Business Ethics*, **38** (1), 119–31.

Rost, J.C. (1995), 'Leadership: a discussion about ethics', *Business Ethics Quarterly*, **5** (1), 129–42.

Sashkin, M. (1988), 'The visionary leader', in J.A. Conger and R.N. Kanungo (eds), *Charismatic Leadership*, San Francisco: Jossey-Bass, pp. 122–60.

Schminke, M., D. Wells, J. Peyrefitte and T. Sebora (2002), 'Leadership ethics in work groups: a longitudinal assessment', *Group & Organization Management*, **27** (2), 272–93.

Shomali, M. (2001), *Ethical Relativism: An Analysis of the Foundations of Morality*, London: Islamic College for Advanced Studies Press.

Singer, P. (2002), *One World: The Ethics of Globalization*, New Haven, CT: Yale University Press.

Stogdill, R.M. (1948), 'Personal factors associated with leadership: a survey of the literature', *Journal of Psychology*, **25**, 35–71.

Stogdill, R.M. (1974), *Handbook of Leadership: A Survey of Theory and Research*, New York: The Free Press.

The American Heritage Dictionary of the English Language (2000), 4th edn, New York: Houghton Mifflin Company.

Tichy, N. and M. Devanna (1986), *Transformational Leadership*, New York: Wiley.

Trevino, L., K. Butterfield and D. McCabe (1998), 'The ethical context in organizations: influences on employee attitudes and behaviors', *Business Ethics Quarterly*, **8** (3), 447–76.

Trevino, L., L. Pincus Hartman and M. Brown (2000), 'Moral person and moral manager: how executives develop a reputation for ethical leadership', *California Management Review*, **42** (4), 128–42.

Weaver, G.R. (2001), 'Ethics programs in global businesses: culture's role in managing ethics', *Journal of Business Ethics*, **30** (1), 3–15.

Westley, F. and H. Mintzberg (1989), 'Visionary leadership and strategic management', *Strategic Management Journal*, **10**, 17–32.

Wood, D.J. (1991), 'Corporate social performance revisited', *Academy of Management Review*, **16**, 691–718.

2 Strategic leadership: strategy, resources, ethics and succession

Michael A. Hitt, R. Duane Ireland and
Glenn W. Rowe

Introduction

For some time, many business scholars and practitioners have been interested in understanding why some firms perform better than others (c.f. Barnett *et al.*, 1994; Miller, 2003). While there may be many reasons for one firm performing better than another, we argue that a prominent reason for differences in performance is the effectiveness of the leadership exhibited throughout an organization (Hitt and Ireland, 2002). Our focus in this chapter is on strategic leadership. Ireland and Hitt suggest that strategic leadership is the 'ability to anticipate, envision, maintain flexibility, think strategically, and work with others to initiate changes that will create a viable future for the organization' (Ireland and Hitt, 1999, p. 43). Complementary to this definition, Rowe (2001) suggests that strategic leadership involves a synergistic combination of managerial and visionary leadership to influence those with whom they work to make decisions on a voluntary basis. Such leadership, Rowe notes, enhances the long-term viability of the organization while simultaneously maintaining its short-term stability. Clearly this ability must be developed and exhibited by people in leadership positions at all levels and in all areas of the organization. Thus it is necessary not only for maintaining current levels of performance but also for ensuring survival of the organization and superior performance over time.

Leaders throughout the organization are responsible for developing and communicating a vision for the organization and for designing a strategy that specifies the actions necessary to achieve this vision over time. To develop and implement this strategy, leaders must effectively manage the firm's resources. This entails building and monitoring the firm's resource portfolio and integrating the various resources to create capabilities needed to take strategic actions. Furthermore these leaders must design specific short-term and long-term actions that leverage and utilize those capabilities in the most effective way. In the process of managing the resources, leaders should communicate a set of values and maintain standards that reflect an appropriate code of ethics. Furthermore these leaders are often called on to be entrepreneurial in their business actions as well as in actions that benefit society (for example, social entrepreneurship). Finally the human capital in organizations is mobile and, thus, people move across organizations over time. Of particular importance are leadership changes. Thus, to maintain the desired level and type of leadership, organizations must plan for and effect leadership succession.

We discuss each of the primary factors noted above in the following sections of this chapter. We begin with a discussion and differentiation of managerial leadership and visionary leadership.

Managerial and visionary leadership
In the previous section, strategic leadership was defined. However visionary leadership is partially different. It is future-oriented, concerned with risk taking, and visionary leaders look beyond their organizations for their personal worth. Under visionary leaders, organizational control is maintained through socialization and the sharing of, and compliance with, a commonly held set of norms, values and shared beliefs (Rowe, 2001). Alternatively managerial leadership provides stability and order, preserving the existing order. Managerial leaders are more comfortable handling day-to-day activities, and are more short term-oriented (Rowe, 2001). In this section, we provide an in-depth examination of managerial leadership and visionary leadership.

Managerial leadership
Only a very few managers will become strategic leaders; a few more will exercise only visionary leadership, while the vast majority will exercise only managerial leadership (Teal, 1996). Several authors suggest that some managers are able to become excellent managers but not excellent leaders, while others have the potential to become excellent leaders but not great managers (Kotter, 1990; Rowe, 2001).

Managerial leaders have passive, impersonal attitudes toward goals. Thus, for managerial leaders, goals are necessities rather than desires. Goals are based on the organization's past and thereby embedded in the organization's history and culture (Zaleznik, 1977). Jack Welch and the late Roberto Goizueta argued that leaders, especially CEOs, need to be insensitive to the past (Morris, 1995), but managerial leaders tend to weight the past heavily. Managerial leaders conceive of work as an enabling process that integrates people and ideas to establish strategies and enable decision making. To achieve the desired outcomes, they bargain, negotiate and/or use punishments/rewards and/or other forms of coercion. Regarding their relations with others, managerial leaders base relationships on their role in the decision-making process; that is, they relate more to accomplishing tasks as opposed to building relationships with people. Managerial leaders may not be empathetic with people with whom they work. Thus they seek out more superficial involvement with others, maintaining a low level of emotional involvement in the relationships. Managerial leaders prefer order to chaos and there is often less order in human relationships. Regarding their sense of self, managerial leaders see themselves as conservators and regulators of the current organization state and personally identify with the existing order. Perpetuating and strengthening the way things are currently done in their organizations enhances these managers' self-worth. Maintaining the order provides them with perceived rewards beyond material or monetary rewards. Of course, if this is true, when the institution managerial leaders have devoted their career to perpetuating and strengthening is restructured, managerial leaders experience emotional pain (Zaleznik, 1977; Rowe, 2001).

Managerial leaders will influence only the behavior or decisions of those with whom they work (Hosmer, 1982). They focus more on day-to-day activities (Schendel, 1989) and they are more comfortable in functional areas of responsibilities. They have more expertise in these functional areas than do visionary leaders or strategic leaders (Hambrick, 1989; Rowe, 2001). Managerial leaders are more likely than visionary and strategic leaders to make decisions that are not subject to value-based or ethical constraints (Evans, 1997; Hosmer, 1982; Sooklal, 1991; Rowe, 2001; Zaleznik, 1990). It should be emphasized that managerial leaders are ethical, moral people, but they may not include values in their managerial decision making because of their focus on financial controls (Rowe, 2001). Managerial leaders support, and engage in, short-term, least-cost behavior activities to enhance the bottom line (Hill and Hoskisson, 1987; Hoskisson and Hitt, 1994; Rowe, 2001; Zaleznik, 1990). They emphasize the exchange and combination of explicit knowledge[1] and ensuring compliance with standard operating procedures (Rowe, 2001). They use a thought process that is linear. Finally managerial leaders believe in determinism (Trigg, 1996), meaning that they believe that their firm's internal environment and external environment largely determine what they do (Mintzberg *et al.*, 1998; Rowe, 2001).

We want to emphasize that being an excellent managerial leader is not bad – the description above is more a recognition of some of the characteristics that define managerial leadership. We believe that organizations need excellent managerial leadership. However, in too many organizations, managerial leadership is predominant and managerial leaders are not wealth creators for their organizations. These leaders at best only maintain wealth that has been created in the past and at worst may be a source of wealth destruction in the long term (Rowe, 2001).

Visionary leadership

Visionary leadership has been offered as a panacea for many of the problems experienced by organizations in the current dynamic global environment (Conger, 1991; Nathan, 1996; Rowe, 2001). However visionary leaders are not always readily embraced by organizations. Allowing the exercise of visionary leadership is risky (Rowe, 2001). Ultimately visionary leaders have the power to influence the thoughts, attitudes and the actions/decisions of people. Having this power in one person entails risk on multiple dimensions. First, there is the risk of equating power with an ability to achieve results quickly. Second, visionary leaders risk losing self-control in their drive to seek and obtain power. Finally, harm may come to the internal development of managerial leaders because of the relative disorder generated by visionary leaders (Rowe, 2001; Zaleznik, 1977). The attitudes of visionary leaders toward goals are the opposite of those held by managerial leaders. Visionary leaders are relatively more proactive, creative and innovative and are more likely to shape ideas rather than react to them. Visionary leaders determine an organization's direction by evoking expectations and images, altering moods and establishing specific objectives and desires. Their influence changes the attitudes of people about what is possible, desirable and necessary. Visionary leaders work hard to develop fresh approaches to problems. They create excitement in the minds of people with whom they work. Visionary leaders work from high-risk positions – in fact, they seek out ventures that are risky, especially when the returns are high. Visionary leaders relate to other people in an empathetic and intuitive manner and are concerned with ideas. With visionary leaders, human relationships are less ordered, turbulent and intense, producing unanticipated outcomes, positive or negative, and may intensify emotional relationships. The key point is that, while they work in organizations, they do not belong to organizations. Their self-identity does not depend on their organizational role or the work they do in their organization. Their sense of identity generally results from major events, especially failures, in their lives (Rowe, 2001; Zaleznik, 1977, 1990).

Visionary leaders have a significant influence on people and concern themselves with ensuring an organization's future through developing and managing people (Schendel, 1989). Visionaries embed themselves in information overload, ambiguity and complexity. Their roles are generally multifunctional and they prefer complex integrative tasks (Hambrick, 1989; Mintzberg, 1973).

Visionaries are more likely to make value-based decisions (Evans, 1997; Hosmer, 1982; Rowe, 2001; Sooklal, 1991; Zaleznik, 1990) and to make investments to ensure long-term viability such as in human capital, innovation and creating/maintaining an effective culture (Hoskisson and Hitt, 1994). Visionary leaders focus on tacit knowledge,[2] developing strategies as communal forms of tacit knowledge that promote the enactment of a vision (Kotter and Heskett, 1992; Schein, 1993). Visionary leaders use non-linear thinking and believe in strategic choice. Visionary leaders believe that the choices they make affect their organizations differentially and these differences affect the environments in which their organizations operate (Child, 1972; Rowe, 2001; Trigg, 1996).

Organizations need visionary leadership to enhance their long-term viability. However organizations led by visionaries who will not allow the constraining influence of managerial leaders are more likely to fail in the short term than those led by managerial leaders. Visionary leaders are willing to take high risks that may create wealth; however they are more likely to overinvest in their vision – more than the returns warrant – and, without the constraining influence of managerial leaders, this could destroy wealth (Rowe, 2001).

Integrating managerial and visionary leadership
Several authors argue that it is not possible for an individual to be both a managerial leader and a visionary leader. The leading proponent of this view is Zaleznik (1977, 1990). On the other hand, several authors suggest that, while there is a paradox in being a strategic leader (the synergistic combination of managerial and visionary leadership: Rowe, 2001), it is possible for individuals to integrate the characteristics of managerial and visionary leadership. Mintzberg (1990) describes the 'cerebral face' (the managerial leader) as a person who is calculative, views the world as components of a portfolio and operates with a sense of rationality. He describes the 'insightful face' as one who stresses commitment, views the world as an integrated portfolio and is rooted in the images of integrity (Mintzberg, 1990). He then argues that management has to be both insightful and cerebral. He suggests that being insightful is making sense of what people do in the organization and developing visions 'that inspire people to subsequent efforts' (Mintzberg, 1990, p. 31).

In addition, he suggests that being insightful becomes increasingly difficult as organizations grow larger and become more diversified, because managers lose the personal knowledge that comes from intimate contact – an essential ingredient for being insightful. When this happens, managers become cerebral. For this reason, Rowe (2001) argues that it is largely impossible to be a strategic leader in an unrelated diversified organization, and suggests that organizations need to be related or diversified in a limited way for strategic leadership to be exercised.

Kotter (1990) argues that management must cope with complexity while leadership must cope with change. He believes that planning and setting budgets, organizing and staffing, and controlling and problem solving help to manage complexity. He suggests that leading for change requires setting a direction, aligning people and getting them committed to a vision, and motivating and inspiring to make the changes. In addition, he argues that some will have the potential to be great managers but not great leaders, while others may become great leaders but not simultaneously great managers. But he believes that it is critical for organizations to develop leader-managers (strategic leaders) and that companies doing so rightly ignore the arguments that individuals cannot simultaneously lead and manage organizations. Finally he suggests that 'strong leadership with weak management is no better, and is sometimes actually worse, than the reverse' (Kotter, 1990, p. 38).

Contrary to Zaleznik, and consistent with others (Kotter, 1990; Mintzberg, 1990) Rowe (2001) suggests visionary leadership and managerial leadership are vital for long-term viability and short-term financial stability. Having visionary and managerial leadership can be accomplished by having two different organizational mind-sets, but with visionary leadership being more influential than managerial leadership; however an organization will be more viable in the long term and better able to maintain its financial stability in the short term, with a critical mass of strategic leaders. Those with a synergistic integration of visionary leadership and managerial leadership demonstrate what Steven J. Ross described as a strategic leader (Loeb, 1993, p. 4):

> There are three categories of people – the person who goes into the office, puts his feet up on his desk, and dreams for twelve hours; the person who arrives at 5 a.m. and works for 16 hours, never once stopping to dream; and the person who puts his feet up, dreams for one hour, then does something about those dreams. (Steven J. Ross, former chairman and co-CEO of Time-Warner)

Managing resources

Effective leaders must successfully manage the resources at their disposal. However visionary leaders are likely to manage resources differently from managerial leaders. Thus our focus is on the way in which strategic leaders, who display characteristics that reflect both types, manage resources.

The notion that resources are a critical component of gaining and sustaining a competitive advantage comes from the resource-based view of the firm (RBV) (Barney, 1991). The RBV is derived from theoretical perspectives in Ricardian and Penrosian economics and prior work on distinctive competencies (Barney and Arikan, 2001). The most simple notion of the value of resources to an organization has been presented by Barney (1991) who argued that, to be a source of competitive advantage, one or more resources must be valuable and rare. Additionally, in order to sustain a competitive advantage created on the basis of valuable and rare resources, they must also be difficult to imitate and nonsubstitutable. The assumptions on which resources with these characteristics are linked to competitive advantage include (1) that firms have heterogeneous sets of resources even within the same industries and (2) resources are relatively immobile across firms. However it is not enough only to hold resources with these characteristics. Actions must be taken to manage, leverage and utilize these resources in order to exploit their value to create and sustain a competitive advantage (Priem and Butler, 2001). And the specific actions needed to exploit these resources are not necessarily self-evident (Barney and Arikan, 2001). Thus effective leadership in managing these resources is critical (Grant, 1991; Sirmon and Hitt, 2003).

The importance of leaders effectively acquiring, developing and monitoring the use of these resources is important in all types of organizations: large corporations, new ventures and family firms as well (Ireland *et al.*, 2003; Sirmon and Hitt, 2003). In managing resources, the culture plays a critical role, and the leader has a key role in establishing the value set for the organization and, thereby, the culture and subcultures that may exist within it (Ireland *et al.*, 2003). Additionally, because resources are dynamic, not static, dimensions within organizations, leaders must continuously focus on them and adapt. This requires a substantial emphasis on organizational learning (Miller, 1996). Leaders in key positions, then, manage resources by structuring the resource portfolio, bundling the resources to develop capabilities and leveraging those capabilities to achieve a competitive advantage (Sirmon *et al.*, 2003).

Resource portfolio
The resource portfolio of an organization entails all tangible and intangible assets controlled by the organization (Makadok, 2003). Developing and managing the resource portfolio involves acquiring resources as needed, continuous building of those resources to increase their value and then divesting resources when they lose their particular value to the firm (Barney, 1986; Denrell *et al.*, 2003; Dierickx and Cool, 1989; Makadok, 2001; Thomke and Kuemmerle, 2002). The resource portfolio is dynamic, with constant additions, continuous development and frequent divestitures of resources. Leaders play a major role in each of these processes.

Leaders play a critically important role in the acquiring of resources, for example. In the acquisition of human capital, they must recruit, attract, select and integrate those hired into the organization. Leaders make the decisions regarding the skills and knowledge bases needed and then take actions to identify and recruit individuals who have those skills and knowledge sets. In addition, leaders want to select individuals who fit well in the organization, especially with the culture. However the culture also can be an attractive characteristic of the organization for recruiting purposes. This is the case at Southwest Airlines, for example. In acquiring resources, leaders purchase the needed resources from strategic factor markets (Barney, 1986) that range from commodity-like resources to complex sets of resources obtained through acquisition (Denrell *et al.*, 2003). Determining the appropriate price to pay for these resources can ultimately determine their value-creating properties for the organization acquiring them. Pricing of these resources, though, is a challenging task because of their complexity (involving, for example, human capital – the knowledge held and the capability of the individual to use that knowledge), the uncertainty in the environment and the potential use, current and future, of this resource in the organization.

Of course, once resources are acquired and integrated into the portfolio of the firm, leaders should seek to add to their value continually. That is, for resources such as human capital, leaders should continuously seek ways to add to their skills and knowledge base. They may do so through formal training programs designed to enhance individuals' explicit knowledge as well as on-the-job training that often increases individuals' tacit knowledge. Both types of knowledge are important to the organization. Explicit knowledge is necessary for a firm to maintain its competitive position (for example, competitive parity); to gain an advantage over its competitors, a firm may need to apply tacit knowledge because its development is socially complex and ambiguous and therefore difficult to imitate (Hitt *et al.*, 2001).

Of course, leaders must overcome inertia and potential problems of core rigidities in order to add value continuously to the current resource set. For example, core rigidities can result from the escalation of commitment on the part of leaders who must monitor the resource portfolio. Prior research suggests that some leaders who make substantial investments can become committed to those investments even though they have shown themselves to be unproductive (Staw *et al.*, 1997). Inertial tendencies must be overcome in order to divest resources that have become unproductive and lost their value to the organization. Often the divesting of assets is not a simple process. Consider the layoff of thousands of employees. While these decisions appear to come easy with the many announcements of large layoffs, they are anything but simple. First, the numbers of people to be laid off must be determined and then the specific individuals with skills of less value for the organization must be identified. Leaders play a crucial part in deciding to divest these resources and in identifying which resources should be divested at a given point in time.

While managing the resource portfolio is the responsibility of great importance for leaders, we noted earlier that holding valuable resources alone will not help an organization create or maintain a competitive advantage or create value as needed to sustain its survival. Resources must be integrated to create capabilities that can be used to gain a competitive advantage.

Bundling resources
Resources generally create more value when integrated with other resources. Therefore leaders must bundle their resources to create the capability to take particular actions. For example, the ability to develop new products and introduce them to the market requires the bundling of scientific expertise in research and development, the knowledge of building quality products in manufacturing and the skills of promotion and marketing of products to the consumers. The bundling of resources to create capabilities has been referred to by different names, such as 'combinative capabilities' (Kogut and Zander, 1992) and 'dynamic capabilities' (Teece *et al.*, 1997). Regardless of the terminology, leaders must have the knowledge and the skills to bundle resources to create effective capabilities. Integration may entail tasks ranging from small combinations of resources designed to perform less complex tasks to the much more complex process of integrating businesses (Brown and Eisenhardt, 1999).

Sirmon *et al.* (2003) suggested that there were at least four types of bundling processes: stabilizing, enriching, tightening and pioneering. A stabilizing bundling process has the intent of making minor incremental improvements in existing capabilities, whereas an enriching bundling process has the intent of extending and elaborating a current capability; a tightening bundling process involves reducing the slack within a particular capability to ensure that it is lean but still can accomplish tasks; and, finally, a pioneering bundling process uses exploratory learning and is unique. The intent is to integrate resources in new ways to create new and unique capabilities. If firms exist in environments that are dynamic and, thus, highly uncertain, enriching and pioneering bundling processes are likely to be more valuable than stabilizing and tightening processes. After the capabilities have been formed, they must be leveraged in order to create a competitive advantage.

Leveraging capabilities
Clearly leaders' visioning capabilities and skills at being entrepreneurial are important in the leveraging process. As noted earlier, resources and capabilities are not of value unless they are used in an appropriate way. Therefore leaders must develop a leveraging strategy that most effectively utilizes the organization's resources and allows it to create a competitive advantage. In particular, these leaders are attempting to leverage the capabilities in order to create more value for customers than competitors are able to do, and so they attempt to develop solutions for customers

(Lin and Germain, 2003). Leaders often use three processes for leveraging: mobilizing, coordinating and deploying resources.

The intent of mobilizing is to identify the capabilities needed and design the configuration of those capabilities necessary to exploit the opportunities (Hamel and Prahalad, 1994). The mobilized capabilities must then be integrated to operate in an efficient manner. The integration involves coordination of the capabilities by the leader. Without such coordination, the configurations of capabilities are unlikely to operate in a cooperative manner. For example, firms often have problems coordinating across the functions of R&D, manufacturing and marketing. These three sets of capabilities must be coordinated in order to develop, manufacture and successfully introduce a new product into the marketplace. Each of these capabilities has separate and varying goals and priorities. A leader must work carefully to integrate these three sets of capabilities so that they cooperate and work toward a common goal (Sirmon *et al.*, 2003). This requires leaders to have effective relational skills (Sirmon and Hitt, 2003). These leaders may form and lead cross-functional teams in order to achieve this coordination (Hitt *et al.*, 1999). The final process involved in leveraging is that of deploying capabilities in order to pursue opportunities that have been identified in the marketplace. Deploying the coordinated configurations of capabilities should be with the intent to create greater value for the customers than competitors, thereby achieving a competitive advantage.

Critical resources
From a leader's perspective, certain resources are likely to be more important than others. According to Sirmon and Hitt (2003) and Ireland *et al.* (2003), the most important resources are financial capital, human capital and social capital. Clearly, with these three sets of resources, other resources important to develop a competitive advantage can be obtained and/or developed. Hitt and Ireland (2002) argue that the two most important resources for strategic leadership are human capital and social capital. We briefly review those below.

Human capital
As noted in the introduction to this chapter, organizations now operate in a knowledge-based economy where knowledge has become a critical component of gaining and sustaining a competitive advantage. Therefore, because an organization's knowledge is largely held by its human capital, leaders' acquisition, development and application of human capital is critically important. Human capital is probably one of an organization's most unique resources and, particularly when integrated with other forms of capital, becomes socially complex, leading to an ambiguous cause and effect

relationship between it and the organizational outcome (Black and Boal, 1994; Itami,1987). Hitt *et al.* (2001) found that firms with stronger human capital tend to experience higher levels of performance. Additionally they found that human capital was important in implementing firm strategies for them to have a positive effect on firm performance. As argued previously, the possession of valuable human capital does not alone guarantee high performance. To gain the full value from human capital, it must be effectively managed, thereby placing heavy emphasis on the leadership within the organization (Lesser and Prusak, 2001). The application of human capital often is accomplished through the use of social capital, another important resource. In fact human capital is often enhanced through the use of social capital (Lepak and Snell, 1999). A leader's internal social capital with associates is a vital component in the ability to manage this human capital. However social capital also has external dimensions, as we examine below.

Social capital
Social capital involves the relationships between individuals and between organizations. Representing capital, these relationships facilitate action and have the potential to create value (Adler and Kwon, 2002). Therefore leaders' social capital with regard to associates enables them to act collectively (Woolcock and Narayan, 2000). Essentially, social capital reflects the value of those relationships. The internal social capital reflects the relationships that leaders have with their associates and with other individuals and work units within an organization. In fact highly effective leaders build great groups, according to Warren Bennis (1997). Thus effective strategic leaders are those who can build collaborative relationships that integrate the talent of individuals and create synergy, allowing the team to display strong capabilities. However these teams only have social capital if trust is engendered among the members (Hitt *et al.*, 2003).

The effectiveness of strategic leaders is predicated on more than managing the internal resources of the firm. Effective strategic leaders are also able to develop and maintain external social capital. External social capital involves the relationships between strategic leaders and others outside the organization who control resources important for the functioning of that organization. Increasingly, few organizations possess all of the resources needed internally to operate and compete effectively and, especially, to gain a competitive advantage. Therefore they attempt to establish networks of relationships with external entities (Gulati *et al.*, 2000). The responsibility to develop and maintain this web of external relationships rests with the organization's strategic leader (Hitt and Ireland, 2002). Many of these relationships involve strategic alliances that afford the organization access to another firm's resources. Of course external firms will rarely allow another organization to use their resources unless there is substantial trust and assumed reciprocity in the relationship. Therefore strategic leaders must be particularly adept at building and maintaining these relationships; many strategic alliances fail because these relationships are ineffective (Ireland *et al.*, 2002).

Important in the effective leadership and management of human capital and social capital are the values displayed by the leaders. The values and the leader's practices should display standards of ethics and social responsibility. Next we discuss how leaders display these value sets and often engage in social entrepreneurship.

Organizational ethics, social entrepreneurship and strategic leadership
Ethics are concerned with the standards for determining what is good or bad, right or wrong (Aronson, 2001). When applied in an organizational context, ethics denote a value system that has been widely adopted by the firm's employees (Harrison and St. John, 2002) and that other stakeholders recognize to be a primary driver of the focal organization's decisions and subsequent actions.

Organizational ethics can be recorded directly in various documents such as an organization's code of conduct. However, from an operational perspective, a firm's ethics can be inferred by observing its actions, perhaps especially during a time of crisis, such as when Johnson & Johnson pulled its Tylenol product from thousands of store shelves to verify that it was doing all it could to deal with potentially dangerous batches of its popular product. Commonly ethics are applied as part of a firm's social responsibilities. Harrison and St. John (2002) argue that social responsibility has four components: economic, legal, moral and discretionary responsibilities. Expanding their decision frame beyond maximization of shareholder wealth, organizational ethics as a part of social responsibility finds decision makers considering the effects of their firm's actions on various stakeholders. With respect to the general public or society as an organizational stakeholder, Messick and Bazerman (1996, p. 10) argue that decision makers should always ask themselves, 'What would the reaction be if this decision and the reasons for it were made public?'

Some believe that organizational ethics are the foundation through which firms may be able to contribute to the societies in which they operate in ways beyond outperforming rivals and maximizing returns to shareholders (Gilbert, 2001) and that the effectiveness of an organization's strategies increases when ethical practices are used to implement them (Hitt *et al.*, 2005). Indeed evidence suggests that ethical actions create positive goodwill (Adler and Kwon, 2002) while, in contrast, unethical practices are a contagious disease affecting the organization's ability to satisfy stakeholders' interests (Brass *et al.*, 1998).

Development and reliance on a value-based organizational culture is an effective means of ensuring that employees comply with and that other stakeholders understand the firm's ethical intentions and the required behaviors associated with them (Trevino *et al.*, 1999). Moreover some executives have been found to believe that a value-based culture and the decisions and actions that are parts of it create a positive and desirable reputation for an organization (Hagen *et al.*, 1998). Long-established positive reputations create reputational capital (Worden, 2003b), which is a 'form of intangible wealth that is closely related to what accountants call "goodwill" and marketers term "brand equity"' (Fombrun, 1996, p. 11). Positive reputations are an important source of competitive advantage. To develop and support an ethical organizational culture, strategic leaders can (1) establish and communicate specific ethical goals to describe the firm's ethical standards, (2) continuously evaluate the ethical goals based on feedback from stakeholders regarding their appropriateness, (3) disseminate the ethical goals (perhaps in the form of an ethical code of conduct) to all stakeholders to inform them of the firm's standards and expectations, (4) develop methods and procedures for employees to follow to reach the ethical goals, and (5) create a work environment in which all people are treated with respect and dignity (Hitt *et al.*, 2005; Murphy, 1995).

Ethics and strategic leadership
Ethical practices are a critical part of effective strategic leadership (Worden, 2003a). Dess and Picken (1999) suggest that, because leaders, and especially strategic leaders, are role models, guiding the ethical values of an organization is a central leadership activity. As role models, and in addition to the actions they take to foster and nurture an ethical organizational culture, strategic leaders should verify that (1) the firm hires individuals who share the organization's ethical values, (2) ethical behavior is consistently recognized and openly rewarded, and (3) their decisions and actions result in unequivocal support for aspects of organizational culture that nurture ethical behavior (Hagen *et al.*, 1998). In slightly different words, when it comes to ethics, strategic leaders must determine the boundaries of acceptable behavior, set the tone for organizational actions and 'demarcate the constant striving for increased profits from those activities which may be detrimental to the values of society in general' (Aronson, 2001, p. 245).

Strategic leaders capable of achieving the outcomes mentioned above engender a positive view of the organization in internal and external stakeholders' minds and make it possible for employees to increase their effectiveness and efficiency as they operate within carefully enunciated and supported behavioral expectations. In addition, because their decisions are intended to link organizational actions to stakeholders' expectations, ethical strategic leaders, as an intangible resource that is difficult for rivals to understand and certainly to imitate, can be a source of competitive advantage (Worden, 2003b). In a sequential fashion, effective strategic leaders are the driving force for developing and successfully using the firm's other competitive advantages (Weerawardena and Sullivan-Mort, 2001), meaning that effective strategic leaders play vital roles in an organization's success.

Various factors are contributing to the increasing importance of organizational ethics and strategic leaders' role in verifying that firms act ethically when striving to meet all stakeholders' needs. Strategic leaders must recognize and respond to this reality. Effectively dealing with this reality increases the likelihood of organizational success (DePree, 1989).

Of the factors contributing to the growing significance of organizational ethics and of ethical strategic leaders, none is more important than societies' desire for organizations to conduct their affairs with a regard for ethical considerations and for strategic leaders to make decisions that will result in their earning of societies' esteem (Aronson, 2001). But, because rapid and dynamic changes in the global business environment pose vexing ethical challenges, it is difficult for strategic leaders to know precisely what decisions should be taken to increase the probability that their firms will act in ways that will satisfy all stakeholders' expectations regarding 'ethical behavior'. Indeed, for the growing number of strategic leaders operating in what Messick and Bazerman (1996) label a 'moral mine field', determining the ethical path for their organizations to follow sometimes may seem to be a virtually impossible task.

An increasing number of strategic leaders have decided that social entrepreneurship (SE) calls for a set of actions with the potential to contribute significantly to strategic leaders' and organizations' efforts to act ethically. Moreover scholars have conceptualized strategic leadership in terms of SE (Weerawardena and Sullivan-Mort, 2001). Because of the attention it is receiving from scholars as well as business practitioners, and although the concept has existed in various forms for many decades, SE is also attracting public policy makers' interests as a means of dealing meaningfully with issues facing their agencies and the societies they serve (Hibbert *et al.*, 2002; Hunt, 2000).

Social entrepreneurship
An evolving concept (Sullivan-Mort *et al.*, 2003), SE has been defined differently. In general, though, researchers and practitioners agree that SE is oriented to bringing about changes that will have positive effects on at least a single if not multiple segments of one or more societies. As

it is related to strategic leadership, SE can be thought of as the use of entrepreneurial behavior to pursue opportunities with the intention of achieving social ends as well as to act in ways that hold decision makers and their firms accountable for reaching objectives (such as profitability) that other stakeholders value (Hibbert *et al.*, 2002). SE integrates the innovative behavior often associated with private sector organizations with the grassroots desire commonly associated with concerns to bring about solutions to public sector problems (Sullivan-Mort *et al.*, 2003). In this context, SE 'involves combining commercial aims with social objectives to reap strategic or competitive benefits' (Hammonds, 2003, p. 54). Thus SE finds firms simultaneously and directly seeking to serve societies' needs while operating profitably, a reality that creates a blurring of responsibilities and actions taken by private sector organizations and public sector agencies (Dees, 1998). In slightly different words, SE is a synthesis of interests, decisions and actions that 'combines the passion of a social mission with an image of business-like discipline, innovation and determination' (Hunt, 2000, A27).

Reflecting SE's complexity, strategic leaders pursue SE-related entrepreneurial opportunities as part of their commitment to society for their firm to act ethically *and* because they believe that exploiting an ethically oriented opportunity will prove to be adequate or superior compensation for the firm's stakeholders relative to the costs of not pursuing competing opportunities or alternatives (Zietlow, 2001). An entrepreneurial opportunity is a situation in which a new good, service, raw material or organizing method can be provided to a market and sold at a price exceeding the cost of its development and distribution (Shane and Venkataraman, 2000).

When engaging in SE, strategic leaders act as entrepreneurs. In the general case, entrepreneurs are change agents whose decisions and actions tend to move entire economies forward, as well as their organizations, as they create new markets and new products, or find ways to serve existing markets innovatively with existing products by identifying and pursuing entrepreneurial opportunities. By shifting economic resources from projects with low levels of productivity and return to entrepreneurial opportunities with potential to generate superior returns, entrepreneurs create value.

As practitioners of SE, which is a specialized case of entrepreneurship, social entrepreneurs view themselves as good stewards of the resources that others have entrusted to them (Brinckerhoff, 2000). The value of social entrepreneurs' work is at its maximum when strategic leaders acting in this manner have accurate knowledge of their world as reflected by their beliefs about *how* the world works, the nature of the causal networks contributing to actions taken in the global economy, and the manner in which their decisions affect the world and its populations (Messick and Bazerman, 1996).

Social entrepreneurs seek to create superior social value through their work (Dees, 1998). Often tackling difficult social problems, SE can be practiced within established profit-seeking organizations, by entrepreneurs starting a new venture, by social enterprises which are set up with a largely social purpose but that are operated as business enterprises, and by voluntary agencies (Boschee, 1995; Thompson, 2002). Regardless of the organizational setting in which they work, social entrepreneurs play the role of change agents for societies at large (Drucker, 1989; Schumpeter, 1934) and are often viewed as leaders who bring about catalytic changes to the public sector agenda as well as a citizenry's perception of the relative importance and merits of various social issues (Waddock and Post, 1991).

Using strategic leadership to engage in social entrepreneurship
Not all strategic leaders have the capacity to engage their organizations successfully in social entrepreneurship projects – projects that tend to be characterized by extreme complexity (Waddock and Post, 1991) and that, when successful, often have positive spillover effects to the general society (Leadbeater, 1997). The capacity to champion an initiative in ways that cause people to believe that the initiative is important and that they can do something about it is vital to strategic leadership success when pursuing SE (Thompson, 2002). Thus the leader's ability to frame a project in important social as well as profitability objectives generates the type of collective purpose (Burns, 1978) that finds people joining the strategic leader to pursue what they jointly believe is an important project. In addition, strategic leaders must have 'judgment capacity', which is conceptualized as a superior ability to deal with complexity and to be able to prioritize activities when leading individuals engaged in an SE project (Sullivan-Mort *et al.*, 2003). Judgment capacity tends to be associated with strategic leaders who have a significant amount of personal credibility with all of the firm's stakeholders. The 'credible' strategic leader fluidly and flexibly uses her or his intra- and inter-firm networks to tap critical resources and to build the relationships required for various SE-related activities to be completed. Commonly the resources brought together through external networks are provided by businesses that are affected by the problem being addressed by the SE project.

In general, four sets of activities are executed as organizations engage in social entrepreneurship (Thompson, 2002). *Envisioning*, the first set of activities, finds the strategic leader specifying or describing the entrepreneurial opportunity that she or he or someone else has identified in ways that are meaningful to multiple parties (such as employees). Consistent with our earlier arguments, the chosen opportunity is one through which the firm can ethically approach solving a social problem while earning a return on the organization's investment of resources that will allow it to continue satisfying the expectations of other stakeholders, including shareholders. The second set of activities, *engaging*, finds the strategic leader generating excitement among organizational actors as they consider various paths to follow to pursue the entrepreneurial opportunity that has both profit and social objectives. Creativity and innovation often characterize the engaging activities. *Enabling* is the third set of activities. Here strategic leaders combine their own judgment with the experiences of their cohorts and employees to determine the resources that must be assembled and integrated to pursue the entrepreneurial opportunity. Leaders' persuasive abilities come into play with this set of activities as they commonly rely on their internal and external social capital (Hitt and Ireland, 2002) to collect and integrate resources from disparate locations. The final set of activities, *enacting*, finds strategic leaders serving as product champions for the social entrepreneurship project and focusing their energies in ways that see the project to a successful conclusion.

In summary the societies they serve and in which they operate as well as some other stakeholders increasingly expect organizations to serve at least some social objectives while earning satisfactory returns on their investments. In addition these parties expect strategic leaders to behave ethically while leading the organizations that are an important part of general societies. Oriented to newness (new goods, new services, new processes and so forth), social entrepreneurship is a special case of entrepreneurship. Effective and informed strategic leaders recognize that the activities associated with social entrepreneurship allow them to lead their firms in the pursuit of entrepreneurial opportunities. When successful, social entrepreneurship creates value for a society (in the form of solving one or more societal problems or issues) while creating value for stakeholders, including shareholders (in the form of superior returns on their capital investments). With further attention from researchers and practitioners, we will learn more about social entrepreneurship as a promising path to consistent displays of organizational and personal ethics. To exercise social entrepreneurship requires effective strategic leaders. This means that succession is important in order to have effective strategic leaders over time. We explore succession next.

Strategic leaders and succession processes

One question that has not been addressed in the literatures on strategic leadership and leader succession is whether a strategic leader can be found through the succession process used to select a new chief executive officer.

To phrase this more pragmatically, are organizations more likely to get a strategic leader through a horse race than through a relay? Vancil's (1987) work on succession was crucial in helping us understand succession processes, especially the relay process and the horse race.

Relay succession

The relay is the most common succession process (Vancil, 1987; Rowe, 1996). In this process, an overt heir apparent is appointed several years (four to eight, generally) before the incumbent CEO is due to retire. After being selected, the heir apparent works together with the incumbent CEO, usually from the chief operating officer/president's position, until the title of CEO is passed to them. It is not unusual for CEOs to appoint two heirs apparent over the period of their tenure, as research by Cannella and Shen (2001) demonstrates. But, eventually, an heir apparent is appointed to the position of CEO. Cannella and Shen identified heirs apparent as those who held the title of chief operating officer (COO) or president, or both, and who were at least five years younger than the CEO. Rowe (1996) identified an heir apparent process as one where the successor CEO held the title 'president' and/or 'COO' for at least two years and where the outgoing CEO remained on the board either as chair or as a board member. After an appropriate period of time (usually two to eight years) the heir apparent is passed the title of 'CEO', analogous to a relay race where the baton is passed to the subsequent runner. We believe that this process is more likely to produce a managerial leader than a horse race.

Our reasoning is as follows. When heirs apparent are appointed, their primary responsibility is to supervise the internal, day-to-day operations of the organization. In the meantime, the CEO has overall responsibility for the external and internal operations and has to operate with a much longer time horizon than day-to-day. While we recognize that they work with the CEO, we believe that, after several years of being responsible for the day-to-day, heirs apparent develop a mind-set that is more appropriate to being a managerial leader. Of course, this will be exacerbated if the CEO is a managerial leader himself or herself.

Horse race succession

A horse race is a much more brutal process. In this process, several potential contenders are selected by the board and CEO and told that they are being considered for the CEO position. They are then appointed to similar levels of authority and responsibility and told that in a relatively short time (usually less than two years but more than six months) one of them will be appointed as the CEO: the one judged by the board and incumbent CEO to have fulfilled his or her responsibilities the best. Rowe (1996) identified horse races as those where there were two or more people with similar authority and one of these became CEO, the above officers were appointed to these positions at approximately the same time and the outgoing CEO severed all ties to the firm in less than a year. In the very famous horse race that occurred at GE to select Jack Welch, there were seven people in the horse race at the beginning. All left GE except the winner, Jack Welch – as we said, a brutal process, in that GE lost an incredible amount of CEO talent. Robert Goizueta was also selected in a horse race to be the CEO of Coca-Cola in 1981.

We selected these two CEOs because Rowe (2001) identified them as being strategic leaders. We believe that it is more likely that firms will select strategic leaders through a horse race because the positions to which each participant in the horse race is appointed mean that they have CEO-like responsibilities. Therefore the board and CEO are in a better position to judge which candidate has the characteristics of a strategic leader. In fact companies like GE may produce strategic leaders who, if they do not win the CEO position in GE, go on to be strategic leaders in the CEO position at other firms. Recent work by Nohria and Groysberg (2003) suggests that, when firms hire executives from GE as their new CEO, they have an immediate positive impact on share price. The average stock market reaction to the hiring announcement is a gain of about $1.3 billion dollars for the hiring firm, with no appreciable change in GE's share price. Moves by 19 former GE executives added approximately $24.5 billion to the share price of the firms that hired them. We need more research on whether the type of CEO selection process helps firms select strategic leaders or managerial leaders.

Conclusions

Strategic leaders display integrated characteristics of both visionary and managerial leaders. They focus on a vision for the future but ensure that short-term goals are achieved. Strategic leaders effectively manage resources, especially human and social capital. They develop and manage a resource portfolio for the organization. They also bundle resources to create capabilities and then configure/integrate the capabilities to create value for customers and achieve a competitive advantage. They must leverage the capabilities effectively to create the competitive advantage.

Effective strategic leaders have high integrity and operate by a code of ethics. They also are called on to act in an entrepreneurial manner and even in the social realm. Thus they sometimes engage in social entrepreneurship. When they do so, society and their organization benefit. To have good strategic leaders over time, organizations must carefully plan the succession process, but the process may not always be a pleasant experience for all involved. Most strategic leaders, for example, are selected in a horse race. Thus the exercise of strategic leadership is not a simple phenomenon but a highly important one for the long-term health of the organization and society.

Notes

1. Explicit knowledge is knowledge that is highly codifiable. It can be verbally expressed and includes computer programs, patents and drawings. It is separable from the person who encoded the knowledge and is highly mobile. Explicit knowledge exists at the individual and organizational levels. The latter includes standard operating procedures, organizational policies, rules, regulations and organizational charts (Hedlund, 1994; Kogut and Zander, 1992).
2. Tacit knowledge is that knowledge so internalized we may not even be aware that we know it. It is characterized by the ability to know more than we can express to others. It is generally so uncodifiable that those who have it may not remember how they acquired the knowledge and may not be aware they have it until they use it. Tacit knowledge exists at the organizational and individual levels. The former includes the organization's routines, culture and other information-based 'invisible assets'. It may not be possible to separate tacit knowledge from the person who possesses it. (Polanyi, 1966; Reed and deFillippi, 1990; Nelson and Winter 1982; Itami, 1987).

References

Adler, P.S. and S.W. Kwon (2002), 'Social capital: prospects for a new concept', *Academy of Management Review*, **27** (1), 17–40.

Aronson, E. (2001), 'Integrating leadership styles and ethical perspectives', *Canadian Journal of Administrative Sciences*, **18** (4), 244–56.

Barnett, W.P., H.R. Greve and D.Y. Park (1994), 'An evolutionary model of organizational performance', *Strategic Management Journal*, **15** (Special Issue), 11–28.

Barney, J.B. (1986), 'Strategic factor markets: expectations, luck and business strategy', *Management Science*, **32** (10), 1231–41.

Barney, J.B. (1991), 'Firm resources and sustained competitive advantage', *Journal of Management*, **17** (1), 99–120.

Barney, J.B. and A.M. Arikan (2001), 'The resource-based view: Origins and implications', in M.A. Hitt, R.D. Freeman and J.R. Harrison (eds), *Handbook of Strategic Management*, Oxford: Blackwell Publishers, pp. 124–88.

Bennis, W. (1997), *Organizing Genius: The Secrets of Creative Collaboration*, Reading, MA: Addison-Wesley.

Black, J.A. and K.B. Boal (1994), 'Strategic resources: traits, configurations and paths to sustainable competitive advantage', *Strategic Management Journal*, **15** (Special Issue), 131–48.

Boschee, J. (1995), 'Social entrepreneurship', *Across the Board*, **32** (3), 20–23.

Brass, D.J., K.D. Butterfield and B.C. Skaggs (1998), 'Relationships and unethical behavior: a social network perspective' *Academy of Management Review*, **23** (1), 14–31.

Brinckerhoff, P.C. (2000), *Social Entrepreneurs: The Art of Mission-Based Venture Development*, New York: John Wiley & Sons.

Brown, S.L. and K.M. Eisenhardt (1999), 'Patching: restitching business portfolios in dynamic markets', *Harvard Business Review*, **77** (3), 72–82.

Burns, J.M. (1978), *Leadership*, New York: Harper and Row.

Cannella, A.A. Jr. and W. Shen (2001), 'So close and yet so far: promotion versus exit for CEO heirs apparent', *Academy of Management Journal*, **44** (2), 252–70.

Child, J. (1972), 'Organizational structure, environment and performance: the role of strategic choice', *Sociology*, **6**, 1–22.

Conger, J. (1991), 'Inspiring others: the language of leadership', *Academy of Management Executive*, **5** (1), 31–45.

Dees, J.G. (1998), 'Enterprising non-profits: what do you do when traditional sources of funding fall short?', *Harvard Business Review*, **76** (1), 55–67.

Denrell, J., C. Fang and S.G. Winter (2003), 'The economics of strategic opportunity', *Strategic Management Journal*, **24**, 977–90.

DePree, M. (1989), *Leadership is an Art*, New York: Doubleday.

Dess, G.G. and J.C. Picken (1999), *Beyond Productivity: How Leading Companies Achieve Superior Performance by Leveraging their Human Capital*, New York: AMACOM.

Dierickx, I. and K. Cool (1989), 'Asset stock accumulation and sustainability of competitive advantage', *Management Science*, **35** (12), 1504–11.

Drucker, P.F. (1989), 'What businesses can learn from nonprofits', *Harvard Business Review*, **67** (4), 88–93.

Evans, R. (1997), 'Hollow the leader', *Report on Business,* November, 56–63.

Fombrun, C. (1996), *Reputation: Realizing Value for the Corporate Image*, Boston: Harvard Business School Press.

Gilbert, D.R., Jr (2001), 'Corporate strategy and ethics, as corporate strategy comes of age', in M.A. Hitt, R.E. Freeman and J.S. Harrison (eds), *Blackwell Handbook of Strategic Management*, Oxford: Blackwell Publishers, pp. 564–82.

Grant, R.M. (1991), 'The resource-based theory of competitive advantage: implications for strategy formulation', *California Management Review*, **33** (3), 114–35.

Gulati, R., N. Nohria and A. Zaheer (2000), 'Strategic networks', *Strategic Management Journal*, **21** (3), 203–15.

Hagen, A.F., M.T. Hassan and S.G. Amin (1998), 'Critical strategic leadership components: an empirical investigation', *S.A.M. Advanced Management Journal*, **63** (3), 39–44.

Hambrick, D. (1989), 'Guest's editor's introduction: putting top managers back in the strategy picture', *Strategic Management Journal*, **10** (Special Issue), 5–15.

Hamel, G. and C.K. Prahalad (1994), *Competing for the Future*, Boston, MA: Harvard Business School Press.

Hammonds, K. (2003), 'Investing in social change', *Fast Company*, **71**, 54.

Harrison, J.S. and C.H. St. John (2002), *Foundations in Strategic Management* 2nd edn, Cincinnati: South-Western Publishing Company.

Hedlund, G. (1994), 'A model of knowledge management and the N-form corporation', *Strategic Management Journal*, **15** (Special Issue), 73–90.

Hibbert, S.A., G. Hogg and T. Quinn (2002), 'Consumer response to social entrepreneurship: the case of the big issue in Scotland', *International Journal of Nonprofit and Voluntary Sector Marketing*, **7**, 288–301.

Hill, C.W.L. and R.E. Hoskisson (1987), 'Strategy and structure in the multiproduct firm', *Academy of Management Review*, **12** (2), 331–41.

Hitt, M.A. and R.D. Ireland (2002), 'The essence of strategic leadership: managing human and social capital', *Journal of Leadership and Organizational Studies*, **9** (1), 3–14.

Hitt, M.A., R.D. Ireland and R.E. Hoskisson (2005), *Strategic Management: Competitiveness and Globalization*, Cincinnati: South-Western Publishing Company.

Hitt, M.A., B.W. Keats and E. Yucel (2003), 'Strategic leadership in global business organizations: building trust and social capital', in W.H. Mobley and P.W. Dorfman (eds), *Advances in Global Leadership*, Stamford, CT: JAI Press, pp. 9–35.

Hitt, M.A., L. Bierman, K. Shimizu and R. Kochhar (2001), 'Direct and moderating effects of human capital on strategy and performance in professional service firms: a resource-based perspective', *Academy of Management Journal*, **44**, 13–28.

Hitt, M.A., R.D. Nixon, R.E. Hoskisson and R. Kochhar (1999), 'Corporate entrepreneurship and cross-functional fertilization: activation, process and disintegration of a new product design team', *Entrepreneurship Theory & Practice*, **23** (3), 145–67.

Hoskisson, R.E. and M.A. Hitt (1994), *Downscoping: How to Tame the Diversified Firm*, New York: Oxford University Press.

Hosmer, L.T. (1982), 'The importance of strategic leadership', *Journal of Business Strategy*, **3** (2), 47–57.

Hunt, A.R. (2000), 'Social entrepreneurs: compassionate and tough-minded', *Wall Street Journal*, 13 July, A27.

Ireland, R.D. and M.A. Hitt (1999), 'Achieving and maintaining strategic competitiveness in the 21st century: the role of strategic leadership', *Academy of Management Executive*, **13** (1), 43–57.
Ireland, R.D., M.A. Hitt and D.G. Sirmon (2003), 'Strategic entrepreneurship: the construct and its dimensions', *Journal of Management*, **29** (6/7), 963–89.
Ireland, R.D., M.A. Hitt and D. Vaidyanath (2002), 'Managing strategic alliances to achieve a competitive advantage', *Journal of Management*, **28**, 413–46.
Itami, H. (1987), *Mobilizing Invisible Assets*, Cambridge, MA: Harvard University Press.
Kogut, B. and U. Zander (1992), 'Knowledge of the firm, combinative capabilities, and the replication of technology', *Organization Science*, **3**, 383–97.
Kotter, J.P. (1990), 'What leaders really do', *Harvard Business on Leadership*, Boston: Harvard Business School Press, p. 37–60.
Kotter, J.P. and J. Heskett (1992), *Corporate Culture and Performance*, New York: The Free Press.
Leadbeater, C. (1997), *The Rise of the Social Entrepreneur*, London: Demos Publishing.
Lepak, D.P. and S.A. Snell (1999), 'The human resource architecture: toward a theory of human capital allocation and development', *Academy of Management Review*, **24** (1), 31–48.
Lesser, E. and L. Prusak (2001), 'Preserving knowledge in an uncertain world', *MIT Sloan Management Review*, **43** (1), 101–2.
Lin, X. and R. Germain (2003), 'Organizational structure, context, customer orientation and performance: lessons from Chinese state-owned enterprises', *Strategic Management Journal*, **24** (11), 1131–51.
Loeb, M. (1993), 'Steven J. Ross 1927–1992', *Fortune*, **127** (2), 4; also in Hitt, Ireland and Hoskisson (2005), *Strategic Management: Competitiveness and Globalization*, 4th edn, Cincinnati: South-Western Publishing Company.
Makadok, R. (2003), 'Doing the right thing and knowing the right thing to do: why the whole is greater than the sum of the parts', *Strategic Management Journal*, **24** (10), 1043–56.
Messick, D.M. and M. Bazerman (1996), 'Ethical leadership and the psychology of decision making', *MIT Sloan Management Review*, **37** (2), 9–22.
Miller, D.A. (1996), 'A preliminary typology of organizational learning: synthesizing the literature', *Strategic Management Journal*, **22**, 484–505.
Miller, D.A. (2003), 'An asymmetry-based view of advantage: towards an attainable sustainability', *Strategic Management Journal*, **24**, 961–76.
Mintzberg, H. (1973), *The Nature of Managerial Work*, New York: Harper and Row.
Mintzberg, H. (1990), 'The manager's job – folklore and fact: retrospective commentary', *Harvard Business on Leadership*, Boston: Harvard Business School Press, pp. 29–32.
Mintzberg, H., B. Ahlstrand and J. Lampel (1998), *Strategy Safari*, New York: The Free Press.
Morris, B. (1995), 'Roberto Goizueta and Jack Welch: the wealth builders', *Fortune*, December **11** (12), 80–94.
Murphy, P.E. (1995), 'Corporate ethics statements: current status and future prospects', *Journal of Business Ethics*, **14** (9), 727–40.
Nathan, M. (1996), 'What is organizational vision? Ask chief executives', *Academy of Management Executive*, **10** (1), 82–3.
Nelson, R. and S. Winter (1982), *An Evolutionary Theory of Economic Change*, Cambridge, MA: Belknap Press.
Nohria, N. and B. Groysberg (2003), 'Coming and going', Economist.com, 23 October, accessed 17 February 2004.
Polanyi, M. (1966), *The Tacit Dimension*, Garden City, NY: Anchor.
Priem, R.L. and J.E. Butler (2001), 'Is the resource-based view a useful perspective for strategic management research?', *Academy of Management Review*, **26** (1), 22–40.
Reed, R. and R.J. DeFillippi (1990), 'Causal ambiguity, barriers to imitation, and sustainable competitive advantage', *Academy of Management Review*, **15**, 88–102.
Rowe, W.G. (1996), 'Persistence and change in CEO succession processes', unpublished dissertation, Management Department, Texas A&M University.
Rowe, W.G. (2001), 'Creating wealth in organizations: the role of strategic leadership', *Academy of Management Executive*, **15** (1), 81–94.

Schein, E.H. (1993), 'On dialogue, culture, and organizational learning', *Organizational Dynamics*, **22** (2), 40–51.

Schendel, D. (1989), 'Introduction to the special issue on "strategic leadership"', *Strategic Management Journal*, **10** (Special Issue), 1–3.

Schumpeter, J.A. (1934), *The Theory of Economic Development*, Cambridge, MA: Harvard University Press.

Shane, S.A. and S. Venkataraman (2000), 'The promise of entrepreneurship as a field of research', *Academy of Management Review*, **25** (1), 217–26.

Sirmon, D.G. and M.A. Hitt (2003), 'Managing resources: linking unique resources, management, and wealth creation in family firms', *Entrepreneurship Theory & Practice*, **27** (4), 339–58.

Sirmon, D.G., M.A. Hitt and R.D. Ireland (2003), 'Dynamically managing firm resources for value creation', paper presented at the Academy of Management, Seattle, Washington.

Sooklal, L. (1991), 'The leader as a broker of dreams', *Human Relations*, **44** (8), 833–56.

Staw, B.M., S.G. Barsade and K.W. Koput (1997), 'Escalation at the credit window: a longitudinal study of bank executives recognition and write-off of problem loans', *Journal of Applied Psychology*, 82 (1), 130–42.

Sullivan-Mort, G., J. Weerawardena and K. Carnegie (2003), 'Social entrepreneurship: towards conceptualization', *International Journal of Nonprofit and Voluntary Sector Marketing*, **8** (1), 76–88.

Teal, T. (1996), 'The human side of management', *Harvard Business on Leadership*, Boston: Harvard Business School Press, p. 147–70.

Teece, D.J., G. Pisano and A. Shuen (1997), 'Dynamic capabilities and strategic management', *Strategic Management Journal*, **18**, 509–33.

Thomke, S. and W. Kuemmerle (2002), 'Assets accumulation, interdependence and technological change: evidence from pharmaceutical drug discovery', *Strategic Management Journal*, **23** (7), 619–35.

Thompson, J.L. (2002), 'The world of the social entrepreneur', *The International Journal of Public Sector Management*, **15** (4/5), 412–31.

Trevino, L.K., G.R. Weaver, D.G. Toffler and B. Ley (1999), 'Managing ethics and legal compliance: what works and what hurts', *California Management Review*, **41** (2), 131–51.

Trigg, R. (1996), *Ideas of Human Nature: An Historical Introduction*, Cambridge, MA: Blackwell Publishers.

Vancil, R.F. (1987), *Passing the Baton: Managing the Process of CEO Selection*, Boston, MA: Harvard University Graduate School of Business Administration.

Waddock, S.A. and J.E. Post (1991), 'Social entrepreneurs and catalytic change', *Public Administrative Review*, **51**, 393–401.

Weerawardena, J. and G. Sullivan-Mort (2001), 'Learning, innovation and competitive advantage in not-for-profit aged care marketing: a conceptual model and research propositions', *Journal of Nonprofit & Public Sector Marketing*, **9** (3), 53–73.

Woolcock, M. and D. Narayan (2000), 'Social capital: implications for development theory, research and policy', *The World Bank Research Observer*, **15** (2), 225–49.

Worden, S. (2003a), 'The role of religious and nationalist ethics in strategic leadership: the case of J.N. Tata', *Journal of Business Ethics*, **47** (2), 147–64.

Worden, S. (2003b), 'The role of integrity as a mediator in strategic leadership: a recipe for reputational capital', *Journal of Business Ethics*, **46** (1), 31–44.

Zaleznik, A. (1996), 'Managers and leaders: are they different?', *Harvard Business on Leadership*, Boston: Harvard Business School Press, pp. 61–88.

Zaleznik, A. (1990), 'The leadership gap', *Academy of Management Executive*, **4** (1), 7–22.

Zietlow, J.T. (2001), 'Social entrepreneurship: managerial, finance and marketing aspects', *Journal of Nonprofit & Public Sector Marketing*, **9** (1–2), 19–43.

3 What leaders and their organizations can do to develop ethical leaders

Robert M. Fulmer

Introduction

Executives in almost every type of organization have been found lacking in integrity and social conscience. To explore how business firms and educational institutions can address the challenge of developing leaders with an appropriate balance between the necessity for operating with profitability and ethical sensitivity, a group of thought leaders came together in mid-2003, better to understand these challenges and ways in which to address them.

Primary participants in this dialogue include the CEO of a major defense and aerospace firm, the director of organizational effectiveness at the world's largest pharmaceutical company, the CEO of the world's leading provider of custom corporate executive education programs, the associate director of a leading NGO with emphasis on balanced leadership, and several academics with experience in leadership development. This chapter grows out of their conversations and examines the roles of top management, boards of directors and others involved in designing initiatives to improve organizational effectiveness. In part recounted in the words of key players, this chapter outlines actions that have been and could be undertaken to develop ethical leadership.

Ethical challenges have become a ubiquitous issue for leaders in a variety of fields. Within the recent past, we have read or seen disappointing reports of Olympic judging caught up in controversy. Award-winning journalists are fired for fabricating sources and stories. Political leaders have been brought before the bar of justice or tried by the court of public opinion. Church leaders are discovered to be covering up crimes committed by their subordinates. And, of course, corporate America and Wall Street are feeling the sting of accusations that go to the heart of investor trust.

In this chapter, I explore what some key business and NGO leaders are saying and doing to address public concerns about various strategies and approaches for developing ethical leadership skills. Ethics, values, leadership and trust are issues of timely immense importance to executives attempting to recover from a substantial downturn in the national and global economies.

After a quick review of the context, several leaders from the ranks of senior executives, academic and human resource development (HRD) specialists will, largely in their own words, describe the perspectives and approaches to the epidemic of unethical behavior in corporations. Individually their comments are insightful and pragmatic. Collectively they form the basis of a systemic approach to the challenges of ethical leadership and suggest some responses that offer potential for raising the level of ethical behavior in organizations.

In the aftermath of numerous scandals involving major corporations across the country, Pepperdine University's Graziadio School of Business and Management held a unique Executive Learning Forum with more than 80 local and national business leaders, experts and graduate students to discuss various strategies and approaches for developing ethical leadership skills. 'Ethics, values, leadership and trust are issues of immense importance to executives attempting to recover from a substantial downturn in the national and global economies,' said Graziadio School dean Linda Livingstone. 'I am pleased and encouraged that we have such a collection of local and national business leaders, who by their participation today are clearly demonstrating their commitment to ethical practices in the conduct of their businesses.'

Business ethics and corporate responsibility

If there is any question that ethics are of widespread concern, a Yahoo search for 'business ethics' generated 2 130 000 hits with at least 16 institutes or centers devoted to this issue. One web-based resource offers 150 comprehensive, interactive course modules covering 1000 topics. Another describes web-based business ethics training and communications solutions for employees and offers courses covering over 180 ethics and compliance topics. The Ethics Officers Association is a rapidly growing organization that provides a reference of practices to assist individuals who have been given specific corporate responsibility for coordinating internal ethical programs. Securities regulators announced the final terms of a $1.4 billion Wall Street research settlement in late 2003, ending almost two years of investigations into charges that analysts issued biased research to gain investment banking business.

More and more business schools are moving to add an ethics component to their curriculum. *The Chicago Tribune* recently highlighted some of the things business schools are doing to help improve the odds that their graduates do not get tangled in scandals like those at Enron and WorldCom. An estimated 90 per cent of business schools now provide some form of training in business ethics.

Toward the end of 2003, Boeing Co. dismissed two senior executives for 'breach of ethics', just four months after the Pentagon punished it for stealing trade secrets from rival Lockheed Martin to help win rocket contracts. In a classic case of 'belatedly locking the barn door', Boeing concurrently announced the appointment of a new unit 'to monitor ethics'.

Does it pay to be ethical?

Research studies in the USA and the UK have shown that a strong sense of ethics can be profitable. Mounting evidence suggests that a company's profitability is bolstered by its reputation as an honest, ethical business partner. Firms that routinely practice high business ethics and principles also attract the highest quality recruits and retain employees longer, according to a study by the Ethics Resource Center (ERC) in Washington.

The financial performance of companies stating a commitment to ethics is better than the performance of those that did not. Verschoor's study (1999) reveals that the excess value a company gives its shareholders over the total amount of their investments increases significantly when an ethics code is clearly stated by a company. Of the 87 companies where an ethics code was clearly stated, the average market value added (MVA) was 2.5 times larger than the MVA of those not mentioning a code of ethics or conduct, the report found. For the 47 companies expressing an extensive commitment to an ethics code, the MVA was three times that of the other companies not expressing an ethics code.

Good ethics is good business

The keynote speaker at the Executive Learning Forum, Daniel Burnham, Raytheon's chairman and CEO, put the recent emphasis on ethics in dramatic context: 'Business integrity is not an oxymoron; it's what smart companies insist upon to sustain their cultures – and to guide the individuals they select for leadership positions. I welcome the opportunity to talk about ethics – and so does our Leadership Team at Raytheon. It's important to speak out right now because it's a key issue facing our country.'

Corporate scandals have been a big contributor to the climate of investor anger and mistrust. Corporate revelations are shocking and disturbing: they go to the heart of investor confidence, even though the vast majority of companies behave responsibly. The source of investor frustration runs deep. Since 9/11, unethical behavior is perceived as *unpatriotic*. This is totally understandable. When people feel that their country is under attack from terrorists, when fire fighters and police officers are asked to lay their lives on the line, when we send our young men and women in harm's way abroad, we need to ask ourselves, 'What are we asking them to fight for? What kind of way of life are we fighting to protect?' Cast in this light, shady, greedy, unethical behavior seems even more shabby and intolerable.

In addition there is the issue of market history. In the 1990s, a historic bull market pulled in millions of new investors. From 1989 to 1998 (according to the NYSE, using Federal Reserve Board data) share ownership increased by some 32 million people. From 1995 to 1998 alone, share ownership rose by 15 million people. These investors had never experienced a bear market. Many had developed expectations that the market would rise indefinitely, that annual returns of 20 per cent, even 30 per cent, were reasonable and sustainable. Now that we are in a bear market, investors are disappointed; they're looking for someone to blame.

Mila Baker of Pfizer added that the 'public concern has been heightened because the behavior that has been showcased in U.S. corporations has been characterized by such blatant abuse. This concern for "ethical consciousness" exists at a time when the concept of leadership legitimacy is being questioned. The increased awareness of ethical issues and ethical dilemmas is a positive outgrowth of abuses in many arenas. There is a legitimate concern over who is responsible for the moral development of the corporation. Public interest around the world is high. CEOs face increased pressures as corporate social responsibility demands increase without any decline in the emphasis on productivity and profitability. A demand for accountability, justice, and fairness is mounting. While there are clashing communities/cultures related to standards of ethical actions, clear, courageous leadership is required. And there is a challenging role for all of us.'

'Business and ethics are fundamentally tied together,' said Blair Sheppard, CEO of Duke Corporate Education, a world leader in customized executive education. 'Today's corporate leaders face a number of challenges to overcome fundamental erosion in confidence and demonstrate their commitment to responsible leadership.'

Balancing demands on business
As several executives suggested, high ethical conduct is no excuse for shoddy products or profits. Conversely high profitability does not excuse shady conduct. Nancy McGaw, associate director for a key policy program at the Aspen Institute, the Business and Society Program (Aspen BSP) described her program's initial purpose: 'At our inception – just five years ago – we set ourselves one of those Big Hairy Audacious Goals that Jim Collins and Jerry Porras talk about. We wanted to influence business practice in such a way that business executives would be better equipped and more inclined to consider the social and environmental impacts of their business decisions. We wanted these executives to be attentive to these impacts as well as to the

economic performance of their enterprise. In other words, our objective was to assure the supply of what we called balanced business leaders.'

In 2000, Aspen BSPs initiated what has become a continuing series of small conferences to learn from experts in leadership development programs around the world – in academia, in corporations and in professional service firms, explaining that, 'We bring together experts who share our commitment to developing leaders who are expert at this daring balancing act, at understanding the complex interdependence between business success and social and environmental progress.

'Our meetings have focused on what it means to be a balanced leader: not just a CEO, mind you, but a leader at any level of the business enterprise. And we have considered what the impacts are of balanced leadership within corporations and for executive education. Our findings indicate that there are key essential skills and qualities that balanced leaders possess. Balanced leaders, educators told us, are ethical, need to be able to span boundaries and listen to diverse constituencies and be willing to be altered by these interactions. Such leaders are enriched by complexity and diversity, not overwhelmed by it, and their decisions acknowledge and honor the often conflicting values and expectations of diverse constituencies.

'Although there was remarkable consensus in the discussions at these meetings about what kind of leaders we said we needed, there was general agreement that, in practice, such leaders are in short supply. Participants at our meetings continue to observe behaviors and attitudes that reflect the absence of these qualities.' They see managers who

- are blindsided by public outrage at the corporation's handling of an environmental or social crisis;
- emphasize the primacy of shareholder interests and marginalize the interests of other stakeholders;
- think economic models will ultimately provide every answer;
- ignore critical constituencies (even within their own companies) when making decisions; and
- consistently place work commitments above other commitments in their lives and expect their colleagues to do the same.

Roles for enhancing ethical, balanced leadership

With universal agreement about the need to develop leaders with a balance between strong ethical sensitivity and the ability to produce profitable results, the Forum participants rose to the challenge of identifying ways that a spectrum of leaders in business education and practice could be a part of the solution rather than simply documenting the need for action. Because of the different perspectives of the various speakers, the totality of their suggestions offers a systems approach to improving ethical practice in organizations. These suggestions are grouped under the headings of various ideas that are appropriate for the CEO and corporate directors, organizational tools and initiatives, as well as challenges for business education.

Dan Burnham, Raytheon's CEO, was outspoken and personal in articulating what he viewed as the responsibility of senior executives.

> Implementing and sustaining ethics programs is important, but we need to do more. Leaders, and leaders-to-be, need to focus on the desired end state, notably, on the vision for their company and the values and the culture of their company.
>
> The CEO must be the chief ethics officer of the firm. He or she cannot delegate integrity. We cannot be distracted by resistance in the organization from those who think the company is already ethical, or that we're trying to be social engineers. The CEO must make everyone understand that the organization's future is dependent on its reputation. It's got to be personal, human, and individual. Every employee must feel empowered and responsible for the reputation of the company. *The leader must demonstrate an interest in uncovering problems and finding solutions.* We should develop an early warning system that identifies problems and even potential problems. This kind of climate can be developed by asking tough questions and telling it like it is. My goal is to act on facts, not emotion. If an unethical behavior is uncovered, it is important to act swiftly and decisively. Objective tools to achieve and measure results help take the subjectivity out of the equation. It is important to surround yourself with those who will tell it like it is.
>
> Top management sets an important tone by *encouraging open and honest communication* so employees feel empowered to raise issues. Raytheon and many other leading firms encourage *their managers to benchmark the firms they admire* – to look beyond the walls and structures of our company and industry. We strive for constancy and try to document how the company has handled similar problems in the past? I think we must *create an environment of inclusion*; that's ethics (and good business) as well. I talk about ethics and integrity routinely, and make sure others see these. You can find at least a couple of speeches on our website that deal with the ethics and integrity.

Burnham suggests at least six things that a CEO can do to improve the ethical climate of a firm and its reputation. But what happens when an organization is being investigated by the Securities and Exchange Commission (SEC), or is accused of wrongdoing by former employees or by the contentious litigation of a class action law suit? Adversity is the real test of leadership and integrity. Trying times test the commitment to a statement of values. Firms that demonstrate their ethicality when they are being publicly challenged will come through this test with their reputations enhanced rather than destroyed. Ralph Larsen, former chairman and CEO of Johnson & Johnson, said that his company's famous credo really boiled down to one core thought, 'personal responsibility'. This credo has become a part of the DNA of Johnson & Johnson and adherence to it a requirement for rising through the ranks at one of America's most admired corporations.

Tools and initiatives for organizations
Any organization that has a CEO with strong ethical values and commitment has a head start in creating an ethical organization, yet no CEO can review the day-to-day decisions and behavior of each employee. Consequently successful firms will translate the desire for ethicality into concrete institutional policies and practices. Pfizer's program for worldwide organizational effectiveness focuses on four key areas: (a) enhancing organization effectiveness in a global context, (b) developing leaders, (c) building productive, healthy and satisfying environments, and (d) improving governance – strategy, structure, process and relationships. Together these elements create a system where ethical leadership can become a core competency and impetus for organizational effectiveness. A best practice study of succession management conducted by the American Productivity and Quality Center found that the exemplars utilized a matrix to assess leaders on both their results and their demonstrated values. Dan Burnham pointed out the importance of making integrity a part of the assessment system and described a similar system at Raytheon.

> What do we look for in a leadership candidate with respect to integrity? What we're really looking for when we recruit leaders are people who have developed an inner gyroscope of ethical principles. We look for people for whom ethical thinking is part of what they do – no different than 'strategic thinking' or 'tactical thinking'. It's the ongoing process of reasoning about what is proper given a set of values and a mission in a very messy world filled with many complexities.
> Here's what it says under integrity in Raytheon's Leadership Assessment Instrument:
>
> • Maintains unequivocal commitment to honesty, truth and ethics in every facet of behavior;
> • Conforms with the letter and intent of company policies while working to effect any necessary policy changes;
> • Actions are consistent with words; follows through on commitments; readily admits mistakes; and
> • Is trusted and inspires others to strive to be trusted.
>
> We believe this kind of person will get better results. We know these are the kind of people who will help us build a successful future.

As Blair Sheppard of Duke Corporate Education commented, 'Firms that know what kinds of developmental needs their people have and are committed to providing those developmental opportunities are obviously ahead of companies that simply assume that the "fit will survive" – without asking, "fit for what?" ... Integrity is probably a more important developmental need than the ability to understand foreign exchange or transfer pricing.'

Pfizer's Mila Baker spoke of ways that ethical leadership can become a core competency and lever for organizational effectiveness.

> First, it is essential to establish ethical leadership as a strategic imperative. Next, care should be taken to develop a 'Strategic Ethical Leadership Agenda' with as much specificity as possible. This agenda should describe actions that demonstrate commitment and acceptable conduct as well as actions that do not measure up to the values of the firm. While it is impossible to make this a comprehensive list, we try to define a set of 'Rules of Engagement' which includes recognition of risk determination and consequences. We have attempted to create a 'Roadmap to Ethical Behavior' by putting a spotlight on ethics by incorporating this subject into all of our change management initiatives. We try to increase the ethical awareness, skills and knowledge of all employees while encouraging dialogue and conversation with others around ethical dilemmas. We institutionalize stories where someone in the firm has dealt successfully with an issue of integrity and try to make that person a 'hero'. Fundamentally, we want to create an environment that is ethically competent AND ethically sensitive. We strive to understand the challenges created by the complexity and scale of our organization and what the implications of this mean for ethical leadership. Perhaps most importantly, every leader should model what he or she is attempting to instill.

The responsibility and opportunity for boards

Since the top of the organization sets the tone for leadership throughout the firm, boards of directors will be asked to assume more responsibility in the development of an ethical climate. Earlier in 2003, Burnham spoke in New England to the National Association of Corporate Directors and challenged members of this important group to meet their goal of representing society and shareholder interest in high standards of content.

At the Pepperdine Executive Learning Forum, he added:

> Being a corporate director provides a way of building confidence in a system that has fueled our national success ... Leadership integrity carries over to corporate governance as well. Every company, no matter how strong and ethical, needs to take a second look at corporate governance, to take advantage of every opportunity for improvement. We've done a close review of our corporate governance. We feel pretty good about the changes we've made:
>
> • We have fewer Board meetings, but with lots of interaction.
> • We try to focus on large questions without ignoring details.
> • We do frequent reviews of the strategic landscape.
> • There are no former Raytheon CEOs on the Board, and we've decided there shouldn't be except under special circumstances.
> • A very substantial portion of our Board is independent.
> • We've named a lead director.

- Before the New York Stock Exchange proposed standards and before legislation (Sarbanes-Oxley) we started digging into the whole area of corporate governance with an eye toward best practices – what we could do better. Since NYSE/Sarbanes-Oxley, we've added to, and taken an inventory of, our practices, and we believe our governance practices are strong and thorough, but we're going to try to keep getting better.
- Moreover, the government has given us tools to reassure investors that we are meeting our fiduciary duties as Board members to be active monitors of corporate performance.
- Oversight, transparency, diligence – they're all critical to confidence. There is no substitute.

Integrity must be felt and lived. But these don't substitute for a well-run business – for strategies that stretch, for risks that are managed and become rewards, for disciplined and predictable execution. Good governance *cannot* fix a lousy business. Bad governance *can* ruin a great business. No institution in America is perfect. But good institutions are led in the right direction by good people and the right values.

Business education has a role

Since the Executive Learning Forum was hosted by an educational institution and attended by both professors and MBA students, it seemed appropriate to consider what contributions could be made at the level of graduate business education. As Nancy McGaw reviewed the seminars and interviews conducted by Aspen BSP, she concluded:

It is difficult to generalize but I think there is one overriding theme from these conversations about leadership development – and it is this: If we want to develop more balanced leaders, we need to shift management education from a focus on mastery to an emphasis on discovery. For too long we have accorded primacy to solving problems with the use of economic and other technical tools.

I recall a story told at one of our convenings by a woman from the Munich office of a major consulting firm. She had worked on teams in Eastern Europe on privatization initiatives. She recalled running the spread sheets, testing scenarios as she had been trained to do, but all the economic modeling in the world couldn't get the team to the 'right' answer when they considered all the lives that would be impacted by the decisions suggested via this economic modeling process. Making those decisions required judgment of quite a different sort.

Many business activities require judgment of a different sort. How to structure a project financing, for example, in a disadvantaged area that needs the jobs and tax revenues that will be generated, but the project is going to disrupt communities and ecosystems. How to decide how much tax avoidance is enough. The list is long.

Recently I attended a presentation by a dean of a business school who was explaining how they built their MBA curriculum around a core query: 'What Does Every MBA Need to Know?' While one would certainly not dispute the need to equip MBAs with the technical skills that are required to get their jobs done, we wonder if we shouldn't also be thinking about building a curriculum around 'What Every MBA Needs to Ask'.

We took that advice and recently asked leadership development experts to name some of the questions that typically don't get asked in MBA curricula or in executive education programs. Let me share four questions that every program design should consider:

1) What is the purpose of our enterprise?
2) Is it possible to articulate that purpose in a way that engages the passions of employees?
3) How do we measure success?
4) What is it that we do as a business when we are at our best that allows us to say that our life has meaning?

I was a corporate banker for 18 years. I can tell you that there would have been some startled – and probably some cranky – responses to such questions if they had been raised in open discussions in the bank in which I worked. Had these questions been open for discussion, they would have given many of us a chance to express some of our deeply held convictions about our work – and some of our misgivings as well. And I believe that the exercise – if undertaken as part of the way we did business and trained our upcoming managers – would not have distracted us from the hard work of making revenue targets and deepening our client relationships. Rather it would have given us a competitive edge.

Danger or opportunity?

The Chinese symbol for change contains symbols for both danger and opportunity. The widespread public concern about ethics in business suggests danger if the voice of the public is not heard but also contains a positive opportunity for change that can improve the quality of management practice and the quality of life in general. As Nancy McGaw reflected on four years of work, she observed:

So much has changed since Aspen BSP started our 'Developing Balanced Leaders' program in the late 1990s. The international, political, economic and social picture looks far bleaker now. So it is fair to ask vis-à-vis developing balanced leaders ... is this a time of great peril – or one of promise? Let me share a finding from a 2003 research report. This study is a follow up to research we conducted between 1999 and 2001 with MBAs at leading international business schools. We undertook that work to learn about MBA students' attitudes about the role of business in society and the influence of an MBA education on these attitudes. Recently, we went back into the field to survey students' attitudes in the wake of corporate scandals, terrorist attacks, a severe economic downturn and threats of war.

One question we asked in both stages of the research was which MBA courses should address issues related to the social responsibility of companies. In the spring of 2001 – when, as you will all remember, things were quite a bit rosier – roughly one-third of the students said they thought accounting courses should have this content. A similar percentage thought such content belonged in finance courses. In November, 2002, 84% of students said yes to accounting and 57% said finance courses should address these issues as well. In fact, with the exception of economics, every discipline showed an increase in the percentage of students who thought social responsibility content belonged in the courses.

There is much to be said about what these findings mean, but I would like to posit this – we are at a propitious moment. There is openness on the part of the purchasers of management education for content that has not previously been sought or, in fact, on offer – and management education should seize the day. It could then take a key role in contributing to a restoration of confidence in leadership's ability to lead with honesty, integrity and consideration for all stakeholders – and we'd begin to produce more of the balanced leaders who are now in short supply.

Suggested strategies

While the rich discussion continued long after the formal session ended and it is impossible to capture all of the thoughts and ideas presented at the Forum, it was clear that the corporate executives as well as representatives from academia, consulting firms and a leading NGO saw a tremendous opportunity in the midst of an unparalleled public concern about ethics and integrity in business.

The major strategies suggested by the participants at the forum include the following:

- the importance of balanced executive leadership that embraces complexity, diversity and social responsibility rather than being overwhelmed by it;
- the need to institute a culture of corporate responsibility at the very highest executive levels as well as within middle management;
- a greater balance between the pursuit of higher performance and profitability and the institution of codes of ethical conduct;
- the incorporation of values and responsibility in the process of executive succession management rather than an overemphasis on performance at all costs;
- the importance of boards of directors as facilitators and enforcers of responsible corporate governance;
- the cultivation and investment in mid-level managers who have the primary responsibility for implementing the corporate vision and values structure;
- the need for more concerted education and training of executives in management and leadership skills.

A note on references

This chapter is based on comments made at Pepperdine's 4th Annual Executive Learning Forum focused on 'The Challenge of Developing

Ethical Leaders', and which included presentations on 'Ethical Leadership and Organizational Effectiveness' and 'Current Challenges in Leadership Development'. Among those speaking at the forum were: Linda Livingstone, dean, Graziadio School of Business and Management, Dan Burnham, chairman and CEO, Raytheon, Inc.; Blair Sheppard, CEO, Duke Corp. Education; Nancy McGaw, Aspen Institute Business and Society Program; Robert M. Fulmer, Graziadio School of Business and Management; Jay Conger, London School of Business; and Mila Baker, director of organizational effectiveness, Pfizer, Inc.

The ethics research cited above draws on C.C. Verschoor (1999), 'Corporate performance is closely linked to a strong ethical commitment', *Business and Society Review*, **104** (4), 407–15. For a comprehensive review of studies on the link between corporate social and financial performance, see J.D. Margolis and J.P. Walsh (2001), *People and Profits? The Search for a Link between a Company's Social and Financial Performance*, Mahwah, NJ: Lawrence Erlbaum Associates.

Details of the best practice study of succession management can be found in J.A. Conger and R.M. Fulmer (2003), 'Developing your leadership pipeline', *Harvard Business Review*, December, 76–84. Aspen's research on the attitudes to ethics, social and environmental issues is reported in Aspen Institute (2003), *Beyond Grey Pinstripes 2003: Preparing MBA's for Social and Environmental Stewardship*, Washington, DC: The Aspen Institute Business and Society Program. The project website, *www.BeyondGreyPinstripes.org*, includes a searchable data base on courses, programs, and research at the 100 business schools that participated in the study.

4   The leadership challenge: building resilient corporate reputations

Charles J. Fombrun

It is a terrible thing to look over your shoulder when you are trying to lead – and find no one there. (Franklin D. Roosevelt)

Introduction

The corporate scandals of 2001–4 made household names out of previously large but relatively obscure companies like Enron, Worldcom, Tyco, Adelphia and Arthur Andersen. Most of these scandals can be traced to deficient organizational cultures that placed individual self-interest above the institutional interests they were hired to defend. They point to a fundamental flaw in late 20th-century models of organization that spurred executive hubris, promoted celebrity over leadership and, in the process, dramatically failed to serve the interests of employees, investors and customers.

In this chapter, I suggest that organizations with responsible leaders at the helm are those that value reputation and manage them as rent-producing economic assets. Drawing on original research conducted by the Reputation Institute, a private research group I founded in 1999, I demonstrate that well-regarded companies rely on a model of leadership that recognizes the interests of multiple constituencies, values how well these constituencies are served, monitors their perceptions and expresses itself to them abundantly, consistently and with authenticity and transparency.

Reputation: a crossroads of literatures

A corporate reputation is a collective representation of a company's past actions and future prospects that describes how key stakeholders interpret a company's initiatives and assess its ability to deliver valued outcomes (Fombrun, 2001). This definition is rooted in convergent perspectives advanced by economists, strategists, organization theorists and marketers.

To economists, corporate reputations are functional traits. Good reputations create favorable impressions among employees, customers, investors, competitors and the general public about what a company is, what it does, and what it stands for (Schlenker, 1980; Tedeschi, 1981). Consumers rely on a company's reputation in judging its products because they cannot directly experience the quality or reliability of those products (Grossman and Stiglitz, 1980). Similarly a good reputation increases investor confidence that managers will act in ways that are reputation-consistent. Since external investors have difficulty assessing the quality of a company's strategy or its ability to execute that strategy, a good reputation helps stabilize relationships between a company and its investors.

Reputations are also signals. A good reputation develops from prior resource commitments executives make to first-order activities likely to create favorable perceptions with outside observers (Myers and Majluf, 1984). Since the features of a good company are hidden from view, companies invest in reputation building to signal the company's attractive qualities and increase stakeholder confidence in the company's offerings. Advertising campaigns, media relations, charitable contributions and conference calls with analysts all constitute 'strategic projections' that companies use to signal their attractive features to potential customers, investors and employees and through which they therefore build reputation (Rindova and Fombrun, 1999).

To corporate strategists, a good reputation is therefore an intangible asset that embodies the history of the company's past interactions with its stakeholders and describes what it stands for (Dutton and Dukerich, 1991). A good reputation impedes mobility and produces returns to a company because it is difficult to imitate (Caves and Porter, 1977; Barney, 1991). By limiting a company's actions and its rivals' reactions, a good reputation is therefore a prominent feature of industry structure (Abrahamson and Fombrun, 1994; Fombrun and Zajac, 1987). Since reputations are *externally* perceived, they are largely outside the direct control of firms' managers (Barney, 1986). Competitors have difficulty duplicating the results of better regarded companies because it takes time for a reputation to coalesce in observers' minds, and empirical studies show that, even when confronted with negative information, observers resist changing their assessments about a company (Wartick, 1992).

Strategic decisions also have social consequences. Social responsibility theorists suggest principles and practices that managers should adhere to in order to induce ethically sound strategic decisions (Carroll, 1979; Wartick and Cochran, 1985). They emphasize that companies have diverse stakeholders with valid claims on the strategies that firms pursue. They therefore advise executives to pursue 'enterprise strategies' that address social concerns in order to secure external support (Sethi, 1979; Freeman, 1984; Post, 1986; Freeman and Gilbert, 1988; Wartick, 1988; Jones, 1995). To them, corporate reputations are a gauge of the legitimacy of a company's actions in an institutional field (Elsbach, 1994; Suchman, 1995).

Economists and strategists typically ignore the sociocognitive processes that actually generate reputational rankings (Granovetter, 1985). In contrast, sociologists argue that rankings are social constructions that come into being through the relationships that companies establish with their constituents (Rao, 1994). Every company has multiple evaluators, each of which applies different criteria in assessing firms. Reputational ratings and rankings therefore represent aggregated assessments of a company's institutional prestige and describe the stratification of the social system surrounding industries.

Faced with incomplete information about a company's actions, observers not only interpret the first-order signals that companies broadcast, but also rely on the evaluative signals refracted by key intermediaries such as market analysts, institutional investors and reporters (Abrahamson and Fombrun, 1994; Fombrun and Rindova, 2004). Media reporters and financial analysts are important intermediaries in an inter-firm network that transmits and refracts information about companies to consumers and investors (Abrahamson and Fombrun, 1992).

Students of marketing and branding regard corporate reputations as an outcome of efforts made by companies to stimulate customer purchases and build customer loyalty. Reputations are valuable insofar as they induce repeat purchases and stabilize corporate revenue streams. Corporate communications are a key ingredient of the marketing mix: they are strategic informational signals designed to familiarize customers and other constituents with the company's offerings, activities and prospects, and thereby induce support. To strengthen customer identification, companies regularly create attractive messages and images that they then communicate in their advertising and public relations campaigns. Often these messages and images are leveraged into communications aimed at other constituencies.

Economists suggest that companies are more likely to invest in reputation building when the quality of the company's products and services is not directly observable. High-quality producers do so to signal their quality to consumers who would not otherwise know. When successful, these investments in building a good reputation allow the company to charge premium prices and earn rents from the repeat purchases that its reputation generates. In contrast, low-quality producers avoid investing in reputation building because they do not expect repeat purchases (Milgrom and Roberts, 1986).

Similar dynamics operate in the capital and labor markets. For instance, managers regularly communicate to investors their economic performance. Since investors are more favorably disposed to companies that demonstrate high and stable earnings, managers try to smooth out their quarterly earnings and keep dividend payout ratios high and fixed, despite earnings fluctuations (Brealy and Myers, 1988). Often the same companies will pay a premium price to hire high-reputation auditors and counselors. They rent the reputations of these agents in order to convey to investors, regulators and other key publics that they are a company of great probity and credibility.

Finally organization theorists generally view reputations as emergent features of companies that are rooted in the shared understandings of employees and managers: their cultures and identities (Albert and Whetten, 1985). Companies develop reputations from their 'self-expressions', communications that are most visible in a company's logos and brands, but also in the company's statements of beliefs and cultural practices (Schultz et al., 2000).

From an organizational viewpoint, a good reputation is therefore a 'social fact', an emergent collective feature of a company that reflects its central, distinctive and enduring identity elements (Albert and Whetten, 1985). Schultz *et al.* (2000) describe how a strong reputation is built from *authentic* representations of a company's inner being: its identity. Their suggestions are consistent with Collins and Porras's (1996) findings that enduring companies have strong core ideologies. Both assert that a company's reputation sits on the bedrock of its corporate identity, the core values that shape its actions, its communications, its culture and its decisions, and with which a company expresses itself to its constituents.

These diverse literatures suggest that reputations are subjective, qualitative assessments of companies by stakeholders. A company that takes its reputation seriously is therefore likely to believe that

- a good reputation conveys the company's *overall attractiveness* to current and potential employees, customers, investors and local communities;
- a good reputation *constitutes a powerful mobility barrier* that gives the company a competitive advantage over rivals;
- a good reputation is therefore an *intangible economic asset* that is worth investing in.

Responsible leaders recognize the significant value embedded in a company's reputation and manage the company's intangible wealth carefully. A company with responsible leadership therefore (a) recognizes the multiple interests of its major stakeholders, (b) values and monitors their opinions, and (c) takes action to address their concerns. As our research indicates a growing number of companies are taking seriously the merits of reputation measurement and management as a way of capturing the company's success at meeting its stakeholder obligations. It is in these companies that we expect to see responsible leadership emerge.

Key dimensions of corporate reputation

Responsible leaders invite systematic monitoring and measurement of how their companies are performing. As we showed in the preceding section, 'reputation' is a construct that gauges how well a company is delivering value to its constituents. To concerned executives, having a valid measure of reputation is therefore essential. For such a measure to deliver, it would have to be universal, reliable and comparative. Unfortunately quantitative measures of corporate reputation proliferate, encouraging chaos and confusion about a company's reputational assets (Fombrun, 1996).

The most visible reputation measure is probably the one popularized in *Fortune*'s annual list of 'America's Most Admired Companies'. Since 1983, the magazine has described how executives rate companies in their own industries on eight attributes of performance: (1) the quality of the company's products and services, (2) the company's innovativeness, (3) value as a long-term investment, (4) financial soundness, (5) ability to attract, develop and retain talent, (6) community responsibility, (7) use of corporate assets, and (8) quality of management. Because of its face validity, the list has spawned a host of imitators and spinoffs around the world.

Close scrutiny of measures like *Fortune*'s, however, indicates serious methodological deficiencies. Some are arbitrarily performed by expert panels, and so are not replicable. Some are carried out with private information, and so are unverifiable. All rely on idiosyncratic attributes, many of which lack theoretical derivation. The result is a cacophony of ratings, few of which are directly comparable, and most of which executives do not trust.

To address these issues, the Reputation Institute worked with the market research firm of Harris Interactive to develop a standardized but versatile instrument that could be used to measure perceptions of companies across industries and with multiple stakeholder segments. As part of that research, we conducted focus groups in the USA and in other countries that began by asking people to name companies they liked and respected, as well as companies they did not like or respect. We then examined why they felt this way. When we analyzed the data from different groups and industries, the findings demonstrated that people justify their feelings about companies with one of 20 attributes that we grouped into six dimensions:

- *emotional appeal*: how much the company is liked, admired and respected;
- *products and services*: perceptions of the quality, innovation, value and reliability of the company's products and services;
- *financial performance*: perceptions of the company's profitability, prospects and risk;

- *vision and leadership*: how much the company demonstrates a clear vision and strong leadership;
- *workplace environment*: perceptions of how well the company is managed, how it is to work for and the quality of its employees;
- *social responsibility*: perceptions of the company as a good citizen in its dealings with communities, employees, and the environment.

On the basis of these attributes, we created an index that summed people's perceptions of companies on these 20 attributes: the 'Reputation Quotient' (or RQ). We then validated the instrument in various countries, and conducted empirical studies using the RQ that benchmarked the reputations of over 200 companies with consumers in five countries: Australia, Denmark, Italy, Netherlands and the USA (Fombrun, Gardberg and Sever, 2000; Alsop, 1999). These studies are now conducted annually and their results are widely diffused in publications like *The Wall Street Journal* and other national media.

Roots of reputation

Expressiveness
The best regarded companies in the second year of the RQ Project, conducted in 2001, were Microsoft (Australia), Lego (Denmark), Ahold (Netherlands), Ferrari (Italy) and Johnson & Johnson (USA). For each company, we therefore examined more closely: (1) their internal and external communications as displayed on their websites, in advertising and through press releases; (2) the citizenship activities they carry out internationally; (3) the visibility of these companies in terms of awards received, media lists on which they appear, and media articles in which they are featured; and (4) interviews with selected executives from some of the companies (Fombrun and Van Riel, 2004).

The results are intriguing: the best regarded companies appeared substantially different from lesser-rated rivals on each of five key dimensions (described below): distinctiveness, visibility, consistency, authenticity and transparency. We therefore propose that these dimensions are core pillars of a model of responsible leadership for the 21st century. They describe the company's 'expressiveness' (Schultz *et al.*, 2000), the strategic posture that comes to light from its communications and initiatives. Figure 4.1 captures these dimensions in a graphic form.

Distinctiveness
Across industries, companies earn stronger reputations when they own a distinctive position in the minds of stakeholders. Companies competing in

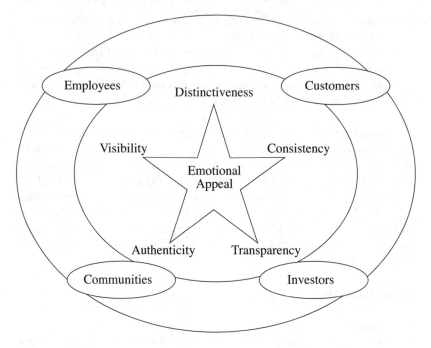

Figure 4.1   Responsible leadership: a reputation model

commoditized industries such as the oil industry or the coffee industry are powerful examples of this process. Most oil companies grapple with negative stakeholder perceptions of oil companies as environmental polluters. To counter these perceptions, responsible companies try to communicate their concern for the environment with active programs and initiatives. In doing so, they run into each other head on. In an effort to build a reputation for responsible leadership in the environmental arena, for instance, in 2000 energy giant BP unveiled a new corporate identity. The blossoming green and yellow motif serves as a metaphorical flower that supports the company's tagline 'beyond petroleum' and its commitment to rely on more environmentally friendly technologies in the future. Under CEO John Brown's leadership, BP's strategy is clearly to claim a stronger share-of-mind as the world's most environmentally friendly company. Its success will depend heavily on what rivals do in this hotly contested terrain, especially as the alternative fuel movement gathers momentum against a backdrop of concern over geopolitical factors and global warming. It also depends heavily on how successful the company is at meeting its stretch goal of moving beyond petroleum.

Visibility

Strong reputations result when companies earn visibility by focusing their actions and communications on a core theme. Take top-rated Coca-Cola: its products are ubiquitous, as is its world-famous logo. All of the company's communications portray a core 'devotion to the product' and its integral role in the lives of people. Contrast that to arch-rival PepsiCo, whose reputation is deliberately that of the also-ran, seeking to leverage the visibility of the 'cola-wars' to chip away at its premium-priced, distinctively branded nemesis. Coca-Cola's continued dominance of the beverage category (despite challenges from Pepsi and other upstarts) is a testament to the advantage of visibility and focus in the design of reputation programs.

Responsible corporate leaders recognize the importance of giving visibility to the company as a whole rather than simply to themselves. Contrary to the popular dictum, familiarity does *not* breed contempt – quite the contrary. In most cases, familiarity helps constituents better understand what companies are doing, and appreciate their efforts, initiatives and results. The result is a stronger emotional bond between the company and its employees, customers, investors and observers. Building an emotional bond between company and stakeholder is the *sine qua non* of responsible leadership in the 21st century.

Contrast that to the individualistic, celebrity model that some companies operate under. Although making CEOs into celebrities adds visibility to the company, all too often it is rooted in individual aggrandizement and hubris at the expense of the company's wellbeing. The fate of Martha Stewart Living Omnimedia (MSLO) demonstrates the inherent riskiness of a model that champions CEO celebrity rather than corporate reputation. In 2004, after founder Martha Stewart was found guilty of obstruction of justice in the notorious insider trading filed against her, the company found itself floundering to retain the support of investors, employees and the public. MSLO's reputation was principally a halo of its founder: the company had not invested in its own reputation building.

There are a few exceptions to the beneficial effects of visibility, notably tobacco companies. Familiarity has tended to hurt the reputations of Philip Morris and RJR. The same was true of AOL-Time Warner in 2001: consumers who were more familiar with the company generally rated it *less* favorably, and depressed its market value. The benefits of visibility therefore depend heavily on the type of exposure that a company achieves. Tobacco companies and AOL-Time Warner, much like Enron, Arthur Andersen, Global Crossings and Worldcom, were visible for all the wrong reasons, and their reputations suffered. In fact visibility is a two-edged sword. On one hand, it can be leveraged to achieve enhanced reputation. Most companies topping national RQ surveys benefit greatly from the visibility of their founders, who have near-mythical status in national folklore (Fombrun and Van Riel, 2004). On the other hand, visibility can also have enduring negative effects on reputation: Exxon's reputation has remained in the doldrums since the Valdez oil spill of 1989, despite settling claims, paying fines, merging with Mobil and launching philanthropic initiatives. Consumers can demonstrate elephant-like memories.

Consistency

Companies build stronger reputations when they are consistent in their actions and communications to stakeholders. In a survey of global firms, we found that better regarded companies were more likely to orchestrate and integrate their initiatives across multiple constituents and functions. Companies with weaker reputations suffered from allowing initiatives to develop in silos.

In general the inconsistency of initiatives and communications that emanate from most companies is staggering. Compartmentalized staff in 'Corporate Affairs' offices (and often in remote foundations) manage relationships with local community groups. 'Investor Relations' groups are responsible for interfacing with analysts. 'Advertising Departments' (and remote ad agencies of record) advise about product and corporate positioning. 'Public Relations' worry about media communications and special events, while 'Human Resources Departments' handle employee communications. These fragmented arrangements virtually guarantee inconsistent presentations of the company to its different constituencies. Not coincidentally, lack of consistency reflects a failure of leadership in the executive suite. No responsible company can long sustain a reputation when its actions and communications are inconsistent.

Authenticity

A good reputation develops when corporate leaders are authentic and genuine in their communications and actions. Stakeholders appreciate authenticity: to be well-regarded, you cannot fake it for long – you have to be real. Being real pays off handsomely: authenticity creates emotional appeal, and there is no reputation without emotional appeal. Statistical analyses of RQ data in all countries indicate that the primary driver of reputation across all the countries we have studied so far is the degree of emotional appeal the company has to respondents.

Again consider Johnson & Johnson. When asked to identify J&J's products, most consumers point to the company's line of baby products. There is no accident here. J&J heavily advertises its consumer products using emotional imagery about children and the nurturing role that parents play in their upbringing. This is so even though the baby products line accounts for no more than 5 per cent of J&J's portfolio of products and services. Babies sell, and the authenticity of J&J is confirmed by its well-known 'credo', the statement of beliefs that everyone at J&J can recite almost verbatim, and which is credited for having made the company 'do the right thing' in the face of crises (like the 1982 and 1985 Tylenol poisonings that cost the company billions of dollars in product recalls, in the development of tamper-proof seals and in post-crisis corporate advertising).

Rival health care products company Bristol-Myers Squibb (BMS) has had a relatively difficult time establishing authenticity with consumers. The maker of countless well-known over-the-counter medications arose from the merger of multiple businesses whose identities have remained relatively distinct. In 1999, BMS sought to find a common point for building its corporate brand. The company signed cyclist Lance Armstrong, winner of the 'Tour de France', to endorse the BMS brand. The theme? Cancer survival: Lance had defeated a severe case of testicular cancer through treatment with one of BMS's drugs. BMS communications sought to build emotional appeal with consumers through Lance's survival story, and his subsequent parenting of a baby. The jury is out on whether consumers will react to the 'cancer survivor' theme that BMS has put out there as a core descriptor of its identity.

Ice-cream maker Ben & Jerry's is another case in point. In the 1999 RQ survey conducted with Harris Interactive, the small Vermont company took fifth position behind Johnson & Johnson and Coca-Cola (Alsop, 1999). The result was surprising because Ben & Jerry's is a considerably smaller company, one without the advertising presence and large revenue base of the other top leading companies. What made it so appealing to the public? Without a doubt, Ben & Jerry's reputation rested heavily on perceptions of the company as authentically humane, socially caring and community-minded, and those perceptions rested on the bohemian leadership style of its founder, supported by 'dress-down' employee gatherings and egalitarian management practices that were very appealing internally and externally.

However, when it comes to leadership and reputation, no company can afford to rest on its laurels. Authenticity can also dissipate. Ben & Jerry's demonstrated this in 2000, when the company was acquired by Dutch giant Unilever and the founders of the Vermont-based company left. To consumers, the spirit of the company departed with them. In our 2000 RQ study, Ben & Jerry's was not nominated and, when we invited the public to rate the company nonetheless, the company's RQ score had dropped a bit. These findings confirm that, in the long run, efforts to manipulate external images by relying purely on advertising and public relations will fail if they are disconnected from the company's identity. A strong reputation is built from *authentic* representations by the company to its stakeholders.

Unfortunately companies have long relied on the counsel of spin-meisters in designing their communications programs. Popular notions of 'strategic philanthropy', for instance, clearly similarly miss the boat by emphasizing the economic benefits that companies should expect from their citizenship programs (Porter, 2002). Doing so virtually guarantees that they appear inauthentic. In both communications and philanthropy, spin is anathema to reputation building. Therefore efforts to manipulate external images purely via advertising, public relations or community relations – rather than in conjunction with a company's core identity – are manifestations of instrumental self-interest by the company, and ultimately fail.

A strong reputation comes from within. It is built from authentic representations of a company, its 'self-expression' (Schultz *et al.*, 2000), or core ideology (Collins and Porras, 1996). A company's communications and citizenship initiatives, to be successful, must sit on the bedrock of the company's *identity*, a set of core values championed and lived by founders, CEOs, boards, senior executives and employees, that are allowed to shape the company's actions, communications, culture and decisions, and with which a company *expresses itself* to its constituents.

Transparency

Finally a good corporate reputation develops when corporate leaders are transparent in the way they conduct the company's affairs. Transparency requires abundant communications delivered in the spirit of 'full disclosure'. When companies make more and better information available about themselves, the public perceives them as more credible and accountable. When we contrast the communications of highly regarded companies to those of direct rivals who are not so well regarded, the results are clear: companies with better reputations disclose more information about themselves and are more willing to engage stakeholders in active dialogue. Their actions reflect increased awareness that communication increases the probability that the company will be seen as genuine and credible, and attracts support and advocacy from its stakeholders.

To investors, adequate disclosure is essential if they, together with analysts, are to make reliable assessments of corporate value. Financial markets depend heavily on the credibility of corporate financial statements and, indeed, on the credibility of the entire system of financial reporting and accountability.

Again consider Martha Stewart, the home-style queen, and the head of media group Martha Stewart Living Omnimedia (MSLO). In mid-2002, charges of insider trading were leveled against her for the advance sale of a block of shares she held in a start-up company, just ahead of bad news. Although amounting to only a few hundred thousand dollars, the effect on the corporate shares of MSLO was catastrophic: a media maelstrom resulted that threatened to engulf the company and sent its shares plummeting by over 80 per cent in an eight-week period.

The wave of corporate scandals that struck the financial markets in 2002, and that began with Enron, had a strong direct effect on the share prices of the companies in question. However the scandals had a much larger effect on the financial system as a whole owing to the loss of public faith it occasioned. In September 2002, economists at the Brookings Institution, a Washington think-tank, released a study that estimated at over \$35 billion the indirect cost of these corporate scandals. The report further judged that loss of faith in the transparency of the financial system would produce another 1 to 2.5 per cent decline in the economy as a whole. Transparency is at the heart of public trust and represents the underbelly of responsible leadership and corporate reputation.

Conclusion: leading from the heart
Research on reputation building suggests that companies build favorable reputations when they are led by executives who 'express' the company well (Schultz *et al.*, 2000). On one hand, expressiveness helps stakeholders make vital decisions by reducing the amount of information processing they have to carry out. The *visibility* of the company and its executives reduces the need for search by making information about the company widely available. *Authenticity* is the voice of the 'gut' – a company whose leadership seems authentic is more likeable and trustworthy, and that may be enough to attract consumers to its products, investors to its stock and employees to its jobs. *Transparency* makes the company's leaders and actions credible, reducing the need for vigilance and verification. *Distinctiveness* makes the company and its leaders stand out, and so reduces the efforts an investor or consumer has to go through to build a sophisticated understanding of the company. Finally *consistency* clarifies the breadth of a company's activities and makes them interpretable. By being expressive, companies effectively 'chunk' information about themselves and present them in attractive packages for stakeholders. By simplifying and pre-digesting information, expressiveness facilitates sense making by stakeholders, reduces the need for additional time-consuming search and increases the likelihood of obtaining supportive behaviors.

On the other hand, expressiveness also helps corporate reputation building by promoting a shared understanding of the company among employees, customers and investors. As Figure 4.1 suggests, visibility, distinctiveness and transparency work together to reveal a company's core purpose, values and beliefs, and so enhance its emotional appeal. Consistency of messaging and initiatives help to shape shared values among internal employees and external stakeholders that bind the company together. Internally expressiveness creates predictability about the firm's key promises and enhances its credibility to employees; externally expressiveness signals authenticity and facilitates a shared understanding of the company among investors, analysts, consumers and the public at large.

Ultimately responsible leadership is a balancing act. It involves balancing the interests of multiple stakeholders, allowing primacy and ascendancy to none. It requires balancing a company's financial and social missions: its investors' demands for performance against its employees' demands for equitable sharing of gains. It involves balancing the interests of the many against the interests of the few.

Our research confirms that all companies increasingly are expected to address broad social concerns. However it also demonstrates that consumers have different expectations of companies in different countries. Italian consumers, for instance, expect companies to put a greater emphasis on social responsibility than do US consumers, with Australians in between. Diversity on the global stage presents a challenge to companies whose operations straddle the cultural divide that will continue to persist in international markets.

Nonetheless the results also suggest that companies with strong, favorable reputations are increasingly aware of having a fundamental duty to defend and balance the interests, not only of shareholder/investors, but of all stakeholders, including employees, investors and the public. Doing so means caring what those stakeholders think. To be credible in their caring, they must measure systematically those perceptions. A growing number of these companies now rely on RQ or RQ-like instruments to benchmark systematically how their actions are reported in the media and how they are interpreted by representative stakeholders. Shrewd executives use these instruments, not only as barometers, but to help them guide strategic business decisions about how and how much to express themselves in the communications they make, the events they sponsor and the citizenship programs they support. Such developments are a promising sign that responsible leadership is taking hold among vanguard companies in the corporate sector. Hopefully others will follow.

References

Abrahamson, E. and C.J. Fombrun (1992), 'Forging the iron cage: interorganizational networks and the production of macro-culture', *Journal of Management Studies*, **29**, 175–94.

Abrahamson, E. and C.J. Fombrun (1994), 'Macro-cultures: determinants and consequences', *Academy of Management Review*, **19**, 728–55.

Albert, S. and D. Whetten (1985), 'Organizational identity', in L.L. Cummings and B.M. Staw (eds), *Research in Organizational Behavior*, vol. 7, Greenwich, CT: JAI Press, pp. 263–95.

Alsop, R. (1999), 'The Best Corporate Reputations in America', *The Wall Street Journal*, 25 September.

Barney, J. (1991), 'Firm resources and sustained competitive advantage', *Journal of Management*, **17**, 99–120.

Barney, J.B. (1986), 'Organizational culture: can it be a source of sustained competitive advantage?', *Academy of Management Review*, **11**, 656–65.

Brealy, R. and S. Myers (1998), *Principles of Corporate Finance*, New York: McGraw-Hill.

Caves, R.E. and M.E. Porter (1977), 'From entry barriers to mobility barriers', *Quarterly Journal of Economics*, **91**, 421–34.

Collins, J. and J. Porras (1996), *Built to Last*, New York: Free Press.

Dutton, J.E. and J.M. Dukerich (1991), 'Keeping an eye on the mirror: image and identity in organizational adaptation', *Academy of Management Journal*, **34**, 517–54.

Elsbach, K. (1994), 'Managing organizational legitimacy in the California cattle industry: the construction and effectiveness of verbal accounts', *Administrative Science Quarterly*, **39**, 57–88.

Fombrun, C.J. (1996), *Reputation: Realizing Value from the Corporate Image*, Cambridge, MA: Harvard Business School Press.

Fombrun, C.J. (2001), 'Corporate reputations as economic assets', in Michael A. Hitt, R. Edward Freeman and Jeffrey S. Harrison (eds), *Handbook of Strategic Management*, Oxford: Blackwell.

Fombrun, C.J. and V. Rindova (2004), 'Corporate reputations as cognitive constructions of competitive advantage', in J. Porac and M. Ventresca (eds), *Constructing Markets and Industries*, London: Elsevier Publishing.

Fombrun, C.J. and E.J. Zajac (1987), 'Structural and perceptual influences on intraindustry stratification', *Academy of Management Journal*, **30**, 33–50.

Fombrun, C.J. and C.B.M. Van Riel (2004), *Fame & Fortune: How the World's Most Successful Companies Build Winning Reputations*, New York: Financial Times/Prentice Hall.

Fombrun, C.J., N. Gardberg and J. Sever (2000), *Journal of Brand Management*, **7**(4), 241–55.

Freeman, R.E. (1984), *Strategic Management: A Stakeholder Approach*, Boston, MA: Pitman.

Granovetter, M.S. (1985), 'Economic action and social structure: the problem of embeddedness', *American Journal of Sociology*, **91** (3), 481–510.

Gregory, J.R. (1998) 'Does corporate reputation provide a cushion to companies facing market volatility? Some supportive evidence', *Corporate Reputation Review*, **1**, 288–90.

Grossman, S.J. and J. Stiglitz (1980), 'On the impossibility of informationally efficient markets', *The American Economic Review*, **70** (3), 393.

Jones, T. (1995), 'Instrumental stakeholder theory: a synthesis of ethics and economics', *Academy of Management Review*, **20**, 404–37.

Milgrom, P.R. and J. Roberts (1986), 'Price and advertising signals of product quality', *Journal of Political Economy*, **94**, 796–821.

Myers, S.C. and N.S. Majluf (1984), 'Corporate financing and investment decisions when firms have information that investors do not have', *Journal of Financial Economics*, **13** (2), 197–222.

Porter, M. (2002), 'The competitive advantage of corporate philanthropy', *Harvard Business Review*, December.

Rao, H. (1994), 'The social construction of reputation: certification contests, legitimation, and the survival of organizations in the American automobile industry: 1895–1912', *Strategic Management Journal*, **15**, 29–44.

Rindova, V. and C.J. Fombrun (1999) 'Constructing competitive advantage', *Strategic Management Journal*, **20**, 111–27.

Schlenker, B.R. (1980), *Impression Management*, Monterey, CA: Brooks/Cole Publishing Company.

Schultz, M., M.J. Hatch and M. Larsen (2000), *The Expressive Organization*, London: Oxford University Press.

Suchman, M. (1995), 'Managing legitimacy: strategic and institutional approaches', *Academy of Management Review*, **20** (3), 571–611.

Tedeschi, J.T. (ed.) (1981), *Impression Management Theory and Social Psychological Research*, New York: Academic Press.

Wartick, S.L. (1992), 'The relationship between intense media exposure and change in corporate reputation', *Business & Society*, **31**, 33–49.

Warwick, S.L. and P.L. Cochran (1985), 'The evolution of the corporate social perfomrance model', *The Academy of Management Review*, **10** (4), 758–70.

PART II

RESPONSIBLE LEADERSHIP AND GOVERNANCE: INDIVIDUAL, GROUP AND RELATIONAL PERSPECTIVES

5 Leadership: making responsible decisions
Michael Useem

Introduction

The most unexplored aspect of leadership and governance is the art and science of responsible decision making. By responsible decisions we mean active choices by managers and directors among plausible options that affect the fate of others, not just themselves. It is an art because it depends upon hunches and intuition; it is a science because it should also be disciplined and analytical. And it is relatively underexplored because such decisions are almost always taken behind closed doors.

To understand how responsible decisions are and should be taken, the closed doors must be opened, and to do so we peer into several such rooms at critical moments of decision. Drawing upon events and studies from a range of public and private sources, we identify a set of personal and organizational capacities that make for optimal outcomes. Our focus is on the drivers of good and timely decisions by those who carry responsibility for others. Distinct criteria emerge from the evidence, and we frame them here as five prescriptive guidelines for making effective decisions in a broad array of situations. It is also evident that responsible decisions divide into discrete bands, and we group them here in three clusters requiring special skills for decision making.

Thinking like a president

Most personal decisions are framed around private utility: what are the individual gains and losses associated with one outcome or another? Most managerial decisions are similarly framed around a division's purpose: what are the benefits and costs for a team or division if one product is launched rather than another?

Predisposition, anxiety and naïveté cloud the calculus, and pure utility is rarely maximized in practice, as has been confirmed by a host of academic assessments ranging from Max Bazerman's *Judgment in Managerial Decision Making* (2002) and J. Edward Russo and Paul J.H. Schoemaker's *Winning Decisions: Getting It Right the First Time* (2002) to Gary Klein's *Intuition at Work* (2003) and Kenneth R. Hammond's *Judgments under Stress* (2000). Still, personal and divisional calculations provide a theoretical benchmark for framing decisions.

Responsible decisions, however, necessitate a distinct framing because they are made for the unique purpose of advancing the entire enterprise, regardless of personal concerns or divisional interests. They depend upon a capacity to transcend private agendas and parochial objectives. That capacity must be exercised even though – and especially when – self-interest conflicts with what the enterprise requires.

One prescriptive device for transcending private agenda and parochial bias in responsible decisions is to draw upon the same criteria in the decision making that ought to be utilized by the person with ultimate authority. The criteria must be adapted to the manager's specific tasks, but, if he or she thinks like the president or chief executive, the manager will have a well-defined set of the criteria for reaching a leadership decision at his or her lesser post.

By way of illustration, consider the decisions of Joshua Lawrence Chamberlain, a Union officer who accepted the ceremonial surrender of the Confederate army of General Robert E. Lee at Appomattox on 12 April 1865. As the US Civil War was coming to an end, Union President Abraham Lincoln had made reconciliation a national priority, and the reintegration of Confederate soldiers was of enormous concern. Although only a mid-grade officer, Chamberlain guided his own decisions by much the same concerns as were his president's, even though there had been no direct communication. 'Before us in proud humiliation,' Chamberlain said of the surrendering soldiers, were those 'whom neither toils and sufferings, nor the fact of death, nor disaster, nor hopelessness could bend from their resolve.' As the bugle sounded, Chamberlain issued an order for his federal troops to strike a respectful pose as the Confederate regiments filed onto the field, a posture that would normally be accorded only a Union general. In doing so, Chamberlain had acted with no order from above, appreciating through his own anticipation what the president would want under the circumstance: 'Was not such manhood to be welcomed back into a Union so tested and assured?' Chamberlain's grand gesture was instantly recognized by the surrendering troops, and it helped initiate the reintegration that Lincoln sought to achieve (Chamberlain, 1994, pp. 260, 281; Winik, 2001).

At times, however, country presidents and chief executives themselves are not thinking as leaders should, instead being more concerned with provincial gain than collective agenda. When leadership thinking falls short at the top, the mid-level decision framing can be built upon the criteria that the top should have been using – and against which the leadership shortcomings had become all too evident.

Consider the moment faced by Enron Corporation vice president Sherron Watkins when she met CEO Kenneth Lay on 22 August 2001. She warned that his company would 'implode in a wave of accounting scandals' from the partnerships that the chief financial officer, Andrew Fastow, was using to hide debt and enrich himself. Lay proved unable to challenge the ruinous practice or to make the other leadership decisions that he should have made to save the company. However, regardless of the CEO's decisions, Watkins had valiantly acted to avert the impending disaster by thinking as if she were responsible for the company's fate even though the chief executive officer was not so thinking (Powers *et al.*, 2002; US Senate, 2002; Swartz and Watkins, 2003; Useem, 2003a).

Similarly WorldCom vice president for internal audit Cynthia Cooper went over her boss's head to tell the board's audit committee on 20 June 2002 that its chief financial officer had been improperly booking revenue to inflate profits by $9 billion. The Federal Bureau of Investigation's Colleen Rowley had done much the same when she wrote a 13-page memo to FBI director Robert Mueller and the Senate Intelligence Committee on 21 May 2002, outlining how upper-level FBI managers had failed to appreciate the early warning signs of what was to become the terrorist attack of 11 September 2001 (Lacayo and Ripley, 2002).

With no guidance from above and contrary pressures all around, these mid-level managers acted with the ultimate good of their organization in mind. Despite inadequate guidance, indifferent attitudes or angry responses from their superiors, they were thinking as their chief executive should have been thinking, and they acted accordingly.

Responsible decisions, whether made on the front line or in the executive office, are thus distinctively defined by whether they transcend personal and parochial concerns. The criteria for choosing one course over another are those that a country president or chief executive would or should have used. This is consonant with what Jim Collins (2001) discovered in his study of a dozen companies that rose from 'good to great'. The most successful business leaders, he found, are those who make authoritative decisions and consistently place enterprise interest ahead of their own.

A personal experience underscores the point. I accompanied a group of 11 MBA students to climb Cotopaxi, one of Ecuador's massive (and still active) volcanoes. With the summit at an elevation of 19 347 ft, Cotopaxi stands nearly a mile higher than any peak in the Alps or central Rockies. As we neared the top around 6 a.m. on summit day, one of our party became increasingly ill from the altitude. He badly wanted to touch the apex like the rest of us, but he also knew that, if he went for it, he would endanger everybody's chances as his illness worsened (Useem, 2003b).

At the same time, the stricken climber decided he would have to ascend as high as possible so that he would not prematurely force his rope-mates down. 'I was exhausted, my head ached, and I was very dehydrated,' he recalled, but he pushed himself to climb within 700 feet of the summit.

There he reached a tiny plateau where he could safely unrope and wait for the rest of his team to reach and return from the summit. He later explained: 'I had wanted to get to a point where, if I couldn't reach the top, at least I wouldn't force the whole team to turn around.'

The afflicted climber's concerns were identical to those of our mountain guides, but he chose not to leave them to the guides to solve alone. He decided on his own what should be done, and he then did what the guides would have wanted and what the team certainly needed. He had made his own strategic appraisal of the moment, and his clear-headed actions allowed the rest of his team to reach the summit of Cotopaxi and safely descend.

A dedication to transcending self-interest is often countermanded by the self-maximizing precepts that run so deeply in the culture of capitalism. Rising above personal advantage in decision making is thus always a challenge, especially in an era of job hopping and downsizing. When a firm has a history of frequent turnover and abrupt layoffs, managers are naturally tempted to give primacy to career over company, whether the subject is long-term expenditures or stock-option allocations. Adding to the challenge, free market theorists have long elevated the pursuit of personal gain into common purpose. 'The social responsibility of business,' economist Milton Friedman has argued, 'is to increase its profits.' By inference, managers should act as micro profit maximizers themselves. The best decisions are those that optimize individual gain and, if all managers make decisions with that in mind, the resulting tide will lift all ships. Or so the theory goes (Friedman, 1970).

The leadership challenge is to prepare an organization's culture to resist that siren call of personal self-interest when faced with responsible decisions. The formula is not complex. If a client, think like a guide. If an officer, think like a commander. If a manager, think like an executive. If an executive, think like a director. If a citizen, think like a president.

Calculating deliberately

Thinking like a chief executive does not depend on strategic brilliance, but it does demand the ability to look ahead and see the whole. What should go right, what could go wrong? Due diligence on the eve of a decision requires a rapid reading of the choices ahead.

The US Navy stressed this capacity in the premium it places on 'forehandedness'. The officer on a ship's bridge is obliged to think ahead and thus anticipate the most unlikely contingencies. 'The single most important attribute for boating,' asserts one manual, is 'forehandedness', a capacity that allows a captain to 'avoid surprises', since they are 'almost universally unwelcome at sea'. One must read ahead (US Navy, 2001).

Learning to look around corners, anticipate countermeasures and envision the future are critical. So too is positioning oneself in the organization to appreciate optimally what is going right and what may yet go wrong. And timely and reliable data are essential foundations for the deliberate calculus.

The disaster of the US space shuttle *Challenger* on 28 January 1986 illustrates the point about as well as any decision failure can. The night before *Challenger's* scheduled launch, temperatures in central Florida plummeted to record lows. NASA flight directors called the top managers of Utah-based manufacturer Morton Thiokol to ask if its solid-fuel booster rockets for the space shuttle would function reliably under the freezing conditions. Faced with the need for a fast decision – launch time was just hours away – the Thiokol managers recommended a 'go'. At 11.38 the next morning, when the space shuttle lifted off with seven astronauts on board, the ground temperature registered 15 degrees colder than on any prior takeoff. Seventy-three seconds later, an O-ring made brittle by the cold cracked in the booster rocket, causing the main rocket to explode.

Later analysis would reveal that ample data had existed in the Thiokol files that evening to tell Thiokol senior managers that the O-rings were almost certain to fail in the cold conditions sure to prevail the next morning. However the managers had not asked for the data because they had not known it was available: it was buried in a faulty filing system. They had made a timely decision, but, in the absence of good information, they had made a flawed one, the most fateful of their careers (Vaughan, 1996).

A prominent governance disaster stemmed from much the same information error. When Disney CEO Michael Eisner hired friend Michael Ovitz in 1995 as his No. 2, he promised Ovitz more than $100 million if he ever fired him. Fourteen months later Eisner did just that. The severance was astonishing: for each failing month on the job, Ovitz was sent off with $7 million, or some $340 000 per day. The Disney compensation committee had evidently devoted just minutes to the CEO's proposed deal with Ovitz and never reviewed the final agreement. The terms of the detail were there for the asking, yet the board evidently never placed the request. The directors gave their assent to the deal that the CEO wanted in an act that a Delaware judge deemed may have been 'consciously indifferent' (Court of Chancery, 2003).

Appreciating uncertainty is also essential for calculating deliberately, since proper risk appraisal is perquisite to mastering it, and risk taking is inherent in responsible leadership. Research studies of military officers reveal that effective commanders are especially good at anticipating, coping with and reducing uncertainty. In anticipating uncertainty, they (1) rely on simpler plans requiring fewer assumptions, (2) are quicker to alter their plans, and (3) more clearly express their plans' intentions. In coping with uncertainty, effective commanders (1) exhibit higher tolerance for unpredictability, (2) are quicker to act on the basis of less than complete data, and (3) better appreciate that the enemy faces the same problems of uncertainty. And in reducing uncertainty, they (1) devote more time to the extraction of meaning from data, (2) structure the battlefield to constrain the enemy's options, and (3) take the view of the enemy to anticipate its actions (Schmitt and Klein, 1996).

Many personal decisions are taken with calculating forethought, or at least they should be. Are the alternatives clear, is the information complete, are the consequences understood? As the consequences grow, though, responsible decision making requires even more deliberate calculation because of the magnitude of impact. Leadership and governance decisions can bolster the livelihood of hundreds of employees and the wealth of thousands of investors. If made with conscious indifference, however, they can destroy assets or even a company.

Acting decisively

A third criterion for the leadership decision template is timeliness, taking action when the moment is right. If premature, deliberate calculation is incomplete, but if belated, opportunity is forgone. Pointing to the cost of missed windows of opportunity, Jack Welch of General Electric has said that he never regretted any of his tough decisions. He only regretted taking too long to make many of them during his 20 years at the helm. He confesses that some of his decisions were wrong, even disastrous, but he did not doubt the need to make them in timely fashion (Welch and Byrne, 2001).

In her comparison of fast-moving and slow-moving computer firms in Silicon Valley, Kathleen Eisenhardt (1990) found vast disparities in company capacities to reach timely decisions. Fast firms required just half the time to reach decisions on product innovations and joint ventures compared with their slower brethren. A key difference, she found, lay in the use of real-time data. Leaders of the fast movers placed a premium on having rich and reliable information on their products and customers, far more so than did the slower firms. The fast movers possessed fine-honed measures of their internal operations, and their managers mined the data for fresh insight. They had better intelligence with which to appraise their own performance and to appreciate where the market was moving. The slow movers, by contrast, tended to engage in tedious planning and forecasting exercises that sometimes required months for completion.

As a case in point, the Internet equipment manufacturer Cisco Systems built a system during the late 1990s for compiling and retrieving detailed data on every major aspect of its business operations. Cisco had traditionally required two weeks to consolidate its year-end results, but by the end of the decade it was closing its books in a single day. Despite Cisco's size (it employed 34 000 and had revenue of $19 billion in 2003), all managers had access to hourly information on revenue, discounts and margins for all products, and they could evaluate backlog order or selling expenses for any operating unit or account manager. As a result, chief executive John Chambers explained, 'first-line managers can look at margins and products and know exactly what the effect of their decisions will be' before they make them, allowing for swifter execution of them.

With real-time data at their fingertips, Cisco managers anticipated an uptick in the Japanese economy in time to put people and resources in place to respond to rising demand for Cisco products. The information system did not prevent it from being blind-sided by an abrupt downturn in demand for its equipment in 2001. Although not a fail-safe management device, the system nonetheless gave company leaders the wherewithal to make decisions that were as informed as possible (Mehta, 2001; Stewart, 2000).

Good information in a leader's hand is one foundation for swiftly getting to the go point. The US Marine Corps has offered several others. It specializes in risky and rapid assaults, and consequently has long worked to foster decisive decision making. It warns its officers that bureaucratic and autocratic leadership styles get in the way of swift action and it trains them to (1) seek a '70 per cent' solution rather than one of 100 per cent certainty; (2) distribute decision authority among their subordinates; (3) define objectives and then let subordinates flesh out the details; (4) tolerate mistakes if learning from them results in better decisions next time; and (5) create a culture in which cycle times are short and the tempo fast. Indecisiveness is deemed a fatal flaw (Freedman, 2000; Katzenbach and Santamaria *et al.*, 2004).

Setting synthetic deadlines in the absence of natural deadlines can drive decisiveness as well. The US administrator in Iraq, Paul Bremer, for example, put forward an artificial deadline to force warring factions in postwar Iraq to reconcile their differences and get on with the task of taking charge. During the months after the early 2003 US attack on Iraq, the Iraqi Governing Council had not even been able to agree on a procedure for drafting a new constitution, let alone write it. But on 15 November 2003, Bremer simply declared that the USA would transfer sovereignty to Iraq on 30 June 2004, period. Though a risky strategy, it had the desired effect of setting a fire under the council, forcing the factions to think about the process – and then resolve their differences and decide on it (Weisman, 2004).

Making good decisions and making timely decisions inherently work against one another since optimizing one means suboptimizing the other. Yet the art of leadership calls for achieving both at the same time: if managers cannot make fast decisions, they should not be in positions of responsibility for others. But, equally, if they cannot make good decisions, they should not be there either. Shooting from the hip is an egregious error, but so too is analysis paralysis. A vital capacity, then, for those with responsibility for others is the ability to find the right balance between deliberate calculation and decisive action.

Bringing self-confidence without overconfidence

Transcendence, due diligence and decisiveness are all essential for decision making, but their effective application also depends on the responsible person's self-confidence. Much decision making is distressing, even painful, and without self-assurance about oneself and the need to delve into the decision, equivocation or avoidance is the paralyzing result. Still, preparing to pull the trigger on hard decisions poses a psychological dilemma. Without confidence, self-questioning can delay a necessary action. Overconfidence, though, can result in under-analysis and an equally subpar result. The US physicist Albert Einstein had the right idea when he talked about the challenge of physics: 'Things should be made as simple as possible, but not any simpler.' Confident, yes; foolhardy, no.

Whereas self-assurance breeds momentum, excess confidence can breed excessive risk. That is what transpired at the investment bank Salomon, where a 'can-do' culture among the leadership team nearly brought the bank to ruin. Salomon bond trader Paul Mozer had made an illegal $3.2 billion bid for US treasury securities on 21 February 1991. Mozer confessed his act to his boss, John Meriwether, more than two months later, and Meriwether immediately took it up to top management on 28 April. Chief executive John Gutfreund, however, failed to report the act to government authorities for more than three months. Salomon's culture had stressed taking financial risks to the limit, placing big bets as near the edge as possible, and its aggressive attitude had helped it become one of Wall Street's largest and most successful players of the era. Yet that same mind-set also encouraged Paul Mozer to cross the line and senior managers to look the other way. John Meriwether and chief executive Gutfreund were so discredited by the delay in reporting the malfeasance that they were forced out within days of its public disclosure.

The Salomon board called upon one of its own members, investor Warren Buffet, to resurrect the company and its shattered credibility. With personal humility and executive resolve, Buffet dismissed the entire management team and completely revamped the company culture. Just three days after taking office, for instance, Buffet told all Salomon officers, 'You are each expected to report, instantaneously and directly to me, any legal violation or moral failure on behalf of any employee.' He provided his home telephone number and added that parking tickets were among the few exceptions to his new disclosure requirements.

Although Salomon paid dearly for the hubris of its prior management (customers fled, shares dropped, fines topped $290 million) the company survived and prospered under a new team which emphasized calculated bets instead of reckless risk taking. A company that had nearly gone bankrupt in 1991 when overconfidence prevailed was sold to Travelers Group in 1997 for $9 billion after self-confidence was restored (Useem, 1998).

If overconfidence nearly brought down an investment bank, it can be fatal in mountain climbing. Consider the decisions made by Arlene Blum, the leader of an all-women's expedition to climb Annapurna, one of the most dangerous peaks in the Himalayas. Blum recruited well: each of the ten climbers was a world-class mountaineer with a fierce resolve to reach the summit. On 15 October 1978, after a grueling and bitterly cold climb from a high camp, two of Blum's team reached the 26 545-foot summit. It was a crowning moment for the expedition, for women and for mountaineering. The climbing world had been waiting to see if Blum's expedition could equal the accomplishment of the all-men's French team that had been the first to ascend Annapurna in 1950.

A day later, though, two other members of Blum's expedition announced that they wanted to touch the summit themselves, a case of personal interest trumping collective objective. At first Blum resisted. Her team had already achieved its goal of placing at least one member on top, and the expedition would gain little if others repeated that feat. Mindful of the grave dangers, one of the Sherpas pressed for an immediate retreat: 'Let's go to Kathmandu and have a party,' he pleaded. But the two mountaineers insisted they be given a chance and, finally, Blum, against her better judgment, relented. Two days later their bodies were found not far below the summit, the victims of what appeared to a fatal fall from its icy approach.

Without a driving urge to succeed, Blum's team would have lacked the will to move supplies up the mountain, much less send the first two climbers to the top. But the team also required an equally keen awareness of risk, and the second two pushed too far, tarring with catastrophe what otherwise would have been a brilliant accomplishment. The title of a *New York Times* article on a disastrous 1996 Everest storm that left eight mountaineers dead captured the essence of this decision-making dilemma: 'Scaling Corporate Heights Without Going Over a Cliff.' Too little confidence would have prevented Arlene Blum's first two climbers from reaching the summit; but too much confidence would send two others over a cliff (Blum, 1982; Useem, 1998).

The overassured manager may not seek to appreciate all the risks entailed in an ambitious decision. But even when the risks are appreciated, the underassured manager may equally jeopardize the organization by failing to display the bias for action that is also essential.

Relying upon the team

Good teams, well led, achieve more than any individual can. That is why top management teams are better predictors of company success than any one executive, even the CEO. Well-formed top management teams are better able to make optimal decisions under tough conditions than any single executive.

It comes as no surprise that equity analysts are as much concerned with a firm's operating executives as with its CEO. Similarly research reveals that successful work teams are overseen more often than others by managers who are particularly good at acquiring critical information and building good relations between the team and outside constituencies. Put differently, when overseeing leaders decide to inform and empower their work teams, the teams perform more effectively (Druskat and Wheeler, 2003).

Industrial research has shown that, as the stress on a worker increases, so does performance, but only until the stress reaches the worker's breaking point, after which performance declines. But the breaking point for individuals in well-formed teams is far higher: Team members support and reinforce one another to do what they could never do on their own, to take decisions that are far better than if left to individuals alone.

Casual observers might have been surprised by the cry of support that went up from many at ABC-TV when Comcast made a hostile bid for Disney in February 2004. After all, Disney had been ABC's parent company for nearly eight years. But industry appreciated the source of relief. Disney had undermined the team culture that had taken root during the years ABC had been owned by Capital Cities, a span that yielded hit after hit, from *The Wonder Years* to *thirtysomething*. Under Disney, the ABC teams lost their free-wheeling autonomy, as studio decisions traveled ever upward for a final OK from the top. With Disney no longer relying on the ABC teams, the network had gone from first to fourth in viewership, trailing even Fox network. If Comcast prevailed, Comcast president Steve Burke would likely work hard to restore ABC's creative independence. He understood Disney culture well, having earlier served as one of its executives, and his father, Daniel Burke, had built the original ABC culture as CEO prior to the Disney takeover.

If disenfranchisement plagued performance at ABC in recent years, team empowerment proved equally potent for ensuring performance at eBay on 11 September 2001. EBay CEO Margaret Whitman was visiting Japan and her chief operating officer, Brian Swette, had traveled to Florida. Not only was the company physically leaderless, the top executives could not even telephone corporate headquarters in San Jose, California for hours after disaster struck. In fact, however, their absence did not prevent performance. Acting swiftly on their own, subordinates at eBay moved to confirm that all 2500 employees were safe, then secured the company website and launched an online auction to raise $100 million for the disaster's victims.

The eBay managers took the right decisions, and chief executive Whitman had already engendered the right skills. Since joining eBay in 1998, when it employed a mere 35, Whitman had invested heavily in recruiting able lieutenants and molding them into a team that was able to lead its 2500 employees even when she was a continent away. 'I did not have to say anything,' she now says of 9/11, 'for the right thing to happen' (Citrin, 2001).

For top teams to make good decisions, the corporate culture must foster a willingness by all to face and make the hard decisions. Built well, teamwork is a foundation for responsible decisions; less well, it can undermine even the most able individual decision maker.

Decision clusters
Responsible decisions can be clustered into several groups, each imposing a distinct set of time demands upon the decision maker. The first cluster is when decisions are to be taken by deadlines not of one's own choosing; the second is when decisions are without definite deadline; and the third is when decisions have the effect of betting the company.

When there is no choice but to make a choice (the first decision cluster) the ticking of the clock concentrates the mind and forces resolution. Bond traders, by way of example, recurrently face decision moments measured in seconds. Wait an extra tick to make the call, and the price of a bond is out of reach. Jump too soon and they can miss a market rally. The manager of a whole floor of bond traders, any of whom can make or lose millions with a click of the mouse, carries special responsibility. Orchestrated well, the floor's instant decisions are the stuff of a great quarter; led poorly, their actions can become a company disaster. That is precisely what faced Rick Rieder when he arrived at work at 7 a.m. every day. Responsible for fixed-income trading at New York investment bank Lehman Brothers, he oversaw a vast trading operation, with more than 150 traders who bet billions on bond movements every day, and another 300 people backing up the operation. He had so prepared his traders to take instant decisions with millions of dollars at stake in virtually every one that he rarely needed to intervene.

This first cluster comprises decisions that are time-driven, recurrent and unrelenting. They require an ability to manage by the clock, execute rapidly and remain steadfast under duress.

As stressful as it may be to make decisions under deadline, it can be harder still to make them when there is no deadline at all, and that defines the second decision cluster. The big choice has to be made sooner or later – to alter a career path, revive a stumbling sales division or transform a policy – but the press of everyday events and the brimming in-box may delay focus on it. Moving quickly is essential, but setting off too soon can also prevent the rumination required.

Consider the rising bank manager who knew that another division was woefully underled and was certain he could do a better job. But getting the job would forcibly evict the faltering manager, and it would require the aspiring manager to master a market with which he was unfamiliar. No cutoff date loomed, but, after six months of deliberation, the aspiring manager grabbed the ring, learned the trade and restored the division.

Or consider Denmark's Minister of Finance, Mogens Lykketoft, who set out to rewrite the country's policies on early retirement during the 1990s. Danish politics dictated coalition and consensus building, and Lykketoft arranged for endless meetings with political partners, parliament leaders and trade associations. The outline of the change had been clear in his mind, but his final decision depended on seemingly endless consultation over several years.

The second big decision cluster, then, comprises decisions at the other end of the spectrum from immediate, time-driven actions. Slow and emergent, though no less consequential, such decisions depend on disciplined consultation and deliberation.

The third cluster includes those rare decisions that place everything on the line. Whether a career, a company or even a life, they are seldom faced, but harrowing when they are. They require strategic thinking and a willingness to risk all.

Early on 6 July 1994, firefighter Don Mackey sent a crew down a slope to dig a fireline to stop the spread of a dangerous blaze on Storm King Mountain in central Colorado. It was a calculated risk: climbing down the slope meant that his firefighters would have to dash back up it in the unlikely event that the fire surged out of control. But that is precisely what happened some five hours later, when a weather front suddenly brought wind gusts of 40 miles an hour. As the fire tore up the slope while the crew was far down it, Mackey yelled 'go, go, go!' to move the team to safe terrain. But it was too late, and Mackey and 11 firefighters on his crew could not evacuate in time. He had bet the company and lost (Useem *et al.*, 2005).

Boeing's chief executive and his engineers had envisaged an aircraft in the 1950s to be called the 707. Though lives were not at stake, if it succeeded Boeing would become the biggest maker of commercial airplanes ever. If not, the enterprise could suffer a slow death. The same decision was faced in the 1970s when Boeing's engineers proposed the 747. In both instances, management bet the company and succeeded beyond its best forecasts. Boeing hoped for a repeat in the 2000s: it wagered the enterprise on a breakthrough aircraft, the 787.

The third cluster of decisions, when leaders bet the enterprise or their career, are infrequent but nonetheless faced sooner or later by most with responsibility for others. They entail a capacity to face up to the most fateful decisions and to invest nearly everything to ensure their execution.

Responsible decisions within all three clusters depend upon application of all five prescriptive decision criteria, but each cluster calls for additional decision criteria as well. In the first cluster, a premium is placed on rapidly absorbing the vital data, sharpening the choices and pulling the trigger. In the second set, stress is on methodical exploration, fine distinctions and extended rumination. In the third cluster, the distinctive edge is personal audacity, resolute commitment and strategic thinking.

Learning to make responsible decisions
Senior executives often say that they had better enjoy making tough decisions if they plan to stay in the game. All the easy decisions are made below; only the intractable ones come up high. An iron stomach and nerves of steel are required, especially when the stakes are high and uncertainty abounds – just those moments when responsible decisions are most consequential. Executive exhortations speak to the point: IBM chief Louis Gerstner demanded that his managers act audaciously during the wrenching restructuring he forced his company through. 'Whatever hard or painful things you have to do,' he said, 'do them quickly' (Gerstner, 2002, p. 68).

But making responsible decisions requires explicit attentiveness to the five criteria set out above: thinking like a president, calculating deliberately, acting decisively, bringing self-confidence without overconfidence, and relying upon the team. All are essential and ignoring any can be fatal. On the evening of his disappointing fourth place finish in the 2004 primary in Iowa, for instance, presidential candidate Howard Dean gathered his supporters, delivered his 'shriek' speech and doomed his candidacy to a footnote in history. He had brought one wrong element in the fivefold skill set to the table: instead of thinking as should a future president – the job he badly wanted – Dean acted more like a sales manager firing up the force.

Responsible decisions also require an appreciation of the variety of leadership decisions and the special capacities required for the major subspecies. Appreciating the five criteria for responsible decision making and three clusters of responsible decisions is a learned capacity. Making good decisions is not, however, a natural capacity for most, and all organizations would do well to prepare their managers and directors for the decisions that lie ahead. Many management development programs already touch on one or more such aspects of leadership decision making. German specialty-chemical maker Degussa, for instance, views bravery and audacity as essential corporate virtues. 'Successful leaders in Degussa,' the company asserts, must have 'courage, determination, and a strong backbone', and it trains all mid-career managers to embrace those qualities. The building of an effective leadership development program depends upon sustained and thoughtful management attention (Conger and Fulmer, 2003; Ready and Conger, 2003), and this should be equally true for one focusing on responsible decision making.

Studies of MBA programs reveal that well designed curriculums can improve a host of management capabilities (for example, Boyatzis *et al.*, 2002), and future managers can be trained for responsible decisions as well. In keeping with that – and in focusing on decision making under duress – the Wharton School takes 90 of its MBA students to Quantico, Virginia for brief immersion in the US Marine Corps' Combat and Leadership Reaction courses. The infamous drill instructors impose an iron discipline on the students, subjecting them to hours of unrelenting verbal harassment. The reason for such a drill with future Marine officers is neither to shock nor to awe (though both are amply achieved), but rather to prepare them for the duress of the battlefield. After enduring months of stress in the relative security of Quantico, Marine commanders are far better prepared to make decisions in combat. Similarly MBA students anticipate that few moments in their future careers would ever feel quite as harsh as a verbal dressing-down at the hands of a Marine drill instructor, and their own future decisions under duress will be better for it.

While our focus has largely been on managers, the decision template developed here can be applied to governing boards as well. Carter and Lorsch (2004, p. 35) have noted that, although demands for governance reform have mainly focused on 'what is visible', the 'real action is in the boardroom itself'. If directors are to lead along with their appointed executives, improving their decisions behind closed doors should also be a company development objective.

Making good and timely decisions is one of the premier requirements of anybody in a position of responsibility. Made well, good choices at that point are the foundation of personal advancement. Made poorly, they can end an otherwise promising career. But, above all, they are an essential foundation of good leadership and governance. Those who carry responsibilities for the fate of others – whether a team, a company or a country – are constantly confronted with hard decisions at the top that must be made well.

References

Bazerman, M. (2002), *Judgment in Managerial Decision Making*, 5th edn, New York: Wiley Text Books.

Blum, A. (1982), *Annapurna: A Woman's Place*, New York: Random House.

Boyatzis, R., E.C. Stubbs and S.N. Taylor (2002), 'Learning cognitive and emotional intelligence competencies through graduate management education', *Academy of Management Learning and Education*, 1 (2), 150–62.

Carter, C.B. and J.W. Lorsch (2004), *Back to the Drawing Board: Designing Corporate Boards for a Complex World*, Boston: Harvard Business School Press.

Chamberlain, J.L. (1994, reprinted), *The Passing of the Armies*, New York, NY and Gettysburg, PA: Stan Clark Military Books.

Citrin, J. (2001), 'A conversation with eBay's Meg Whitman: leadership lessons from America's most successful internet company', *Business 2.0*, 3 October, posted at http://www.business2.com/b2/web/articles/0,17863,514077,00.html.

Collins, J. (2001), *Good to Great: Why Some Companies Make the Leap ... and Others Don't*, New York: HarperBusiness.

Conger, J.A. and R.M. Fulmer (2003), 'Developing your leadership pipeline', *Harvard Business Review*, 81(12), 76–84.

Court of Chancery, State of Delaware (2003), *The Walt Disney Company Derivative Litigation*, C.A. no.15452, 28 May, posted at http://courts.state.de.us/chancery/opinions/15452-126.pdf.

Druskat, V.U. and J.V. Wheeler (2003), 'Managing from the boundary: the effective leadership of self-managing work teams', *Academy of Management Journal*, 46 (4), 435–57.

Eisenhardt, K.M. (1990), 'Speed and strategic choice: how managers accelerate decision making', *California Management Review*, 32 (3), 39–55.

Freedman, D.H. (2000), *Corps Business: The 30 Management Principles of the U.S. Marines*, New York: HarperBusiness.

Friedman, M. (1970), 'The social responsibility of business is to increase its profits', *New York Times Magazine*, 13 September, 32–4.

Gerstner, L.V., Jr (2002), *Who Says Elephants Can't Dance? Inside IBM's Historic Turnaround*, New York: HarperBusiness.

Hammond, K.R. (2000), *Judgments under Stress*, New York: Oxford University Press.

Katzenbach, J.R. and J.A. Santamaria (1999), 'Firing up the front line', *Harvard Business Review*, 77 (3), 107–15.

Klein, G.K. (2002), *Intuition at Work: Why Developing Your Gut Instincts Will Make You Better at What You Do*, New York: Doubleday Currency.

Lacayo, R. and A. Ripley (2002), 'Persons of the Year', *Time*, 160 (27/1), 32.

Mehta, S. (2001), 'Cisco fractures its own fairy tale', *Fortune*, 143 (10), 104–10.

Powers, W.C., Jr, Raymond S. Troubh and Herbert S. Winokur, Jr (2002), 'Report of Investigation by the Special Investigative Committee of the Board of Directors of Enron Corp.', 1 February.

Ready, D.A. and J.A. Conger (2003), 'Why leadership-development efforts fail', *Sloan Management Review*, 44 (3), 83–8.

Russo, J.E. and P.J.H. Schoemaker (2002), *Winning Decisions: Getting it Right the First Time*, New York: Doubleday Currency.

Santamaria, J.A., V.M. Martino and E.K. Clemons (2004), *The Marine Corps Way: Using Maneuver Warfare to Lead a Winning Organization*, New York: McGraw-Hill.

Schmidt, J.E. and G.A. Klein (1996), 'Fighting in the fog: dealing with battlefield uncertainty', *Marine Corps Gazette*, August, 62–89.

Stewart, T.A. (2000), 'Making decisions in real time', *Fortune*, 142 (1), 332–4.

Swartz, M. with S. Watkins (2003), *Power Failure: The Inside Story of the Collapse of Enron*, New York: Doubleday.

US Navy (2001), *Standard Organization and Regulations of the U.S. Navy* (OPNAVINST 3120.32), Washington, DC: US Navy.

US Senate, Permanent Subcommittee on Investigations of the Committee on Governmental Affairs (2002), *The Role of the Board of Directors in Enron's Collapse*, 8 July, Washington,

DC: U.S. Senate, posted at http://news.findlaw.com/hdocs/docs/enron/senpsi70802rpt. pdf.

Useem, M. (1998), *The Leadership Moment: Nine True Stories of Triumph and Disaster and Their Lessons for Us All*, New York: Random House.

Useem, M. (2003a), 'Corporate governance is directors making decisions: reforming the outward foundations for inside decision making', *Journal of Management and Governance*, **7** (3), 241–53.

Useem, M. (2003b), 'Making leadership decisions under uncertainty and stress', in Michael Useem, Paul Asel and Jerry Useem, *Upward Bound: Nine Original Accounts of How Business Leaders Reached Their Summit*, New York: Crown Business/Random House.

Useem, M., J. Cook and L. Sutton (2005), 'Developing leaders for decision making under duress: wildland firefighters in the South Canyon fire and its aftermath', *Academy of Management Learning and Education* (forthcoming).

Vaughan, D. (1996), *The Challenger Launch Decision: Risky Technology, Culture, and Deviance at NASA*, Chicago: University of Chicago Press.

Welch, J. with J.A. Byrne (2001), *Jack: Straight from the Gut*, New York: Warner Books.

Weisman, S.R. (2004), 'U.S. presidential politics and self-rule for Iraqis', *New York Times*, 19 February, p. A11.

Winik, J. (2001), *April 1865: The Month that Saved America*, New York: HarperCollins.

6 Developing strategies and skills for responsible leadership
Kim Cameron and Arran Caza

Introduction

The idea of responsible leadership is not new, and the literature on effective leadership has always been characterized by an element of responsibility (Burns, 1978; Yukl *et al.*, 2002). Responsibility most often has been synonymous with accountability (as in being accountable for performance) or with freedom of action indicating that responsible individuals have discretion or volition (as in having responsibility at work). These two connotations of responsibility are closely related, as people are more likely to be accountable if they are able to act freely (Brown, 1986; Salancik and Meindl, 1984). In these two senses, responsibility means 'response-able', or possessing the capability and the accountability needed to respond. A third connotation of the concept of responsible leadership is less frequently used but equally meaningful. It refers to the ability or inclination to act in an appropriate fashion. Appropriateness is key to this connotation in that it associates responsible action with what is right, correct, or beneficial. Behaving responsibly means doing good (Walsh *et al.*, 2003).

This latter usage of responsibility places the concept in the domain of a newly emerging field of study called Positive Organizational Scholarship (POS). This focuses on the investigation of what goes right in organizations (rather than what goes wrong), what is life-giving (rather than life-depleting), what is experienced as good (rather than bad), what is inspiring (rather than depressing) and what brings elevation to individuals and systems (rather than diminishing). Responsibility used in the first two ways is associated with achieving desired results. Used in the third way, responsibility is associated with the promotion of factors such as interpersonal flourishing, meaning and meaningfulness, virtuous behaviors, positive emotions, high energy connections and appreciative inquiry in organizations (Cameron *et al.*, 2003). It focuses on the highest potentiality of human systems.

Responsible leadership and positive organizational scholarship

Responsible leadership in the POS sense is unashamedly value-biased. It emphasizes an affirmative orientation toward the enablement of positive human potential. Responsible leadership in the POS sense focuses on positive deviance, in that it focuses on extraordinary positive outcomes and the processes that produce them. Elements of responsible leadership using this third definition can be found in disciplines such as positive psychology (for example, Snyder and Lopez, 2002), appreciative inquiry (for example, Cooperrider and Whitney, 1999), prosocial behavior (Batson, 1994), citizenship behavior (Bolino *et al.*, 2002), community psychology (Cowen and Kilmer, 2002), corporate social responsibility (Margolis and Walsh, 2003), ethics (Hursthouse, 1999), creativity (Amabile *et al.*, 1996) and virtue (Tjeltveit, 2004).

Responsible leadership in this positive sense is not a new orientation, of course, since positive phenomena have been studied in organization and management science for decades (for example, Peterson and Seligman, 2003). Yet studies of responsible leadership leading to affirmative, uplifting and elevating processes and outcomes have not been the norm. They have been overwhelmed in the scholarly literature by less positive topics. Responsibility associated with maintaining accountability has dominated responsibility associated with producing goodness. For example, Walsh's (1999) survey found that positive terms (such as virtue, caring, compassion, goodness) have seldom appeared in the business press (such as the *Wall Street Journal*) in the last 17 years, whereas negatively biased words (such as beat, fight, win, compete) have increased fourfold in the same period. In medicine, Mayne (1999) found that studies of the relationship between negative phenomena and health outnumbered by 11 to 1 studies of the relationship between positive phenomena and health. And, in psychology, Czapinski's (1985) coding of research articles found a 2:1 ratio of negative issues to positive or neutral issues.

Responsible leadership in the POS sense does not ignore non-positive conditions, of course, or situations when mistakes, crises, deterioration or problems are present. Most of the time people and institutions fall short of achieving the best they can be or fail to fulfill their optimal potential. However, when organizations should fail but do not, when they bounce back but should not, when they remain flexible and agile but ought to become rigid, they demonstrate positive deviance (Weick, 2003). Responsible leadership in the POS sense, therefore, focuses on enabling positive dynamics to occur, in either conducive or challenging circumstances, and fostering the highest human potentialities.

Several brief descriptions are provided below to illustrate the positive connotation of responsible leadership in organizational settings. They are intended to serve as concrete examples of the way responsible leadership is manifested in organizations.

Timberland, a manufacturer of shoes, boots, and apparel, decided to increase substantially the percentage of organically grown cotton in its clothes in order to reduce exposure to carcinogens by migrant workers who pick corporately-grown cotton. In the absence of any customer demand or regulatory encouragement, and at a substantial expense to the company's bottom line, CEO Mark Schwartz made this decision as a matter of conscience. The intent of Timberland was to try to benefit a disadvantaged group of individuals who would likely never be customers but whose lives could be made better by Timberland's change in policy. (Schwartz, 2002)

In an attempt to marry his theological and free enterprise values, Tom Chappell, founder of Tom's of Maine, created products void of dyes, sweeteners, and preservatives two decades before it became the socially accepted thing to do for health-conscious companies. He also established a policy in his firm in which ten percent of all profits and five percent of employees' time would be donated annually to charitable organizations. The motive was not public recognition or marketing advantage – since these decisions were made at a time when such moves were considered imprudent – but 'just because it is the right thing to do'. (Chappell, 1999)

Merck Corporation created a compound originally intended as an animal antibiotic, but scientists accidentally discovered that it was an effective cure for river blindness, a disease affecting millions of people in the developing world. With no hope of recovering the invested capital needed to create a human application, and at the risk of incurring costs associated with any unanticipated side-effects, Merck developed and distributed the drug free of charge to the developing world, thus helping to eradicate the disease. (Bollier, 1996)

Greg Mortenson, using $623 in pennies donated from American school children and $2000 obtained by selling personal possessions, began a school building program in northern Pakistan aimed at educating formerly illiterate children, especially young women (previously forbidden from receiving an education). To merit a school, a village was required to donate the land, help build the school, and commit to increase the number of young women enrolled by 10 percent each year. In five years, Mortenson's project constructed 28 school buildings – at one quarter of the World Bank's price – and currently educates 8200 formerly-illiterate children, 3400 of whom are girls. (Fedarko, 2003)

When the main buildings of Maulden Mills – maker of Polar Fleece – burned to the ground one night in Massachusetts, its owner, Aaron Feuerstein, made an almost immediate announcement. He promised to continue to pay workers at full salary and to rebuild the plant in the same location, even though substantial cost savings could have been realized by rebuilding in another state or off-shore. Rather than laying off employees, he maintained full pay and benefits. The cost of this decision, coupled with escalating price competition from low-cost off-shore textile manufacturers, put the firm on the edge of bankruptcy six years later. In the midst of difficult negotiations to obtain bank loans and restructured debt, Feuerstein still indicated that he would make the same decision again today. (Derber, 2000)

A local dentist in Columbus, Ohio, after taking over the practice of his deceased father, was involved in a serious automobile accident in which his severe injuries required him to remain bed-ridden for several months. Other dentists in the community, who were direct competitors, volunteered to come into his office to treat his patients. They were paid neither for the hours they worked nor for the patient services they provided. All income remained in the injured dentist's office for his personal use. (Schottenstein, 2003)

These brief examples are not the only forms – nor even the most common forms – of responsible leadership. Nonetheless they serve to illustrate the notion of responsible leadership as positive deviance, and how it can contribute to the elevation of others. The examples also differentiate this form of responsible leadership from the more common understandings of responsibility that are associated with maintaining accountability or possessing discretion.

Enabling responsible leadership
In addition to clarifying the meaning of responsibility, it is also important to acknowledge that leadership has a specific meaning as well. Quinn (2004) asserted that no person is a leader all of the time. Leadership is a *temporary* condition in which certain skills and competencies are displayed. When they are demonstrated, leadership is present. When they are not demonstrated, leadership is absent. People choose to enter a state of leadership when they choose to adopt a certain mind-set and implement certain key skills.

Understanding that leadership is a temporary, dynamic state brings us to a radical redefinition of how we think about, enact, and develop leadership. We come to discover that most of the time, most people, including CEOs, presidents, and prime ministers, are not leaders. We discover that anyone can be leader. Most of the time, none of us are leaders. (ibid., p. 12)

Responsible leadership, then, occurs when positive dynamics are enabled and the highest human potentialities are fostered. It can be demonstrated by almost anyone and revealed in a wide variety of circumstances. The focus of this chapter is on the skills and strategies that are available to responsible leaders which enable and enhance positive outcomes. These include positive work orientation, positive climate, positive communication and positive relationships. The discussion of each of these four factors is followed by a brief discussion of certain practical skills or strategies that can enable them, and reference to validating research is provided. The chapter concludes with a set of research questions that can help guide future investigations.

A positive work orientation
Wrzesniewski (2003), citing research in sociology (Bellah *et al.*, 1985) and psychology (Baumeister, 1991; Schwartz, 1994) pointed out that individuals

typically hold one of three broad orientations toward work: work as a *job*, a *career* or a *calling*. Those who see work as a job do their work solely for the financial or material rewards it provides. They take no particular personal satisfaction from their work, and they pursue their own interests and passions in non-work contexts. In contrast, individuals with a career orientation are motivated by success. They work to achieve the prestige, power, recognition and advancement that come from performing their work well. They desire to be exemplary members of their profession, and they use work to develop more personal capability and notoriety. The third orientation, the sense of work as a calling, motivates individuals to work for the sake of the work itself. The actual tasks involved in their work provide intrinsic benefit and profound meaning. They consider work inherently fulfilling, and they seek for a greater good, regardless of any material rewards offered by work.

Paralleling these work orientations are three types of relationships between members and their organizations: *compliance, identification* and *internalization* (Kelman, 1958; O'Reilly and Chatham, 1996). A compliance relationship produces desired behaviors through punishments and rewards. That is, compliant individuals act for personal material benefit and do not necessarily believe in the content of the action they take (a job orientation). Identification motivates individuals to further or to maintain a relationship with the organization, so that thay are committed to what they are doing as organizational members. Actions are taken to procure the satisfaction of belonging and to reinforce a sense of membership (a career orientation). Internalization is the most profound adoption of organizational goals. Individuals who have internalized the organizational culture and mission have accepted that what they are doing is the right thing to do. Internalization leads individuals to adopt the organization's purposes and priorities as their own (a calling orientation).

The predominance of calling orientations (or internalization in organizations) is associated with more positive outcomes and superior individual and organizational performance. For example, workers with a calling orientation reported higher job and life satisfaction scores compared to those with career or job orientations, as well as high satisfaction with their organization and their work (Wrzesniewski *et al.*, 1997). A stronger identification with the work unit accompanied a calling orientation, as did higher levels of trust and confidence in management, higher levels of commitment, less conflict, more satisfactory relationships with co-workers and higher levels of satisfaction with the work itself (Taylor and Bowers, 1972; Cook and Wall, 1980; Mowday *et al.*, 1979). Since the mean correlation between job satisfaction and performance is 0.30 – as determined by a definitive meta-analysis (Judge *et al.*, 2001) – higher satisfaction scores are likely to be associated with higher performance. In fact higher levels of organizational performance were detected in health care organizations when callings predominated among employees (Wrzesniewski and Landman, 2000).

It is important to remember that this sense of calling is dependent not on the type of work performed but on the interpretation of the profound meaning inherent in the work (Bellah *et al.*, 1985; Wrzesniewski, 2003). Any kind of work, even that typically thought of as physically, socially or morally tainted, can be reframed in a positive light (Ashforth and Kreiner, 1999). Put another way, exactly the same task may be viewed as a calling or a job, depending on the perspective of the individual. For example, in a study of custodians in a Midwest hospital (Wrzesniewski and Dutton, 2001) researchers interviewed a staff member who was assigned to clean up vomit and excrement from the oncology ward when patients came in for chemotherapy. These patients lost control of bodily functions when they were subjected to doses of medications needed to treat their malignancies. This staff member's response to her work was something like this: 'My job is equally important to the physician. I help these people feel human. At their lowest and most vulnerable point, I help them maintain their dignity. I make it okay to feel awful, to lose control, and to be unable to manage themselves. My role is crucial to the healing process.' Even the most noxious and unpleasant of tasks can be reinterpreted as a calling.

Enabling a positive work orientation
Enabling a positive work orientation through a sense of calling among employees is enhanced by helping them identify a sense of meaningfulness in their work. Responsible leaders enable this kind of orientation (where callings and internalization are dominant characteristics of the workforce) through at least four mechanisms reviewed by Pratt and Ashforth (2003). The first is *job enrichment* and *job involvement* (Lodahl and Kejner, 1965; Hackman and Oldham, 1980), meaning that work is designed so as to provide skill variety, task identity, task significance, autonomy and feedback as part of the job. Several strategies to achieve these work attributes have been identified by Hackman and Oldham (1980). The second mechanism is offering *intrinsic motivational factors* such as interesting work, opportunities for creativity, chances for advancement and achievement, peer recognition and personally fulfilling goals (Herzberg *et al.*, 1959; Kanungo and Hartwick, 1987; Amabile *et al.*, 1994). Responsible leadership strategies for achieving these results are enumerated by Pratt and Ashforth (2003). 'The third mechanism is creating an *empowering environment*, including opportunities to develop self-efficacy (a sense of competence), self-determination (a sense of choice), consequence (a sense of impact), meaningfulness (a sense of purpose) and trust (a sense

of security) (Spreitzer, 1992; Mishra, 1992); Cameron (2002c) offered a large number of strategies for enhancing and enabling empowerment. The fourth mechanism is articulating a *clear vision of the future* which is based on source credibility (Kouzes and Posner, 1988), optimism and positive emotions (Fredrickson, 2003) and being interesting (Davis, 1971), meaning that the vision focuses on abundance and opportunity rather than problems or obstacles (Cooperrider and Sekerka, 2003; Powley *et al.*, 2004); Ashforth and Kreiner (1999) presented several strategies for achieving this end. In the case of each of these strategies, in other words, the cited research supports the connection between the enabling factors and a sense of meaningfulness in and at work (also see Pratt and Ashforth, 2003).

A positive climate

Baumeister *et al.* (2001), in a comprehensive review of psychological literature, highlighted the fact that negative occurrences, bad events and disapproving feedback are more influential and longer lasting in individuals than positive, encouraging and upbeat occurrences. One piece of negative feedback amidst several compliments, one significant loss amidst several important gains, one incidence of abuse amidst several incidents of nurturing, one traumatic event amidst several pleasant events or one bad relationship amidst several good relationships all have a disproportionately negative impact on individuals and on organizations. That is, the negative event will engender more coping behaviors, longer lasting reactions and more lingering memories than the comparable positive event.

The title of Baumeister *et al.*'s review gives away its conclusion: 'Bad is Stronger than Good.' People tend to pay more attention to negative than positive phenomena, but for good reason. Ignoring a negative threat could be lethal. That is, from the outset of life, individuals learn that to ignore negative feedback is likely to be not only unpleasant but dangerous or even life-threatening. Ignoring the honking of a horn or the screeching of tires while crossing the street could be fatal. On the other hand, ignoring an enjoyable or satisfying experience would only result in regret at missing a pleasurable occurrence. Seldom does anything life-threatening occur associated with positive phenomena. Consequently individuals in general (and especially leaders in organizations, who are constantly confronted by problems, threats and obstacles) have a tendency to focus on the negative much more than the positive. They are socialized this way from birth. Most leaders, authority figures or models that people encounter are charged with resolving problems, defeating the competition or protecting the innocent from threats (March and Simon, 1958; Riley, 1998; Cameron, 2002a). Negative elements receive much more attention than positive elements in the environment. Responsible leaders, therefore, are unusual in that they choose to emphasize the positive, uplifting and flourishing side of organizational life. It is not that they ignore the negative and adopt a Pollyannaish perspective, but they counter the tendency toward negativity with an abundance of positivity. In the absence of such an emphasis, negative inclinations overwhelm the positive.

The word 'climate' refers to individuals' psychological experience associated with the work environment (Denison, 1996; Smidts *et al.*, 2001), so that a positive climate is one in which positive feelings and interpretations predominate over negative feelings and interpretations. Fredrickson (1998, 2001, 2002, 2003) found, in carefully controlled psychological experiments, that a positive climate produces positive emotions which, in turn, lead to optimal individual and organizational functioning. These positive outcomes are produced both in the immediate term and over the long run. Engendering a positive climate does not depend so much on inherent attributes or events as it does on the approach of the leader. That is, positive emotions can be induced and developed by leaders as they adopt a positive approach to the climate.

Fredrickson (1998) documented a 'broaden and build' phenomenon that is associated with positive emotions. Experiencing positive emotions 'broadens people's momentary thought–action repertoires and builds their enduring personal resources' (Fredrickson, 2003, p. 166). Negative emotions narrow people's thought-action repertoires and diminish their coping abilities. That is, inducing positive emotions (such as joyfulness, love or appreciation) enlarges cognitive perspectives and enhances the ability of individuals to attend to more information, make richer interpretations and experience higher levels of creativity and productivity (Isen, 1987). This also builds enduring personal resources such as intellectual complexity, knowledge, intellectual interest and the capacity to explore (Fredrickson and Branigan, 2001). Positive emotions also modulate negative emotions such as fear, anger, sadness or anxiety and undo their negative physiological effects (Fredrickson and Levenson, 1998). Generating a positive climate, in other words, 'engenders and enhances positive emotions which, in turn, generate upward spirals toward optimal functioning and enhanced performance' (Fredrickson, 2003, p. 169). A positive work climate has also been found to enhance decision making, productivity, creativity, social integration and prosocial behaviors (Staw and Barsade, 1993).

Enabling a positive climate
Responsible leaders resist the tendency to concentrate primarily on the negative, threatening or difficult in the environment. Instead they emphasize positive emotions and positive phenomena in the interest of developing

a positive climate. Two ways to do this are by creating positive energy networks and by focusing on individuals' strengths.

Recent research by Baker *et al.* (2003) discovered that individuals can be identified as 'positive energizers' or 'negative energizers' and that the difference has important implications. Positive energizers create and support vitality in others. They uplift and boost people. Interacting with positive energizers leaves others feeling lively and motivated. In contrast, negative energizers deplete the good feelings and enthusiasm of others. They sap strength from and weaken people. They leave others feeling exhausted and diminished. Positive energizers benefit their organizations by enabling others to perform better (ibid.). In fact, a comparison between information networks (who obtains information from whom), influence networks (who influences whom) and positive energy networks (who energizes whom) revealed that energy networks were far more predictive of success than information or influence networks (Baker, 2000). Being a positive energizer made individuals four times more likely to succeed than being at the center of an information or influence network, and this success was conveyed to those interacting with the energizer (Baker *et al.*, 2003). High performing organizations have three times as many positive energy networks as average organizations (Baker, 2004).

Responsible leaders focus on creating positive energy networks, both by modeling positive energy themselves and by building positive energy networks among others. Positive energizers can be identified and placed in tasks and roles that will allow others to interact with them, thus enhancing the performance of a broadened field of employees. Negative energizers who are essential to the organization for reasons of talent or experience can be placed in non-central positions that minimize the energy-depleting effects they have on others. Leaders can also promote a climate of positivity by recognizing, rewarding and supporting positive energizers.

A second opportunity for the responsible leaders to promote a climate of positivity lies in a focus on individual and organizational strengths. Identifying and building upon people's strengths can produce greater benefit than finding and correcting their weaknesses (Seligman, 2002; Clifton and Harter, 2003). For example, managers who spent more time with their strongest performers, as compared to spending it with their weakest performers, achieved double the productivity. Similarly, in organizations where workers were able to 'do what they do best every day', productivity was one and a half times greater than in the typical organization (Clifton and Harter, 2003).

The reason for this difference lies in the way that people learn. Individuals learn more readily and more completely from positive demonstrations than from negative demonstrations (Bruner and Goodnow, 1956). In other words, telling people what not to do is less helpful than identifying what they should do. People given negative examples (that is, who are told what to fix or to avoid repeating) are much more likely to do exactly what they were told not to do, simply because that is the picture in their mind. For example, if someone says, 'Do not think of a white bear', the first thing to occur is a thought about a white bear. This phenomenon is known as the ideomotor reflex (Bargh and Chartrand, 1999); that is, thinking of an action makes people much more likely to engage in that action regardless of whether they were thinking about doing it beforehand.

This phenomenon is clearly illustrated by a study of how to best enhance the performance of bowlers. In an experimental condition, people were videotaped as they bowled three games. Half the bowlers were then shown video tapes of frames when they knocked all the pins down – spares or strikes – whereas the other half of the bowlers was shown video tape of frames when they did not knock down all the pins. After a period of practice, using the video tapes as models and guides, statistically significant differences were found between the two groups. Those watching themselves succeed (making strikes) were significantly better bowlers than those who watched themselves in a non-success condition (see Cooperrider and Srivastva, 1987). That is, people tend to learn from success more effectively and efficiently than from failure, so responsible leaders emphasize success, build on strengths and celebrate the positive much more than spending time correcting the negative. They enable a positive climate.

Positive communication
Positive communication occurs in an organization when affirmative and supportive language replaces negative and critical language. The power of positive communication is illustrated in a study of 60 management teams who were engaged in their annual strategic planning and budget-setting activities (Losada and Heaphy, 2004). The research focused on investigating why some teams and organizations performed better than others.

Teams were categorized into effectiveness levels based on three measures of performance: profitability, customer satisfaction and 360-degree evaluations of the managers comprising the teams. The three groups were high performing teams (N=15), average performing teams (N=26) and low performing teams (N=19), based on how they scored on the three criteria. To explain differences among the teams, the communication patterns of team members were carefully monitored and categorized by trained raters who were unaware of the performance category of the teams. Four communication categories were used: the ratio of positive to negative comments, the ratio of inquiry to advocacy comments, the ratio of focusing on others compared to focusing on self, and a measure of 'connectivity', or the amount of interaction and information exchanged in the team.

The single most important factor in predicting team performance, which was more than twice as powerful as any other factor, was the ratio of positive comments to negative comments. Positive comments are those that express appreciation, support, helpfulness or compliments. Negative comments express criticism, disapproval or blame. The results of the research showed that, in high performing teams, the ratio of positive to negative comments was 5.6 to 1. Five times more positive comments were made than negative comments in high performing teams. In medium performing teams, the ratio was 1.85 to 1. In low performing teams, the ratio was 0.36 to 1. In low performing teams, in other words, there were three negative comments for every positive comment.

These results demonstrated that high performing teams had very different communication patterns from low performing teams, primarily based on the abundance of positive comments. Effective teams were far more complimentary and supporting than low performing teams. It was not that correction and criticism were entirely absent; that is, these teams were not characterized by a Pollyannaish or rose-colored glasses approach to strategic planning. The ratio, it is important to point out, was not 5 to 0, nor 20 to 1; rather, it was constrained at approximately 5 to 1. Corrective and disagreeing communications were certainly present in high performing teams but just not to the point of dominating or overwhelming the positive. Teams that performed moderately well had about an equal number of positive and negative comments, and teams that performed poorly were more negative than positive (Losada and Heaphy, 2004).

This same 5 to 1 ratio was discovered by Gottman (1994) in his predictive studies of successful marriages and divorces. The best predictor of the sustainability and quality of the marital relationship was found to be the ratio of positive to negative communication events. The 'Gottman index', in fact, has made the 5 to 1 ratio quite well accepted in family therapy and family sociology. Marriages that end in divorce, similar to the Losada and Heaphy (2004) study, are typified by more negative than positive communications (Gottman, 1994).

One explanation for the performance effects of positive communication is that positive communication has been found to create significantly more 'connectivity' (the exchange of information, interpersonal interactions and positive emotions) in organizations. This connectivity is the means by which resources flow and coordinated action takes place (Dutton and Heaphy, 2003). This coordinated exchange, in turn, enables higher productivity and higher quality performance (Losada, 1999; Fredrickson and Levenson, 1998; Fredrickson *et al.*, 2000).

Enabling positive communication

Because bad is stronger than good, and most organizations are fraught with problems and challenges, prescribing positive communication is much easier than practicing it. One obvious way that responsible leaders can enable positive communication is by exemplifying positive talk themselves. Minimizing criticism and negativity, and replacing them with compliments and supportive communication, can enable positive communication to flourish. Leaders' role modeling has a disproportional effect on creating such outcomes (George, 1998). Aside from role modeling, however, two specific levers are available to responsible leaders to enable positive communication: the *reflected best self feedback* process (Roberts *et al.*, in press) and the use of *supportive communication* (Cameron, 2002b).

The reflected best self feedback process is a technique used to capture positive feedback for individuals, to encourage positive communication, and then guide people through a process of uncovering their strengths and the positive evaluations held by others about them. The technique was developed at the University of Michigan and is now being used in several universities and corporations. Each person (student, employee, manager and so on) is asked to identify approximately 20 other people who are acquaintances. These can be friends, coworkers, neighbors or family members. Each of these acquaintances is asked to write three stories in response to the question: 'When you have seen me at my best, what unique value did I create?' or, alternatively, 'When you have seen me make a special contribution, what unique strengths did I display?' In other words, the 20 acquaintances write three stories about when this person was his or her best self. Those 60 stories identify the key strengths and unique talents of the individual, information that is both rare and extremely valuable. The communication is universally positive, and the concomitant positive affect naturally follows (Roberts *et al.*, in press).

This positive communication is analyzed by the person receiving the stories and is summarized into a few key themes. Those themes represent the best self strengths and uniquenesses of the person, and strategies for capitalizing on these strengths are then formulated. The feedback comes in the form of incidents and stories, not numbers or trend lines, so it is connected directly to behaviors that the person has displayed in the past and which can be repeated and enhanced in the future. It captures emotions and feelings as well as intentional actions. These are the strengths that can be built upon and enhanced. This kind of feedback does not even mention weaknesses or shortcomings, so it does not motivate people to focus on areas of deficiency. Instead recipients have strengthened relationships with feedback givers, feelings of reciprocity toward them, an enhanced desire to live up to the positive best self descriptions, elevated positive affect and a reinterpretation of past personal history to be more strength-based.

Of course completely ignoring weaknesses and inadequacies is not healthy, and focusing exclusively on the positive and disregarding critical weaknesses is not apt to be productive in the long run. It is just that most individuals, and most organizations, concentrate overwhelmingly on the negative, and they are likely to ignore, or at least to short-change, the positive. The reflective best self feedback technique is a way to counterbalance that tendency by encouraging positive communication.

A second means by which responsible leaders can enable positive communication is by using *supportive communication*, particularly when corrective, critical or negative messages must be delivered. All communication cannot be complimentary, agreeable or congratulatory, of course, and negative messages must be delivered in any organization or relationship. Therefore certain communication techniques, all designed to preserve and strengthen a positive relationship between communicators while still addressing problems and concerns, are a way to maintain the advantages of positive communication (Cameron, 2002b; Gibb, 1961; Knapp and Vangelisti, 1996). Of the eight elements of supportive communication, the one most appropriate in this context may be the use of description rather than evaluation in identifying and resolving problems (Rogers, 1961). Specifically, when delivering negative messages, describing a situation (rather than evaluating it), identifying objective consequences or personal feelings about it (rather than blaming), and suggesting an acceptable alternative (rather than arguing about who is right) leads to a constructive conversation that focuses on identifying commonalities and collaboration rather than adversarial communication (Gibb, 1961; Cameron, 2002b). Responsible leaders who facilitate positive communication can use these two strategies to help achieve their desired results.

Positive relationships
Heaphy and Dutton (2004) recently reviewed the literature on the connection between positive relationships and physiological health. Abundant evidence has linked the positive effects of social relationships with social phenomena such as power (Ibarra, 1993), career mobility (Burt, 1992), mentoring and resource acquisition (Kram, 1985) and social capital (Baker, 2000). Studies have also shown that social relationships have positive affects on longevity and recovery from illness (Ryff and Singer, 2001). That is, positive social relationships have beneficial effects on a variety of aspects of human behavior and health. Heaphy and Dutton's literature review, however, explains why these positive outcomes occur. Specifically, positive social relationships affect

the *hormonal, cardiovascular* and *immune* systems of the body, thus enhancing health, wellbeing and the nature of the relationships themselves.

Specifically, when people experience position relationships with others, oxytocin (a health-enhancing hormone) is released in the body, leading to lower blood pressure and heart rate and an enhanced ability to handle stress calmly (Taylor, 2002; Ryff *et al.*, 2001). Positive social contacts lessen the allostatic load (the physiological reaction in the body to stress), so the body works less hard to cope under the presence of stressful conditions (Epel *et al.*, 1998). In addition the increase in anabolic hormones associated with positive relationships also has a calming effect on the body and mind (Seeman, 2001). Furthermore, increases in oxytocin cause people to seek social contact with others (Taylor, 2002), which, in turn, leads to a virtuous cycle of positive social contact, with its attendant physiological consequences. Kiecolt-Glaser *et al.* (2003) found that the hormonal effects of positive relationships have a long-term impact on marriages. Married couples were required to discuss a stressful topic and four stress-related hormones (such as adrenacorticotrophic hormone – ACTH) were measured over a 24-hour period. Ten years later, these couples were tracked down, and it was found that the hormonal levels in the original experiment predicted their marital status (married, divorced, separated). Those with elevated stress hormone levels were less likely to be married. The release of good hormones (such as oxytocin) and the decrease of bad hormones (such as ACTH) predicted relationship durability.

Similar findings have been found with regard to the effects of positive relationships on the cardiovascular system. People who experience positive relationships (as opposed to ambivalent or negative relationships) experienced lower blood pressure, systolic heart rate and diastolic heart rate (Holt-Lunstad *et al.*, 2003). When encountering stressful events, people did less cardiovascular work, as evidenced by lower heart rates and blood pressure when they were in positive relationships or felt social support at work (Brondolo *et al.*, 2003; Unden *et al.*, 1991). Social and emotional support at work (especially from supervisors and coworkers) had a direct effect on lowering heart rate and blood pressure (Karlin *et al.*, 2003). Especially interesting was an investigation of caregivers for Alzheimer's patients in which persons with high levels of social support had heart rate patterns associated with lower chronological age compared to care givers with low levels of social support (Uchino *et al.*, 1992). Those with positive relationships were not as old physiologically as those without. In addition a study of 10 000 Israeli men (Medalie and Goldbourt, 1976) found that, among those experiencing high levels of stress, those who had a loving and supportive wife had half the rate of angina pectoris (chest pain). After a heart attack, the presence of social and emotional support doubled the chances of survival six months later in another study (Berkman *et al.*, 2002) and was more predictive than chronological age.

The third factor – the immune system – is also positively affected by positive relationships. Individuals in positive relationships have greater resistance to upper respiratory infections (Cohen *et al.*, 1997), and men reporting greater satisfaction with their social support system had lower levels of a prostate-specific antigen which indicates various prostate diseases. Positive relationships actually enhanced the body's ability to fight off cancer (Stone *et al.*, 1999). Medical students reporting higher levels of social support had stronger immune responses to Hepatitis B vaccines than those with less social support (Esterling *et al.*, 1994), and stronger immunity responses were detected in the bodies of caregivers who experienced higher levels of social support. These immune responses were due primarily to the presence of NK cells (natural killer cells) and T-lymphocytes which fight off colds and disease.

The presence of positive and supportive relationships, in sum, have positive effects on individuals and subsequently on their performance, as well as on their collective performance in an organization, because of their association with very basic physiological processes.

Enabling positive relationships
Fostering positive relationships in organizations is a topic that has been well researched in organizational studies, and many strategies have been identified. Searching the phrase 'relationships at work' on Amazon.com, for example, creates more than 100 000 hits. Buckingham and Clifton (2001) identified a key measure of positive relationships at work as captured by the item: 'Do you have a best friend at work?' When a positive answer is given to this question, the positive effects of relationships mentioned above are significantly higher than when a negative answer is given. One worrisome outcome of best friends working together, of course, is that more time is spent on relationship management than on task accomplishment, but evidence suggests that this is seldom the danger that is feared (Dutton and Heaphy, 2003). Opportunities to form friendships at work actually enhance and increase the productivity of friendship-based work groups (Dutton, 2003).

Aside from friendships, positive relationships at work can also be facilitated by means of another set of factors whose importance was recently uncovered in research. These include the fostering of *compassion*, *forgiveness* and *gratitude* in organizations. These terms may sound a bit saccharine and soft – even out of place in a serious discussion of responsible leadership and effective performance – yet recent research has found them to be very important predictors of organizational success. Companies that scored higher on these attributes performed significantly better than others

(Cameron *et al.*, 2004). When managers fostered compassionate behavior among employees, forgiveness for missteps and mistakes, and gratitude resulting from positive occurrences, their firms excelled in profitability, productivity, quality, innovation and customer retention. Responsible leaders that reinforced these virtues were more successful in producing bottom-line results (Cameron, 2003).

Compassion can be enabled, according to Kanov *et al.* (2004), through three processes: collective noticing, collective feeling and collective responding. When people experience difficulty or negative events, the first step is to notice or become aware of what is occurring; that is, to be on the lookout for colleagues who need help. Second, the expression of collective emotion can be fostered through planned events where people can share feelings (for example, grief, support or love) which help build a climate of compassion (Frost, 1999). Third, collective responding occurs when organized action is taken to foster healing or restoration. In the aftermath of the 11 September 2001 tragedy, many examples of compassion (and non-compassion) were witnessed in organizations around the country. While some responsible leaders modeled caring and compassion in the responses they fostered, others stifled the healing process (see Dutton *et al.*, 2002).

Forgiveness can be enhanced in organizations (McCullough *et al.*, Pargament and Thoresen, 2000; Worthington, 1998) when responsible leaders do at least five things: (1) they acknowledge the trauma, harm and injustice that their organization members have experienced, but they define the occurrence of hurtful events as an opportunity to move forward toward a new goal; (2) they associate the outcomes of the organization (such as its products and services) with a higher purpose that provides personal significance for organization members. This higher purpose replaces a focus on self (for example, retribution, self-pity) with a focus on a higher objective; (3) they maintain high standards and communicate the fact that forgiveness is not synonymous with tolerance of error or lowered expectations. Forgiveness facilitates excellence by refusing to focus on the negative and, instead, focusing on achieving excellence; (4) they provide support by communicating that human development and human welfare are as important in the organization's priorities as the financial bottom line. This kind of support helps employees catch sight of a way to move past the injury; (5) they pay attention to language, so that terms such as forgiveness, compassion, humility, courage and love are acceptable. This language provides a humanistic foundation upon which forgiveness can be developed. An analysis by Cameron and Caza (2002) of several organizations' successful turnarounds after the trauma of downsizing revealed these strategies being demonstrated in institutionalized forgiveness.

Observing acts of compassion and forgiveness, not to mention being the recipient of them, creates a sense of gratitude in people which has been found to have dramatic effects on individual and organizational performance. For example, Emmons (2003) induced feelings of gratitude in students by assigning them to keep journals as part of a semester-long assignment. Some of the students were required to keep 'gratitude journals' on a daily or weekly basis. That is, they wrote down events or incidents that happened during the day (or week) for which they were grateful. Other students were assigned to write down events or incidents that were frustrating, and still other students were assigned to write down events or incidents that were merely neutral. Students keeping gratitude journals, compared to frustrated students and neutral students, experienced fewer physical symptoms such as headaches and colds; felt better about their lives as a whole; were more optimistic about the coming week; had higher states of alertness, attentiveness, determination and energy; reported fewer hassles in their lives; engaged in more helping behavior towards other people; experienced better sleep quality; and had a sense of being more connected to others. In addition they were absent and tardy less often and had higher grade point averages. Feelings of gratitude had a significant impact on student classroom performance as well as people's personal lives. Emmons also found that expressions of gratitude by one person tend to motivate others to express gratitude, so a self-perpetuating, virtuous cycle occurred when gratitude was expressed. Gratitude elicited positive behaviors on the part of other people (for example, they were more likely to loan money or provide compassionate support) as well as behaving reciprocally. For example, a hand-written 'thank you' on a restaurant bill by the server elicited about 11 per cent higher tips, and visits by case workers and social workers were 80 per cent higher if they were thanked for coming (McCullough *et al.*, 2002).

Responsible leaders can engender positive relationships in organizations, therefore, merely by modeling and encouraging acts of compassion, collective forgiveness and expressions of gratitude, as well as by encouraging the formation of friendships at work. As demonstrated by Heaphy and Dutton (2004), such activities produce physiological effects which motivate people toward higher performance as well as fostering virtuous cycles of enriched relationships.

Conclusion and research questions
This discussion has pointed out that responsible leadership can be thought of in three different ways: as accountability, as discretion and freedom, or as enabling appropriate outcomes. Identifying some strategies to facilitate the latter of these three definitions has been the focus of this chapter. Specifically, responsible leadership has been located in the domain

of Positive Organizations Scholarship, and some of the recent literature connected with that field of study has been used to show how a focus on positive dynamics produces extraordinarily positive results. This is in spite of the fact that negative phenomena tend to dominate the attention of individuals and organizations. Because 'bad is stronger than good', mindful and conscientious effort must be placed on positive phenomena in order for the performance benefits to occur. This positive emphasis is contrary to natural tendencies in individuals and organizations. Responsible leadership, therefore, is counterintuitive in that it enhances and enables that which elevates rather than that which overcomes problems.

Four strategies were identified which characterize responsible leadership and which enable especially positive outcomes: *positive work orientation, positive climate, positive communication* and *positive relationships*. These four strategies are not comprehensive, of course, but they illustrate the levers available to leaders who wish to enable positive outcomes. Research evidence has been provided which supports the legitimacy of these strategies.

Research on responsible leadership, of course, is still much underdeveloped in terms of empirical research findings and theoretical maturity. Hence several important research questions are offered below to help guide future research endeavors.

Concept definition

Responsibility and leadership are the subjects of almost 50 000 books, as revealed by a quick scan of Amazon.com. Seldom, however, are the two concepts carefully and precisely defined and measured. The volume of prescriptions far outweighs the volume of credible evidence. A variety of research questions, such as the following, remain unaddressed. How do we know responsibility when we see it? What is and is not responsible leadership in the POS sense? What are the downsides of a focus on the positive? Can organizations succeed without responsible leadership, or can they succeed *with* responsible leadership? How much or how little can be tolerated? What is goodness and appropriateness? Who decides? The central concepts, in other words, provide fruitful territory for more thorough investigations.

Level of analysis

Do the individual dynamics enabled by responsible leaders reproduce themselves in organizations, and vice versa? Why or why not? For example, do positive relationships among individuals have the same kinds of effects on networks of organizations? Do individual interpretations of meaningfulness *at* work produce a sense of meaningfulness *in* the work of the organization? In what way does positive communication and using reflected best self feedback affect organization-level performance? Demonstrating relationships at one level of analysis does not necessarily mean that they will be present in another, and responsible leadership's impact on individuals may be different from that on organizations.

Measurement

Few instruments, methods or reliable indicators have been developed to assess positive phenomena. For example, how should responsibility, or leadership, be assessed? How are positive concepts and variables best identified, measured and explained? What are the key indicators? A need exists to locate and measure the existence of extraordinarily positive states, processes, structures and behavior. What are the markers? Questions relating to what is measured as well as how it is measured are clearly in need of investigation.

New concepts and new relationships

Several nontraditional concepts have been discussed in this chapter in relation to responsible leadership, including positive energy, organizational virtuousness, strengths, positive deviance, positive social relationships, positive climate, meaningfulness and so on. Few of these concepts have been carefully or thoroughly examined, yet they represent a sampling of positive factors that may be associated with responsibility and with leadership. What other aspects of responsible leadership behavior have not been taken into account in explaining positive outcomes? What other environmental, organizational or individual factors might affect positive organizational and individual outcomes? Since most empirical studies account for small percentages of the variance in individual and organizational outcomes, additional variables surely can be uncovered.

Causality

Questions relating to causal directionality are always fruitful areas for investigation, especially in responsible leadership and positive outcomes. What are the causal relationships (directionality) associated with various positive phenomena? Do high-quality relationships lead to cardiovascular fitness, or vice versa? Which comes first, virtuousness (for example, compassion, forgiveness, gratitude) or high performance in organizations? Longitudinal studies are always difficult to conduct, but they would provide important insights about the effects of responsible leadership that heretofore are only assumed.

Enablement

In addition to questions of causal association, issues relating to the enablement of positive outcomes also are salient. Uncovering why and how responsible leadership occurs – and how it affects others – is an underinvestigated issue.

For example, aside from leadership, what are the attributes of the structures, processes, cultures and/or resources that are most conducive, or resistant, to positive dynamics in organizations? What kinds of organizational arrangements are conducive to high-quality relationships, positive energy development, positive climates or the enablement of responsible leadership? What organizational conditions facilitate the development of emotional competence or positive communication, or bring forth the best in people? Studies of enablement, unlike 'best-practice' approaches, seek to identify the processes and mechanisms that enable and encourage positive deviance, responsibility and leadership.

Thus, returning to the point where the chapter began: that, whereas the idea of responsible leadership is not new and the literature on effective leadership has always been characterized by an element of responsibility, the scholarly study of both concepts, responsibility and leadership, is in need of systematic attention. Responsibility in the sense of appropriateness and goodness is both underinvestigated and largely misunderstood, and leadership as a temporary state rather than a permanent attribute or condition requires a rethinking in leadership research. It is hoped that this chapter will stimulate alternative thinking and new venues for investigation, as well as providing guidelines for workable strategies.

References

Amabile, T.M., T.M. Hill, B.A. Hennessey and E.M. Tighe (1994), 'The work preference inventory: assessing intrinsic and extrinsic motivational orientations', *Journal of Personality and Social Psychology*, **66**, 950–67.

Amabile, T.M., R. Conti, H. Coon, J. Lazenby and M. Herron (1996), 'Assessing the work environment for creativity', *Academy of Management Journal*, **39**, 1154–84.

Ashforth, B.E. and G.E. Kreiner (1999), '"How can you do it?" Dirty work and the challenge of constructing a positive identity', *Academy of Management Review*, **24**(3), 413–34.

Baker, W. (2000), *Achieving Success through Social Capital*, San Francisco: Jossey-Bass.

Baker, W. (2004), 'Half-baked brown bag presentation on positive energy networks', unpublished manuscript, University of Michigan Business School.

Baker, W., R. Cross and M. Wooten (2003), 'Positive organizational network analysis and energizing relationships', in K.S. Cameron, J.E. Dutton and R.E. Quinn (eds), *Positive Organizational Scholarship*, San Francisco, CA: Berrett-Koehler Publishers, pp. 328–42.

Bargh, J.A. and T.L. Chartrand (1999), 'The unbearable automaticity of being', *American Psychologist*, **54**(7), 462–79.

Batson, C.D. (1994), 'What act for the public good? Four answers', *Personality and Social Psychology Bulletin*, **20**(Special Issue: The Self and the Collective), 603–10.

Baumeister, R.F. (1991), *Meanings of Life*, New York: Guilford Press.

Baumeister, R.F., E. Bratslavsky, C. Finkenauer and K.D. Vohs (2001), 'Bad is stronger than good', *Review of General Psychology*, **5**(4), 323–70.

Bellah, R.N., R. Madsen, W.M. Sullivan, A. Swidler and S.M. Tipton (1985), *Habits of the Heart: Individualism and Commitment in American life*, New York: Harper & Row.

Berkman, L.F., L. Leo-Summers and R.I. Horowitz (2002), 'Emotional support and survival after myocardial infarction: a prospective, population-based study of the elderly', in J.T. Cacioppo, G.G. Berntson, R. Adolphs, C.S. Carter, R.J. Davidson, M.K. McClintock, B.S. McEwen, M.J. Meaney, D.L. Schacter, E.M. Sternberg, S.S. Suomi, and S.E. Taylor (eds) *Foundations in Social Neuroscience*, Cambridge, MA: MIT Press.

Bolino, M.C., W.H. Turnley and J.M. Bloodgood (2002), 'Citizenship behavior and the creation of social capital in organizations', *Academy of Management Review*, **27**, 505–22.

Bollier, D. (1996), *Aiming Higher: Twenty-five Stories of how Companies Prosper by Combining Sound Management and Social Vision*, New York: Amacom.

Brondolo, E., R. Rieppi, S.A. Erickson, E. Bagiella, P.A. Shapiro, P. McKinley and R.P. Sloan (2003), 'Hostility, interpersonal interactions, and ambulatory blood pressure', *Psychosomatic Medicine*, **65**, 1003–11.

Brown, R. (1986), 'Attribution theory', *Social Psychology*, New York: Free Press, pp. 131–94.

Bruner, J.S. and J.J. Goodnow (1956), *A Study of Thinking*, New York: John Wiley & Sons.

Buckingham, M. and D. Clifton (2001), *Now, Discover Your Strengths*. New York: Free Press.

Burns, James McGregor (1978), *Leadership*, New York: Harper & Row.

Burt, R. (1992), *Structural Holes*, Cambridge, MA: Harvard Business School Press.

Cameron, K.S. (2002a), 'Managing personal stress', in D.A. Whetten and K.S. Cameron, *Developing Management Skills*, Upper Saddle River, NJ: Prentice-Hall, pp. 97–154.

Cameron, K.S. (2002b), 'Coaching, counseling, and supportive communication', in D.A. Whetten and K.S. Cameron, *Developing Management Skills*, Upper Saddle River, NJ: Prentice-Hall, pp. 211–50.

Cameron, K.S. (2002c), 'Empowering and delegating', in D.A. Whetten and K.S. Cameron, *Developing Management Skills*, Upper Saddle River, NJ: Prentice-Hall, pp. 405–50.

Cameron, K.S. (2003) 'Organizational virtuousness and performance', in K.S. Cameron, J.E. Dutton and R.E. Quinn (eds), *Positive Organizational Scholarship*, San Francisco, CA: Berrett-Koehler Publishers, pp. 48–65.

Cameron, K.S. and A. Caza (2002), 'Organizational and leadership virtues and the role of forgiveness', *Journal of Leadership and Organizational Studies*, **9**(1), 33–48.

Cameron, K.S., D. Bright and A. Caza (2004), 'Exploring the relationships between organizational virtuousness and performance', *American Behavioral Scientist*, **47**(6), 766–90.

Cameron, K.S., J.E. Dutton and R.E. Quinn (eds) (2003), *Positive Organizational Scholarship*, San Francisco, CA: Berrett-Koehler Publishers.

Chappell, T. (1999), *Managing Upside Down: the Seven Intentions of Value-centered Leadership*, Boston, MA: William Morrow.

Clifton, D.O. and J.K. Harter (2003), 'Investing in strengths', in K.S. Cameron, J.E. Dutton and R.E. Quinn (eds), *Positive Organizational Scholarship*, San Francisco, CA: Berrett-Koehler Publishers, pp. 111–21.

Cohen, S., W.J. Doyle, D. Skoner, B.S. Rabin and J.M. Gwaltney (1997), 'Social ties and susceptibility to the common cold', *JAMA*, **277**, 1940–44.

Cook, J. and T.D. Wall (1980), 'New work attitude measures of trust, organizational commitment, and personal need non-fulfillment', *Journal of Occupational Psychology*, **53**, 39–52.

Cooperrider, D.L. and L.E. Sekerka (2003), 'Toward a theory of positive organizational change', in K.S. Cameron, J.E. Dutton and R.E. Quinn (eds), *Positive Organizational Scholarship*, San Francisco, CA: Berrett-Koehler Publishers, pp. 225–40.

Cooperrider, D.L. and S. Srivastva (1987), 'Appreciative inquiry in organizational life', *Research in Organizational Change and Development*, **1**, 129–69.

Cooperrider, D.L. and D. Whitney (1999), *Appreciative Inquiry*, San Francisco, CA: Berrett-Koehler Publishers.

Cowen, E.L. and R.P. Kilmer (2002), 'Positive psychology: some plusses and some open issues', *Journal of Community Psychology*, **30**, 449–60.

Czapinski, J. (1985), 'Negativity bias in psychology: an evaluation of Polish publications', *Polish Psychological Bulletin*, **16**, 27–44.

Davis, M.S. (1971), 'That's interesting! Towards a phenomenology of sociology and a sociology of phenomenology', *Philosophy of the Social Sciences* **1**, 309–44.

Denison, D.R. (1996), 'What *is* the difference between organizational culture and organizational climate? A native's point of view on a decade of paradigm wars', *Academy of Management Review*, **21**(3), 619–54.

108   *Responsible leadership and governance in global business*

Derber, C. (2000), *Corporate Nation: How Corporations Are Taking Over Our Lives and What We Can Do About It*, New York: Griffin.

Dutton, J.E. (2003), *Energizing Your Workplace: Building and Sustaining High Quality Relationships at Work*, San Francisco: Jossey-Bass.

Dutton, J.E. and E.D. Heaphy (2003), 'The power of high-quality connections', in K.S. Cameron, J.E. Dutton and R.E. Quinn (eds), *Positive Organizational Scholarship*, San Francisco, CA: Berrett-Koehler Publishers, pp. 263–78.

Dutton, J.E., P.J. Frost, M.C. Worline, J.M. Lilius and J.M. Kanov (2002), 'Leading in times of trauma', *Harvard Business Review* (January), 54–61.

Emmons, R.A. (2003), 'Acts of gratitude in organizations', in K.S. Cameron, J.E. Dutton and R.E. Quinn (eds), *Positive Organizational Scholarship*, San Francisco, CA: Berrett-Koehler Publishers, pp. 81–93.

Epel, E., B.S. McEwen and J.R. Ickovics (1998), 'Embodying psychological thriving: physical thriving in response to stress', *Journal of Social Issues*, **54**, 301–22.

Esterling, B.A., J.K. Kiecolt-Glaser, J. Bodnar and R. Glaser (1994), 'Chronic stress, social support and persistent alterations in the natural killer cell response to Cytokines in older adults', *Health Psychology*, **13**, 291–9.

Fedarko, K. (2003), 'He fights terror with books', *Parade*, **6**(April), 4–6.

Fredrickson, B.L. (1998), 'What good are positive emotions?', *Review of General Psychology*, **2**, 300–19.

Fredrickson, B.L. (2001), 'The role of positive emotions in positive psychology: the broaden-and-build theory of positive emotions', *American Psychologist*, **56**, 218–26.

Fredrickson, B.L. (2002), 'Positive emotions', in C.R. Snyder and S.J. Lopez (eds), *Handbook of Positive Psychology*, New York: Oxford University Press, pp. 120–34.

Fredrickson, B.L. (2003), 'Positive emotions and upward spirals in organizations', in K.S. Cameron, J.E. Dutton and R.E. Quinn (eds), *Positive Organizational Scholarship*, San Francisco, CA: Berrett-Koehler Publishers, pp. 163–75.

Fredrickson, B.L. and C. Branigan (2001), 'Positive emotions', in T.J. Mayne, and G.A. Bonnano (eds), *Emotions: Current Issues and Future Directions*, New York: Guilford, pp. 123–51.

Fredrickson, B.L. and R.W. Levenson (1998), 'Positive emotions speed recovery from the cardiovascular sequelae of negative emotions', *Cognition and Emotion*, **12**, 191–200.

Fredrickson, B.L., R.A. Mancuso, C. Branigan and M.M. Tugade (2000), 'The undoing effect of positive emotions', *Motivation and Emotion*, **24**(4), 237–59.

Frost, P.J. (1999), 'Why compassion counts', *Journal of Management Inquiry*, **8**, 127–33.

George, J.M. (1998), 'Salesperson mood at work: implications for helping customers', *Journal of Personal Selling and Sales Management*, **18**, 23–30.

Gibb, J.R. (1961), 'Defensive communication', *Journal of Communication*, **11**, 141–8.

Gottman, J.M. (1994), *What Predicts Divorce: The Relationship between Marital Processes and Marital Outcomes*, New York: Lawrence Earlbaum.

Hackman, J.R. and G.R. Oldham (1980), *Work Design*, Reading, MA: Addison-Wesley.

Heaphy, E.D. and J.E. Dutton (2004), 'Embodied connections: understanding the physiological effects of positive connections at work', working paper, Center for Positive Organizational Scholarship, University of Michigan Business School.

Herzberg, F., B. Mausner and B.B. Snyderman (1959), *The Motivation to Work*, New York: Wiley.

Holt-Lunstad, J., B.N. Uchino, T.W. Smith, C. Olsen-Cerny and J.B. Nealey-Moore (2003), 'Social relationships and ambulatory blood pressure: structural and qualitative predictors of cardiovascular function during everyday social interactions', *Health Psychology*, **22**, 388–97.

Hursthouse, R. (1999), *On Virtue Ethics*, Oxford: Oxford University Press.

Ibarra, H. (1993) 'Network centrality, power, and innovation involvement: determinants of technical and administrative roles', *Academy of Management Journal*, **36**, 471–501.

Isen, A.M. (1987), 'Positive affect, cognitive processes, and social behavior', *Advances in Experimental Social Psychology*, **20**, 203–53.

Judge, T.A., C.J. Thoreson, J.E. Bono and G.K. Patton (2001), 'The job satisfaction–job performance relationship: a qualitative and quantitative review', *Psychological Bulletin*, **127**(3), 376–407.

Kanov, J.M., S. Maitlis, M.C. Worline, J.E. Dutton, P.J. Frost, and J.M. Lilius (2004), 'Compassion in organizational life', *American Behavioral Scientist*, **47**, 808–27.

Kanungo, R.N. and J. Hartwick (1987), 'An alternative to the intrinsic–extrinsic dichotomy of work rewards', *Journal of Management*, **13**, 751–66.

Karlin, W.A., E. Brondolo and J. Schwartz (2003), 'Workplace social support and ambulatory cardiovascular activity in New York City traffic agents', *Psychosomatic Medicine*, **65**, 167–76.

Kelman, H.C. (1958), 'Compliance, identification, and internalization: three processes of attitude change', *Conflict Resolution*, **2**(1), 51–60.

Kiecolt-Glaser, J.K., C. Bane, R. Glaser and W.B. Malarkey (2003), 'Love, marriage, and divorce: newlywed's stress hormones foreshadow relationship changes', *Journal of Counseling and Clinical Psychology*, **70**, 537–47.

Knapp, M.L. and A.L. Vangelisti (1996), *Interpersonal Communication and Human Relationships*, Boston, MA: Allyn and Bacon.

Kouzes, J.M. and B.Z. Posner (1988), *What Followers Expect from Leaders: How to Meet People's Expectations and Build Credibility*, San Francisco: Jossey-Bass.

Kram, K. (1985), *Mentoring at Work: Developing Relationships in Organizational Life*, Glenview, IL: Scott Foresman.

Lodahl, T.M. and M. Kejner (1965), 'The definition and measurement of job involvement', *Journal of Applied Psychology*, **49**, 24–33.

Losada, M. (1999), 'The complex dynamics of high performance teams', *Mathematical and Computer Modelling*, **30**, 179–92.

Losada, M. and E.D. Heaphy (2004), 'Positivity and connectivity', *American Behavioral Scientist*, **47**(6).

March, J. G. and H.A. Simon (1958), *Organizations*, New York: John Wiley & Sons.

Margolis, J.D. and J.P. Walsh (2003), 'Misery loves companies: rethinking social initiatives by business', *Administrative Science Quarterly*, **48**, 268–305.

Mayne, T.T. (1999), 'Negative affect and health: the importance of being earnest', *Cognition and Emotion*, **13**, 601–35.

McCullough, M.E., R.A. Emmons and J. Tsang (2002), 'The grateful disposition: a conceptual and empirical topography', *Journal of Personality and Social Psychology*, **82**, 112–27.

McCullough, M.E., K.I. Pargament and C. Thoreson (2000), *Forgiveness: Theory, Research and Practice*, New York: Guilford.

Medalie, J.H. and U. Goldbourt (1976), 'Angina pectoris among 10,000 men: psychological and other risk factors as evidenced by a multivariate analysis of a five-year incidence study', *The American Journal of Medicine*, **60**, 910–21.

Mishra, A.K. (1992), 'Organizational response to crisis: the role of mutual trust and top management teams', unpublished doctoral dissertation, University of Michigan Business School.

Mowday, R.T., R.M. Steers and L.W. Porter (1979), 'The measurement of organizational commitment', *Journal of Vocational Behavior*, **14**, 224–47.

O'Reilly, C.A. and J.A. Chatham (1996), 'Culture as social control: corporations, cults and commitment', in B.M. Staw and L.L. Cummings (eds), *Research in Organizational Behavior*, vol. 18, Greenwich, CT: JAI Press, pp. 157–200.

Peterson, C.M. and M.E.P. Seligman (2003), 'Positive organizational studies: lessons from positive psychology', in K.S. Cameron, J.E. Dutton and R.E. Quinn (eds), *Positive Organizational Scholarship*, San Francisco, CA: Berrett-Koehler Publishers, pp. 14–28.

Powley, E.H., R.E. Fry, F.J. Barrett and D.S. Bright (2004), 'Egalitarian participation meets command and control: democratic transformation through the Appreciative Inquiry summit', *Academy of Management Executive*, **18** (3), 67–81.

Pratt, M.G. and B.E. Ashforth (2003), 'Fostering meaningfulness in working at work', in K.S. Cameron, J.E. Dutton and R.E. Quinn (eds), *Positive Organizational Scholarship*, San Francisco, CA: Berrett-Koehler Publishers, pp. 309–27.

Quinn, R.E. (2004), *Building the Bridge as You Walk on it: A Guide to Leading Change*, San Francisco, CA: Jossey-Bass.

Riley, S. (1998) *Critical Thinking and Problem Solving*, Upper Saddle River, NJ: Prentice-Hall.

Roberts, L.M., J.E. Dutton, G. Spreitzer, E.D. Heaphy and R.E. Quinn (in press), 'Composing the reflected best-self portrait: building pathways for becoming extraordinary in work organizations', *Academy of Management Review*.

Rogers, C.W. (1961), *On Becoming a Person*, Boston: Houghton Mifflin.

Ryff, C.D. and B. Singer (eds) (2001), *Emotion, Social Relationships and Health*. Oxford: Oxford University Press.

Ryff, C.D., B. Singer, E. Wing and G.D. Love (2001), 'Elected affinities and uninvented agonies: mapping emotion with significant others onto health', in C.D. Ryff and B. Singer (eds), *Emotion, Social Relationships and Health*, New York: Oxford University Press, pp. 133–75.

Salancik, G.R. and J.R. Meindl (1984), 'Corporate attributions as strategic illusions of management control', *Administrative Science Quarterly*, **29**(2), 238–54.

Schottenstein, A. (2003), 'Virtue and organizations', senior research project, University of Michigan Undergraduate Research Opportunity Program.

Schwartz, B. (1994), *The Costs of Living: How Market Freedom Erodes the Best Things in Life*, New York: W.W. Norton.

Schwartz, J. (2002), 'Dean's lecture series', University of Michigan Business School.

Seeman, T. (2001), 'How do others get under our skin? Social relationships and health', in C.D. Ryff and B. Singer (eds), *Emotion, Social Relationships and Health*, New York: Oxford University Press, pp. 189–210.

Seligman, M.E.P. (2002), 'Positive psychology, positive prevention, and positive therapy', in S.J. Lopez (ed.), *Handbook of Positive Psychology*, New York: Oxford University Press, pp. 3–9.

Smidts, A., A.T.H. Pruyin and C.B.M. Van Riel (2001), 'The impact of employee communication and perceived external prestige on organizational identification', *Academy of Management Journal*, **44**(5), 1051–62.

Snyder, C.R. and S.J. Lopez (2002), *Handbook of Positive Psychology*, New York: Oxford University Press.

Spreitzer, G.M. (1992), 'When organizations dare: the dynamics of individual empowerment in organizations', unpublished doctoral dissertation, University of Michigan Business School.

Staw, B.M. and S.G. Barsade (1993), 'Affect and managerial performance: a test of the sadder-but-wiser versus happier-and-smarter hypotheses', *Administrative Science Quarterly*, **38**, 304–31.

Stone, A.A., E.S. Mezzacappa, B.A. Donatone and M. Gonder (1999), 'Psychosocial stress and social support are associated with prostate-specific antigen levels in men: results from a community screening program', *Health Psychology*, **18**, 482–6.

Taylor, J.C. and D.G. Bowers (1972), *Survey of Organizations: A Machine Scored Standardized Questionnaire Instrument*, Ann Arbor, MI: Institute for Social Research, University of Michigan.

Taylor, S.E. (2002), *The Tending Instinct: How Nurturing is Essential for Who we are and How we Live*, New York: Time Books.

Tjeltveit, A.C. (2004), 'Implicit virtues, divergent goods, multiple communities', *American Behavioral Scientist*, **47**, 395–414.

Uchino, B.N., J.K. Kiecolt-Glaser and J.T. Cacioppo (1992), 'Age related changes in cardiovascular response as a function of a chronic stressor and social support', *Journal of Personality and Social Psychology*, **63**, 839–46.

Unden, A.L., K. Orth-Gomer and S. Elofsson (1991), 'Cardiovascular effects of social support in the work place: twenty-four-hour ECG monitoring of men and women', *Psychosomatic Medicine*, **53**, 50–60.

Walsh, J. P. (1999), 'Business must talk about its social role', in T. Dickson (ed.), *Mastering Strategy*, London: Prentice-Hall, pp. 289–94.

Walsh, J.P., K. Weber and J.D. Margolis (2003), 'Social issues and management: our lost cause found', *Journal of Management*, **29**, 859–81.

Weick, K.E. (2003), 'Positive organizing and organizational tragedy', in K.S. Cameron, J.E. Dutton and R.E. Quinn (eds), *Positive Organizational Scholarship*, San Francisco, CA: Berrett-Koehler Publishers, pp. 66–80.

Worthington, E.L. (1998), *Dimensions of Forgiveness: Psychological Research and Theological Perspectives*, Philadelphia, PA: Templeton Foundation Press.

Wrzesniewski, A. (2003), 'Finding positive meaning in work', in K.S. Cameron, J.E. Dutton and R.E. Quinn (eds), *Positive Organizational Scholarship*, San Francisco, CA: Berrett-Koehler Publishers, pp. 296–308.

Wrzesniewski, A. and J.E. Dutton (2001), 'Crafting a job: revisioning employees as active crafters of their work', *Academy of Management Review*, **26**(2), 179–201.

Wrzesniewski, A. and J. Landman (2000), 'Occupational choice and regret: Decision antecedents and their outcomes', unpublished manuscript.

Wrzesniewski, A., C.R. McCauley, P. Rozin and B. Schwartz (1997), 'Jobs, careers, and callings: people's relations to their work', *Journal of Research in Personality*, **31**, 21–33.

Yukl, G., A. Gordon and T. Taber (2002), 'A hierarchical taxonomy of leadership behavior: integrating a half century of behavior research', *Journal of Leadership and Organizational Studies*, **9**(1), 15–31.

7 Leadership and the social construction of charisma[1]

Rakesh Khurana

The first hurdle for myself is the laugh test: if we actually named this guy and told the employees and shareholders that he was the new boss, what would they think? Then there is the tendency to find people who look like the job. You start by whacking down the job to a set of alternatives. So you consider things like performance, the company, the company they are coming from, who they have worked with. From there you start to find people who look like the position. (William Pounds, former dean, MIT Sloan School of Management, and corporate director)

Introduction

Charismatic leadership is back, and this is something that should surprise us. It is probably not surprising that, in the realm of religion, a figure such as John Paul II should have emerged to lead the world's Catholics following years of tumult in the post-Vatican II Catholic Church; or that, among the dispossessed and disenfranchised of the Islamic world, we should have seen the rise of a charismatic such as Osama bin Laden. After all, as our foremost student of charismatic leadership, Max Weber, would remind us, charisma itself is a phenomenon associated with religion generally, and with politics in societies not yet governed by the rationalizing forces of capitalism and liberal democracy. Yet the resurfacing of charismatic leadership in American politics (with Ronald Reagan as the prime exemplar) and business (in the person of the charismatic CEO) in the last two decades presents a more puzzling situation, at least from a Weberian perspective. How could charisma have reappeared under the highly bureaucratized and rationalized conditions of American society at the end of the twentieth century?

No academic discipline would seem to have more potential for shedding light on this question than sociology. Yet, in the last few decades, sociology has essentially dropped the subject of leadership from its agenda (see Ganz, 2000). Why did research on this topic stop? I believe this development can be traced to the influence of C. Wright Mills (1956), whose work putting leadership in the context of power led sociological discussion of the topic into a cul-de-sac, leaving the field open to psychologists, psychoanalysts, the business consulting 'instrumentalists' and the rest.

As sociologists should certainly understand, however, there is much more to the question of how individuals acquire authority – which is what leadership, in the final analysis, is about – than the issues of power, the psychology of leaders and followers, the 'work of leaders' and so forth. In particular, the issue of how leadership is constructed by followers and by societies at large is one that sociology might fruitfully pursue in order to understand the re-emergence of charismatic leadership in recent times. For, as I will argue, what we are witnessing today is not so much a return of the charismatic leader that Weber described as the attribution to certain individuals of a pseudo-charisma that is clearly a social construction. In the process of transformation that charismatic leadership has undergone in modern America, meanwhile, charisma itself has assumed a very different social function from the disruptive, anti-traditional and anti-institutional one that Weber ascribed to it.

To understand this transformation, it is helpful to examine certain ideas about charismatic leadership in particular, and leadership in general, in the sociological tradition. What will be attempted in this chapter is first to trace the progress of certain sociological ideas in the writings of Max Weber and Georg Simmel that are pertinent to the phenomenon of leadership, and then to develop a modern theory of leadership by combining and extending these ideas within the empirical setting of the CEO labor market.[2]

Sociological approaches to leadership

Leadership as legitimate authority
Weber (1947) defines authority as 'the probability that a command with a given specific content will be obeyed by a given group of persons'. Authority, he argues, is central to the smooth workings of a society. A widely shared allegiance to a particular authority gives rise to the social order. Weber conceptualizes a well known typology of three types of shared authorities: (1) rational–legal authority, which rests upon the belief in the legality of enacted rules and the extent to which those exercising authority have a formal right to issue commands; (2) traditional authority, which rests upon the belief that obedience is owed to an occupant of a particular social role, such as a patriarch or a tribal leader; (3) charismatic authority, where authority emanates from a single leader who is believed by his followers to possess extraordinary or superhuman qualities.

Weber's view of the charismatic leader was that, in contrast to legal or traditional heads, he was an opponent of routinization and represented the impulse for disruption and change in the prevailing social order. According to Weber, the charismatic individual was the revolutionary force of society. Whereas traditional or rational–legal sources of authority were external factors influencing human behavior, charisma was a transformational force that changed people from within. Weber saw charismatic leadership confronting habits, rules and conventions head-on and, therefore, as the key to unlocking the iron cage of bureaucracy and societal stasis.

Weber, of course, recognized that charismatic authority, even though grounded in individual traits, resembled other types of authority in constituting a social relationship. He acknowledged, in other words, that even charismatic individuals gain power and come to be regarded as 'leaders' only insofar as others believe in their authority. For this reason, for example, heroes must continue to perform daring and successful deeds, and prophets must demonstrate by the accuracy of their prophecies that they possess genuine insight into the divine will (Trice and Beyer, 1986; Hunt, 1984). 'If proof of his charismatic qualification fails him for long ... it is likely that his charismatic authority will disappear' (Weber, 1968, p. 50). In short, the charismatic leader must live up to the expectations of his followers or see his authority vanish. Weber also recognized that there were particular social conditions, that is, times of great social, political, religious or economic stress, under which societies and their subordinate structures were most likely to turn to charismatic authority as providing a solution to the crisis.

These features of charismatic authority notwithstanding, however, Weber saw charisma as a quality inherent in certain individuals. 'What [the charismatic leader] despised,' he wrote, 'is traditional or rational' behavior since charisma is 'specifically outside the realm of every-day routine' (ibid., p. 52). In their purest form, charismatic leaders reject the use of their 'gifts of grace' for material exploitation and gain. They see their work as constituting a calling or mission. Consequently, Weber hypothesized, charismatic leaders emerged not from some bureaucracy or recognized body of experts but rather from the crowd, particularly from among those who live on the margins of conventional society. Charismatics, in Weber's view, stand apart from the dominant social system, and are motivated by their own inner values rather than those infused by the social order.

It is clear from Weber's writings that he regarded charisma as a rare phenomenon, since an individual must have exceptional personal qualities to engender this label. It should also be clear that the modern social institutions, with their elaborate safeguards of checks and balances against concentrated individual authority and universalistic culture founded on a deference toward rational–legal authority, would not likely be receptive to genuine charismatic authority should it ever present itself (Scott and Meyer, 1994). Instead modern forms of charismatic authority are better understood by examining the social context (Hunt, 1984). As noted earlier, Weber hinted that, in modern societies, an orientation toward charismatic authority was more likely to be linked to the properties of the social situation rather than the properties of a person. For example, a crisis, such as a dramatic change in the political or economic conditions of an institution, can be seen as creating conditions under which followers are attracted to the idea that an exceptional person could provide a solution to that crisis and therefore may attribute charismatic qualities to an individual, even when none of those qualities exist.

For Weber's contemporary Georg Simmel (Simmel, 1902), leadership also took the form of a dominating authority and could be studied for its content in terms of origin, style and effects. According to Simmel, there are two means by which leaders acquire authority over a group (Hunt, 1984). First, leaders acquire their dominance over a group by virtue of outstanding qualities such that 'a group comes to place its faith and trust in their abilities', or, second, because formal roles in social institutions, such as a university, church, government department or the military, may provide individuals with 'reputations and status that they would have been unlikely to acquire' without such institutional support. In the former case, which resembles Weber's concept of charismatic leadership in obvious respects, the leader's authority is derived from *ascribed* qualities that exert influence on the followers. In the second case it is conferred by the *achieved* quality of a leader's place within a hierarchy (see Hunt, 1984, for extended interpretation). This conception of leaders gaining authority through the prestige of the institutions with which they are associated clearly identifies this authority as a social product rather than something conceived as emerging from the personal qualities of the leader.

For Simmel, as for Weber, the leader and led have an interactive relationship, since it is impossible to base authority solely on coercion. Thus the led always have the option of following or not following. Yet, in his discussion of leadership and how its various forms are experienced by followers, Simmel uncovers an interesting irony that, once again, distinguishes his thinking from Weber's. For Simmel says that those under the sway of institutionally based leadership may feel themselves (like the followers of Weber's charismatic leader) to be following the leader in a spontaneous fashion, and thus may experience their act of devotion as a liberation from the institutionalized authority that the prestige leader actually embodies even as they reaffirm that authority (Hunt, 1984). Moreover those who recognize authority in an appointed office rather than in the person of a leader may feel themselves to be more 'free' than those who become enchanted by a hero or a prophet. Thus, we might conclude, it is fallacious to assume that a particular type of leadership necessarily elicits a particular kind of response from the followers. It may also then be true that charisma can be a constricting, conservative force as well as the disruptive one that Weber described.

In any event, Simmel views leaders as subject to the response of their followers, and describes them as often 'leading a group in the group's own direction'. The leader is conceptualized as the 'unitary expression' of the group's will rather than as an expression of division within it. He is seen as critical to the coherence of the group. Admittedly Simmel was focused on small groups rather than (as was Weber) societies and large institutions. Even so, his conception of leadership points to the possibility of charisma as something aligned with, rather than opposed to, institutionalization and rationalization.

Since the time of Weber bureaucratization and rationalization have proceeded quickly and charismatic authority has been thought to have disappeared. Multinational corporations and large public bureaucracies now account for the major portion of our institutions. They are now the most pervasive and influential institutions in society. Under such circumstances, the emergence of charismatic leadership would seem to have been an unlikely occurrence. However charisma has reappeared in recent years in both public and corporate settings. The term 'charismatic' has been increasingly applied to figures leading these organizations, while their successes and failures have been attributed to the possession or lack of charisma.

In contrast to previous sociological conceptions of charisma, this chapter will argue that charisma in this contemporary setting is a social phenomenon that is highly organized and socially structured. Moreover it is a post hoc type of attribution made with the benefit of hindsight.

Charismatic leadership as a social construction

In recent years, the term 'social construction' has become more widely used in sociological and organizational research. The central idea behind this term is that reality is not objective and given, but something that is created through an intensely social process (Berger and Luckmann, 1967). Specifically, social constructionists argue that all aspects of social reality, such as family, identity, money, organization and leadership are socially negotiated through continuing processes of institutionalization hardening into a taken-for-grantedness.

In the last two decades, new institutionalism (also referred to as neoinstitutionalism and hereafter referred to as institutional theory) has been the perspective that has explicitly linked social construction to organizational choices. Characterized by skepticism toward atomistic accounts of social process and a 'conviction that institutional arrangements and social processes matter', this perspective highlights the view that actors behave in 'socially determined ways' because they are embedded within pre-existing organizational systems (see Dimaggio and Powell, 1991, for an introduction to this perspective). In contrast to rational choice views of social institutions, this perspective emphasizes that institutions do not merely mirror the preferences, interests and power of the units constituting them; the institutions themselves shape those preferences, interests and that power.

When applied to the study of leadership, an institutional perspective rejects an asocial interpretation of managerial decision making. It also rejects the rational view of leadership choice as based on rational analysis, localized decision making and far-sighted planning, turning instead toward cognitive and cultural mechanisms, and an interest in supraindividual units of analysis that cannot be conceptualized as aggregations or direct consequences of individuals' attributes or motives (Zucker, 1977, p. 25; Dimaggio and Powell, 1991). In doing so, a new institutional perspective focuses less on local activities, such as the decisions of a board of directors choosing its leader on the basis of the functional needs of the organization, and more on the social context within which such decisions are made (like the role of executive search firms, investors and the media which legitimate particular models of leadership). Rather than focusing on the variation, the emphasis is on understanding the sources of the universal homogeneity of these organizations and their taken-for-granted practices and even existences (Meyer and Rowan, 1977; Ocasio, 1999). The origins of actors' preferences are now on the table, along with the feedback between actors' interests and the institutions they comprise. In other words, a new institutional perspective on leadership emphasizes that one reason why leaders are of such similar social type is simply that 'individuals cannot conceive of appropriate alternatives'. Because of their power in shaping the process by which choices are even considered, institutions create 'the lenses through which actors view the world and the very categories of structure, action, and thought' (Dimaggio and Powell, 1991, p. 13).

In the context of leadership succession, there are two central mechanisms by which individual action and society interact: the categorizing of acceptable versus unacceptable candidates and the practical actions of organizing CEO succession. Many sociologists increasingly take the view that categories are not simply a representational system for classifying and labeling external reality but actually constitute part of social reality (Zuckerman, 1999). Recent work by Zuckerman and Kim (2003), for example, highlights the point that meaning expressed through the categories used to analyze a film (for example, popular versus art-house) does not refer to an external reality. Podolny and Hill-Popper (2004), too, argue that a specific category does not achieve its meaning in relation to external reality, but only in relation to other categories; that is, the meaning of a category is constructed through the play of differences. In the context of the CEO succession process, the categories of acceptable and unacceptable candidates objectify directors' experiences by classifying and organizing them into a meaningful whole. These categories act as an interpretive scheme in the sense that directors' experiences of reality, such as their perceptions of cause-and-effect relationships, become objectified through them. They also become the primary medium through which these objectifications are transmitted between people and are translated into actions that result in their subsequent reproduction elsewhere.

A second way of understanding the social construction of leadership is to look not only at interpretive schemes but at practical actions. Giddens (1987) argues that a greater part of the social construction of reality takes place in 'practical consciousness', through the observation of the way actions and decisions are made in everyday life. Bourdieu (1977), in his theory of practice, argued along similar lines. By elaborating the concept of *habitus* as a theory for bridging the distinction between individual and social, he points out how everyday actions become central components in social construction, since they constrain and enable the social construction of reality in specific ways.

The combination of the two mechanisms of categories and actions contributes to the legitimation of certain processes and outcomes as objective. By being sensitive to specific categorical expressions and practical actions used in the succession process and making comparisons across different settings, we can begin to understand how discourses about leadership, the role of performance and so on are socially constructed.

The remainder of this chapter, pursues the phenomenon of leadership succession in a context in which the inherent nature of authority had seemed to be resolved: the large business enterprise. Using a careful field-based study of the attribution of leadership qualities in the context of CEO search, it will present a theory of leadership attribution based on a structural form. To explain the link between CEOs and the board of directors that appoints them, evidence will be presented to support the following propositions: (1) board members attribute leadership qualities to people who already hold the CEO position; (2) board members attribute leadership qualities to people who come from high performing firms; (3) board members attribute leadership qualities to people who come from well regarded and other high-status firms.

Analysis of board role in CEO succession: a field study

The research reported in the remainder of this chapter draws heavily on a published study of executive succession in US corporations (see Khurana, 2002, for additional detail on the scope and methodology of this study). In that study, CEO turnover and CEO succession were studied at the 850 largest US companies from 1980 to 1996. In the data presented here we focus on one significant component of the larger study through an in-depth field study of the board's role in CEO succession. The directors interviewed were involved directly or indirectly through their board tenures with over 100 successions in Fortune 500 companies. Archival, interview and observational data about the directors' biographies and their affiliations were also collected.

Organizing the CEO succession process

Launching the search: the search committe The process of board-led CEO succession starts with the board appointing a search committee. The search committee manages the administrative tasks of succession. The chair of the search committee is usually the director responsible for the executive development and compensation committee. It is the search committee that hires the executive search firm that almost always assists with the search.

Whether a search committee exercises significant control over the succession process is most dependent on the recent performance of the firm. If the firm has performed satisfactorily, the outgoing CEO is asked to participate, but not to take control of the process. In such cases, the appointment usually passes to the heir apparent, whose identity had been known well in advance. To the extent that the board conducts a search in this situation, it is fairly superficial and symbolic. This was the situation at a north-east bank in 2000. The outgoing CEO, who by all accounts had performed well, had made his preference for his successor clear to the board and to financial analysts. The board went through the motions of forming a search committee and conducting a 'search'. One consultant hired to bless the heir apparent admitted that there was no real serious data gathering or comparison of this candidate with others, either inside or outside. He summarized the process in this way:

> We had a short list, some internal and external candidates, but I can't say it was meaningful. Everyone knew that [D] was [M]'s favored chosen successor. The search committee went through the motions and I was asked to evaluate the internal candidates.... I went around to talk to the other executives about [D]. I asked them to provide examples of when he had been visionary, his leadership style. As you can imagine, everything was described very positively. When I asked for negative examples and feedback, people were silent. They knew the endgame.... The board acted upon the outgoing CEO's recommendation and appointed his successor with little reaction from either the press or Wall Street.

In some successions, there is a 'horse race' between known competing candidates. In the most recent instance, GE's new CEO, Jeffrey Immelt, was explicitly pitted against two other internal candidates. While GE's board and search committee made an admirable show to investors and the business media of having been actively involved in the search, the decision to elect Immelt was mostly made by the retiring CEO, Jack Welch. Not surprisingly the decision was declared in the press release to have been supported unanimously by the board.

When firm performance has been poor or no obvious successor to an outgoing CEO has emerged, the search process takes on a quite different character. When the current CEO is thought to be performing poorly, or when the CEO position is vacant, boards come under tremendous pressure to appoint a new CEO. A firm pays a price financially and in terms of organizational image when it remains leaderless for too long. Directors know that a firm's executives, managers and line employees all experience a great deal of uncertainty when the CEO position is empty. Moreover Wall Street and the business media both exert unrelenting pressure on boards to announce a new chief executive as quickly as possible. One consequence of this pressure to announce a new CEO expeditiously is that the board's search process is oriented toward completing the search as quickly as possible.

In an attempt to reassure these external constituencies with a rush to find a new CEO, many boards tend to adapt much of the form and practices used for internal successions to external successions. Because most boards have not had extensive experience with outside succession, they fall back on following many of the formal structures and practices used for internal succession. This is not to say that directors are not consciously aware of this copying process. In many cases, it offers a quick and viable solution with little expense, since boards are in a rush to complete the search. As one director said, 'Once you've done a search, you have a sense of what one should look like. This then becomes the basis upon which you do other searches.' This transmission of the meaning of an institution is based on the social recognition of that institution as a 'legitimate solution' to a 'well-understood' problem. All transmission of institutional solutions obviously implies control and legitimating procedures (Powell and Dimaggio, 1983). These are attached to the institutions themselves and administered by the transmitting personnel. Because many large companies share directorships, there are few major differences among companies in terms of how the search committee is organized.

One of the first questions the search committee chair faces is deciding on the committee's size. The board often vigorously debates this question. Some board members argue that a large committee will better represent the interests of the board as a whole. Others argue that a small committee will be more focused and efficient. Interestingly these debates do not drastically affect the outcome. In 75 per cent of the field cases examined, the search committee was between four and seven members. The smallest committee found consisted of three members and the largest 11.

Consistent with a taboo on creating distinctions among board members, as well as with the usual practice in internal searches, the size of the search committee is more vigorously debated than is its composition. The most common method for determining the composition of the search committee is asking for volunteers. The individuals who volunteer for the assignment are disproportionately directors who are retired executives or directors from non-business backgrounds, such as nonprofits and education, who have more time than do their peers to devote to the search. In the field cases examined, there was on average only one non-retired director on the committee.

One unintended result of the uniform application of the process used for internal searches to external ones (particularly the voluntary method for composing a committee) is that boards do not always pay as careful attention to the composition of the search committee as the ramifications of the process would suggest they should, even though the make-up of the search committee is critical to succession outcomes. In some cases examined, search committees were composed of members who had little familiarity with the company and its history. In these cases, most of the information search committee members had about the company, its products and its other executives was limited to the information they received in quarterly meetings. Moreover, because the future CEO will want some familiarity with the board members he or she will work with, the committee needs individuals who are likely to stay on. This is difficult when most of the search committee is made up of executives who have already retired.

Search committees also need directors with diverse functional backgrounds. In several of the instances studied, CEO succession decisions were biased by directors' narrow backgrounds. Consider the case of one technology company with a strong engineering culture. Although the company's products were considered the most technologically advanced in its market, poor marketing had slashed its market share. The CEO succession decision was biased by the narrow backgrounds of committee members. The search committee, largely directors with backgrounds in operations or research and development, recommended a CEO with a strong technical background but little marketing experience. Unsurprisingly the company's market share continued to erode.

Defining the position: the specification sheet   Despite the way in which the constitution of the search committee seems to belie directors' stated belief in the importance of the job of choosing a new CEO, board members are not utterly oblivious to the needs of the firm as a factor in a CEO search.

Directors, in fact, portray the CEO succession process as a unique chance for them to assess the firm's objectives. The opportunity to search for a new CEO, in the words of one director, is 'a clean slate to find the person to help meet the company's objectives'. CEO succession, according to another director, offers one of the few real opportunities for board members to assess the current state of the organization and the future that they desire for it.

Such statements notwithstanding, there is little evidence that board members engage in any extensive discussion of a firm's objectives during the actual search process. Even in cases where the firm has been performing poorly, or the organization needs a new strategic direction because of a changed environment, most CEO searches do not begin with an analysis of the problems facing the organization. Instead many search committees jump immediately into the task of writing a specification sheet.

The specification sheet is a formal document that describes the requirements for the new CEO. It is usually developed with the assistance of an executive search firm conducting one-on-one meetings with each of the board members, and is considered a critical element of the search process. Al Zeien, the former CEO of Gillette and a member of several corporate boards, emphasizes the importance of the specification sheet for the search process:

> From my own experience, on an outside board, the search firm [and the search], is only as good as the spec [sic] that the board agrees upon at the outset, and the spec has got to be pretty specific because that is really the basis by which the process is going to take place.

Search consultants also stress the importance of the specification sheet; according to one, the spec sheet 'lays out the required qualifications . . . the desired qualifications . . . and forces the client to prioritize and focus'. Because of the commonly held view that the specification sheet provides the guidelines against which candidates can be both identified and evaluated, executive search firms emphasize the development of the specification sheet as a strategic component of the search process, and their particular approach to assembling a specification sheet as an important way for them to differentiate themselves from their competitors. It is, as one consultant put it, 'the consultative component of the process, and perhaps our most value-added'.

In view of these descriptions, it comes as a surprise that search committee members rarely refer back to the specification sheet once it has been drawn up and initially circulated. Instead of functioning as a set of guidelines for the search, the specification sheet assumes importance only during the process of compiling it, when it is used as a Rorschach print on which directors project their hopes, desires, fears, interpretations and solutions. In discussions ostensibly devoted to identifying the qualities that the search committee seeks in the next CEO, some directors use the specification process to air privately their grievances against the outgoing CEO, blaming him for the firm's problems. Other directors use the process of compiling the specification sheet to engage in self-congratulatory behavior, for example by describing their roles in ousting the previous CEO. Almost every director also uses it as an opportunity to discuss his or her 'theories of leadership' and ideas about the qualities of a good leader. The resulting list is usually so long that, if taken seriously, it would deter many candidates by its sheer length. In compiling this list of desired qualities, moreover, directors give little attention to their relative importance.

Khurana (2002) shows a specification sheet for a CEO search at a major software company and a specification sheet for a CEO search at an insurance company. Both of these lists are entirely typical of those used in external CEO searches. Three aspects of these specification sheets immediately stand out as noteworthy. The first striking feature of these specification sheets is their emphasis on individual characteristics. The content of both lists consists largely of a collection of personal traits rather than a set of concrete skills or a discussion of the situational context of the search. The characteristics that the boards seek in a new CEO are numerous. The CEO should be 'aggressive'; the CEO should be able to 'balance reward with risk'; the CEO should be able to 'provide direction'; the CEO should be able to 'work closely with the team to develop a direction'. Judging from these lists of qualities, a CEO's ability to perform effectively in the position is determined by individual attributes. There are almost no references to the particular challenges facing the firm or any other contextual issue.

The second noteworthy feature of the two sample specification sheets is the similarity between them. A blind read would make it difficult to know that one sheet comes from a software firm and the other from an insurance company. Part of this similarity is due to the fact that each of the characteristics listed is difficult to argue against. Traits such as 'proven leader' and 'motivator' apparently do not need to be defined. They are in many ways irreducible, because their rightness appears to be grounded in nature and reason: after all, who is against leadership and motivation? The individual characteristics that search committees seek in a CEO are furnished by society's idealized definitions of leadership writ small. They are congruent with prevailing notions (those found in the business press, for example) of what a CEO should be like. Thus this laundry list of characteristics sheds light on the way societal beliefs penetrate into the CEO search process.

The third remarkable feature of these specification sheets is the ambiguous and contradictory nature of many of the requirements when they are considered in relation to one another. For example, the board of the insurance company is looking for a CEO who will both 'establish challenging goals' and 'safely' deliver a return on equity of 'between 13 and 15 per cent'. The individual should 'concentrate on increasing . . . stockholder value' but only in a way that is 'balanced appropriately with risks'. The incoming candidate should be at the 'forefront of insurance issues' but 'accommodations can be made in industry knowledge for those candidates outside the industry'. Looking at either of the sample specification sheets, one can only conclude that no one person could fulfill all of the requirements on either of them. How is it possible, for example, to be team-oriented and a consensus builder while being directive? To be a risk taker without taking too many risks? To be flexible and yet stand up for one's beliefs? This would be a no-win situation for candidates and board members alike if anyone ended up taking the specification sheet the least bit seriously.

How do we account for these anomalies and deficiencies in the specification sheet? The knee-jerk explanation might be that the people conducting the search have not worked hard enough or been given the appropriate incentives to pinpoint the traits or skills essential to the organization's near-term success. Yet such an interpretation ignores the context formed by the modern view of what a CEO should be like. Because it is difficult to know ex ante what CEO characteristics are needed to improve performance, directors are left to guess about which criteria are likely to be associated with success. Consequently they resort to the barely definable buzzwords seen on the specification sheet – terms such as 'leadership', 'team-builder' and 'integrity' – terms which are more closely associated with a charismatic orientation toward succession rather than rational succession processes.

Moreover, even if directors could more precisely define the characteristics they were looking for in a CEO, the search process would continue to exist in tension with the information problems associated with external CEO appointment. Selecting a CEO is an information-intensive decision. The information needed for selecting a CEO is usually highly particular and fine-grained. That is, it is usually information that can be derived only through direct experience in working with and observing the candidate. Some examples of particular factors about which information is needed include candidates' dispositions, working styles and mannerisms; how they work with others; and, most importantly, whether they can really do what they say they are capable of doing. For internal candidates, this information is more easily gathered, since the board and the sitting CEO have better knowledge and experience of the individuals under consideration. Moreover a detailed record of insider candidates' promotion history, performance reviews and accomplishments can be found in their personnel and performance review records.

For outside candidates, this particular information is not so easily gathered. In particular, because of the confidentiality inherent in CEO searches, it is not possible to interview peers or subordinates for particular information about the candidate. Instead such information needs to be gathered through more informal means. Yet, even as directors gather the particular information they require through their own social networks, they give careful consideration throughout the search to the way the external constituents who form their audience will perceive it. Directors are concerned to establish that those who will evaluate the outcome see the search process as legitimate and defensible. Both the structurally and culturally derived attributes of the external search are used to create a composite of a potential candidate with the dual goal of reducing uncertainty for directors and legitimating the external CEO succession choice in the eyes of outsiders.

Creating the candidate pool: the social matching process
It is, of course, potentially desirable for boards to consider the interests of outside parties when selecting a new CEO. After all, a company's shareholders, the business press and the larger community that the business press is writing for will all be affected in some way by the decision. Yet the focus on external constituents does have some important unintended consequences. Most significantly, it has led to an emphasis on the 'acceptability' of a candidate at the expense of considering whether an individual possesses the necessary skills for the position. As a result of this emphasis, search committees focus on a fairly narrow pool of candidates and evaluate them by means of the kind of conservative decision process described in the quotation from a corporate director that prefaces this chapter. These features of the search process, in turn, are evident in the final choices that directors make when selecting a new CEO.

While the CEO succession process appears, at first glance, to offer limitless opportunities for invigorating an organization or introducing fundamental change, many search committees express frustration with the limited pool of candidates from which they end up choosing. The reason for this outcome can be found in the process that search committees use to identify and qualify the candidate pool.

Identifying the candidates   Following the compilation of a specification sheet, directors, often with the assistance of an executive search firm, begin putting together a long list of candidates. The majority of these candidates are suggested by board members themselves, based on their knowledge of the industry and of the profiles of CEO talent at other firms. Consistent with Michael Useem's (1984) and others findings that the leading internal candidates for a vacant CEO position are already board members at other companies, the plausible external candidates are also already board members (Khurana, 2002). As a result the identification of potential candidates is often based on the suggestion of a board member. While executive search firms will sometimes add one or two names, their contributions to this phase of the process are negligible.

Consider the entirely typical case of a search at a publishing firm. Here the search committee came up with a list of 40 names. Of those names 30 came from the directors themselves, who were asked by the search firm to list potential candidates. The search firm added ten names to the list, including the names of four women or members of minority groups. Within a few days, with the help of the search firm, the search committees narrowed the initial list down to 20 names, almost all of them of candidates who were actively employed. The search firm then gave the search committee a booklet containing a photograph and a short profile of each of these candidates. These profiles included only general information on the candidates' work histories and educational credentials, as well as estimates of their most recent compensation. One director described the booklet as a 'Who's Who of global publishing that included high profile CEOs of other prominent publishing firms and promising top executives from related industries such as entertainment'.

The search firm then began to contact candidates in the book. Without revealing the identity of their client, the search consultants sought to identify candidates who would seriously consider leaving their existing positions. When the consultants came back with a short list of ten candidates the board began to narrow the list even further. Throughout this process, the board was guided by three criteria for winnowing the candidate pool: the current position of the candidate, the performance of the candidate's current firm and the stature of that firm.

These criteria form the critical matter of the CEO labor market. At one level, as we shall see, they are apparently reasonable responses to the conditions of the market outlined above. The relevance of these criteria – experience, performance and status – seems so self-evident, so reasonable, that directors rarely question them or feel the need to justify using them.

At another level, however, these criteria form the basis of a durable sorting process that results in a narrow definition of the candidate pool and a distinct privileging of one set of candidates over another. Examined with a critical eye, they turn out not to be aligned with the technical or efficiency goals of the CEO search. Rather they are essentially extraneous considerations that cause search committees to shine a spotlight on certain candidates, thereby leaving others in the shadows. The mechanism governing this sorting process is one that can best be described as social matching. Social matching is a filtering process that takes place when individual and organizational actors are confronted with choices from which it is difficult to select because of limited information, and because the choices themselves cannot be reliably distinguished from one another (March and March, 1977). Minimally, social matching is a convention. However its impact is not benign. Social matching is one of the basic mechanisms contributing to a closed CEO labor market. It leads to closure because directors seize upon one or more easily identifiable external characteristics of potential candidates to construct a narrowly defined candidate pool. By relying on social matching to identify the plausible candidate pool, directors are caught in an unforeseen trap of focusing on a narrow set of candidates and unwittingly undermining the original intent of a broad search. To return to the imagery of the spotlight, some of those candidates on whom the spotlight shines may later founder as CEOs. Meanwhile other candidates who might perform perfectly well are either entirely invisible to the directors or never given serious consideration, ultimately depriving organizations of the chance to consider the full set of qualified candidates.

The characteristics of candidates on which directors fasten are conditioned on what Douglas (1986) calls 'habit of thought'. Habits of thought are organizing and classificatory principles that are endowed with the character of common sense, theories that seem self-evident. Directors' ideas about the criteria necessary to be included in the candidate pool actively influence the characteristics of that candidate pool. They also affect directors' perceptions about that pool. For example, when searching for external candidates, boards of directors typically limit the pool to candidates coming from organizations that have been performing well. As a result, many firms pass over talented executives from underperforming firms because their directors still perceive organizational performance as a reliable measure of CEO ability, even when experience and academic research have shown that link to be tenuous. Other circumstances (such as market conditions or the skills and experience of the company's senior management team) known to have a profound impact on corporate performance are not considered in sorting through the candidates. Thus reliance on the performance of the firm from which the candidate is coming for evaluating a candidate's record, although at one level a perfectly defensible response, is actually problematic.

Directors' ways of thinking that lead to the selection of criteria for use in the social matching process stem from the same sources as do their ideas about the qualities necessary to become a CEO. The external environment furnishes much of the grist for the mill of the social matching process.

Position matching: already a CEO or president   One factor that contributes to the narrowness of the set of candidates that search committees seriously consider is that many committees feel that a potential candidate needs to have previous experience leading a large corporation. For example, 75 per cent of outsider CEO appointees during the period of 1985–2000 were either CEOs or presidents in their previous jobs. According to one director, a candidate's having already been in the CEO position or its equivalent 'gives you a sense of how they are likely to act – it reduces uncertainty'. Directors point out that the fact that an individual is already a CEO indicates that another board has already rendered a favorable judgment about that person. From directors' point of view, there is an energy saving from coding a candidate on the basis of his previous position. As Gigi Michelson, a longtime director at GE and other large firms, puts it, a board would not appoint someone to a CEO position if it 'did not already have a judgment about the person, their personal stability, some knowledge of [their] family life and outside background, outside activity, outside of the corporation and so on'.

While directors sincerely believe that having already occupied a leadership position is an important qualification for the job of CEO, their reliance on position matching in identifying candidates also makes it easier for the board to defend its chosen candidate to the outside world. By choosing a candidate who has already had experience as a CEO or president, the board conforms to outsiders' expectations concerning the traits or characteristics a defensible candidate will need. Board members thus turn individual responsibility into external accountability .

Of course the expectations to which directors try to conform create advantages for certain classes of candidates and disadvantages for others. Thus focusing on candidates with prior CEO experience, particularly at large companies, can prove to be a liability. While no two CEOs are the same, and each will have a unique personality and style of leadership, often such differences are minor. Although directors do not make a link between their selection process and the uniformity of candidates that they observe, they do often comment on this uniformity and describe it as a problem. Several directors interviewed complained about the shortage of 'real leadership' and the 'cookie-cutter' character of several of the CEO candidates whom they had considered. 'A lot of the candidates are corporate survivors, not leaders,' said George Kennedy about a search he had led at the industrial conglomerate Brunswick. Similarly Henry Wendt, former CEO of Smith-Kline Beecham and director of other boards, said, 'We're in the most severe shortage of CEO talent in corporate history. Most of the people I see are not leaders, they are managers who know how to work the system and have worked it well. Times are different. We need leaders, not politicians. We need to find people who can define what the organization is about. Charismatic people who help people understand what they need to do. Executors who know how to get things done. People who integrate leadership into their everyday activities. It is really difficult to find a real leader based on my experience in searching for CEOs.'

Such observations are not surprising. As Mills (1956) noted, 'the top executives of the big companies are not, and never have been, a miscellaneous collection of Americans; they are a quite uniform social type which has had exceptional advantages of origin and training, and they do not fit many of the stereotypes that prevail about them'. Whatever their origins, CEOs of large corporations settle into the executive suite after a selection process lasting years. Socialization in the executive suite, and self-selection en route to it, significantly reduce the variability of the types of candidates who are seriously considered for vacancies in the CEO job. Those at the top of an organization are all corporate survivors and, implicitly or explicitly, understand how to navigate a complex bureaucracy skillfully.

In any event, categorizing candidates as to whether or not they have already been CEOs highlights the fact that the process is one not so much of conscious exclusion as of narrowly drawn expectations. By selecting candidates on the basis of classifications perceived as legitimate by others, they are at the same time establishing a pattern of actions. The micro-level decisions of any single board adhering to such classifications in defining the consideration set of candidates create the basis for a broader pattern in the selection process. These classifications, though grounded in pragmatic reasoning, also straitjacket the minds of directors. The convention of choosing an individual who has already occupied the position of CEO overcomes any tendency of the individual board to select candidates that deviate from the orthodox qualifications. It trims the board's decisions to fit the conventions. Directors thereby substitute a convention for deliberative thinking and decision making.

Performance sorting: coming from a high performing company   In almost every search studied, candidates were categorized according to the performance of their current firms or corporate divisions. In the minds of directors, sorting candidates along the criteria of performance is a reasonable means of gauging the quality of a potential CEO. In the case of Hewlett-Packard, for example, several HP directors described choosing outsider Carly Fiorina over several internal candidates because of their association of Fiorina with the strong performance of Lucent Technologies. Lucent's stock had indeed performed extraordinarily well since the company had been spun out of AT&T. Yet, while the HP directors had attributed Lucent's success to its executives, much of this 'success', it was later revealed, was due to creative accounting and liberal financing of sales to customers. Another relevant factor that these directors seemed to ignore was that investors had bid up almost every technology-related stock in 1999.

Directors everywhere admire CEO candidates whose firms have performed at a level above the average for their industry. As one director states, 'We are after people who do better than the average in the pack.' What is striking about this performance sorting is the casual assumption that CEOs directly affect organizational performance, an assumption that has found little empirical support in scholarly studies of the topic (see Pfeffer, 1978, 1997, for a review of these studies). Directors, however, rarely cast a critical eye on the supposed connection between firm performance and executive quality, and are dismissive of the research that does so as inherently flawed. One director describes any such study as 'inherently unscientific, since you can never run the controlled experiment of what the firm would have been like without the CEO' and dismisses statistical techniques as well as studies that match comparable firms to one another in order to gauge the impact of an individual CEO on performance as 'academic mumbo-jumbo, with no regard for reality'. It is as if, when directors do not like the empirical facts, they simply create their own narratives. In such a milieu, any theory or causal relationship is justifiable. Meanwhile there is little evidence of directors trying to break down the performance of a candidate's organization into its constituent parts, so as to determine what role the candidate may have played and what might be attributable to factors such as the environment, the quality of the company's employees, the competitive structure of its industry, or even luck.

Even granting, for the sake of argument, the possible validity of the contention that the research on the relationship between firm performance and executive quality is inherently flawed, a question arises as to why directors are so resistant to any suggestion that the widely credited relationship between the two might be spurious. It is difficult to convey to the reader how deeply rooted this belief in the dependent relationship between the CEO and firm performance is among members of corporate boards, who hold it with virtually religious conviction. Openly to question it is taboo. (In the case of three board members interviewed in the early stages of this study, I lost credibility with them when I suggested in a casual manner that the CEO's role is largely symbolic and that most empirical studies have shown that they have little control over firm performance.) One reason it may be difficult for directors to talk objectively about the relationship between CEOs and firm performance is that it touches on intimate beliefs. Directors have internalized the link between CEOs and performance to the point of sancralizing it. Every director defends the logic. Thus directors' existing theories about the relationship between CEO quality and firm performance precondition their responses to a challenge and even determine what can be counted as a reasonable question. Their ideas place firm limits on their ability to make objective judgments about the posited relationship.

Another reason it is difficult to question the belief in the relationship between CEOs and corporate performance is that it enjoys such broad support and legitimacy, especially among an external constituency of business media and analysts, who often reduce firm performance to the qualities of a single individual. That is, part of the inability to question this linkage can be attributed to the hold that these institutions have on directors' thought processes. Merton (1968) has written about the power that a social fact can have over human behavior. Once a complete and reinforcing system of opinions has been formed, it offers strong resistance to anything that contradicts it. Thus internal coherence and external legitimacy are authoritatively interlocked in the directors' beliefs and actions. The external institutions of the business media and analysts systematically reinforce the individual perceptions of directors into forms compatible with the relations they authorize. They fix processes that appear to be dynamic, even as their own influence remains invisible. As a result, the relationship between firm performance and the CEO is endowed with a logic of rightness, to the point that belief in it can become a rigid constraint on meaningful change. Hypotheses about the relation between CEO quality and firm performance become axioms.

A striking example of this tendency is provided by directors' reaction to views that challenge this relationship. Three things are apparent. First, a contradiction to the idea seems implausible. What does not fit into the system is largely ignored. Exceptions are rationalized by rejecting the process by which those exceptions were identified, questioning the methodology used to identify those exceptions, or justifying them in terms that do not contradict the system.

As we have already noted, the belief in the link between CEO quality and firm performance is not without its substantive consequences. Without directors explicitly realizing it, this emphasis on the performance of the firms with which CEO candidates are linked sometimes leads to the inclusion in the pool of otherwise mediocre candidates and to the exclusion of candidates who seemed to have performed admirably under challenging circumstances. By connecting firm performance to CEO quality as a sorting mechanism for eliminating potential candidates, directors create a system for segmenting people on the basis of a measure that is empirically flawed.

Status matching: coming from a firm of similar or higher repute   Prestige is particularly important in CEO searches, and search committees see the status of the institution from which a CEO candidate comes as amplifying or reducing the status of their own institutions. Board members have their own version of Q ratings and hiring a high-status CEO is viewed as a symbolic marker of belonging to a particular class of firms. One director summarized this phenomenon this way:

> While the search process is becoming professionalized, the way things work at this level is a lot on the basis of appearances. The process is basically driven by the board, and most boards are looking for either one or two things in a CEO-peer, which suggests executives who are similar to them, or more higher [*sic*] profile people who bring prestige and stature to the company simply because of who they are and their obvious accomplishments. So by and large, this is a biased set of selection criteria.

Directors' concern with the status of the CEO has parallels to concerns with status in most areas of society. Status, as Veblen (1973) noted, can be used to signal quality, wealth and, by inference, power. Limiting the candidate pool as a way of either enhancing or maintaining the status of the firm is important in directors' view of the world. In sociology, Podolny's (1994) research has strongly underscored the importance of status in markets. Specifically he argues that, under uncertainty, organizations use their affiliations with other economic actors as signals of quality and worth. Thus, if an economic actor's affiliates in a network form of organization possess considerable legitimacy or status, that actor may derive legitimacy or status from them. This legitimacy or status may in turn have a number of positive economic benefits for the actor, ranging from survival, to organizational growth, to profitability (Goode, 1978). In the case of an organization whose future is uncertain, appointing a CEO of high status can produce advantages for the organization such as increased confidence in the prospects of the firm.

One of the basic insights of research on status, however, is that there may not always be a tight coupling between the status of an individual and his or her underlying quality. The business journal *Barrons* has commented on what it calls a 'familiar script': 'A star manager with a track record of success elsewhere comes in as a savior of an ailing firm. Not only is he expected to be the catalyst to the recovery, but his very presence is seen by the market as a vote of confidence that the company can indeed be fixed.' This was the case at auto parts manufacturer Federal Mogul in November 1996. The appointment of Richard Snell as CEO prompted a Merrill Lynch analyst to write: 'Frankly, we are surprised and somewhat relieved that the company was able to secure someone of Mr. Snell's stature.' The stock price jumped from $22 to $25 per share. As he had done in his previous position at Tenneco Automotive, Snell then went on an acquisition spree. He took Federal Mogul from a $2 billion company to a $6 billion company while the stock price went from $70 per share in mid-1998 to just $11. The same story can be repeated for Xerox, Eastman Kodak and Hewlett-Packard, all companies in recent years that have hired high-status outsider CEOs.

That CEOs have a status that can be transferred from one company to another has become a deeply ingrained idea in directors' new view of the role of CEOs. In any event, given the importance that directors attach to the status of CEO candidates, every candidate list is in some way a stratified one. Thus, while CEO candidates may appear similar with respect to their prior titles, education and background, from the perspective of the directors there is no list of candidates that can be described as flat or undifferentiated along the lines of status.

Directors' placing of a primary value on status is directed at outside audiences. 'Like anything else, who we select as a CEO is interpreted by both the insiders and outsiders of the company,' as one director notes. Ironically, in a reaction against what they see as the conformism of the candidates in the firm's internal labor market, directors engage in their own type of conformism. The more they consider the evaluations of outsiders, the more they conform to the opinions of these outsiders.

But relying on status is constraining. In our interviews, we found that the sheen of a candidate's status dazzles directors and reduces their level of discrimination. In the pursuit of status, directors stop trusting their own responses to particular individuals. It is not easy to resist the social pressure of status. Directors sometimes praise high-status individuals who, without their celebrity and repute, would leave most of us cold. Status considerations also lead directors to feign indifference to individuals whom they secretly admire and in whom they have confidence. In the quest for status, directors forgo the opportunity to choose a candidate who might truly represent 'new blood' and be 'reinvigorating' in favor of one who, but for his celebrity, might not even be considered for the position.

Conclusion
One way to avoid the reduction of difficult richness to neo-Freudian reductionism is by linking the themes in sociological conceptions of leadership just described. The development of leadership and the preservation of the concept of leadership depend on uncovering the exact dynamics of their interplay. Between the blur of trying to say too much at once and the banality produced by dismissing the social mystery of leadership there remains the possibility of articulating just what it is that causes some people to see leadership in others, and what it is they see. Re-examining leadership through the lens of social construction allows for such an approach.

A social constructionist approach connects the symbolic value leaders possess and their relation to the social structure. The intersection of these points is concentrated and consists in the point or points in a society where its leading ideas come together with its leading institutions to create an arena in which the events that most significantly affect their members take place. In trying to understand leadership, social constructionism allows us to examine how particular positions in society are constructed, reproduced and exercised in a little understood arena of the formal selection of leaders. A social constructionist approach enables us to look at the interpretations of leadership shared by individuals. It emphasizes the coexistence of local and global understanding of leadership.

Leadership succession is such a center. Leadership succession is of interest in any realm of social life that is sufficiently focused – in politics or religion. Who is selected offers a portal into an institution's beliefs and structure. At the center of any complex organization there is both a governing elite and a set of symbolic forms expressing the fact that it is legitimate in governing. No matter what the process by which the members are chosen, democratically (rarely) or appointed (often), they justify their existence and order their actions in terms of a series of actions to invoke legitimacy in their choices (Scott, 1995). In other words, if succession is at the center of organizational life, and if such centers are cultural phenomena and thus socially constructed, investigation into the process of succession and into its very nature are very similar endeavors.

The aim of this chapter has been to describe the main features of the way in which a social construction of leadership takes place in the CEO selection process. A central feature of this approach is that it identifies a mechanism that allows for an ongoing reproduction of advantage through the identification of social characteristics, such as current position in an organization, organizational performance and organizational status, that are key ingredients in the social categorization of a person as a 'leader'. Considered as either a process for filling vacancies or one for advancing careers, the external CEO search appears at first glance to offer almost unlimited opportunities for identifying candidates. But, owing to the process of social matching, it becomes a mechanism for opportunity hoarding by restricting the candidate pool only to those who possess certain structural and positional attributes. Both searching firms and candidates can plausibly consider only a match that maintains, or preferably increases, their reputations, and this mutual interest in reputation enhancement sets constraints that severely limit the positions to which candidates can aspire and the vacancies which appear attractive to potential candidates. Thus there is a process of self-selection that serves to limit the participants in a search.

The social construction process in the CEO labor market has direct implications for rent extraction and the reproduction of inequality. Because the corporate elite forms a distinctive and identifiable network, they control valuable resources (cf. access to the CEO position) that support network activities such as continual recruitment from a restricted set of individuals. Moreover such restrictions are subsequently supported through an extensive set of beliefs and practices that sustain network control of the resource. These restrictions, in turn, generate rent-extracting opportunities. In the case of the CEO labor market, these rent extraction opportunities present themselves in the CEO compensation process. Because boards of directors are notoriously social organizations, where the goal is not to maximize profits but to avoid personal embarrassment while maintaining social cohesion within the board and the larger corporate community, directors do not drive a hard bargain when negotiating CEO pay. For directors, it is simply bad form to nitpick over a couple of million dollars with another member of the group, particularly one who helps set director fees or serves on the compensation committee of other corporations. Moreover boards often legitimate the compensation of their CEOs by hiring a compliant executive compensation consultant and then arguing that the pay is set in an arm's-length market transaction. One implication, then, is that executive compensation would have a weak relation to firm performance and result in a pay-setting process that is economically distortive. Recent corporate scandals around CEO pay levels and corporate disclosure practices suggest this may be true.

Finally a social constructionist perspective towards leadership studies allows the reconsideration of a topic that sociologists have neglected for too long. The notion of charisma derives from 'charisms' meaning 'divinely inspired gifts'. Many attempts have been made by scholars in the field of psychology, political science and organizational theory to conceptualize these 'gifts' as individual traits. The contribution of a social constructionist perspective, as it is practiced in CEO succession, is recognizing that these 'gifts' lay not within the leaders but, instead, in followers embedded within a social context attributing these gifts to individuals.

Note

1. The empirical research of this chapter draws heavily on Khurana (2002).
2. The author's interpretation is based on other reviews, especially Edward (1982) and Hunt (1984).

References

Berger, P. and T. Luckmann (1967), *The Social Construction of Reality*, New York: Doubleday.
Bourdieu, P. (1977), *Outline of a Theory of Practice*, Cambridge: Cambridge University Press.

Dimaggio, P.J. and W.W. Powell (1991), *The New Institutionalism in Organizational Analysis*, Chicago: The University of Chicago Press.
Douglas, M. (1986), *How Institutions Think*, Syracuse, NY: Syracuse University Press.
Edward, S. (1982), *The Constitution of Society*, Chicago: University of Chicago Press.
Ganz, M. (2000), 'Resources and resourcefulness: strategic capacity in the unionization of California agriculture, 1959–1966', *American Journal of Sociology*, **105**, 1003–62.
Giddens, A. (1987), 'Structuralism, post-structuralism and the production of culture', *Social Theory and Modern Sociology*, Oxford, Cambridge: The Polity Press.
Goode, W.J. (1978), *The Celebration of Heroes: Prestige as a Social Control System*, Berkeley: University of California Press.
Hunt, S.M. (1984), 'The role of leadership in the construction of reality', in Barbara Kellerman (ed.), *Leadership: Multidisciplinary Perspectives*, Englewood Cliffs, NJ: Prentice-Hall.
Khurana, R. (2002), *Searching for a Corporate Savior: The Irrational Quest for Charismatic CEOs*, Princeton: Princeton University Press.
March, J.C. and J.G. March (1977), 'Almost random careers: the Wisconsin school superintendency, 1940–1972', *Administrative Science Quarterly*, **22**, 377–409.
Merton, R.K. (1968), *Social Theory and Social Structure*, New York: Free Press.
Meyer, J.W. and B. Rowan (1977), 'Institutionalized organizations: formal structure as myth and ceremony', *American Journal of Sociology*, **83**, 340–63.
Mills, C.W. (1956), *The Power Elite*, New York: Oxford University Press.
Ocasio, W. (1999), 'Institutionalized action and corporate governance: the reliance on rules of CEO succession', *Administrative Science Quarterly*, **44**, 384–416.
Pfeffer, J. (1978), 'The ambiguity of leadership', in M.W. McCall, Jr and M.M. Lombardo (eds), *Leadership: Where Else Can We Go?*, North Carolina: Duke University Press.
Pfeffer, J. (1997), *New Directions for Organizational Theory: Problems and Prospects*, Oxford: Oxford University Press.
Podolny, J. (1994), 'Market uncertainty and the social character of economic exchange', *Administrative Science Quarterly*, **39**, 458–83.
Podolny, J. and M. Hill-Popper (2004), 'Hedonic and transcendent conceptions of value', *Industrial and Corporate Change*, **13**, 91–116.
Powell, W.W. and P.J. Dimaggio (1983), 'The iron cage revisited: institutional isomorphism and collective rationality in organizational fields', *American Sociological Review*, **48** (2), 147–60.
Scott, W.R. (1995), *Institutions and Organizations*, Thousand Oaks, CA: Sage.
Scott, W. Richard and John W. Meyer (1994), *Institutional Environments and Organizations*, Thousand Oaks, CA: Sage.
Simmel, G. (1902), *The Sociology of George Simmel*, New York: Free Press.
Strauss, A. and J. Corbin (1990), *Basics of Qualitative Research: Grounded Theory Procedures and Techniques*, Newbury Park, CA: Sage.
Trice, H.M. and J.M. Beyer (1986), 'Charisma and its routinization in two social movement organizations', *Research in Organizational Behavior*, **8**, 113–64.
Useem, M. (1984), *The Inner Circle*, New York: Oxford University Press.
Veblen, T. (1973), *The Theory of the Leisure Class, with an introduction by John Kenneth Galbraith*, Boston: Houghton Mifflin.
Weber, M. ([1947] 1978), *Economy and Society*, Berkeley: University of California Press.
Zucker, L.G. (1977), 'The role of institutionalization in cultural persistence', *American Sociological Review*, **42**, 726–43.
Zuckerman, E. (1999), 'The categorical imperative: securities analysts and the legitimacy discount', *American Journal of Sociology*, **104** (5), 1398–1438.
Zuckerman, E. and T-Y. Kim (2003), 'The critical trade-off: identity assignment and box-office success in the feature film industry', *Industrial and Corporate Change*, **12**, 27–67.

8 Foundations of responsible leadership: from self-insight to integrity and altruism

John Alexander and Meena Wilson

Introduction

Ethical scandals in major corporations and other important institutions in the United States in the early 2000s dominated media headlines and triggered rounds of finger pointing, mixed with soul searching. Much of the debate surrounding these high-profile misdeeds concentrated on macro solutions such as greater regulation and increased oversight from government, courts and corporate boards. Significantly less emphasis has been placed on the roles and the responsibilities of individual leaders in today's ethically challenging corporate environment. But when the last courtroom verdict from these episodes has been handed down and the last regulatory reform enacted, leaders will still face, on a daily basis, difficult and complex ethical dilemmas. The same opportunities to make decisions for good or ill will exist. New laws and regulations, while necessary, will not eliminate the problem. The cure for this disease, we believe, begins within the individual and stems from personal integrity.

Integrity, at its core, is the kind of honesty that leads to trustworthiness. A person of integrity tells what he or she believes to be the truth and bases his or her actions on a well-defined sense of right and wrong, always seeking to do the right thing. It is behaving in a manner that, in dictionary terms, exhibits 'moral excellence' (*The Oxford Dictionary of Current English*, 1998, p. 460). Integrity is one of those basic qualities whose presence or absence helps us define a person's character. For responsible leadership, we believe integrity must be intertwined with altruism: concern for the welfare of others.

We contend that integrity and altruism can and should be developed during one's adult career. Considering the increasingly complex ethical climate in which leaders today find themselves, a better understanding of how these qualities can be developed and encouraged is crucial not only to avoiding high-profile ethical scandals, but also to creating a healthier organizational climate in which integrity, altruism and, by extension, trust are the bedrocks of human behavior.

But how is this seemingly idealistic state to be achieved? The simplest answer is that the leader must first look inward, into the inner core of his or her beliefs, values and identity. Self-insight contributes to the development and valuing of integrity. It is this valuing of personal integrity that stands out as pivotal in situations where ethical dilemmas are involved. In other words, integrity, fostered by self-insight and fused with altruism, is the leader behavior most likely to support ethical business practices.

In this chapter we discuss the nature of an ethical dilemma. We look at definitions of integrity and altruism, and consider the connection between them and the contribution they make to the ethical life of an organization. The shared understanding of these terms becomes the springboard for addressing the ways in which integrity and altruism can be developed and encouraged through self-insight. By focusing primarily on the behavioral realm, we discuss leadership development strategies that hone self-insight and make integrity and altruism possible.

Foundational concepts

What contribution does the leader's integrity and altruism make to the ethical life of an organization? Metaphorically here is what seems to be true: under hazardous conditions such as hurricanes, tornados or earthquakes that have damaged the physical environment, people seek out individuals with physical strength and basic survival skills for the aid they need. Such individuals have developed physical fitness, a knowledge base and a skill set to respond to physically threatening situations. Others turn to them and rely on their strength. Similarly we believe that integrity fused with altruism is ethical fitness and a source of strength for addressing situations created by human maelstroms. The ostensible threat is that individuals or groups will inflict harm on each other by self-serving, negligent or deliberately malevolent behaviors. In this instance, people turn to the person with a different kind of strength, which shows up as integrity, altruism and ethical fitness, and watch what they do and say to guide their own behavior.

Moving from the metaphor, we looked at the literature associated with ethical dilemmas, integrity and altruism, and their connections to leadership.

Ethics in the context of work

Views vary on what constitutes an ethical dilemma. Books and articles on ethical decision making abound in both academic and business publishing. The frameworks developed by LaRue Hosmer and Rushworth Kidder seem the most encompassing and relevant. These frameworks highlight the fact that distinguishing right from wrong is not often simple. A choice of one course of action over another typically involves a struggle.

Hosmer proposes that moral dilemmas originate in two basic sets of questions (Hosmer, 1994, p. 5). The first set relates to whether decisions will lead to beneficial or harmful outcomes, toward whom, and the extent of benefit or harm that will occur. For example, is it ethical to let go of some employees to strengthen a firm's ability to survive in a volatile market? Which value trumps the other: the negative impact of layoffs on some employees, or the potentially negative impact of a firm going out of business altogether, with a greater loss of jobs?

The second set relates to the nature of mutual obligations. What do managers and employees owe each other and the society to which they belong? Where are the ethical lines drawn in cases of excessive CEO compensation completely detached from performance or when plants and facilities are shut without regard for the human costs involved? How are ethical decisions made in regard to issues such as worker safety, quality and product safety, and environmental impact?

For Kidder, ethical dilemmas are choices, not between right and wrong, but between two different kinds of right (Kidder, 1995, p. 18). Kidder discusses ethical dilemmas in terms of choices between truth and loyalty, short term and long term, justice and mercy, and individual versus community. For example, if an employee reveals justifiable concerns about his own competence to his assigned human resources coach, should the coach then be loyal to the employee or truthful with the employee's supervisor? To care for his family, should the father of two young boys realize the short-term benefit of spending time with them in sports and community activities? Or should he pursue an evening MBA program that his boss has recommended and achieve the long-term benefit of career advancement and financial security? What if a product malfunction posing a serious safety hazard is traced to the negligence of one employee with a record of nine years of competent work? Does the company owe mercy to the individual? Or must the safety-based policies of the company be justly enforced and the employee fired for the benefit of its community of employees?

Barbara Toffler's research helps relate Hosmer's and Kidder's frameworks to the workplace. In her study, she found that managers commonly use the term *ethics* in four ways: basic truths concerning right and wrong; rules of behavior; institutional or cultural codes; and the integrated unity of a person's character (Toffler, 1986, p. 10). Basic truths, rules and codes can guide managers when it comes to making ethical choices, but resolving complex ethical dilemmas such as those described by Hosmer and Kidder require something more. It is our premise that this fourth element, 'the integrated unity of a person's character' (integrity) fused with concern for the welfare of others (altruism) is the foundation of the individual leader's capacity to work through ethical dilemmas.

Integrity as a component of leadership

In the academic and popular literature, hundreds of formulae have been advanced for achieving success as a business leader. But the continual reinvention of such formulae testifies that no single approach befits every leader for every situation. What stands out, however, is that over the last decade the success formula increasingly includes words such as integrity, ethics, principles, heart, soul, authenticity and the like.

In our experience with thousands of managers, we too have seen a high value placed on integrity. Participants in our programs typically rank personal integrity as the core component of effective leadership. Research also documents the importance of integrity as the most highly rated personal characteristic at all levels of management. Responding to an American Management Association poll to assess their values, 6000 US executives and managers cited integrity as the quality they most admire in superiors, peers and subordinates. Integrity was interpreted as 'truthful, trustworthy, has character, has convictions' (Posner and Schmidt, 1984, p. 209). A decade later, honesty was valued above every other quality (Posner and Schmidt, 1992, p. 86). In the GLOBE cross-cultural study of management traits across more than 62 different countries involving more than 17 500 managers from over 1000 organizations, integrity – being honest, trustworthy and just – was one of five universally endorsed traits of the performance-oriented style of leading (House *et al.*, 2003).

What makes integrity so central to effective leadership? We believe that it is the tight coupling of integrity with trust. If people around the leader do not trust him or her, then little else matters. According to James Hackett, Chairman and CEO of Steelcase Inc., 'The formulaic value of integrity, knowing why it is important, does more than just build character – it actually allows you to lead' (Hackett, 2003, p. 141). He takes pride in having made the right but unpopular decision to spend $40 million on recalling flammable panels and replacing them with a stricter fire code product. Describing public sector initiatives, Michael Fullan explains how system-level changes in school districts can hardly be implemented without leadership based on relationships and trust (Fullan, 2004). The economic life of countries and cultures according to F. Fukuyama is predicated on the moral bonds of social trust. Without social trust, the numerous economic transactions between individuals and organizations would not operate smoothly (Fukuyama, 1995, pp. 8–12). The link between trust and integrity also shows up in a dictionary definition of trust: 'reliance on the integrity, strength, ability, [and] surety of a person; [it is a] confident expectation' (*The Random House Dictionary of the English Language*, 1967, p. 1521).

A caveat: while evidence of integrity is an essential component of leadership, it is only one of many qualities that define effective leadership. Evidence of integrity by itself is no guarantee of leader effectiveness.

Altruism as a component of leadership

The word altruism comes from the Latin *alter* meaning 'other'. Altruism is linked to empathy and is demonstrated by unselfish behavior. Whereas empathy is an emotional state, altruism is the motivation to contribute to the welfare of another (Sober and Wilson, 2001).

Some social scientists believe that all acts of altruism ultimately reflect self-interest, through the expectation of reward, approval from society or credit with God. Others believe that altruism makes evolutionary sense, contributing to group survival. Many religions, including the Christian, Moslem, Jewish and Tibetan Buddhist faiths, each have belief systems supporting altruistic behaviors.

But for altruism to take hold as habitual behavior, family or social traditions must reinforce it. For example, when very young children are taught how to give and the importance of doing things on behalf of others, it can result in an ingrained belief that it is important to give back to society in some way. Similarly leaders and managers who practice altruism may help to embed altruistic behaviors within employees and within the organizational culture.

Unfortunately we do not know much about workplace altruism. This concept has not attracted much research attention. R.N. Kanungo and M. Mendonca hypothesize that the 'absence of a single unifying construct of altruism has led organizational theorists to ignore a variety of altruistic behaviors in the workplace such as those related to mentoring, empowerment, team building, and citizenship' (Kanungo and Mendonca, 1996, p. 79). They also contend that moral behavior is deeply ingrained in human nature, but the norms for executive behavior – including promoting cutthroat competition for the benefit of individuals, shareholders and investors – are often at odds with altruism (ibid., p. 80).

Even so, Kanungo and Mendonca, among others, equate ethical leadership and altruism with effective leadership. Kanungo and Mendonca assert that ethical leadership and altruism are not compatible with self- or individually oriented power and achievement motives (ibid., pp. 48–50). McClelland's early and extensive research on managerial motivation corroborates this view that managers with personalized power concerns are less effective as leaders because they are more impulsive in using power. Similarly managers with individual achievement motives focus on personal improvement and on doing things better by themselves (McClelland and Burnham, 1976, p. 103); they are less effective as leaders because they are not as concerned with the welfare of others or their organization. Writing about the leadership in companies that make the leap from 'good' to 'great', Jim Collins observes that companies are more likely to be great when leaders are incredibly ambitious, but they exemplify 'ambition first and foremost for the company and concern for its success', not themselves (Collins, 2001, p. 25).

Our experience working with managers supports the connection between effective leadership, integrity and altruism. Although we have not conducted formal research in this area, we have consistently heard managers tie a disposition to genuinely care about coworkers and the organization to the perception of whether a leader does or does not have integrity.

Setting the stage for self-insight

What we understand about the process of achieving integrity and becoming altruistic is embedded in our belief that self-awareness is a critical component of leadership development. Our knowledge and our processes have evolved over nearly 35 years of program-based interactions with tens of thousands of managers at the Center for Creative Leadership (CCL). These programs are feedback-intensive (Table 8.1) and continually link back to participants' work context: their work challenges, work pressures and work relationships. They also draw on the participants' experiences in their families, school settings, early career and community. What we have learned is that leadership development is intimately linked to personal development. And personal development is predicated on an understanding of self.

The tools and techniques of personal development that have been at the core of CCL's approach to leadership development provide managers with many 'snapshots' of themselves in action. Through a combination of assessments, experiences and a variety of feedback mechanisms, CCL affords managers with a series of images in which they see themselves in the midst of a range of situations from a variety of angles. Just as photographs in an album reveal changes in a person's outer physical appearance over time, the use of several different lenses to capture images of behavior, preferences and perceptions creates a collage of the individual's interior landscape. Program participants are then immersed in these views of themselves. They assess whether that overall image is consistent with their self-image and whether they are pleased with the impression they are making on coworkers. The immersion, a concentrated exercise in self-insight, gives rise to new frames for understanding oneself. It provides an opportunity to step back and see the whole, and to look for patterns, inconsistencies, implications and opportunities for growth.

The data collected on participants are longitudinal and comprehensive. The snapshots typically include a reflective analysis of previous activities and jobs dating back to high school: strengths, weaknesses and what participants learned about themselves; an inventory of descriptions used by themselves and friends; personality assessments using valid and reliable instruments; 360-degree feedback obtained by asking bosses, colleagues and

Table 8.1 Components of a typical feedback-intensive program

Monday	Tuesday	Wednesday	Thursday	Friday
• Introduction of framework for leadership development • Discussion of leadership development methods • 360-degree feedback assessment instrument • Introduction to learning partners & feedback method • Personality & learning styles assessment	• Introduction of framework for coaching • Coaching role plays • Personality needs assessment instrument • Group activity with facilitated feedback & video debrief	• Group activity • Change style assessment instrument • Leadership assessment instrument • Outdoor action learning	• Staff feedback • Peer feedback	• Personal planning and goal setting

143

subordinates to assess managerial effectiveness; simulations and role-playing exercises that are videotaped and observed by peers and psychologists; non-traditional exercises, such as acting, sculpting and drawing, that generate alternative perspectives on oneself; a review of past track record and future work possibilities to create an imaginative life story; and journalling and storytelling to encourage reflection.

The personal images captured are played back in many different ways during the program, providing in-the-moment mirrors of behavior. Using a structured approach, other participants react with their perceptions. The climate is friendly, supportive and even humorous. This holistic, experiential and interactive approach with significant time for feedback and reflection escalates the process of self-analysis and insight.

Of course, feedback, reflection and behavior change occur in contexts other than leadership development programs. For example, they can occur on the job, especially with difficult assignments, personal hardships and even from reading books and late-night conversations with friends or spouses. However, CCL's use of a consistent and focused methodology provides an unusual and extensive application of valuable processes. This methodology creates key moments – the 'eureka!' or flash of insight – that precede integration of new learning and desire for change. Our research shows that, through this focused viewing and evaluation of self, an 'unfreezing' process is set in motion, motivating people to change themselves (Van Velsor, 1985).

The premise underlying this methodology is that people can continually add to their understanding about themselves and others. They are then able to adjust their sense of who they are and how they should behave. In the context of work, managers and leaders can assimilate what they learn and use that insight to improve their ability to carry out the tasks of leadership.

Lest we give the impression that at CCL we have found a simple key to self-insight and behavior change, we will be clear about what we have learned: the journey is lengthy and difficult, and personal development (including the development of integrity and altruism) are the by-products of a lifelong effort to examine and re-examine personal perspectives, attitudes and behaviors.

Developing integrity

If integrity at its core is honesty and trustworthiness, can the leader acquire it? Or is integrity deeply embedded in one's personality at an early age? In our work, we often address other traits and preferences that, whether 'hardwired' by nature or experience, appear at first to be solid and not malleable. Yet we have often found that individuals are receptive to realigning their inner selves, personal desires and skill development because of their ambition to be productive and lead a purposeful life. So, just as a manager can address personal characteristics such as impatience, conflict avoidance, arrogance and so forth, we suggest it is possible that integrity can evolve over time, including in adulthood. This approach to adapting or changing perspectives, attitudes and behaviors involves four key tactics:

1. addressing discrepancies between self-perception and other perception;
2. learning the language for understanding personality-based leadership strengths and limitations;
3. committing oneself to capitalize on strengths and overcome limitations; and
4. choosing to learn and develop through job challenges, supportive relationships and transitions.

These tactics encompass a multitude of practices that develop and strengthen personal consistency and predictability, which in turn contribute to honesty and trustworthiness.

To demonstrate how these tactics play out in the development of leadership, we introduce Rick Greywall, Miguel Williams, Jean Hummel and Carl Laskow, fictitious managers who reflect the experiences of many real-life managers with whom CCL has worked. We use the stories of these managers to ground an otherwise theoretical discussion, to illustrate how subtle (and not well-understood) shifts in perspectives and attitudes occur, and to show how these shifts can make a difference in leadership behaviors and effectiveness.

Addressing the discrepancies between self-perception and other-perception
Most emotionally healthy adults carry idealized portraits of themselves. But to what extent do others validate the picture we have of ourselves? More than 30 years ago, CCL pioneered the use of multi-rater feedback, a process of formal assessment to help individuals understand themselves and gauge their effectiveness. In many organizations today executives and managers engage in this process, commonly referred to as '360-degree feedback'. Multi-rater feedback instruments provide data from others – typically one's boss, peers and direct reports – that allow the individual manager or executive to compare his or her own ratings with those of others. Managers become aware, often for the first time, that bosses, superiors, peers and direct reports view them differently. These comparisons allow the individual to get a fix on his or her leadership strengths and limitations.

Since the data are derived from assessment instruments that are solidly based on research, they provide a systematic assessment of leadership fitness, measuring one's skill at managing self, managing relationships and managing work. At a minimum, 360-degree assessments raise awareness; optimally they serve as a wake-up call and a platform for change.

Through 360-degree assessment, manager Rick Greywall learns that he is highly regarded by peers and direct reports for his decisiveness and resourcefulness, has the ability to learn and pick up something quickly, and is respected for doing whatever it takes. He earns kudos for using a participative style to lead employees through change. But he also finds out that he is perceived as unable to confront problem employees. Through the 360-degree feedback, Rick's coworkers and subordinates report that he does not identify potential performance problems early on, and he procrastinates when dealing with issues of incompetence. His failure to hold honest conversations with poor performers is an indicator that he cannot be trusted to build a high-performing team – essential for meeting the demands of his job.

Rick's experience illustrates how elements of a manager's personality are initially uncovered through 360-degree assessments and feedback-intensive programs. Personal temperament, the imprint of people and experiences, tensions between conflicting inclinations and much more are brought to light. With these insights, inescapable inconsistencies also surface. Managers have to ask themselves: who do I think I am, who do I want to be and how do others see me? The differing answers have to be reconciled. By focusing on specific behaviors, managers can begin to work through the incongruities and choose a course of action. As regards developing personal integrity, managers are led to ask themselves: what do I want to do, what am I actually doing and what is the right thing to do?

More broadly, these data serve as notice that perceptions about performance differ. If serious perceptual discrepancies emerge, there are two possibilities: either self-perception is more grandiose than warranted, or it is unduly modest. Grandiose individuals are humbled through the feedback process, while self-effacing individuals confront their misguided humility and learn how their lack of leadership self-assurance reduces the productive capacity of their organization.

Again Rick is a case in point. Though well aware of his strategic ability and his 16-year track record for introducing and driving change, he is surprisingly diffident about his leadership capabilities. He is pleased to discover the extent to which he is highly regarded and gains self-confidence as a result. Ironically the only dimension on which he rates himself more favorably than his coworkers do is on his ability to confront problem employees.

In regard to integrity, a manager may be surprised to find that others rank him, for example, low on credibility and lacking in follow-through, clearly calling into question his personal sense of integrity. Using this information, he can then explore the patterns of behavior that have led to this perception gap and take steps to improve.

Learning the language for understanding personality-based leadership strengths and limitations

A wide range of difference exists in the way individuals feel, think and act, and every language has words describing personality variation. For example, we describe coworkers as quick-witted, abrupt, cautious, selfish, inventive, pessimistic, reliable, intelligent, persevering, skeptical and so forth. But surprisingly few leaders and managers understand the role personality plays in their interactions with others. This limitation has a significant consequence: managers lack insight about how their personality obstructs their effectiveness. Their traits and preferences may work at cross-purposes with their goals and good intentions.

Personality disrupts productivity in many ways. Consider extroverted manager Miguel Williams. He is spontaneous and socially at ease. He needs and enjoys group interactions. But what if he is the assigned manager of an R&D or IT unit that is typically populated by professionals, almost anti-social by comparison, who wish to be left alone? While Miguel considers his social habits to be team building, his subordinates see it as wasting time. Jean Hummel is a structured manager who is most comfortable with well-planned projects. What if her cross-functional team includes peers who prefer open-ended problem solving? Jean may see her efforts as practical and results-oriented, while her team is frustrated by her non-responsiveness to new information and emerging contingencies. Manager Carl Laskow is highly intuitive and works with a like-minded team of direct reports. They typically use anecdotes, imagination and ability to see patterns and make connections to construct future scenarios for their unit. But will their approach and recommendations be considered valuable by peers or bosses who are far more data-driven?

Such situations are a fact of life in most organizations. Those very elements of personality that are a manager's strong suit create static in the communication channels when he or she is working with people with different personalities. Though the central task of leadership and management is to engage others to get work done, most leaders and managers cannot converse intelligently about personality variation. Without a language giving them a more precise understanding of coworkers, managers are at a loss when it comes to knowing 'where others are coming from'. They are susceptible to making inaccurate assessments and unnecessarily judgmental evaluations.

But this need not be the case. Personality studies have evolved considerably over the past 80 years. The cumulative efforts of psychologists have led to a cross-culturally validated and systematic language for describing personality differences. Research has also demonstrated links between personality and managerial effectiveness. In our experience, providing managers with the framework and language for addressing personality variation generates powerful insight into both self and others. They begin to see how varying perspectives, attitudes, preferences and perceptions often interfere with genuine collaboration. They begin to discern personality-based strengths and limitations, modify or eliminate ineffective behaviors and leverage effective behaviors in managing themselves and others.

The implications for developing integrity lie in the way self-insight is combined with newly learned frameworks for approaching interpersonal relationships and leadership. This inculcates the ability to work with others in a constructive, respectful way and contributes to building trust. We will return to this idea in connection with developing altruism.

Commitment to capitalize on strengths and overcome limitations
Self-insight can motivate self-management; managers typically leave CCL programs with a commitment to alter dysfunctional or ineffective behaviors. In their desire to be successful, they feel compelled to discipline those attitudes and behaviors that limit personal effectiveness or cause distrust. They are also driven to take full advantage of assets that enhance their leadership effectiveness.

Of course the work of changing behaviors is complex and can be discouraging. Earlier we described extroverted Miguel Williams, structured Jean Hummel and intuitive Carl Laskow. Though they came to see how their natural personality strengths and related behaviors were interfering with team productivity, they each struggled with the way to change or adapt such seemingly 'fixed' traits. The way to start, we have found, is to understand the underlying drivers of the behaviors. This is where, in CCL programs, a feedback specialist or coach plays a central role.

In a five-day development program, for example, the fourth day is typically devoted to receiving and reflecting on feedback. Up to this point, participants have gathered lots of information about themselves, expanding their understanding about how personality and preferences interact in the workplace. Now they are trying to make sense of it all. At this point, managers have a one-on-one session with a highly trained feedback specialist who helps them to find the links between their life experiences, personality and managerial effectiveness. When the manager and feedback specialist sit down to analyze personal data, new insights are gained. Often managers' initial analyses of their dilemmas are not accurate or complete. Through discussion with his feedback specialist, Miguel begins to see how his sociability helps him to cover up his lack of organization and attention to project details. Jean learns that her commitment to thorough planning is driven by a high need to impose control over others' behaviors while resisting control by them. Carl becomes aware that his overreliance on intuitive insight is, in part, driven by his belief that he 'never was good at numbers and finance'.

These insights may seem obvious and trivial to observers, but they have a great impact on managers participating in the programs. Prior to meeting the feedback specialist, participants have begun to draw a self-portrait, based on volumes of data and new ways of thinking about leadership. Though many have inklings about their talents and shortcomings, the feedback session helps bring their nascent self-portrait into sharper focus. Areas for self-improvement become apparent. Career and life priorities are reviewed and often modified. The data-driven evidence and implications are faced head-on. By the end of the program, participants are motivated to capitalize on strengths and overcome limitations.

This work of honestly assessing situations and relationships, and becoming accountable for resolving problems, we argue, is the work of developing integrity. In essence, managers voluntarily choose to begin the process of seeing clearly and taking action to integrate (that is, to make whole and consistent) different elements of their personality. The effort, as well as results, of doing this work can contribute to a greater sense of the importance of integrity as both a personal value and a professional asset.

Choosing to learn and develop through job challenges, supportive relationships and transitions
As we know, leadership is not for the faint of heart. It requires stamina and an ability to accept and learn from hardships. The more one takes risks, the more one is likely to stumble, or fall outright. But the more varied the developmental challenges leaders and managers are willing to take on, the greater the opportunity to learn and apply new skills, provided they learn how to learn from these experiences (Van Velsor *et al.*, 2004, pp. 208–10).

Research shows that effective leaders are those who learn from their mistakes and apply what they have learned in new situations. Along the way, they benefit from a multitude of supportive relationships such as those provided by feedback givers, dialogue partners, counselors, cheerleaders, coaches, mentors and role models (McCauley and Douglas, 2004, p. 87). The ideal outcome is when the cumulative insights about oneself stimulate a desire to grow and change: to acquire new perspectives that subsume old ones and that are transformative. Evidence that this state has been attained comes when participants report that they will never see a certain situation, challenge or issue in the same way again. Their perspective on that prior condition has been forever altered, and will elicit a different and presumably more effective response in the future.

As noted earlier, the underlying assumption is that program participants are capable of assimilating what they learn about themselves and applying those insights to improving their productivity. Layers of abilities – for managing one's self, interrelating with others and facilitating work in an organizational setting – begin to be built up. This is how individuals begin to develop into leaders who can be trusted because they are effective, honest and caring. The choice to learn and do the work required for development is essential for those who wish to serve in leadership roles that invariably require facing ethically challenging dilemmas.

Beyond personal integrity
These four tactics drive CCL's approach to leadership development and contribute to the development and valuing of personal integrity. But leadership is inherently social and interactive. So how does our view of integrity move individual leaders beyond a self-absorbed preoccupation with their own inner workings? Our current best sense of what happens as a result of self-analysis and insight is as follows. It is eye opening to learn that different people perceive people and situations differently; but that is only the beginning of the work to include other perspectives in one's thought processes and decisions. Similarly managers who begin to understand and appreciate the complexity of their own motivations become poised to observe and respond to the differing motivations of others. The effort to overcome managerial shortcomings creates an appreciation of how difficult it is to change habits of thinking and acting. From that, more patience and tolerance of others may be developed. And those who assume that, as leaders, they are a work-in-progress are more likely to influence coworkers to undertake their own developmental journey.

By considering how integrity is developed as a personal value and professional asset, we also begin to see its connection to altruism, and how both contribute to developing ethical organizations.

Developing altruism
Let us suppose that altruism, like many other qualities such as aggressiveness, optimism or creativity, follows a normal distribution curve. This would mean that most individuals operate from a mix of self-interest and concern for others, with some people more likely to behave selfishly and others unselfishly. What, then, would it take for individuals to behave more consistently on the altruistic end of the curve? Are there ways to nudge or encourage managers and leaders to show more altruism? What behaviors would altruism involve?

We believe that altruism is fostered by the same methodology that supports the development of individual integrity. Whether this is an incidental by-product of the self-insight and motivation established through CCL's processes, or a more direct link, we do not know. What does seem to be true is this: in practicing effective leadership behaviors, individuals learn to relate to coworkers, open up to new perspectives and discover connections. These outcomes then, it seems, lead to new opportunities for learning and demonstrating altruistic behaviors.

US Major General James Dozier gives a striking example of how self-awareness, new perspectives and commitment to behavior change can affect others. He credited his leadership development experience at CCL in 1981 with saving his life when captured by Italian terrorists of the Red Brigade in 1982. Through his development program, he became acutely aware of how his behavior affected others. This realization sensitized him to behaving appropriately with his captors. He was aware that, if he behaved in a calm and predictable way, his trigger-happy captors would be less likely to execute him (Dozier, 2004).

Adjusting behavior in response to a life-and-death situation is not what we typically think of when we consider altruism. Yet, given the view that altruism stems from the ability to step outside one's perspective and consider another's vantage point, General Dozier demonstrated altruism to powerful effect. Other participants make consequential, if less dramatic, changes in the months following the program. An astonishing behavioral shift occurs, it seems, when managers truly comprehend how their words and actions shape the behavior of others toward them. For example, a lead negotiator on contracts with external vendors sensed that his subordinates did not always give him the information he needed to close negotiations successfully. But from feedback he learned that he becomes hostile and moody when things are not going his way. He realized that his own volatile reactions led to his subordinates withholding vital information.

Once this insight takes hold, many opportunities for demonstrating altruism seem to arise. Among these opportunities, three points of decision stand out: the choice to lead, the commitment to recognize and respect others, and the effort to support the development of others. By recognizing and saying 'yes' to these opportunities, managers activate their ability to behave altruistically. Here again, we draw on CCL's experience in working with thousands of leaders to highlight how these opportunities contribute to the development of altruism.

Choosing to lead

What is leadership? What are the tasks of leadership? What are the obligations of managers to the organization and their subordinates? Surprisingly few managers have a clear idea of what leadership means. All too often, leadership is what goes with reaching a higher rung on the career ladder and involves making the numbers and keeping bosses or boards happy. Only recently – as making the numbers becomes more difficult because of globalization, competition, the maturity of product life cycles and so forth – have we put leadership behaviors under the magnifying glass. We propose that the core tasks of leadership – setting a direction, gaining the commitment of others and aligning the efforts of the group or team – are the starting point for understanding effective leadership behavior. Within these tasks lie numerous opportunities to demonstrate altruism.

But it is incorrect to assume that those who occupy senior positions in organizations understand the tasks of leadership and know what it means to behave like a leader. This is similar to thinking that those who birth children instinctively know how to parent them well. Such assumptions are inaccurate inasmuch as leadership, like parenting, requires role-related behaviors that have to be learned. And without the awareness or valuing of certain tasks or behaviors, neither leaders nor parents are likely to exhibit or develop them.

Managers who attend CCL developmental programs frequently report that the experience was the first time they had a clear view of what effective leadership entails. In a recent evaluation of one of CCL's flagship programs, 74 men and ten women executives from 25 countries were interviewed from 30 to 120 days after their program participation. Fifty-five per cent reported that they were beginning to 'notice when they were not behaving like a leader' and so were enabled to behave differently (Ascalon *et al.*, 2004). The interviewees were referencing their newfound knowledge that effective leadership involves specific tasks and behaviors; this simply had not been highlighted for them previously.

Once the dimensions of the leader's work have been identified, managers can recognize and actively choose to practice the behaviors that go with the role. This is what we mean by the phrase 'choosing to lead'. It is similar to an individual choosing, or not choosing, to assume the tasks of being a parent: for example, by putting meals on the table regularly, driving youngsters to swimming and music lessons, supervising daily chores and homework, listening to sagas of youthful romance and so forth. In both instances, whether leading or parenting, individuals become accountable for influencing the lives of others in a positive way. The choice calls for some measure of unselfishness on their part.

If people do not understand that effective leaders must show a certain level of unselfish care for the organization and for the people with whom they work, they will not aspire to do so. They will instead equate leadership effectiveness with only the more tangible or measurable aspects of their work.

Learning to recognize and respect others

At the end of a CCL leadership development program, it is common for participants to set goals around improving work and family relationships (Center for Creative Leadership, 2000, p. 5). As they work on their relationship goals in the weeks and months following the program, these managers start to practice new behaviors. Increased recognition and respect for others becomes the unanticipated outcome of their new behaviors. Again, a broader view of others is a necessary precursor to altruism.

In several evaluation studies, when asked to describe what they are doing differently in their efforts to be more effective leaders, program participants report making behavior changes tied to building relationships (Van Velsor, 1985; Palus and Warren, 1991). Some describe taking the time to be more available to coworkers, engaging with them and listening to their ideas. Others talk about learning to be less confrontational and more level-headed, calm and patient. As confidence and communication skills improve, managers are better able to know when to be assertive and when to hold back. They begin to involve others by trusting, delegating and collaborating, and note that they feel less alone by doing so (Ascalon *et al.*, 2004).

These managers describe a range of tactics in their attempts to develop new habits and better relationships. One manager makes it a practice to walk out of the building and into the fresh air for a few moments to regain equilibrium before returning to difficult meetings. Many learn to pay more attention to individual differences and show more respect and compassion. By reversing their customary behaviors, they open up some very different ways of working with colleagues. There is more candor and trust – on both sides. A light seems to be turned on, and they are now able to notice more about their coworkers, respect them more and engage more fully in establishing effective relationships.

To be sure, the process described above is not invariable. As efforts to evaluate the short- and long-term impact of programs continue, we learn more about ways in which adult development can be optimized. For example, self-doubt, lack of motivation, time and workload pressures and inattentive bosses obstruct developmental progress. Progress is boosted by international diversity in the classroom, follow-on coaching and alumnae interactions. Post-program evaluations indicate that, compared with managers who lack support, those who build a support network of coworkers, coaches and friends are able to make statistically significant behavior changes (Van Velsor, 1985; Palus and Warren, 1991; Ascalon *et al.*, 2004). And there is some evidence that managers who participate in programs during times of personal or organizational transition experience a bigger developmental push (McCauley and Hughes-James, 1994, p. 50; Musselwhite, 1985).

Once the process of learning to relate to others has started, each step seems to lead to the next. The ability to scan and acknowledge different perspectives, attitudes, preferences and perceptions in a team or work group is an important characteristic of leadership. Therefore the more managers observe and appreciate differences, the more coworkers feel recognized and respected. They are free to share their opinions. Learning to be altruistic may not be the original objective for managers seeking to be more effective, but almost inadvertently they expand their capacity to be considerate and caring of others.

Supporting the development of others
Organizational structures have changed dramatically over the last decade. Economic factors, combined with the dismantling of hierarchies, downsizing and delayering, matrixed reporting relationships and the influx of international and Gen-X employees, have made the workplace a fluid environment. High on the agenda of many organizations is the issue of attracting, developing and retaining talented employees. Employees, too, place ever more value in bosses and organizations that contribute to their development. In this environment, supporting and guiding employees is both an altruistic and a pragmatic gesture.

A corresponding change has ensued in the way leadership development is approached. For filling their most senior positions, large organizations are turning away from a sink-or-swim philosophy and looking for ways to develop leadership talent effectively and systematically. CCL interventions typically begin with a focus on individual leader development (incorporating the four tactics previously discussed) and then build upon that foundation to improve relationships and expand organizational leadership capacity collectively. Coaching, too, promises to be a valuable tool for grooming executives and managers to think and act like leaders. Top executives and managers who take on the responsibility for developing others can serve as powerful resources for modeling and encouraging integrity and altruism.

Implications and future directions
We believe that the nurturing of integrity and altruism is woven into our approach to leadership development. Using four essential tactics, individuals can gain self-insight and develop personal consistency and predictability. Extending these processes further, we note three key opportunities for demonstrating integrity and making altruism more popular in the workplace.

Summarized, here is what we recommend to leaders and managers who wish to be exemplary in their development:

- Cultivate the habit of looking at the differences between how you perceive yourself and how others perceive you.
- Try to understand the drivers behind your behavior (and that of others) and make the kinds of adjustments that make it possible for you to collaborate effectively.
- Make a commitment to grow and challenge yourself continually to utilize strengths wisely and overcome weaknesses.
- Learn and develop through job challenges, supportive relationships and transitions.
- Choose to lead while recognizing, respecting and supporting others.

Essentially these tactics and opportunities help individuals to get to know themselves and others, and to commit themselves to their own and others' development in service of productive collaboration. When ethical dilemmas (as described by Hosmer and Kidder) have to be confronted, these individuals are better equipped to choose an ethical course of action. While they may still undergo an emotional struggle, these managers have learned new habits for assessing and responding to complex and ambiguous situations.

These new habits tie such leaders back to ethical behavior. Ethics are the value-based standards of conduct and customs that promote the good of the whole community. We suggest that managers participating in programs that intensify self-insight relative to a leadership framework are given the tools to pay attention in a different way to the work of leadership. Their experience lays the groundwork for more mindful leadership behaviors.

This raises at least three implications for practice: why is this kind of leadership development not more pervasive? How can workplace integrity and altruism be more valued? How much longer will it be before followers start holding leaders accountable for meeting higher standards of performance? Two broad directions for future research also surface: why are better integrated individuals more honest and trustworthy? How can workplace altruism and its impact be assessed?

We believe that the intentional learning and personal development generated through an insight-based approach to leadership development places a renewed value on honesty, trust and care. The increased valuing of integrity and altruism in oneself leads to expecting it in others. Managers are motivated to demonstrate integrity and altruism through their words and actions and are interested in seeing these qualities developed in others. When leaders and organizations operate from these expectations, the bar on acceptable standards of leadership is raised. Those who take on the tasks of leadership are informed by their commitment to integrity and altruism, which seems to us to be precisely the type of ethical behavior needed in today's organizations.

References

Ascalon, E., E. Van Velsor and M. Wilson (2004), 'Leadership Development Program Europe Impact Study: a presentation at the LDP Network Conference', February, Scottsdale, AZ.

Center for Creative Leadership (2000), 'Feedback training plus: making magic happen in the classroom', proprietary manual, Greensboro, NC.

Collins, J.C. (2001), *Good to Great: Why Some Companies Make the Leap ... and Other's Don't*, New York: Harper Collins.

Dozier, J. (2004), 'A conversation with 2003 distinguished alumni award recipient Major General Dozier', colloquium presented at the Center for Creative Leadership, Greensboro, NC, 10 February.

Fukuyama, F. (1995), *Trust: The Social Virtues and the Creation of Prosperity*, NewYork: The Free Press.

Fullan, M. (2004), *Change Forces: The Sequel*, London and Philadelphia, PA: Falmer Press.

Hackett, J. (2003), 'Leadership dilemmas: ethical challenges can make or break a CEO', in N.M. Tichy and A.R. McGill (eds), *The Ethical Challenge: How to Lead with Unyielding Integrity*, San Francisco: Jossey-Bass, pp. 135–58.

Hosmer, L.T. (1994), *Moral Leadership in Business*, Boston: Irwin.

House, R.J., P.J. Hanges and M. Javidan, P.W. Dorfman and V. Gupta (2004) (eds), *Culture, Leadership, and Organizations: The GLOBE Study of 62 Societies*, Thousand Oaks, CA: Sage.

Kanungo, R.N. and M. Mendonca (1996), *Ethical Dimensions of Leadership*, Thousand Oaks, CA: Sage.

Kidder, R. (1995), *How Good People Make Tough Choices: Resolving the Dilemmas of Ethical Living*, New York: William Morrow and Company.

McCauley, C.D. and C.A. Douglas (2004), 'Developmental relationships' in C.D. McCauley and E. Van Velsor (eds), *The Center for Creative Leadership Handbook of Leadership Development*, San Francisco: Jossey-Bass, pp. 85–115.

McCauley, C.D. and M.W. Hughes-James (1994), 'An evaluation of the outcomes of a leadership development program', Center for Creative Leadership, Greensboro, NC.

McClelland, D.C. and D.H. Burnham (1976), 'Power is the great motivator', *Harvard Business Review*, March–April, 100–110.

Musselwhite. C. (1985), 'The impact of timing on readiness to learn and transfer of learning from leadership development training, a case study', unpublished doctoral dissertation, North Carolina State University, Raleigh.

Palus, C. and A. Warren (1991), [APEX survey], unpublished raw data.

Posner, B.Z. and W.H. Schmidt (1984), 'Values and the American Manager: An Update', *California Management Review*, **26** (3), 202–216.

Posner, B.Z. and W.H. Schmidt (1992), Values and the American Manager: An Update Updated, *California Management Review*, 34 (3), 80–94.

Sober, E. and D.S. Wilson (2001), in E. Fisher (producer), *The Infinite Mind: Altruism*, National Public Radio broadcast, New York: Lichtenstein Creative Media.

Stein, J. (ed.) (1967), *The Random House Dictionary of the English Language*, New York: Random House.

Thompson, D. (ed.) (1998), *The Oxford Dictionary of Current English*, 2nd edn, New York: Oxford University Press.

Toffler, B. (1986), *Tough Choices: Managers Talk Ethics*, New York: John Wiley & Sons.

Van Velsor, E. (1985), [leadership development program impact study report],unpublished raw data.

Van Velsor, E., R.S. Moxley and K.A. Bunker (2004), 'The leader development process', in C.D. McCauley and E. Van Velsor (eds), *The Center for Creative Leadership Handbook of Leadership Development*, San Francisco: Jossey-Bass, pp. 204–33.

PART III

RESPONSIBLE LEADERSHIP AND GOVERNANCE: ETHICS, SOCIAL IMPACT AND THE GLOBAL COMMON GOOD

9 Integrating leadership with ethics: is good leadership contrary to human nature?
Joanne B. Ciulla

Introduction

Leadership is a human activity. People engage in leadership all over the world. All leaders do similar things as leaders. They initiate activities, they motivate people, and they move people towards various goals. Some use persuasion, others force. Some are democratic and aim to promote the greatest good, while others are autocrats who aim to maximize their own good and the good of their friends and cronies. Individual leaders vary across cultures and within cultures. They may have different leadership styles, attitudes, values, beliefs and practices, depending on the culture, institution or organization. This is not a chapter about traits, cultural differences, universal values or particular ethical problems facing business leaders, nor is it about leadership in one area or another. This chapter looks at a fundamental question about leadership. What is it about human nature that makes ethical leadership in any context or culture difficult?

The chapter examines leadership in terms of the basic philosophic question concerning human nature. To what extent does free will shape our lives and to what extent are our lives determined by our genes and by fate (Dennett, 1995; 2003)? This question is particularly salient to the study of both ethics and leadership. We begin by exploring the relationship between moral values and practical knowledge or ethics and effectiveness. We then go on to discuss risk and moral accountability or moral luck. Then we examine the problems of self-control, self-interest and altruism. Later in the chapter, we look at what biology tells us about self-interest, cooperation and reciprocity. In the end, we focus on nepotism. Throughout human history, leaders, meaning people who hold leadership positions, were indeed born (not made) into the family business or the family political dynasty. The majority of businesses in the world today are family businesses and many heads of state are members of a family dynasty. The natural inclination of leaders to look after their family, friends and clan is both a source of strength and a source of corruption in business, politics and a variety of other organizations. In conclusion we argue that ethical leadership is a moral struggle because, in a sense, it does not come naturally.

Some definitions

Before we get started, a short note on the words 'ethics', 'morality' and 'leadership' is in order. Some people like to make a distinction between ethics and morality, arguing that ethics is about social values and morality is about personal values. Like most philosophers, I use the terms interchangeably. As a practical matter, courses on moral philosophy cover the same material as courses on ethics. There is a long history of using these terms as synonyms of each other, regardless of their roots in different languages. In *De Fato* (II. i) Cicero substituted the Latin word 'morale' for Aristotle's use of the Greek word 'ethikos'. We see the two terms defining each other in *The Compact Oxford English Dictionary*. The word 'moral' is defined as 'of or pertaining to the distinction between right and wrong, or good and evil in relation to the actions, volitions, or character of human beings; ethical' and 'concerned with virtue and vice or rules of conduct, ethical praise or blame, habits of life, custom and manners' (p. 1114). Similarly the dictionary defines ethics as 'of or pertaining to morality' and 'the science of morals, the moral principles by which a person is guided' (p. 534). Aside from linguistic considerations, it is not useful to divide ethics into public and personal ethics. Ethics is about relationships with other people and living things and, as such, the personal is the public. If we start separating public and private ethics, we find ourselves sliding into ethical relativism, which makes for tough going when leaders have to make real decisions about what is right and wrong both at home and in international contexts.

I have written extensively on why debates over the definition of leadership are really debates about the values related to leadership (Ciulla, 1995, 1999). Joe Rost (1991) argued that leadership studies could not progress without a common definition of leadership. He collected 221 definitions of leadership, ranging from the 1920s to the 1990s. All of these definitions generally say the same thing: leadership is about a person or persons somehow moving other people to do something. Where the definitions differ is in how leaders motivate their followers, their relationship to followers, who has a say in the goals of the group or organization, and what abilities the leader needs to have to get things done. I have argued that leadership scholars who worry about constructing the ultimate definition of leadership are asking the wrong question but trying to answer the right one. The ultimate question about leadership is not, what is the definition of leadership? We are not confused about what leaders do, but we would like to know the best way to do it. The whole point of studying leadership is to answer the question, what is good leadership? The use of the word 'good' here has two senses, morally good leadership and technically good leadership (that is, effective at getting the job-at-hand done). The problem with this view is that, when we look at history and the leaders around us, we find some leaders who meet both criteria and some who only meet one. History only confuses the matter further. Historians do not write about the leader who was very ethical but did not do anything of significance. They rarely write about a general who was a great human being but never won a battle.

Ethics and effectiveness
History defines successful leaders largely in terms of their ability to bring about change for better or worse. As a result, great leaders in history include everyone from Gandhi to Hitler. Machiavelli was disgusted by Cesare Borgia the man, but impressed by Borgia as the resolute, ferocious and cunning Prince (Prezzolini, 1928). While leaders usually bring about change or are successful at doing something, the ethical questions waiting in the wings are the ones found in the various definitions mentioned earlier. What were the leader's intentions? How did the leader go about bringing change? And was the change itself good? I have argued that a good leader is an ethical and an effective leader (Ciulla, 1995). While this may seem like stating the obvious, the problem we face is that we do not always find ethics and effectiveness in the same leader. Some leaders are highly ethical but not very effective. Others are very effective at serving the needs of their constituents or organizations but not very ethical in other ways.

This distinction between ethics and effectiveness is not always a crisp one. Sometimes being ethical is being effective and sometimes being effective is being ethical. In other words, ethics is effectiveness in certain instances. There are times when simply being regarded as ethical and trustworthy makes a leader effective and other times when being highly effective makes a leader ethical. Given the limited power and resources of the secretary-general of the United Nations, it would be very difficult for someone in this position to be effective if he or she did not behave ethically. The same is true for organizations. In the famous Tylenol case, Johnson & Johnson actually increased sales of Tylenol by pulling Tylenol bottles off their shelves after someone poisoned one of them. The leaders at Johnson & Johnson were effective because they were ethical.

The criteria that we use to judge the effectiveness of a leader also are not morally neutral. For a while, Wall Street and the business press lionized Al Dunlap (Chainsaw Al) as a great business leader. Their admiration was based on his ability to downsize a company and raise the price of its stock. Dunlap apparently knew little about the nuts and bolts of running a business. When he failed to deliver profits at Sunbeam, he tried to cover up his losses and was fired. In this case, and in many business cases, the criterion for good leadership is limited to whether he or she makes a profit for the firm. It does not take great skill to get rid of employees, and taking away a person's livelihood requires a moral and a practical argument. Also one of the most striking aspects of professional ethics is that often what seems right in the short run is not right in the long run, or what seems right for a group or organization, is not right when placed in a broader context. For example, Mafia families may have very strong internal ethical systems, but they are highly unethical in any larger context of society.

There are also cases when the sheer competence of a leader has a moral impact. There were many examples of heroism in the aftermath of the terrorist attack on the World Trade Center. The most inspiring and frequently cited are the altruistic acts of rescue workers. Yet consider the case of Alan S. Weil, whose law firm Sidley, Austin, Brown & Wood occupied five floors of the World Trade Center. After watching the Trade Center towers fall to the ground and checking to see if his employees got out safely, Weil got on the phone and within three hours had rented four floors of another building for his employees. By the end of the day he had arranged for an immediate delivery of 800 desks and 300 computers. The next day the firm was open for business with desks for almost every employee (Schwartz, 2001). We do not know if Weil's motives were altruistic or avaricious, but his focus on doing his job allowed the firm to fulfill its obligations to all of its stakeholders, from clients to employees.

On the flip side of the ethics effectiveness continuum are situations where it is difficult to tell whether a leader is unethical, incompetent or stupid. As Terry Price has argued, the moral failures of leaders are not always intentional. Sometimes moral failures are cognitive and sometimes they are normative (Price, 2000). Leaders may get their facts wrong and think that they are acting ethically when, in fact, they are not. For example, in 2000, South African president Thabo Mbeki issued a statement saying that it was not clear that HIV caused AIDS. He thought the pharmaceutical industry was just trying to scare people so that they could increase their profits (Garrett, 2000). Coming from the leader of a country where, at the time, about one in five people tested positive for HIV, this was a shocking statement. His stance caused outrage among public health experts and other citizens. It was irresponsible and certainly undercut the efforts to stop the AIDS epidemic. Mbeki understood the scientific literature, but chose to put political and philosophical reasons ahead of scientific knowledge. (He has since backed away from this position.) When leaders do things like this, we want to know if they are unethical, misinformed, incompetent or just stupid. Mbeki's actions seemed unethical, but he may have thought he was taking an ethical stand. His narrow mind-set about this issue made him recklessly disregard his more pressing obligations to stop the AIDS epidemic (Moldoveanu and Langer, 2002).

In some situations leaders act with moral intentions, but because they are incompetent they create unethical outcomes. Take, for instance, the unfortunate case of the Swiss charity Christian Solidarity International. Their goal was to free an estimated 200 000 Dinka children who were enslaved in Sudan. The charity paid between $35 and $75 a head to free enslaved children. The unintended consequence of their actions was that they actually encouraged slaving by creating a market for it. The price of slaves and the demand for them went up. Also some cunning Sudanese found that it paid to pretend that they were slaves so that they could make money by being liberated. This deception made it difficult for the charity to identify those who really needed help from those who were faking it. Here the charity's intent and the means it used to achieve its goals were not unethical in relation to alleviating suffering in the short run; however, in the long run, the charity inadvertently created more suffering. However one might also argue that slavery is wrong, hence it is also wrong to participate in any commerce with a slave trader. After all, the problems with the scheme did stem from buying back the slaves (Ciulla, 2003).

The ethics-and-effectiveness question parallels the perspectives of deontological and teleological theories in ethics. From the deontological point of view, intentions are the morally relevant aspects of an act. As long as the leader acts according to his or her duty or on moral principles, the leader acts ethically, regardless of the consequences. From the teleological perspective, what really matters is that the leader's actions result in bringing about something morally good or 'the greatest good'. Deontological theories locate the ethics of an action in the moral intent of the leader and his or her moral justification for the action, while teleological theories locate the ethics of the action in its results. We need both deontological and teleological theories to account for the ethics of leaders. Just as a good leader has to be ethical and effective, he or she also has to act according to duty and with some notion of the greatest good in mind (Ciulla, 2001).

In modernity we often separate the inner person (intentions) from the outer person (behavior). Ancient Greek theories of ethics based on virtue do not have this problem. In virtue theories you basically are what you do (Aristotle, 1984). A number of business ethics scholars use virtue ethics to patch the Cartesian split between what people are and what they do (Solomon, 1992; Sisson, 2003; Hartman, 1988). The utilitarian John Stuart Mill saw this split between the ethics of the person and the ethics of his or her actions clearly. He said the intentions or reasons for an act tell us something about the morality of the person, but the ends of an act tell us about the morality of the action (Mill, 1987). This solution does not really solve the ethics-and-effectiveness problem. It simply reinforces the split between the personal morality of a leader and what he or she does as a leader. Going back to an earlier example, Weil may have worked quickly to keep his law firm going because he was so greedy he did not want to lose a day of billings, but, in doing so, he also produced the greatest good for various stakeholders. We may not like his personal reasons for acting, but in this particular case, the various stakeholders may not care because they also benefited. If the various stakeholders knew that Weil had selfish intentions, they would, as Mill said, think less of him but not less of his actions. This is often the case with business. When a business runs a campaign to raise money for the homeless, they may be doing it to sell more of their goods and improve their public image. Yet it would seem a bit harsh to say that they should not have the charity drive and deny needed funds for the homeless. One might argue that it is sometimes unethical to demand perfect moral intentions. Nonetheless personally unethical leaders who do good things for their constituents are still problematic. Even though they provide for the greatest good, their people can never really trust them.

Moral luck
The historian's assessment of good leaders is sometimes contingent on what philosophers call 'moral luck'. Moral luck is another way of thinking about the free will/determinism problem in ethics. People are responsible for the free choices they make. We are generally not responsible for things over which we have no control. The most difficult ethical decisions leaders make are those where they cannot fully determine the outcome. Philosopher Bernard Williams describes moral luck as intrinsic to an action based on how well a person thinks through a decision, and whether his or her inferences are sound and turn out to be right. He says moral luck is also extrinsic to a decision (Williams, 1981). Things like bad weather, accidents, terrorists, malfunctioning machines and so on can sabotage the best-laid plans. Moral luck is an important aspect of ethics and leadership because it helps us think about ethical aspects of risk assessment.

Consider the following two examples. First, imagine the case of a leader who is confronted with a situation where terrorists are threatening to blow up a plane full of people. The plane is sitting on a runway. The leader gets a variety of opinions from her staff and entertains several options. Her military advisors tell her that they have a plan. They are fairly certain they will be able to free the hostages safely. The leader is morally opposed to giving in to terrorists but also morally opposed to killing the terrorists if it is not necessary. She has duties to a variety of stakeholders and long-term and short-term moral obligations to consider. She weighs the moral and technical arguments carefully and chooses to attack, but she is unlucky. Things go wrong and the hostages get killed.

Now consider the case of another leader in the same situation. In this case the negotiations are moving forward slowly, and his advisors tell him that an attack is highly risky. The leader is impatient with the hostages and his cautious advisors. He does not play out the moral arguments. For him it is simple – 'I don't give a damn who gets killed – these terrorists are not going to get the best of me!' He chooses to attack. This leader is lucky. The attack goes better than expected. One of the terrorists trips and loses his weapon. He is subdued, his colleagues are overpowered and the hostages are freed without harm (Ciulla, 2004).

Some are very careful about risking human lives, but they are unlucky, whereas others are not very careful about risking human lives but very lucky. Most really difficult moral decisions leaders make are risky, because they frequently have imperfect or incomplete information and lack control over all of the variables that will affect the outcome. Leaders who fail at something are worthy of forgiveness when they act with deliberate care and for the right moral reasons, even though followers may not always forgive them or lose confidence in their leadership. Americans did not blame President Jimmy Carter for the botched attempt to free the hostages in Iran, but it was one more thing that shook their faith in his leadership. He was unlucky because, if the mission had been successful, it might have strengthened people's faith in him as a leader and improved his chances of retaining the presidency.

The irony of moral luck is that leaders who are reckless and do not base their actions on sound moral and practical arguments are usually condemned when they fail and celebrated as heroes when they succeed. That is why Immanuel Kant said that, because we cannot always know the results of our actions, moral judgments should be based on the right moral principles and not contingent on outcomes (Kant, 1993). The reckless, lucky leader does not demonstrate moral or technical competency, yet, because of the outcome, often gets credit for having both. Since history usually focuses on outcomes, it is not always clear how much luck, skill and morality figured in the success or failure of a leader. This is why we need to devote more study to the ethics of leaders' decision-making processes in addition to their actions and behavior.

Moral standards
People often say that 'leaders should be held to a higher moral standard', but does that make sense? If true, would it then be acceptable for everyone else to live by lower moral standards? The curious thing about morality is that, if you set the moral standards for leaders too high, requiring something

close to moral perfection, then few people will be qualified to be leaders or will want to be leaders. For example, how many of us could live up to the standard of having never lied, said an unkind word, or reneged on a promise? Ironically, when we set moral standards for leaders too high, we become even more dissatisfied with our leaders because few are able to live up to our expectations. We set moral standards for leaders too low, however, when we reduce them to nothing more than following the law or, worse, simply not being as unethical as their predecessors. A business leader may follow all laws and yet be highly immoral in the way he or she runs a business. Laws are moral minimums that do not and cannot capture the scope and complexity of morality. For example, an elected official may be law abiding and, unlike his or her predecessor, live by 'strong family values'. The official may also have little concern for the disadvantaged. Not caring about the poor and the sick is not against the law, but is such a leader ethical?

History is littered with leaders who did not think they were subject to the same moral standards of honesty, propriety and so on as the rest of society. One explanation for this is so obvious that it has become a cliché: power corrupts. David G. Winter (2002) and David McClellend's (1975) work on power motives and on socialized and personalized charisma offer psychological accounts of this kind of leader behavior. Michael Maccoby (2000) and a host of others have talked about narcissistic leaders who, on the bright side, are exceptional and, on the dark side, consider themselves exceptions to the rules. Others have written about the way success corrupts leaders and how they lose strategic focus and abuse their power to get what they want and cover it up if they get caught (Ludwig and Longenecker, 1993).

E.P. Hollander's (1964) work on social exchange demonstrates how emerging leaders who are loyal to and competent at attaining group goals gain 'idiosyncrasy credits' that allow them to deviate from the groups' norms to suit common goals. As Price (2000) has argued, given the fact that we often grant leaders permission to deviate or be an exception to the rules, it is not difficult to see why leaders sometimes make themselves exceptions to moral constraints. This is why I do not think we should hold leaders to different or higher moral standards than ourselves. If anything, we have to make sure that we hold them to the same standards as the rest of society. What we should expect and hope is that our leaders will fail less than most people at meeting ethical standards, while pursuing and achieving the goals of their constituents. So when we say leaders should be held to a higher moral standard what we really mean is that leaders must be more successful at living up to moral standards, because the price of their failure is greater than that of an ordinary person. The really interesting question for leadership development and organizational and political theory is, what can we do to keep leaders from the moral failures that stem from being in a leadership role? The checks and balances of a democracy and corporate boards and auditors are some of the formal structures we use to prevent the moral failure of leaders. We also need to develop self-discipline in aspiring leaders.

Altruism
Some leadership scholars use altruism as the moral standard for ethical leadership. In their book, *Ethical Dimensions of Leadership*, Rabindra Kanungo and Manuel Mendonca write, 'Our thesis is that organizational leaders are truly effective only when they are motivated by a concern for others, when their actions are invariably guided primarily by the criteria of the benefit to others even if it results in some cost to oneself (Kanungo and Mendonca, 1996, p. 35). When people talk about altruism, they usually contrast altruism with selfishness, or behavior that benefits oneself at a cost to others (Ozinga, 1999). Altruism is a very high personal standard and, as such, is problematic for a number of reasons. Both selfishness and altruism refer to extreme types of motivation and behavior. Edwin Locke brings out this extreme side of altruism in a dialogue with Bruce Avolio (Avolio and Locke, 2002). Locke argues that, if altruism is about self-sacrifice, then leaders who want to be truly altruistic will pick a job that they do not like or value, expect no rewards or pleasure from their job or achievements, and give themselves over totally to serving the wants of others. He then asks if anyone would want to be a leader under such circumstances? One might also ask, would we even want such a person as a leader? While I do not agree with Locke's argument that leaders should act according to their self-interest, he does articulate the practical problem of using altruism as a standard of moral behavior for leaders.

Avolio's argument against Locke is based on equally extreme cases. He draws on his work at West Point, where a central moral principle in the military is willingness to make the ultimate sacrifice for the good of the group. Avolio also uses Mother Teresa as one of his examples of altruistic behavior. In these cases, self-sacrifice may be less about the ethics of leaders in general and more about the jobs of soldiers and missionaries. The Locke and Avolio debate pits the extreme aspects of altruism against its heroic side. Here, as in the extensive philosophic literature on self-interest and altruism, the debate spins round and round and does not get us very far. Ethics is about the relationship of individuals to others, so, in a sense, both sides are right and wrong.

Altruism is a motive for acting, but it is not in and of itself a normative principle (Nagel, 1970). Requiring leaders to act altruistically is not only a tall order, but it does not guarantee that the leader or his or her actions will be moral. For example, stealing from the rich to give to the poor, or Robinhoodism, is morally problematic (Ciulla, 2003). A terrorist leader who becomes a suicide bomber might have purely altruistic intentions, but the means that he uses to carry out his mission – killing innocent people – is not considered ethical even if his cause is a just one. One might also argue, as one does against suicide, that it is unethical for a person to sacrifice his or her life for any reason because of the impact that it has on loved ones. Great leaders such as Martin Luther King, Jr and Gandhi behaved altruistically, but their leadership was ethical because of the means that they used to achieve their ends and the morality of their causes. We have a particular respect for leaders who are martyred for a cause, but the morality of King and Gandhi goes beyond self-sacrifice. Achieving their objectives for social justice while empowering and disciplining followers to use nonviolent resistance is morally good and, some would say, morally awesome leadership.

Altruism is also described as a way of assessing an act or behavior, regardless of the agent's intention. For example, Stephen Worchel, Joel Cooper and George Goethals define altruism as acts that 'render help to another person' (Worchel *et al.*, 1988, p. 394). If altruism is nothing more than helping people, then it is a more manageable standard, but again simply helping people is not necessarily ethical (Price, 2003). It depends on how you help them and what you help them do. It is true that people often help each other, without making great sacrifices. If altruism is nothing more than helping people, then we have radically redefined the concept by eliminating the self-sacrificing requirement.

Manuel Mendonca offers a further modification of altruism in what he calls 'mutual altruism' (Mendonca, 2001). Mutual altruism boils down to utilitarianism and enlightened self-interest. If we follow this line of thought, we should also add other moral principles, such as the golden rule, to this category of altruism. It is interesting to note that Confucius explicitly calls the golden rule altruism. When asked by Tzu-Kung what the guiding principle of life is, Confucius answers, 'It is the word altruism [*shu*]. Do not do unto others what you do not want them to do to you' (Confucius, 1963, p. 44). The golden rule crops up as a fundamental moral principle in most major cultures (Wattles, 1996). The golden rule tells us how to transform knowledge of one's own self-interest into concern for the interests of others. In other words, it provides the bridge between altruism and self-interest (others and the self) and allows for enlightened self-interest. This highlights another reason why altruism is not a useful standard for the moral behavior of leaders. The minute we start to modify altruism, it not only loses its initial meaning, it starts to sound like a wide variety of other ethical terms, which makes it very confusing.

Plato believed that leadership required a person to sacrifice his or her immediate self-interests, but this did not amount to altruism. In Book II of the *Republic*, Plato writes,

> In a city of good men, if it came into being, the citizens would fight in order not to rule ... There it would be clear that anyone who is really a true ruler doesn't by nature seek his own advantage but that of his subjects. And everyone, knowing this, would rather be benefited by others than take the trouble to benefit them. (Plato, 1992, 347d)

Rather than requiring altruistic motives, Plato is referring to the stress, hard work and (sometimes) thankless task of being a morally good leader. He is saying that, if you are a just person, leadership will take a toll on you and your life. He goes on to say that the only reason a just person accepts a leadership role is out of fear of punishment. He tells us, 'Now the greatest punishment, if one isn't willing to rule, is to be ruled by someone worse than oneself. And I think it is fear of this that makes decent people rule when they do' (ibid., 347c). Leadership here is not motivated by altruism but by enlightened self-interest. Plato's comment sheds light on why we sometimes feel more comfortable with people who are reluctant to lead than with those who really want to do so. Today, as in the past, we worry that people who are too eager to lead want the power and position for themselves, or that they do not fully understand the responsibilities of leadership. Plato also tells us that, while leadership is not in the just person's immediate self-interest, it is in their long-term interest. He goes on to argue that it is in our best interest to be just, because just people are happier and lead better lives than unjust people.

While we admire self-sacrifice, morality sometimes calls upon leaders to do things that are against their self-interest. This is less about altruism than it is about the nature of both morality and leadership. We want leaders to put the interests of followers first, but most leaders do not pay a price for doing that on a daily basis, nor do most circumstances require them to calculate their interests in relation to the interests of their followers. The practice of leadership is to guide and look after the goals, missions and aspirations of groups, organizations, countries or causes. When leaders do this, they are doing their job; when they do not do this, they are not doing their job. Looking after the interests of others is as much about what leaders do in their role as leaders as it is about the moral quality of leadership. Implicit in the idea of leadership effectiveness is the notion that leaders do their job. When a mayor does not look after the interests of a city, she is not only ineffective, she is unethical for not keeping the promise that she made when sworn in as mayor. When she does look after the interests of the city, it is not because she is altruistic, but because she is doing her job. In this way, altruism is built into the way we describe what leaders do. While altruism is not the best concept for characterizing the ethics of leadership, scholars' interest in altruism reflects a desire to capture, either implicitly or explicitly, the ethics-and-effectiveness notion of good leadership.

Biology, reciprocity and cooperation
Biologists offer some intriguing insights into human nature that are relevant to understanding the role of altruism and self-interest in leadership and ethics. For example, in his provocative book, *The Selfish Gene* (1976), Richard Dawkins argues that Darwin's notion of the survival of the fittest is not about individual survival, but rather about survival of the gene pool. On his account, people appear to act altruistically by sacrificing themselves for their kin, but in effect are simply protecting their gene pool. Dawkins says that genes are voracious replicators. He argues we are born selfish and cannot depend on our genes to build societies where people cooperate unselfishly. Fortunately, Dawkins tells us, we do not have to do what our genes want because people are more than their genes. Culture provides practices and experiences that people imitate and replicate across generations. Dawkins calls these 'memes'. Memes include everything from the belief in God and an afterlife, to making pots. They are the parts of culture that have strong survival value and are passed on generation after generation. Dawkins says, 'When you plant a fertile meme in my mind you literally parasitize my brain, turning it into a vehicle for the meme's propagation in the same way that a virus may parasitize the genetic mechanism of a host's cell' (Dawkins, 1976, p. 192).

If genes are selfish and memes are culturally constructed, is cooperation unnatural? Do humans need leaders because we were born with uncooperative genes? Again, if we turn to the animal kingdom, we find some curious examples of reciprocity and cooperation, behaviors that are not selfish. Consider the case of the stickleback fish. Sticklebacks risk their lives to inspect the threat of predators, and they do this in pairs. A stickleback will tolerate defection of a fish that has cooperated in the past more than it will tolerate defection from one who has not. When a stickleback goes out on patrol, it will pick the fish that cooperated best in the past. Researchers have found similar behavior among vampire bats. When a vampire bat feeds, it will often share its meal with a bat that is hungry. Bats tend to share first with bats that have shared with them in the past, then with other bats from their cave, and then with bats from other caves. This sort of behavior shows that other species in nature seem to cooperate and practice reciprocity.

Reciprocity, according to Matt Ridley (1996), requires repetitive interactions, recognition and memory of what others have done, and an ability to keep score. Many animals are born knowing what every child is taught: if you don't cooperate, no one will want to play with you. Reciprocity cast this way is certainly not altruism, but self-interest, albeit of an enlightened kind. Biologists define as altruistic behavior in which an animal either does not reproduce or risks its life so that close relatives can survive. For example, bees risk their lives to defend the hive. They do this so that their genes survive. Ridley says that, in this case, 'their courage is gene selfish' (ibid., p. 179). He goes on to argue that the ability of humans to act altruistically towards others is passed on genetically from altruistic behavior that they practice towards their family. In an era of globalization, the tendency of animals and humans to favor family, friends and neighbors is not only very evident, but also a key consideration for leaders.

It is ironic that some biologists focus on the selfish nature of human beings, while a growing number of behavioral economists are talking about our cooperative side. The research of these two groups converges in interesting ways. Dawkins believes that society needs to be set up in ways that allow altruistic and cooperative memes to flourish. Economist Robert Frank asserts that societies based on the assumptions of the 'rational economic man' teach people to be self-interested. Frank found that business students who had been taught to maximize their own interests performed worse in prisoner dilemma games than astronomy majors (Frank *et al.*, 1993). In the game, players may cooperate with each other or defect. Defection leads to a higher payoff, but if both players defect they achieve a worse result than if they had cooperated. The game is played many times so that experience can guide the players' behaviors. Tit for tat is the best strategy. Players cooperate on the first move and then do what the other players do on subsequent moves. The best strategy in the game is to be cooperative, but not a pushover. Players must try not to be jealous of opponents' success and they must show forgiveness when an opponent defects. In the game, the unselfish players outperform the greedy ones in the long run. Cooperative successes benefit strong and weak opponents. This is also the case with evolution: stronger rules for cooperation outplay weaker ones. Darwin's notion of individual advantage accounts for cooperation as the best long-term strategy (Axelrod, 1984).

Cooperation in the tit-for-tat scenario is based on reciprocity. There is, however, a moral difference between reciprocity that has an immediate payoff (for example, I give you money and you give me an espresso) and reciprocity that is done without knowledge or anticipation of a future payoff. The latter looks more like altruistic motivation and also conforms to some of our ideas of morality (especially the idea of a good will in

Kant's moral theory). For a real life example of long-term reciprocity, consider the case of Merck & Co. After World War II, tuberculosis thrived in Japan. Most Japanese could not afford to buy Merck's powerful drug, streptomycin, to fight it. Merck donated a large supply of the drug to the Japanese public. The Japanese did not forget Merck's kindness. In 1983, almost 40 years later, the Japanese government allowed Merck to purchase 50.02 per cent of Banyu Pharmaceutical. At the time this was the largest foreign investment in a Japanese company (Useem, 1998). The Merck case illustrates ethical behavior and long-term reciprocity. The company did not know, and perhaps did not expect, that there would be any future payoff, so we could say its motivation was altruistic. But there is a sense in which most moral action is based, not simply on good will, but on the conscious or unconscious sense that, in the long run, and in some unknown way, it is beneficial to behave ethically. From a biological perspective we may sense that, when we are ethical, it is more likely that people will 'want to play with us' in the future. In Merck's case it turned out that the Japanese wanted to play or do business with them 40 years later.

Reciprocity is central to leadership because it is the essential element of moral concepts such as loyalty, trust, justice and fairness (Becker, 1986). Reciprocity is so basic to human relationships and moral concepts that it is surprising leadership scholars have not focused more on the moral implications of transactional leadership. Transactional leadership, especially viewed in terms of long-term reciprocity, promises richer insights into the social and moral dynamics of leadership than the current emphasis on transformational leadership (Burns, 1978), which is often portrayed by scholars as the most ethical kind of leadership.

Are ethical leaders 'unnatural'?
The themes of altruism, self-interest, cooperation and reciprocity are parts of ethics as well as leadership. For example, Kant believed that a moral action is an act of the will that goes against what we might be naturally inclined to do. For Kant, ethical action always hurts a bit. The will keeps us in check against many of our inclinations. According to Thomas Hobbes (1983), the job of the leader (sovereign) is to enforce the social contract. Citizens would give up some of their liberty to pursue their self-interest to get protection from the state so that they could pursue their self-interests without fear. Kant and Hobbes fall into the selfish gene camp because they put leaders, ethics and laws in charge of keeping us from doing some things that may come naturally. Religion has also done its bit to keep us in line, often through intensive reciprocal arrangements. God or the gods are leaders who keep score, threaten eternal damnation or a long time-out in purgatory to anyone who does not control his or her natural urges and inclinations.

The relationship of followers to their God or gods is often portrayed as transformational, but in practice is frequently transactional. Throughout history, people have made deals with their gods through sacrifices, promises, pleading, gifts and prayers. There is a strong parallel with the reciprocal relationships people have with their gods and their leaders.

Mill (1987) had a different view of human nature than Kant and Hobbes. His approach is perhaps most relevant to leaders. First, Mill places more confidence in the human ability to cooperate and act on the basis of what is good for others. People learn through their own experience and the experiences of history and their culture. This collective experience and knowledge is analogous to what Dawkins calls 'meme replicators'. One objection to utilitarianism is that most people cannot or do not know what the greatest good is for the greatest number of people. Mill points out that, usually, we do not make utilitarian judgments that concern everyone in the world. We know from our own experiences what other people want and usually we make choices based on what is good for a specific group of people, not the whole world. Another objection to Mill's theory is that the utilitarian calculation concerning how to determine what will bring about the greatest happiness or serve the common good is too cold and calculating. It does not consider individual relationships. To this Mill replies that morality is about objective ideas and the minute you start molding your idea of the good to the relationship you have with individuals, you lose it. Mill recognized the importance of moral consistency and was not about to make exceptions for family and friends. Moral consistency is an essential part of trust. It is what makes reciprocity work and it facilitates cooperation. All of these things are central to effective leadership in any context and in any culture.

Mill, like Kant, seems to argue that morality is a kind of counterweight to the way we might naturally behave. Utilitarianism captures the most distinctive challenge of leadership. Leaders are, at least in principle, supposed to look out for the good of more people than the ordinary person. In a sense, leaders of multinational organizations must be superutilitarians, because of the sheer size and the complexity of calculations about greatest good for the greatest number. Yet, if we are naturally selfish and naturally inclined to look after our own genes, clans, friends, communities and countries, then morality that concerns a wide array of distant strangers may be a struggle against nature (Wolfe, 1989). Philosopher Peter Singer (1982) offers a more hopeful view. He believes that humanity has made moral progress, by expanding the circle of people to whom we have moral obligations. Howard Gardner (1995) also notes that some of the best leaders are those who are the most widely inclusive of other groups. Utilitarian leaders – meaning those who put the greatest good above the interests of their families, friends and clans – are quite extraordinary. This kind of leadership is challenging because it is, in a sense, unnatural, whereas selfish leadership based on cronyism and individual gain is quite natural. Perhaps this is why there is still so much of the latter in the world today.

Family values

One reason why people even ask, 'Are leaders born or made?' is that the majority of leaders throughout recorded human history have been born into families of leaders. From pharaohs, to emperors, to kings, to leaders of a number of countries today, leaders have sought to keep leadership in their gene pool. This is how they look after their families, friends and, it is hoped, their constituents. Family genes also play a role in the way leaders build coalitions and enlist cooperation. Families matter when we talk about leadership because many countries in the world (democratic or undemocratic) are ruled by family dynasties. It is sometimes easy to forget that most businesses in the world are family-owned. Almost 95 per cent of American businesses are family-owned, including 40 per cent of the Fortune 500 companies (Bellow, 2003). In Asia, family dynasties control 46.6 per cent of the GDP in the Philippines, 84.2 per cent in Hong Kong and 76.2 per cent in Malaysia (*Economist*, 2001, p. 6).

Nepotism is a complicated problem for leaders of every stripe. People who are not in leadership positions are free to aid their family members in any way they can. Leaders can, too, but sometimes at the cost of other goals, such as competent administrators or getting the best price for goods and services. The ancient Chinese realized that nepotism was a problem for leaders. In the words of an old Chinese proverb, 'When a man becomes an official, his wife, children, dogs, cats, and even chickens fly up to heaven' (Bellow, 2003, p. 95). One of Confucius's greatest contributions to an ethical doctrine is that which described how to balance the duties of filial piety with duties to the public and principles of merit (Confucius, 1963). The Latin root of the word 'nepotism' is *nepos*, which means nephew or grandson. The word comes from the Italian *nipóte*, which refers to any male or female family member. The actual word 'nepotismo' originated in the fourteenth or fifteenth century and was used to describe the corrupt practice of popes who appointed relatives and illegitimate children to offices.

When we look around the world today, we often see the tension between leaders' obligations to family and clan and obligations to organizations and others outside the clan. By clan, I not only include family, but friends of the leader and the leader's family. Consider the following case that might be used in a business ethics class.

Imagine that you are the regional director of a large multinational manufacturing concern who oversees operations in several foreign countries. A year ago, you promoted a talented, hard working, local employee to run one of your factories. On a visit to the region you decide to stop in and visit the factory. When you arrive at the manager's office, you notice that the secretary has the same last name as the manager. You mention this to him and he tells you that she is his sister. He takes you on a tour of the plant and as you walk around the manager is greeted by various people working there as 'uncle', 'cousin' and 'father'. You ask him, 'Is this some sort of custom or are all of these people your relatives?' He replies, 'Yes, I have a duty to take care of my family.' You then discover that, of the 80 employees on the payroll over half are members of the manager's extended family.

The first reaction of most American MBA students is that the manager is unethical. Hiring one's relatives is unethical because the manager's relatives may not be the most qualified workers. Yet they also might be hard working and smart, like the manager. One might also argue that the factory manager does not own the factory and therefore does not have the right to keep the jobs within his family.

Some might think that these things only happen in developing and/or undemocratic countries, yet they are common in the Western world too. Consider what happened in the aftermath of the 2000 presidential elections in the USA. The election pitted a son of a president against the son of a senator. When George W. Bush won, he appointed Michael Powell, son of Colin Powell, chairman of the FEC, and Eugene Scalia, son of Supreme Court Justice Antonin Scalia, the chief labor attorney. In addition to these appointments, Bush made the vice president's daughter, Elizabeth Cheney, deputy assistant secretary of state and her husband chief counsel for the Office of Management and Budget.

If the primary obligation of the leader is to make choices based on the greatest good for the organization or state, there is, in principle at least, nothing wrong with appointing family members and friends' family members to jobs, as long as they are the best qualified. However, in a democracy, the other moral principle at stake is equal opportunity. When qualified people do not have equal access to compete for a job on merit, it undermines public trust and perceptions of fairness. The same is true in organizations that claim to hold merit as the criterion for advancement. The Bush appointees may be well qualified for their jobs, but there may also be others out there who, if given a chance to compete for the job, would be better.

One might argue that nepotism in business is different from politics because a family business is private. Adam Bellow (2003) argues that people do not mind if leaders appoint relatives to jobs as long as they are competent. William Ford runs the Ford motor company, Jane Lauder heads Estée Lauder, and Bill Wrigly manages his family's chewing gum business.

On the one hand, we do not think that it is unfair that William Ford is CEO of Ford; he has a right to do so because it is his family's business. On the other hand, it would matter if an incompetent family member ran Ford because his or her incompetence would have a negative impact on a number of stakeholders. For example, stockholders and financiers complained when Rupert Murdoch appointed his 30-year-old son James to run BSkyB, Europe's largest satellite broadcaster (*Economist*, 2003). There were also concerns when Liz Mohn, the founder's wife, took over as family representative on the board of the international publishing giant Bertelsmann (*Economist*, 2004).

One intriguing question for future research is whether you get better or worse leaders as a result of nepotism. If genes shape our dispositions, leadership might be a genetic predisposition like music or art. The Bach and Brueghel families each produced great musicians and artists. On the one hand, leadership, like music or art, may also be a family business. Families of artists or leaders can provide the right combination of nature and nurture to foster certain talents. On the other hand, family connections and power may shield a person from developing important leadership skills and competing with others on merit. Leadership, unlike art and music, requires a complex set of social tasks with people outside the clan. Perhaps leaders develop better skills when they have to make it on their own. Some leadership scholars have noticed that a striking number of leaders lost their fathers as children. Gardner notes that 60 per cent of British prime ministers lost their fathers when they were young. He suggests that children who lose a parent when they are young are forced 'to formulate their own social and moral domains' (Gardner, 1995, p. 24).

Leadership, ethics and our common biology

We should never underestimate the pull of our biology that is inherent in conflicts between loyalty to family and friends and a leader's obligation to serve the best interests of the organization, group or country. It is more difficult to trust and feel moral obligations to strangers than it is to family and friends. The physical environment thrives on diversity. We know that, when societies close themselves off from outsiders, they become neurotic, vulnerable and weak, like an overbred dog (Diamond, 1997). The same is true for communities and organizations where leaders only look after the interests of their families and friends. Over time, nepotism, cronyism and, for that matter, nationalism become fertile breeding grounds for corrupt leadership.

The ability to build trust in strangers is not easy because leaders must first trust others before others will trust them (Solomon, 1998). Good leadership requires an enhanced capacity to feel morally obligated to a wide range of others. This is not a skill, but a kind of knowledge and perspective on the world. As James Q. Wilson notes (1993), people all over the world seem to have a moral sense that allows them to make moral judgments about distant others. Robert Wright argues that our common biology is the basis for our sense of morality. As humans we have many of the same inclinations and feelings, but they get channeled in different ways by different cultures (Wright, 1994). Leadership appears to be an unnatural act in the sense that it requires self-restraint and imagination to care for the wellbeing of strangers. It is also a natural act in that cooperation does seem to come naturally to humans and other species and is often the best way to serve our self-interests.

Leadership scholars need to bring in other disciplines such as biology to develop a fuller picture of human nature than we get from the literature in psychology and organizational behavior. A rich picture of human nature serves as the foundation for understanding what ethical and effective leadership looks like for people everywhere, not just the ones in a particular culture or organization. We know that we are shaped by nature and nurture and governed by our free will and fate. The complicated relationship between these dichotomies offers insight into how to develop leaders who know when to act naturally and when to resist doing so. As Stephen Pinker observes, the voice of the species is 'that infuriating, mysterious, predictable, and eternally fascinating thing we call human nature' (Pinker, 2002, p. 24).

References

Aristotle (1984), *The Politics*, trans. Carnes Lord, Chicago: University of Chicago Press.
Avolio, B.J. and Edwin E. Locke (2002), 'Contrasting different philosophies of leader motivation: altruism versus egoistic', *The Leadership Quarterly*, **13** (4), 169–71.
Axelrod, R.M. (1984), *The Evolution of Cooperation*, New York: Basic Books.
Becker, L. (1986), *Reciprocity*, London and New York: Routledge & Kegan Paul.
Bellow, A. (2003), *In Praise of Nepotism*, New York: Doubleday.
Burns, J.M. (1978), *Leadership*, New York: Harper Torchbooks.
Ciulla, J.B. (1995), 'Leadership ethics: mapping the territory', *The Business Ethics Quarterly*, **5**(1), 5–28.
Ciulla, J.B. (1999), 'The importance of leadership in shaping business values', *Long Range Planning*, **32** (2), pp. 166–72.
Ciulla, J.B. (2001), 'Trust and the future of leadership', in Norman Bowie (ed.), *Companion to Business Ethics*, New York: Basil Blackwell, pp. 334–51.
Ciulla, J.B. (2003) 'The ethical challenges of non-profit leaders', in R. Riggio (ed.), *Improving Leadership in Non-Profit Organizations*, Mahwah, NJ: Erlbaum, pp. 63–75.
Ciulla, J.B. (2004), 'Ethics and leadership effectiveness', in J. Antonakis, A.T. Cianciolo, and R.J. Sternberg (eds), *The Nature of Leadership*, Thousand Oaks: Sage Publications, pp. 302–27.
Confucius (1963), 'Selections from the Analects', in Wing-tsit Chan (ed. and trans.), *A Source Book in Chinese Philosophy*, Princeton: Princeton University Press.
Dawkins, R. (1976), *The Selfish Gene*, New York: Oxford University Press.
Dennett, D. (1995), *Darwin's Dangerous Idea: Evolution and the Meanings of Life*, New York: Simon & Schuster.
Dennett, D. (2003), *Freedom Evolves*, New York: Viking.

Diamond, J.M. (1997), *Guns, Germs & Steel: the Fates of Human Societies*, New York: W.W. Norton.

Economist (2001), 'Keeping it in the family', *Asian Business Survey*, **7**, 4–6.

Economist (2003), 'Like father like son', 6 November, 82.

Economist (2004), 'In the court of queen B', 4 March, 77.

Frank, R.H., T. Gilovich and D.T. Regan (1993), 'Does studying economics inhibit cooperation?', *Journal of Economic Perspectives*, **7** (2), 159–71.

Gardner, H. (1995), *Leading Minds: An Anatomy of Leadership*, New York: Basic Books.

Garrett, L. (2000), 'Added foe in AIDS war: skeptics', *Newsday*, News Section, 29 March, A6.

Hartman, E. (1988), *Conceptual Foundations of Organization Theory,* Cambridge, MA: Ballinger.

Hobbes, T. (1983), *Leviathan*, London: Dent.

Hollander, E.P. (1964), *Leaders, Groups and Influence*, New York: Oxford University Press.

Kant, I. (1993), *Foundations of the Metaphysics of Morals*, trans. J.W. Ellington, Indianapolis, IN: Hackett Publishing Company.

Kanungo, R. and M. Mendonca (1996), *Ethical Dimensions of Leadership*, Thousand Oaks, CA: Sage.

Ludwig, D. and C. Longenecker (1993), 'The Bathsheba syndrome: the ethical failure of successful leaders', *The Journal of Business Ethics*, **12** (4), 265–73.

Maccoby, M. (2000), 'Narcissistic leaders', *The Harvard Business Review*, **78** (1), 69–75.

McClelland, D. (1975) *Power: The Inner Experience*, New York: Halsted Press.

Mendonca, M. (2001), 'Preparing for ethical leadership in organizations', *Canadian Journal of Administrative Sciences*, **18** (4), 266–76.

Mill, J.S. (1987), 'What utilitarianism is', in *Utilitarianism and Other Essays*, ed. Alan Ryan, New York: Penguin Books, pp. 276–97.

Moldoveanu, M. and E. Langer (2002), 'When "stupid" is smarter than we are', in Robert Sternberg (ed.), *Why Smart People Can Be So Stupid*, New Haven: Yale University Press, pp. 212–31.

Nagel, T. (1970), *The Possibility of Altruism*, Oxford: Clarendon Press.

Ozinga, J.R. (1999), *Altruism*, Westport, CT: Praeger.

Plato (1992), *Republic*, trans. G.M.A. Grube, Indianapolis, IN: Hackett Publishing.

Pinker, S. (2002), *The Blank Slate: the Modern Denial of Human Nature*, New York: Viking.

Prezzolini, G. (1928), *Nicolo Machiavelli, the Florentine*, trans. Ralph Roeder, New York: Brentanos.

Price, T.L. (2000), 'Explaining ethical failures of leadership', *The Leadership and Organizational Development Journal*, **21** (4), 177—84.

Price, T.L. (2003), 'The ethics of authentic transformational leadership', *Leadership Quarterly*, **14** (1), 67–81.

Ridley, M. (1996), *The Origins of Virtue: Human Instincts and the Evolution of Cooperation*, New York: Penguin Books.

Rost, J. (1991), *Leadership for the Twenty-First Century*, New York: Praeger.

Schwartz, J. (2001), 'Up from the ashes, one firm rebuilds', *New York Times*, 16 September, section 3, p. 1.

Singer, P. (1982), *The Expanding Circle*, New York: New American Library.

Sisson, A.G. (2003), *The Moral Capital of leaders*, Cheltenham, UK and Northampton, MA, USA: Edward Elgar.

Solomon, R.C. (1992), *Ethics and Excellence: Cooperation and Integrity in Business*, New York: Oxford University Press, pp. 87–108.

Solomon, R.C. (1998), 'Ethical leadership, emotions and trust: beyond "charisma"', in Joanne B. Ciulla (ed.), *Ethics, The Heart of Leadership*, Westbury, CT: Quorum Books.

The Compact Oxford English Dictionary (1991), Oxford: Clarendon Press.

Useem, M. (1998), *The Leadership Moment*, New York: Times Business Books.

Wattles, J. (1996), *The Golden Rule*, New York: Oxford University Press.

Williams, B.A. (1981), *Moral Luck*, Cambridge: Cambridge University Press.

Wilson, J.Q. (1993), *The Moral Sense*, New York: Free Press.
Winter, D. (2002), 'The motivational dimensions of leadership: power, achievement and affiliation', in R.E. Riggio, S.E. Murphy and F.J. Pirozzolo (eds), *Multiple Intelligences and Leadership*, Mahwah, NJ: Lawrence Erlbaum Associates, pp. 196–207.
Wolfe, A. (1989), *Whose Keeper? Social Science and Moral Obligation*, Berkeley: University of California Press.
Worchel, S., J. Cooper and G. Goethals (1988), *Understanding Social Psychology*, Chicago: Dorsey.
Wright, R. (1994), *The Moral Animal: Why We Are the Way We Are*, New York: Vintage Books.

10 Corporate responsibility, accountability and stakeholder relationships: will voluntary action suffice?
Sandra Waddock

Introduction

Stakeholder theory has advanced significantly in the years since Ed Freeman popularized the term in his book *Strategic Management: A Stakeholder Approach* (Freeman, 1984). From an almost fully corporate centric 'spoke and wheel' model of stakeholder 'management,' stakeholder theory has moved toward understanding that stakeholder *relationships* are at the heart of stakeholder theory (Evan and Freeman, 1988; Freeman and Gilbert, 1988) and ultimately of corporate performance itself (Andriof and Waddock, 2002; Andriof *et al.*, 2003), a reality that progressive companies understand clearly. Indeed recent work on networks suggests that organizations and individuals can be stakeholders to an issue, forming networks for local and global action (Waddell, 2003).

Companies, in the emerging stakeholder view (Post *et al.*, 2002a), are recognized as inextricably embedded in a web of relationships with stakeholders, some constructive, some destructive (Mitchell *et al.*, 1997). All of these relations combine to constitute the context in which the company operates, not to mention the foundation of the company itself (Waddock, 2002a; Andriof and Waddock, 2002). As testimony to the progress of stakeholder thinking, the term 'stakeholder' and its economic analog 'stakeholder capitalism' have entered popular parlance.

Contrasted to the theoretical mainstream terminology of stakeholder management (for example, Post *et al.*, 2002a, 2002b; Johnson-Cramer *et al.*, 2003), the concept of stakeholder relationships underscores the mutuality, the give and take, and the element of power sharing that is explicit in the terms 'stakeholder engagement' (Svendsen, 1998; Andriof and Waddock, 2002) and 'stakeholder relationships' (or relationship management). Stakeholder theory suggests that companies and their managers should recognize that they are in relationship with each other, that their actions, as Freeman (1984) stated long ago, mutually affect each other. That is the theory, anyway. Stakeholder *practice*, or what I have elsewhere termed 'leading corporate citizenship' (Waddock, 2002b), may be a different story. The wave of corporate scandals during the early 2000s in the United States has exacerbated the calls for greater corporate responsibility, transparency and accountability that have been coming from labor, human rights, environmental and anti-corruption activists, not to mention anti-globalization forces, during the past dozen or so years. The spectacular collapses of former corporate stars like Enron, WorldCom and accounting giant Arthur Andersen have led to renewed interest in legislation and regulation because some stakeholders, including the purportedly dominant stakeholder, investors, have been badly hurt by these scandals. Employees have been laid off, pension funds destroyed, supply chain and customer relationships disrupted and the accuracy of financial reports called into question, with the result that public opinion about business has hit an all-time low. What trust there was that companies would do the right thing evaporated in the swell of scandal. Even the much vaunted first among (non)-equal stakeholders (shareholders) have been ill treated by the shenanigans of top managers, with some (potential) pensioners (such as Enron's) losing most of their life savings and other shareholders also losing most of their investment.

Although not new to the above scandals, the consequence of the distrust of companies and their executives is that significantly greater openness in corporate reporting, transparency and accountability is demanded by many stakeholders. Employees with investments in corporate pension funds care not only about their jobs but also about the security of their pensions, as do many labor unions. Social investors and many social activists care about the responsibility of companies with respect to specific issues related to corporate decisions (for example, labor practices, environmental sustainability, outsourcing and job creation). Customers are concerned about the conditions in which products are produced, and regulators want to prevent further abuses.

By the end of the 1990s, activists had become significantly concerned about labor and human rights practices in the increasingly long supply chains of consumer goods, clothing and toy companies, among others. Anti-globalization protests erupted around the 1999 World Trade Organization meeting in Seattle and then in different settings around the globe as protesters attempted to draw attention to the impacts of transnational firms (and WTO, IMF and World Bank policies) on communities, employees, countries and the natural environment. Additionally there is increasing recognition that corporate responsibility initiatives need to be embedded in stakeholder practices and relationships and not be mere window dressing or public relations activities. Even meaningful 'do good' activities such as strong philanthropic programs and foundations, excellent public–private partnerships and investment in local communities no longer suffice to build trust in companies (cf. Lydenberg, 2003).

Internal responsibility management

Company responses to public outrage about scandals and related unethical practices vary dramatically. Responses can range from company leaders burying their collective heads in the sand and hoping the problem will go away, to denying that a problem exists in the first place. (One highly placed financial executive recently told a gathering of faculty discussing business ethics that in his entire career he had never seen an ethical problem, simply failing to recognize that moral issues are inextricably embedded in many management practices. As is now known from numerous scandals that surfaced in the financial services industry, ethical problems are rampant.)

More proactive companies, however, take systemic management approaches to managing their stakeholder and ecological responsibilities, developing responsibility management systems similar to quality management systems. Such responsibility management approaches are particularly relevant for companies with long supply chains in developing countries who have suffered diminished reputation as a result of having been the targets of anti-sweatshop, anti-child labor and human rights activists (for example, Waddock and Bodwell, 2002). Companies that proactively manage their stakeholder responsibilities see doing so as a means of living up to their own codes through systems elsewhere termed total responsibility management (TRM) systems (Waddock *et al.*, 2002; Waddock and Bodwell, 2002). Analogous in many respects to total quality management (TQM) approaches, TRM approaches represent companies' mostly voluntary initiatives to 'manage' the criticisms they have received from human and child labor activists, labor unions, social investors and anti-corruption agitators, among others. Coping with these criticisms means developing systemic approaches to managing responsibilities (for example, Waddock and Bodwell, 2002) that take into account the risks, investments and interests of numerous stakeholders. From the perspective of many stakeholders, however, such boundary-spanning mechanisms and internal corporate management systems provide largely for one-sided communications, with the weight of power and voice still resting in the hands of corporate officers and managers.

The scandals and related developments of the late 1990s and early 2000s put companies on the spot to demonstrate to internal stakeholders, including employees, suppliers and labor unions, as well as to external stakeholders, including activists of all stripes, NGOs and governments, that they are, in fact, being and not just 'looking' responsible. Simple corporate *social* responsibility (CSR) activities, demonstrated by the types of 'do good' or discretionary activities incorporated into the corporate community relations programs that emerged during the 1980s (for example, Burke, 1999), volunteer and philanthropic efforts designed to 'give back' without changing fundamental business practices, no longer satisfy many stakeholders that companies are in fact good corporate citizens. Simultaneously companies are under intense pressure from investors and the financial community in general to produce (short-term) bottom-line results, pressures that have sometimes translated into taking shortcuts to generate short-term profits, while potentially harming certain stakeholders (even investors) or the natural environment in the longer term. As will be discussed, external to companies, voluntary initiatives that create the fundamentals of what can be called a responsibility assurance system are now developing globally. The question is, will voluntary responsibility assurance, combined with internal responsibility management, satisfy the distrustful public?

External voluntary initiatives
Because some critics claim that much of the internal corporate activity, including extensive self-regulatory programs, philanthropic activity and community relations, is nothing but window dressing, several striking recent examples of voluntary corporate efforts to self-regulate, provide greater transparency and live up to accepted ethical and responsibility standards have emerged. Many of these voluntary initiatives aimed at developing more responsible practices carry an implicit hope of avoiding a new wave of regulation (for example, Vietor, 1989). They are part of what I have elsewhere (Waddock, 2003a) termed an emerging 'responsibility assurance system' that works in conjunction with the also recently developing internal responsibility management systems.

Three main elements of responsibility assurance are currently notable globally in the intersection of business, government, and civil society:

- generally accepted standards and principles,
- credible monitoring, verification and certification policies and processes,
- generally accepted social and ecological reporting standards.

Notable recent voluntary initiatives that attempt to establish standards, principles and codes of conduct include the UN's Global Compact, the Global Sullivan Principles, CERES, the ISO 14000 environmental standards series and the OECD Guidelines for Multinational Corporations. Industry groups oriented toward improving problematic practices through developing industry-wide codes of conduct include the Fair Labor Association, the chemical industry's Responsible Care initiative and the Direct Marketing Association's code of conduct, among numerous others. The scandals and growing ecological problems, however, illustrate the relative ineffectiveness of such initiatives (some of which have been in place for years) to actually control corporate behaviors, change practices or eliminate ethical problems.

The second element of responsibility assurance involves establishing credible monitoring, verification and certification systems, such SAI's SA 8000 labor standards and AccountAbility's AA 1000 standards, both of which are intended to verify that companies live up to their rhetoric with respect to labor and stakeholder relationships, respectively. The key term here is 'credible'. To the extent that trust in the responsibility and integrity of corporate practices has been eroded (or, more likely, never existed in the first place), corporate critics are unlikely simply to believe companies that say they are managing, for example, their supply chains, use of environmental resources or marketing practices, more responsibly. The need for credibility in monitoring and related responsibility audit systems (for example, Waddock and Smith, 2000) suggests that they will need to be undertaken by external agents associated with independent organizations that have established believable processes and audit practices. Traditional accounting/audit companies may not, at least at this point, have the necessary background to undertake such broader audits credibly (for example, O'Rourke, 1997, 2000), particularly in light of their current ethical problems and the collapse of former accounting giant Arthur Andersen as a result of ethical lapses.

The third element of responsibility assurance is a responsibility equivalent of generally accepted accounting principles (GAAP). Just as global financial reporting is beginning to emerge in the wake of globalization over the past 20 years and the attendant need for comparability of financial information across companies in different nations,[1] so too is there a need for generally accepted accounting reporting principles for triple bottom-line elements of social and ecological reporting. The most notable current initiative around responsibility reporting is the Global Reporting Initiative (GRI), founded in 1999 by a coalition of business, NGOs, labor unions and others led by CERES founder Joan Bavaria. Sometimes criticized for being too cumbersome and complex, the GRI nonetheless represents an important step forward globally in thinking about how to ensure comparability of social or triple bottom-line (economic, social and environmental) elements across companies in different countries. Indeed the progress of the Global Reporting Initiative and its link to the UN Global Compact suggest that a comprehensive standard may already be emerging, despite criticisms of GRI for its complexity of application.

Voluntary action: the UN global compact

One of the notable developments around corporate responsibility in recent years has been the United Nations' foray into the world of corporate practices through Secretary General Kofi Annan's Global Compact (GC) initiative,[2] which articulates nine fundamental principles related to human rights, labor rights and the environment. A company joins when the CEO submits a letter to Annan agreeing to uphold the nine principles and participate in a learning community, where companies agree to share their good (responsible and principle-related) practices in a learning forum, in publicly available cases and in stakeholder dialogues. The Global Compact promotes use of the GRI reporting standards, which in turn are linked to both SA 8000 and AA 1000 monitoring and verification procedures, thus creating a systemic approach to voluntary responsibility assurance and management (see also Kell and Levin, 2003; Ruggie, 2001).

About 2000 companies around the world had joined the Global Compact initiative by mid-2004, albeit participation from US firms has been relatively limited to date, with only 44 US signatories in early 2003. Many of the companies participating in these and related programs are doing so because of the external pressures they are now facing for greater transparency and accountability and, not incidentally, in the hopes that, by voluntarily agreeing to monitor their practices or uphold a set of principles, they will avert mandated standards, reporting requirements or verification by governments.

A recent North American learning forum conference on the GC highlights some of the reasons why companies align themselves with such voluntary initiatives, as well as some of the difficulties that others experience in signing on (for elaboration, see Waddock, 2003b). Downsides and risks of joining initiatives like the GC include (largely unfounded) fears by legal counsel that signing a set of aspirational principles will subject the company to possible litigation, as well as lack of understanding of certain key principles, a fear of what is in the fine print and associated sense of vulnerability or exposure through the visibility associated with becoming a signatory. Additionally there is concern about the overall effectiveness of such voluntary initiatives, that corporate critics, particularly NGOs, might charge companies with 'bluewashing', or wrapping themselves in the (blue) UN flag, and that the GC itself has yet to accomplish much of significance. Furthermore some companies are concerned about reporting problems transparently, recognizing the difficulties of translating global principles into action at the local level, where resources, cultural considerations and realities are considerably more complex.

On the positive side, companies sign on to the Global Compact and similar initiatives (such as the Global Sullivan Principles or the Caux

Principles), for a variety of reasons, including the aspiration to live up to the nine principles (which revolve around human rights, labor standards and environmental sustainability), because signing on has the potential to establish a leadership role, particularly for early signatories, and because the GC, unlike some other codes and sets of principles, is simple, clear and straightforward, relying on principles already agreed to by most of the world's nations. Additionally, from a responsibility management perspective, the GC's 10 principles create a context for action and alignment of the company's espoused values with practice, provide opportunities to raise difficult or formerly 'off the table' issues (such as human rights, the right to free association or sustainability) and thereby provide opportunities for internal learning and change. Additionally the GC provides a ready-made forum for multi-stakeholder engagement, including NGOs, labor unions and activists, among others. There is some potential in such engagement for risk management, not only in the sense of being proactive about possible risks, but also of being part of the process of shaping the future rules of the game by which businesses will have to play.

Multi-stakeholder engagement
Stakeholder theorists argue that the demands facing companies today represent a new reality for companies, who now need to find ways to engage with their stakeholders in mutually responsive, not in the old one-sided, ways and mutually develop and implement the standards to which companies need to adhere. This so-called stakeholder engagement (Svendsen, 1998; Calton and Payne, 2003) is based on techniques of dialogue (Isaacs, 1999) that reflect interactivity, power sharing and mutuality, rather than one-sided communication.

In theory, engagement provides for stakeholder voice in company decisions and permits greater openness and transparency about company practices and impacts. Stakeholder dialogue can also theoretically provide important information and input into company practices and strategies and help companies head off unfounded external criticisms of their activities. Stakeholder networks and engagement through dialogue (Payne and Calton, 2002; Calton and Payne, 2003) are at the heart of emerging theory on stakeholder relationships. Royal Dutch Shell's 'Tell Shell' program is one notable example of a company's attempt to create an on-line dialogue with stakeholders, and the company has also engaged numerous stakeholders in intensive focus groups as it has attempted to move through a transformation toward greater corporate responsibility in recent years (Mirvis, 2000; Lawrence, 2002), although recent problems with oil reserves accounting suggest that problems still abound.

The landscape of corporate stakeholder engagement and voice has arguably been altered by the emergence of multi-sector engagement and responsibility initiatives that sometimes result in voluntary adoption of codes, principles, reporting practices and even external monitoring and responsibility assurance, as noted above. All of this voluntary activity indicates that many progressive company executives would prefer voluntary standards to government mandate. Government mandate around corporate stakeholder and environmental responsibilities might force companies to become more transparent and accountable by mandating reporting standards, content and audit procedures. Mandate might impose higher standards of practice across the board than currently exist. Since there is currently no global governance structure with any enforcement capabilities, it is also conceivable that different nation states would evolve different standards and reporting requirements, creating a nightmare scenario in which multinational firms were subject to different regulations in every country in which they operate. Yet, in a world where the public trust that did exist with respect to companies has been lost to scandals, will voluntary action suffice?

Is voluntary action enough?
Unfortunately it is not just scandals that rocked public trust in large companies over the past few decades. To scandals we can add executive greed evidenced in excessive CEO compensation rates (US CEO compensation is now estimated to be somewhere between 411 and 475 times that of the average worker). Additionally many employees and their communities have struggled with the aftermath of down or 'right'-sizings that have resulted in sometimes massive corporate layoffs, erosion of employee loyalty and the loss of local jobs related to outsourcing practices aimed at finding (and exploiting) the lowest wage countries. In turn, companies within outsourced supply chains are frequently criticized for poor labor relations, sweatshop and otherwise abusive working conditions and egregious environmental practices. Add in outright deception by major tobacco companies about the health effects of their products, the central role of the gaming industry in providing public monies (McGowan, 2001), deceptive advertising and marketing practices, rampant failures to uphold their public trust by public accountants (especially the now mostly defunct Arthur Andersen) and numerous issues related to ecological sustainability, globalization and free trade, and it becomes clear why public trust in companies is at a low ebb. Corporate critics will not rest easy with industry self-regulation, especially in light of growing recognition of the lack of corporate 'conscience' (Goodpaster and Matthews, 1982) because of the corporation's inherent nature as an engine for economizing (Frederick, 1995).

To understand the discomfort with transnational enterprise, consider the power of global corporations today. The UN estimated in 2002 that there were some 65 000 transnational corporations with more than 850 000 foreign affiliates (UN, 2003) whose power in the global economy is growing. Transnational corporation (TNC) sales figures now represent as much as one-tenth of world GDP and one-third of exports (ibid.). By 2002, some 51 of the world's largest economic entities were not countries but transnational companies, and these firms accounted for some 4.3 per cent of world GDP (UNCTAD, 2002). Efficiency moves (doing the most with the fewest employees and resources) or what Frederick (1995) calls 'economizing' in these companies is being driven by three major forces: policy liberalization or opening up of national markets, technological changes with associated rising costs and (a consequence of the first two forces) increasing competition (UNCTAD, 2002). Many of these companies seem to lack domestic 'roots' and a sense of place that would provide a rationale for values other than profitability and growth aimed at 'maximizing' shareholder returns; thus they frequently overlook commitment to local communities. Driven by intense pressures from global (and domestic) capital markets and an economic system that gives primacy to shareholders, many companies seem unable to focus on their impacts on stakeholders other than those ostensible (however distant or short-term) shareholders.

It is in this competitive context that overt and voluntary responsibility management systems and related voluntary responsibility assurance systems are arising – as a direct result of pressures coming from the broader array of stakeholders who increasingly demand that their voices be heard (for example, Waddock *et al.*, 2002). Responsibility management approaches, combined with adoption of internally generated, industry-based or global codes of conduct, joining enterprises like the Fair Labor Association and using, for example, the SA 8000 labor standards to ensure that international labor standards are being met, and even issuing triple or multiple bottom-line reports following GRI standards represent the cutting edge of stakeholder relationship management today. Such voluntary steps by companies, however, are unlikely to satisfy stakeholders hurt in the recent wave of scandals or other acts suggesting corporate excesses or corporate abuses of power to those desiring more 'civil' corporations (Zadek, 2001) or a more 'civil economy' (Bruyn, 1999).

Given the realities of TNC behavior as well as that of small companies, many corporate critics want to hold companies' feet to the proverbial fire of public scrutiny, transparency and open accountability. Ethical lapses, accounting misrepresentations and evidence of greed have destroyed the fundamental trust on which business transactions rest. Yet trust and related social capital are arguably at the very core of effective markets and, presumably, effective social systems more generally (for example, Fukayama,

1996; Hosmer, 1995; Putnam, 2000), as well as successful economic clusters (Porter, 1998).

Although voluntary initiatives like the Global Compact attempt to foster greater confidence in the integrity of companies, their reach to date is relatively small. Consider that a total of 2000 companies are signatories (not all of which are multinational corporations – MNCs) in a context of more than 65000 total MNCs (of which, it will be remembered, only 44 in early 2003 were US companies). About 45 per cent of the world's 250 largest companies are now producing a sustainability or social report, with the content in these reports gradually broadening, but many companies are still largely driven by (legal) compliance rather than by values (KPMG, 2002) and there is little consistency in what is reported or how reports are generated, with few reports externally audited and verified. Other companies take steps toward responsibility management and assurance only because of significant stakeholder pressure, such as the anti-Nike campaigns that forced Nike into monitoring its suppliers' labor practices as a way of protecting its brand and reputation.

The Conference Board estimated that in 1999 some 2000 companies were issuing 'nontraditional' reports (covering sustainability, environmental or social issues), although about 60 per cent of companies surveyed regularly issued philanthropic reports (Conference Board, 2001), albeit the number has likely grown substantially since that time. The Conference Board, a business association, along with other observers including some of the large accounting firms, NGOs, labor unions and civil society organizations, believes that some day the issuance of such nontraditional reports could become standard operating procedure (ibid.).

These data indicate that the number of companies engaging in responsibility management and assurance activities, while growing rapidly, is still small relative to the total number of companies in the world. Furthermore there are millions of small and medium-sized enterprises (SMEs) whose executives have yet even to begin thinking about adherence to codes of conduct or global principles, never mind participating in responsibility assurance programs of any sort. Indeed one of the major concerns raised at the second annual global UN Global Compact Learning Forum held in Berlin in December 2002 was how to bring SMEs into better alignment with what the many progressive MNCs are now doing, when resources are scarcer, management time and skill are at a premium, and SME-specific know-how about corporate citizenship and integrity is lacking.

Still more complicating, not all of the corporate sustainability and/or social (nontraditional) reports are externally verified or audited, and there are wide disparities in what is actually reported. In some respects, unless following guidelines like GRI's, companies can still report what, when and how they like. There is as yet no requirement other than peer and stakeholder pressures that creates a context in which multiple bottom-line reports are issued. There is as yet little apparent consistency across companies and nations when it comes to what is reported and how, despite the efforts of the GRI to create social accountability GAAP. For example, the Conference Board reports that, when the United Nations Environmental Program (UNEP) and the British firm SustainAbility analyzed 196 companies' sustainability reports in 2000, using a scale of 196, the average score was 84 and only six companies scored above 100 on that ranking – and all of those companies were European (ibid.). Clearly there is yet a distance to go in demonstrating sufficient corporate transparency, responsibility and accountability that public trust can be rebuilt, particularly in light of the scandals that have erupted into public view since those studies were undertaken.

Despite efforts to forestall mandate through voluntary action by many large companies and despite the current lack of an effective global governance system that has sanctioning powers, it is quite likely that the voluntary initiatives in evidence among progressive companies today are interim steps rather than the end state (cf. Helleiner, 2001). At this point, there is no global institution with the power to set reporting guidelines or to create a mandated responsibility assurance program that has taken an interest in such activity. The UN, which is one of the few worldwide governance bodies, has limited resources and virtually no enforcement powers, and the World Trade Organization and World Bank seem to have little interest in such standardization of corporate practice. Furthermore, as Mike Moore, former Director General of the World Trade Organization (WTO), recently pointed out, the UN comprises a bewildering array of institutions with overlapping functions, conflicting rules and their own standards of accountability (or lack thereof) (Moore, 2003). The WTO itself, which does have a good deal of power, is the subject of much anti-globalization criticism and, as one critic recently charged, seems 'designed to strip sovereignty from nations, removing critical public policy decisions from democratic control', with implications of its decision 'imperil[ing] efforts to protect human health and the environment' (Mokhiber and Weissman, 2003, p. 1).

What will be enough?
Economy is not, as former US Labor Secretary Robert Reich pointed out, the same thing as society. Those who would wish to 'civilize' companies or the global economy (for example, Zadek, 2001; Helleiner, 2001; Bruyn, 1999) through standards of practice, reporting guidelines, and responsibility management and assurance implicitly recognize this reality. According to some stakeholders, economic development also implies healthy societies

built around local values, democracy and equity to all citizens, and not just rewards for a priveleged few (who may not even live locally) (Rodrik, 2001). Culture, national values, local standards and norms, tradition and heritage, and the social capital embedded in healthy communities are among the elements that create not just economies but societies. Economic development according to some stakeholders also implies healthy societies, built around some of those local values (and not homogenized), societies that evidence democracy and equity to all citizens, not just rewards for a privileged few (who may not even live locally) (Rodrik, 2001).

Some stakeholders (such as the activists who began the series of protests at the WTO meeting in Seattle in 1999) recognize that businesses do play a key role in fostering effective societies. They also believe that a business's role needs to encompass other human values than growth, efficiency and profit, despite the perhaps inherent tendency of businesses developed in Western civilization to economize (Frederick, 1995). Although the voices of activists against globalization can sometimes seem cacophonous, fundamentally they may well be seeking much the same outcomes with respect to businesses: companies that are responsive and responsible to the very human needs of the societies in which they operate, not just to the strictures of capital markets (cf, Cavanagh *et al.*, 2002).

Human needs are manifested through principles like the nine principles of the UN Global Compact, which focus on basic human rights, labor rights, and environmental sustainability. They are manifested through demands for greater responsibility, transparency and accountability that seek to put a human face on the large and seemingly uncontrollable behemoths that many corporations have become. They are manifested in the need for healthy communities imbued with social capital (Putnam, 2000) and for groupings of businesses linked together in effective economic clusters (Porter, 1998). Progressive companies, those who are engaged in responsibility management and responsibility assurance initiatives, seem to recognize this more expansive stakeholder-integrated perspective.

It is clear that, despite the progress that has been made to date, much remains to be done to bring all companies into line with these more human and humane values, somehow to shift perspective (or create a shift of mind, what Peter Senge, 1990, calls *metanoia*) away from economy as the guiding force for world development toward the integration of human society into nature that is the way that the world, *qua* planet Earth, really operates. Voluntary responsibility assurance is a good first step and may be the only feasible step toward this integration until some effective form of global governance, not now in existence, emerges.

In the end, however, something more than self-governance and voluntary action may be needed to build the world in which companies are responsible enough to their stakeholders to merit being trusted (again?). That something is possibly going to be a global governance mechanism drawing on the emerging responsibility assurance system but potentially going well beyond it in setting forth expectations about corporate responsibility, transparency and accountability practices. Such a mechanism would establish a playing field that not only is level for companies operating across national borders (which is actually desired by many thoughtful corporate leaders as an alternative to having to meet multiple standards), but also levels the capacities of other, possibly less resource-rich but equally important, stakeholders to engage in shaping societies. Simultaneously it will be important to find ways to generate new businesses that are not only ecologically sustainable (today a distant dream: cf. Hawkens *et al.*, 1999; McDonough and Braungart, 2002), but also sustain their local communities (Korten, 1999).

Notes
1. Re the anticipation of global generally accepted accounting principles or GAAP, see for example, http://www.kpmg.com.hk/Press%20releases/pressrel_GAAP_convergence03. html).
2. See www.unglobalcompact.org for further information.

References
Andriof, J. and S. Waddock (2002), 'Unfolding stakeholder engagement' in Jörg Andriof, Sandra Waddock, Bryan Husted and Sandra Rahman (eds), *Unfolding Stakeholder Thinking*, Sheffield: Greenleaf, pp. 19–42.

Andriof, J., S. Waddock, B. Husted and S. Rahman (eds) (2002), *Unfolding Stakeholder Thinking: Theory, Responsibility and Engagement*, Sheffield: Greenleaf.

Andriof, J., S. Waddock, B. Husted and S. Rahman (2003), *Unfolding Stakeholder Thinking 2: Relationships, Communication, Reporting and Performance*, Sheffield: Greenleaf.

Bruyn, S.T. (1999), *A Civil Economy*, Ann Arbor: University of Michigan Press.

Burke, E.M. (1999), *Corporate Community Relations: The Principle of the Neighbor of Choice*, Westwood, CT: Praeger.

Calton, J.M. and S.L. Payne (2003), 'Coping with paradox: multistakeholder learning dialogue as a pluralist sensemaking process for addressing messy problems', *Business & Society*, **42** (1), 7–42.

Cavanagh, J., J. Mander, S. Anderson, D. Barker, M. Barlow, W. Bellow, R. Broad, T. Clarke, E. Goldsmith, R. Hayes, C. Hines, A. Kimbrell, D. Korten, H. Norberg-Hodge, S. Larrain, S. Retallack, V. Shiva, V. Tauli-Corpuz and L. Wallach (2002), *Alternatives to Economic Globalization*, San Francisco, CA: Berrett-Kohler.

Conference Board (2001), 'The road to sustainability: business' first steps', posted at: http://www.pwcglobal.com/Extweb/NewCoAtWork.nsf/docid/5889E328182C2E2285256B61005 A6497.

Evan, W.M. and R.E. Freeman (1988), 'A stakeholder theory of the modern corporation: Kantian Capitalism', in T. Beauchamp and N. Bowie (eds), *Ethical Theory and Business*, Englewood Cliffs, NJ: Prentice-Hall.

Frederick, W.C. (1995), *Values, Nature, and Culture in the American Corporation*, New York: Oxford University Press.

Freeman, R.E. (1984), *Strategic Management: A Stakeholder Approach*, Boston, USA: Pitman.

Freeman, R.E. and D.R. Gilbert, Jr (1988), *Corporate Strategy and the Search for Ethics*, Englewood Cliffs, NJ: Prentice Hall.

Fukuyama, F. (1996), *Trust: Human Nature and the Reconstitution of Social Order*, New York: Touchstone Books.
Goodpaster, K.E. and J.B. Matthews, Jr. (1982), 'Can a corporation have a conscience?', *Harvard Business Review*, **60** (1), 132–41.
Hawken, P., A. Lovens and L.H. Lovens (1999), *Natural Capitalism: Creating the Next Industrial Revolution*, Boston, MA: Little, Brown.
Helleiner, G.K. (2001), 'Markets, politics and globalization: can the global economy be civilized?', *Global Governance*, **7** (3), 243–64.
Hosmer, L.T. (1995), 'Trust: the connecting link between organizational theory and philosophical ethics', *Academy of Management Review*, **20** (2), 379–403.
Isaacs, W. (1999), *Dialogue and the Art of Thinking Together*, New York: Doubleday Currency.
Johnson-Cramer, M.E., S.L. Berman and J.E. Post (2003), 'Re-examining the concept of "stakeholder management"', in J. Andriof, S. Waddock, B. Husted and S. Rahman (eds), *Unfolding Stakeholder Thinking 2: Relationships, Communication, Reporting and Performance*, Sheffield: Greenleaf, pp. 145–61.
Kell, G. and D. Levin (2003), 'The global compact network: an historic experiment in learning and action', *Business and Society Review*, **108** (2), 151–82.
Korten, D. (1999), *The Post-Corporate World: Life After Capitalism*, San Francisco, CA: Berrett-Koehler.
KPMG (2002), International Survey of Corporate Sustainibility Reporting 2002, posted at http://www.kpmg.de/library/surveys/satellit/Sustainibility_survey_Power_Utilities.pdf.
Lawrence, A.T. (2003), 'The drivers of stakeholder engagement: reflections on the case of Royal Dutch/Shell', in J. Andriof, S. Waddock, B. Husted and S. Rahman (eds), *Unfolding Stakeholder Thinking 2: Relationships, Communication, Reporting and Performance*, Sheffield: Greenleaf, pp. 185–200.
Lydenberg, S.D. (2003), 'Trust building and trust busting: corporation, government, and responsibilities', *Journal of Corporate Citizenship*, **11**, 23–7.
McDonough, W. and M. Braungart (2002), *Cradle to Cradle: Remaking the Way We Make Things*, New York: North Point Press.
McGowan, R.A. (2001), *Government and the Transformation of the Gaming Industry*, Cheltenham, UK and Northampton, MA, USA: Edward Elgar Publisher.
Mirvis, P. (2000), 'Transformation at Shell: commerce and citizenship', *Business and Society Review*, **105** (1), 63–85.
Mitchell, R.K., B.R. Agle and D.J. Wood (1997), 'Toward a theory of stakeholder identification and salience: defining the principle of who and what really counts', *Academy of Management Review*, **22** (4), 853–86.
Mokhiber, R. and R. Weissman (2003), 'Throwing precaution to the wind', Corp-Focus, posted at http://lists.essential.org/pipermail/corp-focus/2003/000152.html.
Moore, M. (2003), 'Multilateral meltdown', *Foreign Policy*, **135**, March/April, 74–6.
O'Rourke, D. (1997), 'Smoke from a hired gun: a critique of Nike's labor and environmental auditing in Vietnam as performed by Ernst & Young', report published by the Transnational Resource and Action Center, San Francisco, 10 November, available on the Internet at www.corpwatch.org/trac/nike/ernst/.
O'Rourke, D. (2000), 'Monitoring the monitors: a critique of PricewaterhouseCooper's labor monitoring', white paper, 28 September.
Payne, S.L. and J.M. Calton (2003), 'Towards a managerial practice of stakeholder engagement: developing multi-stakeholder learning dialogues', in J. Andriof, S. Waddock, B. Husted and S. Rahman (eds), *Unfolding Stakeholder Thinking 2: Relationships, Communication, Reporting and Performance*, Sheffield: Greenleaf, pp. 121–36.
Porter, M.E. (1998), 'Clusters and the new economics of competition', *Harvard Business Review*, **76** (6), 77–90.
Post, J.E., L.E. Preston and S. Sachs (2002a), *Redefining the Corporation: Stakeholder Management and Organizational Wealth*, Stanford, CA: Stanford Business Books.
Post, J.E., L.E. Preston and S. Sachs (2002b), 'Managing the extended enterprise: the new stakeholder view', *California Management Review*, **45** (1), 6–29.

194   *Responsible leadership and governance in global business*

Putnam, R.D. (2000), *Bowling Alone: The Collapse and Revival of American Community*, New York: Simon & Schuster.
Rodrik, D. (2001), 'Trading in illusions', *Foreign Policy*, 123, March/April, 54–63.
Ruggie, J.G. (2001), 'Global_governance.net: The global compact as a learning network', *Global Governance*, 7 (4), 371–9.
Senge, P.M. (1990), *The Fifth Discipline*, New York: Doubleday.
Svendsen, A. (1998), *The Stakeholder Strategy: Profiting from Collaborative Business Relationships*, San Francisco, CA: Berrett-Koehler.
UNCTAD (2002), 'United Nations Conference on Trade and Development', posted at http://r0.unctad.org/en/press/pr0247en.htm.
United Nations (2003), *World Investment Report 2002*, New York and Geneva: United Nations Press; online at http://r0.unctad.org/wir/pdfs/wir02ove_a4.en.pdf.
Vietor, R.H.K. (1989), *Strategic Management in the Regulatory Environment*, Englewood Cliffs, NJ: Prentice-Hall.
Waddell, S. (2003), 'Global action network: a global intervention to make globalization work for all', *Journal of Corporate Citizenship*, 12, Winter, 27–42.
Waddock, S. (2002a), *Leading Corporate Citizens: Vision, Values, Value Added*, New York: McGraw-Hill.
Waddock, S. (2002b), 'Fluff is not enough: managing responsibility for corporate citizenship', *Ethical Corporation*, 4, March/April, 12–13.
Waddock, S. (2003a), 'What will it take to create a tipping point for corporate responsibility!', paper presented at the annual meeting of the Academy of Management, Seattle, WA, August.
Waddock, S. (2003b), 'Learners and leaders: evolving the global compact in North America', Boston College working paper.
Waddock, S.A. and C. Bodwell (2002), 'From TQM to TRM: the emerging evolution of total responsibility management (TRM) systems', *Journal of Corporate Citizenship*, 2 (7), 113–26.
Waddock, S.A. and N. Smith (2000), 'Corporate responsibility audits: doing well by doing good', *Sloan Management Review*, 41 (2), 75–83.
Waddock, S.A., C. Bodwell and S.B. Graves (2002), 'Responsibility: the new imperative', *Academy of Management Executive*, 16 (2), 132–48.
Zadek, S. (2001), *The Civil Corporation: The New Economy of Corporate Citizenship*, Sterling, VA: EarthScan Publications.

11 The influence of CEO transformational leadership on firm-level commitment to corporate social responsibility

David A. Waldman and Donald Siegel

Introduction

There is growing scholarly interest in assessing the antecedents and consequences of corporate social responsibility (CSR). Following the work of McWilliams and Siegel (2001), we define CSR as actions on the part of the firm that appear to advance, or acquiesce in the promotion of, some social good, beyond the immediate interests of the firm and its shareholders and beyond that which is required by law. Thus CSR involves using the firm's resources to advance societal interests. CSR strategies may result in a company embodying socially responsible attributes in their products (such as the use of organic or pesticide-free ingredients) or also lead to situations where consumers are made aware of the fact that the good they are purchasing has been produced in a socially responsible manner (for example, when cosmetic firms report that ingredients in their products are not tested on animals). Other stakeholders, including employees, suppliers, community groups, government and some shareholders, may also derive satisfaction from a firm's CSR actions.

While a variety of motives could affect the propensity of firms to engage in CSR, management scholars have recently focused attention on instances when managers appear to be using CSR instrumentally. That is, they can promote CSR either for their own benefit (Friedman, 1970; Wright and Ferris, 1997), which follows from agency theory, or to enhance firm profitability, based on a resource-based view (Russo and Fouts, 1997) or on a theory of the firm/strategic perspective (McWilliams and Siegel, 2001).

For example, a basic assumption of the McWilliams and Siegel (2001) model is that managers of publicly held firms attempt to maximize profits. The authors assert that there is an optimal level of CSR, which will simultaneously maximize profit *and* satisfy demand for CSR emanating from various stakeholder groups. To determine the optimal level of investment in CSR, firms may assess the (strategic) costs and benefits of engaging in this activity. Thus the authors attempt to integrate stakeholder theory and the theory of the firm. More importantly their model assumes that firms carefully consider the strategic implications of CSR. It also asserts that firms pursuing product differentiation, image or reputation-building strategies will have an incentive to be socially responsible. Indeed the authors identified several strategic variables that constitute predictors of CSR, such as R&D spending and advertising intensity. In sum, according to McWilliams and Siegel (2001), the pursuit of CSR is essentially calculative and can be understood in terms of a cost/benefit framework.

While this framework is useful, it does not take into account the personal attributes or qualities (such as leadership qualities) of key decision makers such as CEOs, which may also affect the extent to which firms engage in CSR. Instead McWilliams and Siegel (ibid.) suggested an overlap between personal qualities and instrumental/strategic variables such as product differentiation. For example, using the case of Ben and Jerry's Ice Cream, they purported that 'CSR may be a popular means of achieving differentiation, because it allows managers to simultaneously satisfy personal interests and to achieve product differentiation' (ibid., p. 119). It follows that an understanding of leadership qualities might not add to our understanding of the pursuit of CSR strategies beyond more calculative approaches.

Nevertheless there may indeed be a potential, unique role for CEO leadership qualities, behavior or values in determining the propensity of firms to engage in CSR. CEOs are charged with the responsibility of formulating corporate strategy and are often deeply involved in promoting the image of their respective firms through social responsibility. Furthermore they may dramatically change the strategic direction of the firm, including decisions pertaining to CSR. For instance, numerous CEOs of large corporations played a prominent role in the 1997 US Presidential 'summit' on voluntarism in Philadelphia, led by General Colin Powell, perhaps the most conspicuous CSR event in history. At this summit, many CEOs pledged that their companies would dedicate additional human resources to CSR activities.

It is also interesting to note that, despite the compelling arguments in favor of the instrumental use of CSR, corporate executives may also be driven to adopt CSR practices for moral or ethical reasons that characterize effective leaders (Daft, 2002). Jones (1995) asserted that stakeholder theory encompasses an ethical/normative dimension, implying that managers may engage in CSR because their moral or ethical values compel them to do so – regardless of more calculative, cost–benefit explanations.

Models of effective leadership have increasingly emphasized values and related characteristics of leaders that might influence strategy formulation and implementation, including decisions and actions taken toward the implementation of CSR (House and Aditya, 1997). Thus it is somewhat surprising that there has been virtually no direct theoretical or empirical analysis of the relationship between CEO leadership characteristics and CSR.

The purpose of this chapter is to help fill this gap. More specifically, we focus on transformational leadership theory and extend it in new directions by applying it to firm-level commitment to CSR. Our major goal is to provide a theoretical conceptualization linking CEO transformational leadership and CSR. The chapter begins with a description of transformational leadership and its relevance to strategy formulation and implementation. Next we outline a theoretical model of such leadership in relation to firm-level commitment to CSR. This is followed by a discussion of our exploratory empirical analysis of some of our hypotheses. We conclude with a consideration of future research directions.

Transformational leadership at the strategic level
For several decades, strategy researchers have devoted considerable attention to the antecedents and consequences of the strategic decisions of senior managers. The essence of strategic leadership theory is that strategic decisions represent 'weak situations' (Mischel, 1977), in the sense that available stimuli are often complex, ambiguous and uncertain (Cannella and Monroe, 1997; Finkelstein and Hambrick, 1996). In such situations, the choices of decision makers can vary widely, including the choice to pursue CSR-based strategies. Accordingly weak situations allow decision makers to insert their own individual characteristics (such as leadership qualities) into such choices (Finkelstein and Hambrick, 1996; House and Aditya, 1997).

The initial phase of research on strategic leadership focused on background and demographic characteristics of CEOs, such as age, functional track, education and socioeconomic history, in order to examine whether such characteristics influence strategic decision making (Hambrick and Mason, 1984). The empirical evidence suggests that such factors have limited explanatory power, and that it might be more beneficial to employ more direct measures of a top-level manager's personality, values, beliefs or leadership characteristics (Boal and Hooijberg, 2001; Cannella and Monroe, 1997; Priem *et al.*, 1999). We conjecture that transformational leadership factors may be especially relevant to strategic decision making in general, and CSR in particular.

In the past, leadership theory has been viewed as the domain of organizational behavior and micro-oriented perspectives. Indeed a quick perusal of most organizational behavior textbooks shows how leadership processes are typically cast at the dyadic and small group levels. One example is the path–goal theory, which focuses on the leadership actions that should be taken to increase subordinates' motivation to attain personal and work-related goals (Evans, 1970; House, 1971). Thus the theory is most readily applied to supervisory-level leadership behavior and subordinate performance, rather than the promotion of such higher-level organizational phenomena as CSR.

A number of individuals have suggested that leadership theory should be directed toward broader organizational phenomena and the actions and decisions that occur at the upper echelons (Sashkin, 1988; Yukl, 1999). For example, Beyer and Browning (1999) advised scholars to consider whether leadership behavior and characteristics result in collective or system-wide outcomes, as well as the more commonly researched phenomena involving follower perceptions/behaviors. Fortunately, newer frameworks of leadership can be applied to provide an integration of micro-level behavior, such as that shown by an individual leader, and macro-level phenomena such as CSR (House *et al.*, 1995). This is the direction we pursue, in which we assess the connection between CEO transformational leadership and firm-level commitment to CSR.

The field of leadership has experienced an infusion of theory that House and Aditya (1997) referred to as the 'neocharismatic paradigm'. Specifically the neocharismatic paradigm stresses how exceptional leaders articulate visions that are based on strongly-held ideological values and powerful imagery, stimulate thinking that leads to innovative solutions to major problems and emphasize radical change and high performance expectations. They also foster substantial follower confidence, intrinsic motivation, identity, trust and admiration in the leader, and emotional appeal (Conger and Kanungo, 1998; Pawar and Eastman, 1997; Shamir *et al.*, 1993).

Transformational leadership theory represents a prominent example of the neocharismatic paradigm that may provide new possibilities for upper echelons theory in general, and for the understanding of CSR in particular. Bass (1985, 1998) has been a strong proponent of transformational leadership as a model for understanding extraordinary effort and performance in organizations. In addition to the above qualities and behaviors, Bass emphasized the difference between transformational and transactional leadership and how the latter is based on satisfying the self-interest of the leader and his/her followers. In contrast, transformational leadership has been defined in terms of how such leaders stress self-sacrifice for the good of the larger group or collective (Bass, 1985, 1997, 1998; Howell and Avolio, 1992). Although Bass emphasized the internal organization, in more recent writings it is clear that he is also implying the larger community beyond a leader's organization (Bass and Steidlmeier, 1999). Furthermore transformational leadership is achieved by elevating followers' motivational needs and expanding their understanding and perspectives, as well as by challenging the status quo and followers' expectations and assumptions (Bass, 1997; Bass and Avolio, 1994). Bass and Steidlmeier (1999) distinguished the above conceptualization, which they referred to as *authentic* transformational leadership, from what they characterized as *inauthentic* or *pseudotransformational* leadership. The latter is less concerned with the common good and leadership based on morality and, instead, is more concerned with personal agendas and self-aggrandizement of the leader. In our theoretical model, we deal with both forms of transformational leadership and their potential effects on commitment to CSR.

A model of transformational leadership and commitment to CSR

The above arguments provide a basis for understanding the potential relationship between CEO transformational leadership and commitment to CSR in the form of strategic decisions and choices. To help form precise theoretical connections, we note that Bass (1985) originally distinguished between two components of transformational leadership: emotional and intellectual. Bass broke down the emotional component into the two factors of charisma and inspirational leadership. In a subsequent essay, Bass (1997) acknowledged the lack of independence of these two factors, a finding discussed in detail by Lowe *et al.* (1996). Accordingly, for our purposes below, we will simply examine a single, emotional factor referred to as charismatic leadership. Indeed charisma is often viewed as the core of transformational leadership in that it accounts for most of the variance in outcomes and, accordingly, is sometimes used exclusively in transformational leadership research (for example, Waldman *et al.*, 2001). However, for the theoretical reasons described below, we also included intellectual stimulation in our model, which Bass (1985) referred to as the intellectual component of transformational leadership. As described in detail below, we will make a case for this component also being logically related to the commitment to pursue firm-level CSR.

At this juncture, it is useful to note that Bass (1985) identified an additional component of transformational leadership, individualized consideration. We will not include this factor in our model, for two reasons. First, numerous research findings have shown a lack of independence between the Bass (1985) measure of individualized consideration and other transformational leadership factors (Bass, 1997; Lowe *et al.*, 1996). While the same can be said about intellectual stimulation, Lowe *et al.* (1996, p. 415) referred to it as the 'third child' of transformational leadership and they implored researchers to investigate more thoroughly the potential effects of intellectual stimulation, especially at organizational levels. Although not referring specifically to intellectual stimulation, Locke (2003) also lamented that the intellectual side of leadership is underdeveloped and said that it should be further incorporated into leadership theory, especially at strategic levels. Second, individualized consideration focuses on how a leader deals with individual followers in terms of their mentoring, coaching and development. Because of the individual-level focus, a clear conceptual linkage with higher-level organizational phenomena, such as CSR, may be difficult to establish. At the same time, we recognize that a general concern for people and felt responsibility toward people may be relevant to leadership and CSR. Thus we include responsibility disposition in the model shown in Figure 11.1.

Socialized versus personalized charisma
The model depicts aspects of transformational leadership as antecedents of commitment to firm-level transformational leadership. In addition, we portray dispositional antecedents to alternative forms of charismatic leadership (that is, socialized versus personalized), as described below. Charismatic leadership is rooted in Max Weber's (1947) consideration of a particular class of leaders. Weber viewed charismatic leaders as those who are able to flourish at times of crisis, are able to communicate their visions effectively, and who attract followers to their views. Followers perceive charismatic leaders as exceptionally gifted, even larger-than-life individuals, possessing attractive visions in response to looming crises.

The more recent neocharismatic leadership theories mentioned above have moved away from Weber's original context of crises, focused largely in the societal domain, into a stream that examines the impact of charisma on organizational processes and outcomes (House, 1999). Unlike Weber (1947) and related theoretical approaches (Trice and Beyer, 1986), organizationally-focused theories of charisma view such leadership as a matter of degree; rather than an all-or-none phenomenon. Furthermore, although uncertainty and turbulence in the external context of an organization has been considered as a moderating factor (Waldman *et al.*, 2001), charismatic leadership has been considered relevant even in the absence of a crisis (Bass, 1997; Conger and Kanungo, 1998).

Our definition of charismatic leadership is based largely on the work of Bass (1985), Conger and Kanungo (1998) and House and colleagues (for example, House and Shamir, 1993). Specifically we define charisma as a *relationship* between an individual (leader) and one or more followers based on leader behaviors combined with favorable attributions on the part of followers. Key behaviors on the part of the leader include providing a sense of mission and articulating an inspirational vision based on powerful imagery, values and beliefs. Additional behaviors include demonstrating determination when accomplishing goals, communicating high performance expectations and acting in ways to build a powerful image. Favorable attributional effects on the part of followers include the generation of trust and confidence in the leader, making followers feel good in his/her presence, and strong admiration or respect based on the leader's accomplishments and the values and beliefs that he or she espouses (Waldman and Yammarino, 1999).

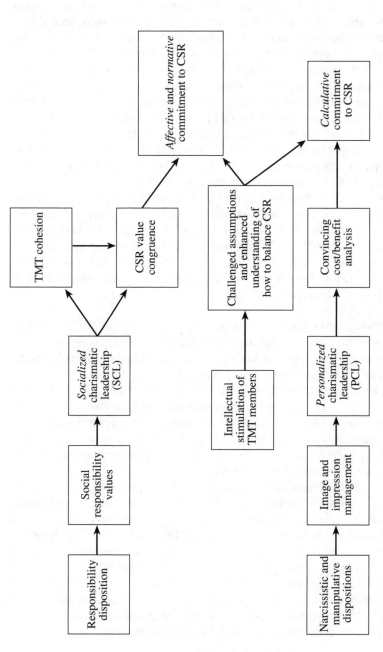

Figure 11.1   A model of CEO transformational leadership and firm-level commitment to corporate social responsibility

The conventional view in the neocharismatic literature is that this type of leadership will result in beneficial outcomes for individuals, groups and organizations. Indeed much of the theory and empirical research on charismatic leaders points to a number of positive consequences, such as higher performance ratings, more satisfied and motivated employees, and high effectiveness ratings by subordinates and superiors (Bass, 1985; Lowe *et al.*, 1996; Shamir *et al.*, 1993). However some recent writing on the topic is advising caution in understanding the outcomes of charismatic leadership. Two types of charismatic leadership have been identified: socialized charismatic leadership (SCL) and personalized charismatic leadership (PCL). The key distinction lies in the leader's underlying disposition and power motives, or the extent of an individual's unconscious desire to have an impact on others or one's environment (House and Howell, 1992). These two forms of charisma are highlighted in Figure 11.1.

Socialized charismatic leaders (SCL) tend to apply restraint in their use of power, and they use their influence to achieve goals and objectives for the betterment of the collective entity, rather than for personal gain (House and Howell, 1992). We propose that a sense of responsibility is the dispositional basis of socialized charisma. Individuals with a strong sense of responsibility have beliefs and values reflecting high moral standards, a feeling of obligation to do the right thing and concern about others (Winter, 1991).

Although not referring to charisma specifically, Burns (1978) originally advanced the argument that transformational leadership is tantamount to moral leadership, and that both followers and leaders progress to higher levels of moral development as a result of such leadership. Along similar lines, Kuhnert and Lewis (1987) and Kuhnert (1994) outlined a constructive/ developmental personality theory of understanding the world and resulting behavior on the part of leaders. This theory would suggest that socialized charismatic leaders are likely to progress to a higher stage of development involving deeply held personal values and standards (for example, integrity, self-respect and maintaining the societal good).

Bass and Steidlmeier (1999) also addressed moral values, suggesting that authentic transformational leaders reach higher levels of moral development, including a sense of obligation to the larger community. Although not specifically referring to such leadership, Daft (2002) used the Kohlberg (1976) stages of moral development to demonstrate how some leaders are able to progress to Kohlberg's post-conventional stage in which they act in an independent and ethical manner, regardless of the expectations of other individuals. Turner *et al.* (2002) recently demonstrated an empirical relationship between transformational leadership and higher stages of moral development according to the Kohlberg (1976) typology.

Along similar lines, Kanungo (2001) and Mendonca (2001) argued that charismatic leadership, in contrast to transactional leadership, is rooted in strong ethical values. The essence of this argument is that such leaders are guided by morally altruistic principles that 'reflect a helping concern for others even at considerable personal sacrifice or inconvenience' (Mendonca, 2001, p. 268). Furthermore their fortitude gives charismatic leaders the courage to face risks and work at overcoming obstacles in the pursuit of what they consider to be worthwhile CSR goals (Mendonca, 2001). Thus they use their responsibility disposition and social responsibility values and standards to guide their actions and policies as leaders. Through their charismatic appeal, followers are persuaded to do so as well. We propose that the leader strengthens this appeal by presenting CSR-related goals in terms of the values they represent. Followers will admire such leaders since their visions are likely to be partially based on values of altruism, justice and humanistic notions of the greater good (Bass and Steidlmeier, 1999). In turn, subsequent action toward the accomplishment of goals becomes more meaningful for followers because such action is consistent with valued aspects of their self-concepts (Shamir *et al.*, 1993). Accordingly followers want to identify with the socialized charismatic and the values that s/he represents. In sum, these arguments would suggest:

P1   *Responsibility disposition and social responsibility values help to build socialized charisma on the part of a leader.*

In contrast, PCLs tend to be motivated almost exclusively by self-interest and use their power to achieve their personal goals. They also tend to be self-centered or narcissistic, exploitative and manipulative in their relationship with others (Kets de Vries, 1993; Maccoby, 2004). To help gain favorable charismatic attributions of followers (for example, confidence and feelings of strong admiration), they will rely largely on image and impression management (Gardner and Avolio, 1998). That is, PCLs will manipulate events to enhance and aggrandize their image and personal accomplishment. They will orchestrate events to symbolize their own greatness (Gardner and Avolio, 1998) and will also emphasize allegiance to themselves, rather than the organization and its vision. For example, PCLs may engage in unconventional acts to enhance their image of grandeur so that followers will be in awe of them. In addition, rather than focusing confidence building in the direction of the group and its members (as is the case for the SCL), the PCL focuses confidence building more in his or her own direction as the one individual who can take the group to a better future.

Numerous authors have suggested that vision formation is a central element of charismatic leadership (for example, Bass, 1985; Conger and

Kanungo, 1998; House and Shamir, 1993). Furthermore, vision formation presents an interesting contrast between socialized and personalized charismatic leadership processes. We propose that the SCL will emphasize the development of a shared vision. According to Senge (1990), a leader's vision becomes shared when it builds upon a desire on the part of followers to pursue a common important undertaking, and when it connects to their individual visions and goals. Nanus (1992) suggested that it can be a worthwhile endeavor for major constituents (employees, internal and external customers, and so forth) to get involved in vision formulation in order to ensure that it is truly shared – advice that is likely to be heeded by the SCL. Conversely the PCL is not so concerned with shared vision or participation in vision formation. Instead the PCL will articulate his or her own vision and how that vision can alleviate uncertainty and fear that followers might have regarding the environment or their future. Overall there is more emphasis on the leader as an extraordinary person, rather than an emphasis on the actual vision.

An important difference between the SCL and PCL is the extent of consensus among their employees' responses towards them. The PCL's behaviors will engender heterogeneity in terms of charismatic attributions of the leader. Some followers may be quite attracted to the leader's actions, accomplishments and confidence. They may trust the leader and feel secure in terms of their own positions, as long as they remain loyal. Conversely other followers may not be so enamored of the PCL. They may attribute personalized goals to the leader and display a lack of trust in his/her actions and motives. In contrast, we would expect a greater degree of consensus among the followers of the SCL due to a stronger belief in a collective vision and a strong sense of perceived humility. In sum, we predict:

P2   Narcissistic and manipulative dispositions, combined with image and impression management, will help to build personalized charisma on the part of a leader.

Commitment to corporate social responsibility
The above distinction between socialized and personalized charisma sets the stage for understanding how these aspects of leadership can have differential effects on a firm's commitment to the pursuit of CSR. Below we will explore those effects, as well as introducing the potential influence of an additional aspect of transformational leadership, intellectual stimulation. However we must first define the term 'commitment'.

Commitment has received considerable attention in the organizational literature. As defined by Jernigan *et al.* (2002, p. 564), organizational commitment 'represents both an attitude that describes an individual's linkage to the organization and a set of behaviors by which individuals manifest that link'. Researchers have recognized that organizational commitment is a complex and multifaceted construct. For example, Meyer *et al.* (1993) proposed a three-factor model that includes affective (emotional attachment or identification), normative (felt obligation to continue employment) and continuance (felt instrumental or exchange-based need to continue employment) components. Because of the instrumental nature of the continuance component, others have referred to it as 'calculative' commitment (Jernigan *et al.*, 2002; Penley and Gould, 1988). Although the three-factor model has generally been supported empirically (for example, Hackett *et al.*, 1992; Meyer *et al.*, 1993), moderate to high relationships are typically common with regard to affective and normative organizational commitment.

For the present model, we borrow from the organizational commitment literature and suggest three comparable components. *Affective* commitment to CSR entails an emotional or moral attachment to the values underlying CSR. *Normative* commitment involves a feeling of obligation to the pursuit of CSR since it is seen as the right thing to do. *Calculative* commitment involves an intention to pursue CSR because of the exchange value that CSR might entail. In other words, decision makers may perceive favorable consequences for themselves (for example, an image of being an individual who is concerned about the environment), or for their organizations (for example, reduced pressure from environmentalists to change a firm's policy toward the environment). Such perceptions are formed in relation to perceived costs (for example, the additional capital, labor or materials that must be devoted to the pursuit of better environmental performance).

As depicted in Figure 11.1, we argue that socialized charisma will indirectly influence affective and normative CSR commitment on the part of strategic decision makers through its effects on top management team (TMT) cohesion and value congruence with decision makers (that is, TMT members who can make decisions relevant to the pursuit of CSR policies and practices). Waldman and Yammarino (1999) provided arguments linking CEO charismatic leadership to TMT cohesion. We argue here that, as suggested above, *socialized* charisma will help build cohesion through the formation of shared vision. In addition, followers of an SCL will tend to have a strong internalization of the leader's values and goals (value congruence). That is, these values are likely to increase the intrinsic valence of goal accomplishment, especially objectives linked to CSR, which enable the decision maker to attach his or her self-concept to the broader good of society (Shamir *et al.*, 1993). Thus high-level followers who are executives themselves will coalesce around the SCL's vision and socially oriented values and become morally (rather than calculatively) committed to institute policies and strategies in line with CSR in their own units (Shamir and Howell, 1999). Moral commitment will be affective or emotional in nature, as well as a feeling of obligation or doing what is perceived to be right. In short, we predict:

P3   *The relationship between socialized charisma and affective and normative commitment to CSR will be mediated by TMT cohesion and CSR value congruence.*

A different picture emerges with the PCL. Instead of relying upon shared values, commitment and cohesion, the PCL will recognize the positive, image-building benefit of pursuing CSR. That is, she or he will recognize that there are both personal and organizational benefits to be gained by pursuing policies and practices relevant to CSR. We propose that the PCL will engage decision makers in a cost–benefit analysis to convince them of the relative benefits of CSR. Followers are likely to be convinced because of their admiration and devotion to the leader. Moreover, on the basis of our previous arguments, it is entirely possible that the PCL will manipulate data or information to make CSR appear to be especially beneficial. Furthermore, in an attempt to maximize his or her own public image, she or he may attempt to take personal credit for CSR actions taken by the firm. The end result will be calculative commitment. That is, instead of generating moral commitment or a feeling of obligation, the PCL will foster an instrumental or exchange-based desire to pursue CSR. Decision makers will be motivated to pursue CSR simply because the benefits of doing so outweigh the costs. In sum, we suggest:

P4   *The relationship between personalized charisma and calculative commitment to CSR will be mediated by a convincing cost-benefit analysis.*

Intellectual stimulation and commitment to CSR
Bass (1985) referred to intellectual stimulation when considering the intellectual component of transformational leadership. Intellectual stimulation involves leader actions geared toward the arousal and change in problem awareness and problem solving on the part of followers, as well as beliefs and values. Intellectually stimulating leaders help followers question old assumptions and beliefs so that they can view complex problems and issues in more innovative ways (Bass, 1997). The relevance of intellectual stimulation at the strategic leadership level has been considered in the literature. For example, Wortman (1982) described the importance of top-level executives engaging themselves and subordinates in the intellectual

task of conceptualizing and articulating a firm's broader environmental context, as well as the threats and opportunities posed by that context. More recently, Boal and Hooijberg (2001) also emphasized the importance of the intellectual or cognitive aspects of strategic leadership.

Stratified systems theory (SST) sheds light on ways in which intellectual stimulation may be specifically relevant to strategic leadership. SST focuses on the cognitive side of leadership and strategy, asserting that effective strategic leaders are those with high levels of conceptual capacity (Jaques and Clement, 1991; Lewis and Jacobs, 1992). Conceptual capacity involves the ability to think abstractly and integrate complex information, providing an antecedent to leadership action. SST emphasizes that conceptual capacity is most relevant in terms of the way the leader develops a useful understanding of the strategic environment. Thus the concept is in line with the work of Conger and Kanungo (1998), who stressed the leader's ability to recognize both opportunities and constraints in the environment, and they noted how the ability to do so varies widely among strategic leaders.

More relevant to the present study, conceptual capacity includes the ability to integrate or process information pertinent to the environment (that is, breadth of perspective) and to deal with a high level of abstraction. Lewis and Jacobs (1992) stressed that conceptual capacity is more important at higher levels of management, especially in the context of strategy formulation. Such a capacity allows strategic leaders to develop insight and construct visions over long time horizons using their own judgment processes unconstrained by the boundaries, values, beliefs or points of view of others.

We propose that an intellectually stimulating leader will use conceptual capacity to scan and think broadly about the environmental context and the manner in which a wide variety of organizational stakeholders may be served. They will possess complex mental maps that contain a systematic view of the external forces that have an impact on the organization. Their mental maps include a dynamic picture of how the various external forces interact with each other and, as a result, present a richer perspective of firm performance and competitive advantage that goes beyond simple cost leadership or product differentiation (Porter and Kramer, 2002). Intellectually stimulating leaders realize that success in such an environment requires strong relationships with a variety of key stakeholders.

Indeed stakeholder theory is relevant to understanding the potential linkage between transformational leadership and CSR, especially with regard to intellectual stimulation. It specifies that a firm is composed of a number of different constituencies, such as employees, suppliers, customers, shareholders and the broader community (Donaldson and Preston, 1995; Freeman, 1984). All of these constituencies have a strategic and/or moral stake in the firm, and they are each guided by their own interests and values. The problem facing senior management, and especially the CEO, is to enhance the welfare of the firm while simultaneously balancing the needs of the various constituents. Many scholars claim that shareholders are by far the most important claimant, since they are the owners of the company. However Bass and Steidlmeier (1999) asserted that, because of his/ her broad-ranging moral and justice values, the authentic transformational leader will attempt to balance the interests of all stakeholders.

We propose that the intellectually stimulating leader will use his or her understanding of complex environmental conditions to enhance followers' thinking regarding how the demands of achieving performance goals can be balanced with the desire to pursue CSR. For example, their own ideas and beliefs are likely to stimulate followers' thinking about how socially responsible outcomes can be achieved, while simultaneously generating adequate returns for shareholders. These ideas and beliefs may induce followers to reconsider their own prior beliefs that enhanced performance can only be achieved at the expense of CSR. That is, followers will view the issue of integrating strategy and CSR from a different perspective such that CSR will be viewed more as an opportunity, rather than a threat. There is a strengthened realization that the company does not exist in isolation from its community and society surrounding it. For example, improving education in society may be viewed as a social good, but intellectually stimulating leaders may also attempt to show how improving the educational level of the workforce can enhance competitive advantage (Porter and Kramer, 2002). The upshot is that followers will attempt to balance CSR concerns in their own strategic decision making.

As depicted in Figure 11.1, we purport that the ultimate effect of CEO intellectual stimulation will be on all three components of CSR commitment. Affective and normative commitment will be influenced as the leader challenges old beliefs or negative attitudes pertaining to CSR, while simultaneously relaying his own beliefs and values. In addition, calculative commitment will be affected by helping followers to rethink the benefit of CSR and how such policies might be implemented in an effective manner. For example, the intellectually stimulating CEO might help followers to re-examine basic assumptions that might have suggested to them that CSR simply cannot be cost-effective. In sum, we argue:

P5   The relationship between intellectual stimulation and affective, normative and calculative commitment to CSR will be mediated by the extent to which followers' negative beliefs and assumptions are challenged, and their understanding of how to balance CSR in decision making is enhanced.

The findings of Meyer *et al.* (1993) imply that affective and normative commitment components have a stronger impact on the logical outcomes of organizational commitment (such as turnover) than those associated with calculative commitment. Likewise we expect that affective and normative commitments to CSR are likely to have a stronger effect on the extent of CSR practices, as compared to calculative CSR, especially over time. They will also generate an intrinsic or inspired desire to work toward the realization of CSR. In contrast, the motivation to pursue CSR may be more fleeting when that desire is more calculative in nature. That is, with calculative commitment, motivations to engage in CSR can be unstable and fleeting. However the intrinsic motivation generated by affective and normative commitment is likely to be more stable and pervasive (that is, influencing various aspects of CSR). In sum, we suggest:

P6　*The association between affective and normative commitment to CSR and subsequent CSR practices will be stronger and more enduring, as compared to calculative commitment.*

An exploratory study

Sampled firms
We conducted an exploratory study to examine the basic question suggested by our model: does transformational leadership predict CSR? A total of 95 US and 55 Canadian firms were considered for participation. In order to be considered for inclusion in the sample, a firm had to conform to three criteria: (1) net sales greater than one billion dollars, (2) the CEO had at least two years of tenure, and (3) at least six individuals per firm at the vice president, senior vice president, or general manager level who could be identified in a corporate directory. The first criterion was based on the notion that it would be easier to obtain performance data for larger firms. The CEO tenure criterion was used in order to allow the CEO time to demonstrate charismatic leadership and implement such policies as CSR. The third criterion was necessary in an attempt to obtain input from multiple managers per firm allowing for non-response to the survey.

Nearly twice as many American firms were solicited because there was a greater proportion of American firms that met the aforementioned criteria. These firms represented a wide range of industries such as telecommunications, retailing, utilities, food processing, banking and manufacturing (for example, automotive). A total of 56 firms (51 US and five Canadian) were subsequently used in our analyses. These firms met the above criteria, and CSR data (described below) were available for them.

The study included a survey administration at the end of 1992. Several managers from each of our included firms were approached for participation. These managers were employed in a wide range of areas including general management, marketing, finance, accounting, human resources, strategic planning, engineering and legal services. Each respondent was a senior manager who was considered capable of the leadership qualities of his or her CEO. The survey response rate was approximately 28 per cent. Given the importance of these managers in their respective organizations, and the potential sensitivity of survey items dealing with CEO leadership, such a response rate can be considered reasonable and acceptable (Finkelstein, 1992). Despite attempts to obtain at least two managers per firm, 12 of the 125 respondents were the sole representatives of their firms. The other respondents represented 44 firms (either two or three respondents per firm).

Measures and procedures
We assessed CEO charismatic leadership and intellectual stimulation using 13 items based on the Multifactor Leadership Questionnaire (MLQ) (Bass, 1985) that were considered by the authors to be especially relevant to leadership at the strategic level. These items were originally developed for subsequent use in the work of Howell and Avolio (1993) and were refined in a revision of the MLQ (Bass and Avolio, 1990). Each participant was asked to think about the CEO of his or her respective firm, and then to rate that individual on each item on a five-point scale with anchors ranging from 'not at all' to 'frequently, if not always'. Each respondent was asked to provide the name of the CEO of that person's firm to ensure that respondents from a respective firm rated the same individual. This precaution was necessary because of the possibility of CEO turnover at or about the time of the survey.

Nine of the items were intended to assess charismatic leadership, while the other four items were chosen for intellectual stimulation. A factor analysis using principle components as the extraction procedure and varimax rotation was conducted to determine the appropriateness of proceeding with two separate measures. The results confirm a two-factor solution.[1] Specifically two factors with eigenvalues greater than one were extracted, which accounted for 60 per cent of the common variance. The first factor clearly represents charismatic leadership (alpha = 0.90), while the second factor represented intellectual stimulation (alpha = 0.86). Using tests for determining the appropriateness of aggregating scores from multiple respondents, we combined respondents' perceptions of charismatic leadership and intellectual stimulation to produce averaged, aggregated scores for the 44 respective firms for which multiple respondents were available. The other

12 firms were represented by single respondents. For the firm-level analyses reported below, the correlation between the two leadership measures was 0.46, indicating only a moderate amount of covariation.

We were able to link data on CEO leadership characteristics to firm-level information on CSR provided to us by the firm of Kinder, Lydenberg and Domini (KLD). The KLD data provide ratings of CSR for investors who want to 'screen' investment portfolios to exclude companies that violate their social principles. This information, which pertains to CSR for 537 publicly traded firms over the period 1991–6, is based on surveys, financial statements, articles on companies in the popular press and academic journals, and government reports. Sharfman (1996) found that these data represent a significant improvement on existing self-reported measures of corporate social performance (see Aupperle, 1991, in terms of construct validity). In addition the KLD data have been used in several recent CSR studies (Hillman and Keim, 2001; McWilliams and Siegel, 2000; Waddock and Graves, 1997a).

This information is used to assess CSR based on 12 indicators consisting of two categories. The first category consists of qualitative measures of CSR, including community relations, diversity, employee relations, environment performance, product quality and non-US operations (for example, usually environment and labor relations), as well as a residual category called 'other', which evaluates the level of executive compensation, disputes with tax authorities, and the social performance of organizations in which the firm has invested (for example, a company may have a minority interest in a firm with social concerns).

For example, a company's level of environmental social responsibility is assessed in terms of several actions, including the extent to which the firm uses clean energy and alternative fuels, recycles, derives substantial revenue from products that promote or generate environmental benefits, yields hazardous waste and toxic emissions, and violates environmental statutes. Actions on the part of a firm with respect to diversity include the extent to which women and minorities are represented in senior management positions (including the CEO), the extent of contracting to women and minority-owned businesses, employment of the disabled and the extent to which a firm has been involved in controversies relating to affirmative action. For information regarding other indicators, see Waddock and Graves (1997a).

The second category of KLD data contains CSR indicators that are referred to as 'exclusionary' screens, since many portfolio managers will automatically exclude firms that engage in these activities from their portfolios. These five indicators are alcohol, tobacco, gambling, military contracting and nuclear power. Graves and Waddock (1994) and Sharfman

(1996) have demonstrated that, together, both categories adequately capture the domain of what management scholars consider to be CSR.[2]

Unfortunately we had incomplete information on four aspects of CSR for the entire sample period (1991–6): alcohol, tobacco, gambling and non-US operations. The end result is that we have measures for eight indicators of CSR for 537 firms. We conducted a factor analysis with principle components as the extraction procedure and varimax rotation to assess the factor structure of the eight indicators. We computed averages over the sample period (that is, averaging annual scores on the CSR aspects for 1991–6), which were then used in the factor analysis. Three factors with eigenvalues exceeding one were extracted, which accounted for 56 per cent of the common variance. The third dimension was excluded from subsequent analyses since it was represented by a single indicator, nuclear power. We labeled the two remaining dimensions *strategic* CSR and *social* CSR. Strategic CSR was indicated by environmental, product quality, other, employee relations and military (alpha = 0.77). Social CSR was represented by the community and diversity indicators (alpha = 0.80). Our purpose in using this terminology is to highlight the point that the first dimension appears to be capturing aspects of CSR that relate more clearly to the firm's competitive strategy (for example, differentiation, reputation building). In contrast, the latter dimension appears to be based more on concern for social issues.[3]

Note that our categorization of CSR, based on the results of the factor analysis, yields slightly different categories of CSR than those presented in Waddock and Graves (1997b) and Hillman and Keim (2001), which were also based on KLD data. In those studies, the authors asserted that five dimensions of CSR (employee relations, diversity issues, environmental issues, product issues and community relations) represent 'stakeholder management' aspects of CSR, while all other dimensions constitute 'social issue' participation. However they did not formally test this assertion using factor analytic procedures.

We included *Compustat*-derived control measures of firm size (total assets), R&D intensity (average annual ratio of R&D to sales) and prior profit levels (industry-corrected return on equity for the seven-year time period prior to survey administration).

Findings
Several correlational findings are particularly noteworthy. First, neither charisma nor intellectual stimulation was significantly correlated with a composite measure of social CSR averaged across 1993–6 (that is, post survey administration). Second, a comparable, composite measure of strategic CSR was also not significantly correlated with charisma, although

the correlation was positive ($r = 0.20$, $p > 0.05$). However we did obtain a significant, positive correlation between intellectual stimulation and strategic CSR ($r = 0.36$, $p < 0.05$). Third, the results reveal positive associations between strategic CSR and firm size ($r = 0.24$, $p < 0.10$), R&D intensity ($r = 0.39$, $p < 0.05$) and prior profit levels ($r = 0.27$, $p < 0.10$), findings that are consistent with theoretical and empirical evidence presented in Waddock and Graves (1997a) and McWilliams and Siegel (2000). Fourth, social CSR is also significantly related to R&D intensity ($r = 0.33$, $p < 0.05$). Fifth, only a modest correlation was obtained between social and strategic CSR ($r = 0.25$, $p < 0.10$).

We used a two-step, regression procedure with social and strategic CSR (1993–6) as the dependent variables. This procedure was followed since we propose that transformational leadership may influence the propensity of firms to engage in CSR, in addition to those factors associated with a theory of the firm perspective on CSR (Waddock and Graves, 1997a; McWilliams and Siegel, 2000). Therefore, following Waddock and Graves (1997a), we include measures of lagged profitability and firm size as control variables in the first step. The inclusion of profits is based on the Waddock and Graves (1997a) finding that better financial performance results in higher CSR. These authors also included an industry dummy variable in their analyses. We chose instead to normalize the KLD data (for all 538 observations) by using two-digit SIC codes over the sample period. Thus our measures of strategic CSR and social CSR were each constructed relative to other firms in the same sector. Based on the work of McWilliams and Siegel (2000), R&D intensity was included as a control variable in the first step in each model. We also controlled for two aspects of CEO tenure: length of tenure as the firm's CEO prior to survey administration, and length of tenure as CEO during the four-year period following survey administration that included KLD measures (that is, 1993–6).[4] Finally, in order to generate a more conservative test of our hypotheses, we also included lagged measures of strategic CSR and social CSR, respectively, as control variables in the first step. The lagged measures represent average levels of the respective CSR variables for the years 1991 and 1992.

The models for strategic CSR fit better than those for social CSR, as evidenced by the higher R^2 values for the corresponding regressions. Consistent with Waddock and Graves (1997a) and McWilliams and Siegel (2000), we found that increases in firm size, and R&D intensity (but not prior profitability) appeared to induce higher levels of CSR. This applied to both strategic and social CSR. Neither measure of CEO tenure appeared to have any explanatory power. However, contrary to expectations, CEO charisma did not have significant predictive power with respect to either strategic or social CSR. In contrast, our key empirical finding is that CEO intellectual stimulation at a given point in time (1992) has a positive impact on the propensity of firms to engage in *strategic* CSR in the future (that is, 1993–6), beyond any variance accounted for by firm size, performance, R&D intensity and the lagged effect of CSR (R^2 change $= 0.05$, $p < 0.05$).

Conclusions and future directions

The findings of our exploratory study indicate that a key dimension of CEO transformational leadership, intellectual stimulation, has a positive impact on subsequent CSR activity. However it is interesting to note that the findings appeared to hold only for strategically-oriented CSR, not for more socially-oriented CSR. Such results imply not only that intellectually stimulating leaders are attempting to pursue corporately responsible actions, but also that they focus their efforts on areas that are most germane to strategic concerns of the firm, such as enhancing product quality or reputation and environmental performance. In contrast, CSR issues that have more of a social basis (that is, community relations and diversity) are not significantly related to transformational leadership.

This study should be considered a preliminary and incomplete test of the model in Figure 11.1 for several reasons. First, a number of antecedent and mediating variables were not included. For example, with regard to charismatic leadership, we did not measure actual CEO values pertaining to CSR or ethics per se. We encourage research that more directly assesses the moral and ethical qualities of leaders (Craig and Gustafson, 1998; Parry and Proctor-Thomson, 2002). It is conceivable that integrity or other moral aspects of charismatic leadership more directly stimulate CSR activity, rather than the aspects of charisma assessed in the exploratory study that included vision, admiration for the leader and high expectations and determination on the part of the leader.

Second, attempts should be made to assess personalized charisma directly, although such measurement may be challenging. For instance, Figure 11.1 depicts the socialized and personalized charisma in dichotomous terms, yet they probably exist more as a continuum. Moreover the two forms of charismatic leadership may be somewhat fluid in nature, changing over time for particular leaders. Indeed the tendency may be to shift from a socialized power motive to a more personalized power motive, rather than vice versa. Kets de Vries (1993) discussed how such tendencies may actually be associated with aging processes and a leader's fear of losing strength, power and even virility as he or she grows older. These fears could cause an otherwise socialized charismatic to resort to manipulation and image building to maintain power, while gradually losing genuine concern for the greater good of the organization. As a result, some followers may eventually reject the influence of a leader whom they initially accepted (Shamir and Howell, 1999).

The upshot is that personalized behaviors are likely to engender heterogeneity in terms of charismatic attributions of the PCL on the part of followers. Over time, some followers may be enamored of the leader's accomplishments, charm and other personal qualities. These followers may trust the leader and feel secure regarding their own positions, as long as they remain loyal. Conversely other followers may not be so enamored. Instead they may attribute personalized goals to the leader, especially in the absence of a shared vision.

Kozlowski and Klein (2000) characterized such heterogeneous emergence of an organizational phenomenon as a configural or compilation model. They noted that, while such phenomena have only occasionally been theorized in the organizational literature, they are nevertheless quite common in organizations. In short, emergent phenomena or constructs (such as charismatic leadership) are not necessarily shared or uniform and, instead, may be nonuniform or marked by differentiation, disagreement, coalition formation and so forth. Indeed Kozlowski and Klein (2000) suggested that, in one situation or type, a phenomenon may emerge in a uniform or composition form (such as socialized charisma). Conversely, in another situation or type, the phenomenon may emerge in a nonuniform or compilation form (such as personalized charisma).

Third, our differential results for social versus strategic CSR raises issues pertaining to the definition and measurement of the CSR construct. For example, as noted earlier, the KLD data represent ratings of CSR by a firm of industry analysts. The goal of KLD is to provide information for investors who want to 'screen' investment portfolios to exclude companies that violate their social principles. Thus KLD is simply providing a service for individuals with a liberal social agenda. However we would argue that, for theory development and research purposes, it may be problematic for such a bias to determine parameters for the definition and measurement of the CSR construct.

For example, the extent to which a firm engages in military contracting serves as one of the 'screens' in the KLD rating process. In other words, all other factors equal, a firm that engages in military contracting would tend to receive a lower score on CSR. The inclusion of such a screen is biased toward a particular agenda, rather than being representative of broader thinking regarding the nature of CSR. Note also that the KLD data do not include a consideration of shareholders and whether they are treated in a responsible manner. That is unfortunate, since the type of corruption surrounding the recent Enron and Worldcom scandals would commonly be considered to be corporately irresponsible by society at large, in terms of its ultimate effects on shareholders, employees and the greater economy.

The results of our study suggest that a cognitive component may come into play, requiring leadership that is oriented toward problem solving and getting followers to reconceptualize or engage in issues such as CSR. Perhaps our significant findings pertaining to intellectual stimulation especially make sense because of the way this factor of transformational leadership engages all three aspects of commitment to CSR, as shown in Figure 11.1. An intellectually stimulating CEO may take a more inclusive view of the role of his or her firm within society and pursue a strategic and focused approach to CSR that enhances both the firm's competitive position and its place in a broader societal context (Porter and Kramer, 2002). Thus, to understand better the importance of leadership at the strategic level, researchers may need to take into account transformational leadership factors in addition to charisma, such as intellectual stimulation.

Additional leadership research may be warranted that goes beyond our study and model. Although we have implied the broader involvement of lower-level executives in decision making relevant to CSR, an implicit assumption of this chapter is that it is the CEO who is primarily formulating and attempting to implement the firm's CSR policies. Consequently a related assumption is that the appropriate level of analysis for examining leadership and CSR policies is the corporate or organizational level. However leadership and CSR relationships may be more appropriate for study at lower units of analysis (such as at divisional level). Moreover CSR may be at least in part a function of the process and philosophy of the board of directors, rather than just the CEO.

We would like to encourage future quantitative and qualitative research that directly assesses the role of leadership in CSR formulation and implementation at multiple levels of analyses. As an example of a more qualitative approach, we can envision a multiple case study design comparing organizations, and divisions within those organizations, in terms of their involvement in CSR. These organizations could be analyzed in depth in terms of the CEO's role in formulating and implementing CSR, the roles of lower-level executives and managers, and the role of the board of directors. Research along these lines could help provide a richer understanding of linkages between leadership and CSR across the levels of an organization.

Notes

1. In order to maximize our sample size, the factor analysis was conducted using a larger sample of 234 individuals that included all of the original survey respondents (including firms for which CSR data were not available) from both the US and Canadian firms. For more specific empirical results, please contact either of the authors.

2. For details about the scoring of KLD data, please contact either author.
3. We do not wish to imply that diversity and community initiatives cannot be used for strategic purposes under certain circumstances, only that most firms engage in these activities largely to advance a social cause. It seems plausible to us that the dimensions that we call 'strategic' are much more likely to be matrixed into a firm's business and corporate-level strategies, as compared to the indicators loading on 'social' CSR. For example, the measurement of diversity appears to represent an effort to adhere to the social movement of embracing diversity (for example, employment of the disabled), rather than using diversity in a strategic manner. Conversely the measurement of such strategic CSR indicators as environmental performance, at least in part are more geared toward the firm's competitive strategy (for example, deriving substantial revenue from products that promote or generate environmental benefits).
4. Although there was little CEO turnover during the 1993–6 period, we excluded the five companies whose CEOs departed and re-estimated the regression findings.

References

Aupperle, K.E. (1991), 'The use of forced choice survey procedures in assessing corporate social orientation', in L.E. Post (ed.), *Research in Corporate Social Performance and Policy*, vol. 12, Greenwich, CT: JAI Press, pp. 269–79.

Bass, B.M. (1985), *Leadership and Performance beyond Expectations*, New York: Free Press.

Bass, B.M. (1997), 'Does the transactional–transformational leadership paradigm transcend organizational and national boundaries?', *American Psychologist*, **52**, 130–39.

Bass, B.M. (1998), *Transformational Leadership: Industrial, Military and Educational Impact*, Mahwah, NJ: Lawrence Erlbaum Associates.

Bass, B.M. and B.J. Avolio (1990), *The Multifactor Leadership Questionnaire*, Palo Alto, CA: Consulting Psychologists Press.

Bass, B.M. and B.J. Avolio (1994), 'Introduction', in B.M. Bass and B.J. Avolio (eds), *Improving Organizational Effectiveness through Transformational Leadership*, Thousand Oaks, CA: Sage, pp. 1–9.

Bass, B.M. and P. Steidlmeier (1999), 'Ethics, character and authentic transformational leadership behavior', *Leadership Quarterly*, **10**, 181–217.

Beyer, J.M. and L.D. Browning (1999), 'Transforming an industry in crisis: charisma, routinization and supportive cultural leadership', *Leadership Quarterly*, **10**, 483–520.

Boal, K.B. and R. Hooijberg (2001), 'Strategic leadership research: moving on', *Leadership Quarterly*, **11**, 515–49.

Burns, J.M. (1978), *Leadership*, New York: Harper Row.

Cannella, A.A., Jr and M.J. Monroe (1997), 'Contrasting perspectives on strategic leaders: Toward a more realistic view of top managers', *Journal of Management*, **23**, 213–37.

Conger, J.A. and R.N. Kanungo (1998), *Charismatic Leadership in Organizations*, Thousand Oaks, CA: Sage Publications.

Craig, S.B. and S.B. Gustafson (1998), 'Perceived leader integrity scale: an instrument for assessing employee perceptions of leader integrity', *The Leadership Quarterly*, **9**, 127–45.

Daft, R.L. (2002), *The Leadership Experience*, (2nd edn), Cincinnati, OH: South-Western.

Donaldson, T. and L.E. Preston (1995), 'The stakeholder theory of the corporation: concepts, evidence and implications', *Academy of Management Review*, **20**, 65–91.

Evans, M.G. (1970), 'The effects of supervisory behavior on the path–goal relationship', *Organizational Behavior and Human Performance*, **5**, 277–98.

Finkelstein, S. (1992), 'Power in top management teams: dimensions, measurement, and validation', *Academy of Management Journal*, **35**, 505–38.

Finkelstein, S. and D.C. Hambrick (1996), *Strategic Leadership: Top Executives and their Effects*, Minneapolis and St. Paul: West Publishing.

Freeman, R.E. (1984), *Strategic Management: a Stakeholder Approach*, Boston, MA: Pitman.

Friedman, M. (1970), 'The social responsibility of business to increase its profit', *New York Times*, 13 September, pp. 122–6.

Gardner, W.L. and B.J. Avolio (1998), 'The charismatic relationship: a dramaturgical perspective', *Academy of Management Review*, **23**, 32–58.

Graves, S. and S. Waddock (1994), 'Institutional investors and corporate social performance', *Academy of Management Journal*, **37**, 1035–46.

Hackett, R.D., P. Bycio and P. Hausdorf (1992), 'Further assessments of a three-component model of organizational commitment', in J.L. Wall and L.R. Jauch (eds), *Academy of Management Best Papers Proceedings*, Madison, WI: Omnipress, pp. 212–16.

Hambrick, D.C. and P.A. Mason (1984), 'Upper echelons: the organization as a reflection of its top managers', *Academy of Management Review*, **9**, 193–206.

Hillman, A.J. and G.D. Keim (2001), 'Shareholder value, stakeholder management and social issues: what's the bottom line?', *Strategic Management Journal*, **22**, 125–39.

House, R.J. (1971), 'A path–goal theory of leadership effectiveness', *Administrative Science Quarterly*, **16**, 321–38.

House, R.J. (1999), 'Weber and the neo-charismatic leadership paradigm: a response to Beyer', *The Leadership Quarterly*, **10**, 563.

House, R.J. and R, Aditya (1997), 'The social scientific study of leadership: quo vadis?', *Journal of Management*, **23**, 409–74.

House, R.J. and J.M. Howell (1992), 'Personality and charismatic leadership', *Leadership Quarterly*, **3**, 81–108.

House, R.J. and B. Shamir (1993), 'Toward an integration of transformational, charismatic and visionary theories of leadership', in M. Chemmers and R. Ayman (eds), *Leadership: Perspectives and Research Directions*, New York: Academic Press, pp. 81–107.

House, R.J., D.M. Rousseau and M. Thomas-Hunt (1995), 'The meso paradigm: a framework for the integration of micro and macro organizational behavior', *Research in Organizational Behavior*, **17**, 71–114.

Howell, J.M. and B.J. Avolio (1993), 'Transformational leadership, transactional leadership, locus of control and support for innovation: key predictors of consolidated business-unit performance', *Journal of Applied Psychology*, **78**, 891–902.

Jaques, E. and S.D. Clement (1991), *Executive leadership: a practical guide to managing complexity*, Arlington, VA: Cason Hall.

James, L.R., R.G. Demaree and G. Wolf (1984), 'Estimating within-group inter-rater reliability with and without response bias', *Journal of Applied Psychology*, **69**, 85–98.

Jernigan, I.E., J.M. Beggs and G.F. Kohut (2002), 'Dimensions of work satisfaction as predictors of commitment type', *Journal of Managerial Psychology*, **17**, 564–79.

Jones, T. (1995), 'Instrumental stakeholder theory: a synthesis of ethics and economics', *Academy of Management Review*, **20**, 404–37.

Kanungo, R.N. (2001), 'Ethical values of transactional and transformational leaders', *Canadian Journal of Administrative Sciences*, **18**, 257–65.

Kets de Vries, M.F.R. (1993), *Leaders, Fools and Imposters*, San Francisco: Jossey-Bass.

Kohlberg, L. (1976), 'Moral stages and moralization: the cognitive-developmental approach', in T. Likona (ed.), *Moral Development and Behavior: Theory, Research, and Social Issues*, Austin, TX: Holt, Rinehart and Winston, pp. 31–53.

Kozlowski, S.W.J. and K.J. Klein (2000), 'A multilevel approach to theory and research in organizations: contextual, temporal, and emergent processes', in K.J. Klein and S.W.J. Kozlowski (eds), *Multilevel Theory, Research and Methods in Organizations: Foundations, Extensions and New Directions*, San Francisco: Jossey-Bass, pp. 3–90.

Kuhnert, K.W. (1994), 'Transforming leadership: developing people through delegation', in B.M. Bass and B.J. Avolio (eds), *Improving Organizational Effectiveness through Transformational Leadership*, Thousand Oaks, CA: Sage, pp. 10–25.

Kuhnert, K.W. and P. Lewis (1987), 'Transactional and transformational leadership: a constructive/developmental analysis', *Academy of Management Review*, **12**, 648–57.

Lewis, P. and T.O. Jacobs (1992), 'Individual differences in strategic leadership capacity: a constructive/developmental view', in R.L. Phillips and J.G. Hunt (eds), *Strategic Leadership: a Multiorganizational-level Perspective*, Westport, CT: Quorum Books, pp. 121–37.

Locke, E.A. (2003), 'Foundations for a theory of leadership', in S.E. Murphy and R.E. Riggio (eds), *The Future of Leadership Development*, Mahwah, NJ: Lawrence Erlbaum Associates, pp. 29–46.

Lowe, K.B., K.G. Kroeck and N. Sivasubramaniam (1996), 'Effectiveness correlates of transformational and transactional leadership: a meta-analytic review of the MLQ literature', *Leadership Quarterly*, **7**, 385–425.

Maccoby, M. (2004), 'Narcissistic leaders: the incredible pros, the inevitable cons', *Harvard Business Review*, **82**, 92–101.

McWilliams, A. and D. Siegel (2000), 'Corporate social responsibility and financial performance: correlation or misspecification?', *Strategic Management Journal*, **21**, 603–9.

McWilliams, A. and D. Siegel (2001), 'Corporate social responsibility: a theory of the firm perspective', *Academy of Management Review*, **26**, 117–28.

Mendonca, M. (2001), 'Preparing for ethical leadership in organizations', *Canadian Journal of Administrative Sciences*, **18**, 266–276.

Meyer, J.P., N.J. Allen and C.A. Smith (1993), 'Commitment to organizations and occupations: extension and test of a three-component conceptualisation', *Journal of Applied Psychology*, **78**, 538–51.

Mischel, W. (1977), 'The interaction of person and situation', in D. Magnusson and N.S. Ender (eds), *Personality at the Crossroads: Current Issues in Interactional Psychology*, Hillsdale, NJ: Erlbaum.

Nanus, B. (1992), *Visionary Leadership*, San Francisco: Jossey-Bass.

Parry, K.W. and S.B. Proctor-Thomson (2002), 'Perceived integrity of transformational leaders in organisational settings', *Journal of Business Ethics*, **35**, 75–96.

Pawar, B.S. and K.K. Eastman (1997), 'The nature and implications of contextual influences on transformational leadership: a conceptual examination', *Academy of Management Review*, **22**, 80–109.

Penley, L.E. and S. Gould (1988), 'Etzioni's model of organizational involvement: a perspective for understanding commitment to organizations', *Journal of Organizational Behavior*, **9**, 43–59.

Porter, M.E. and M.R. Kramer (2002), 'The competitive advantage of corporate philanthropy', *Harvard Business Review*, **80**, 56–69.

Priem, R.L., D.W. Lyon and G.G. Dess (1999), 'Limitations of demographic proxies in top management team heterogeneity research', *Journal of Management*, **25**, 935–53.

Russo, M.V. and P.A. Fouts (1997), 'A resource-based perspective on corporate environmental performance and profitability', *Academy of Management Journal*, **40**, 534–59.

Sashkin, M. (1988), 'The visionary leader', in J.A. Conger and R.N. Kanungo (eds), *Charismatic Leadership: the Elusive Factor in Organizational Effectiveness*, San Francisco: Jossey-Bass, pp. 122–60.

Senge, P.M. (1990), *The Fifth Discipline: the Art and Practice of the Learning Organization*, New York: Doubleday.

Shamir, B. and J.M. Howell (1999), 'Organizational and contextual influences on the emergence and effectiveness of charismatic leadership', *The Leadership Quarterly*, **10**, 257–83.

Shamir, B., R.J. House and M.B. Arthur (1993), 'The motivational effects of charismatic leadership: a self-concept based theory', *Organization Science*, **4**, 577–94.

Sharfman, M. (1996), 'The construct validity of the Kinder, Lydenberg & Domini social performance ratings data', *Journal of Business Ethics*, **15**, 287–96.

Trice, H.M. and J.M. Beyer (1986), 'Charisma and its routinization in two social movement organizations', in B.M. Staw (ed.), *Research in Organizational Behavior*, vol. 8, Greenwich, CT: JAI Press, pp. 113–64.

Turner, N., J. Barling, O. Epitropaki, V. Butcher and C. Milner (2002), 'Transformational leadership and moral reasoning', *Journal of Applied Psychology*, **87**, 304–11.

Waddock, S. and S. Graves (1997a), 'The corporate social performance – financial performance link', *Strategic Management Journal*, **18**, 303–19.

Waddock, S. and S. Graves (1997b), 'Quality of management and quality of stakeholder relations', *Business and Society Review*, **36**, 250–79.

Waldman, D.A. and F.J. Yammarino (1999), 'CEO charismatic leadership: levels-of-management and levels-of-analysis effects', *Academy of Management Review*, **24**, 266–85.

Waldman, D.A., G.G. Ramirez, R.J. House and P. Puranam (2001), 'Does leadership matter? CEO leadership attributes under conditions of perceived environmental uncertainty', *Academy of Management Journal*, **44**, 134–43.

Weber, M. (1947), *The Theory of Social and Economic Organization*, trans. T. Parsons, 1st American edn, New York: Oxford University Press.

Winter, D.G. (1991), 'A motivational model of leadership: predicting long-term management success from TAT measures of power motivation and responsibility', *The Leadership Quarterly*, **2**, 67–80.

Wortman, M.S. (1982), 'Strategic management and changing leader–follower roles', *Journal of Applied Behavioral Science*, **18**, 371–83.

Wright, P. and S. Ferris (1997), 'Agency conflict and corporate strategy: the effect of divestment on corporate value', *Strategic Management Journal*, **18**, 77–83.

Yukl, G. (1999), 'An evaluation of conceptual weaknesses in transformational and charismatic leadership theories', *Leadership Quarterly*, **10**, 285–305.

12 Is there free will in business? Leadership and social impact management

Mary C. Gentile

Introduction

When I first went to work at a business school – well, not just any business school actually but the Harvard Business School in the mid-1980s – I experienced culture shock. This was a time when even the student newspapers at business schools crowed that students would attempt a hostile takeover of their grandmothers if they could make a profit at it.

I was fresh out of graduate school with a doctorate in the Humanities and nothing had prepared me for this new world. I was excited by the energy, the clarity of intention and the sheer logic of the place. It seemed the opposite of everything I had known. I would joke with my friends that, when my fellow doctoral students in literature and film used to ask 'how are you?', I would be considered suspect – either shallow or ignorant – if I had answered without the requisite level of angst, seasoned with knowing despair. At the business school, on the other hand, the accepted response to that greeting was 'Great, just great!' delivered in a firm and confident tone with direct eye contact and preferably accompanied by an energetic shake of one's right arm and closed fist. What looking glass had I stumbled through?

Business school and the corporate offices of senior executives I was privileged to frequent as a result of my then job as researcher, case writer and eventually faculty member at such a school were halls of purposefulness and confidence. Whereas the test of intelligence had previously been the ability to take a single passage of poetry or fiction and open it up, revealing multiple layers of meaning and nuance, the performance test here seemed to be the ability to define a problem so precisely and cleanly that all irrelevancy fell away and one was left with a clearly solvable equation or a single principle to optimize. It was a beautiful and heady world, albeit one to which I was unaccustomed.

Almost 20 years after my introduction to that world, we now live in a time when the once astonishing merger and acquisition (M&A) deals of the 1980s (remember *Barbarians at the Gates*?) are surpassed and even dwarfed on a regular basis and when CEOs, having risen to the status of popular heroes in the late 1990s, are now facing a heightened public scrutiny as a result of widely publicized and stunning excesses and abuses over the past few years. But despite this fall from grace, the belief in the power and the efficacy of business has not diminished; rather it is the public's trust in the business agenda and its methods that has been tarnished. In fact the degree of public and government scrutiny and even cynicism that business and its leaders encounter today is a direct reflection of the amount of power and control and capacity they are believed to wield.

And this brings us to a fundamental irony about leadership in this arena. Business leaders and aspiring business leaders in free market contexts are attracted to the potential to make an impact, to build something tangible, to manage and control an enterprise and, of course, to make money. This is a world of 'can do' attitudes, of belief in the individual's capacity to make a difference by sheer dint of talent and hard work. And yet, when it comes to the arena of social impacts and the global common good, these business practitioners all too often protest that their hands are tied. When it comes to running their business in a manner that explicitly serves society, through the value it creates and also the value it preserves, they too often appear to believe that the market prevents them from doing as much as they might wish. How can the arena of free market capitalism, so steeped in the orthodoxy of individualism and a belief in the mastery of one's own fate, be so constrained? Is there free will in business?

Social impact management

To try to answer this somewhat existential question, it is essential first to define the terrain within which business practices have an impact or over which business exerts its will. At The Aspen Institute's Business and Society Program (Aspen BSP),[1] we call this terrain the field of Social Impact Management[2] and we describe it as the field of inquiry at the intersection of business practice and wider societal concerns that reflects and respects the complex interdependency between the two. Social Impact Management is about managing this interdependency to mutual benefit. It is about recognizing that, in an increasingly global economy where business and environmental and political actions have faster and faster repercussions for other parts of the world, 'business and society' is a false dichotomy.

Social Impact Management, therefore, is not about 'business as the bad guy', but rather about business (or business practitioners) as those who need to look where they are going and examine what they are doing, in order to ensure both their own long-term viability and also that of the wider society within which they operate. Business is an exceedingly powerful player in an increasingly interdependent world, and it leaves very large footsteps in its wake. It needs to watch where it steps.

In order to take this kind of care, Social Impact Management requires asking a new and broader set of questions regarding the traditional terrain of business. For example, when determining business strategy it is common to explore a firm's purpose in terms of its objectives for competitive positioning. What is less common is for that strategy discussion to consider the firm's intentions and their implications for consumers, employees and community members, given the different choices around growth objectives and product development. These broader questions consider both short- and long-term views, a wider set of actors and stakeholders, and a more complex set of metrics.

Thus Social Impact Management, as a way of thinking about business decisions, explicitly considers three questions.

- Purpose: what is the purpose – in both societal and business terms – of a business or business activity?
- Social context: are the legitimate rights and responsibilities of relevant stakeholders considered? Is a proposed strategy evaluated, not only in terms of predicted business outcomes, but also in terms of its broader impacts – for example, on quality of life, the wider economy of a region, and security and safety?
- Metrics: how are performance and profitability measured? What is being counted and what is not being counted? Are impacts and results measured across both short- and long-term time frames?

While these questions are difficult to answer,[3] they are not significantly different by nature from the judgments and choices business managers make all the time. Business practitioners are familiar, if not comfortable, with decision making under conditions of incomplete information, asymmetrical information, time pressures, multiple party negotiations and so on. Furthermore wider society has impacts on business functioning and business has impacts on wider society, whether or not those impacts are actually identified, quantified and incorporated into an organization's decision-making processes. Social Impact Management simply raises the specter – and the possibility – of conscious choice.

Yet one cannot entertain the possibility of conscious choice without a free will, and that brings us back to our original question: is there free will in business? In Aspen BSP's and my own work with business practitioners and business scholars, we have encountered various permutations of this question, along with possible avenues for addressing it. Let us explore some of those questions and responses, seen through the three lenses of Social Impact Management: purpose, social context and metrics.

The purpose of business: 'raising the stakes?'

One of the most common ways in which business practitioners constrain their thinking and their action around Social Impact Management has to do with their definitions of purpose: the purpose of business writ large, of their firms and of their individual careers.

At the broadest level, we might frame this as a dialogue between those who would argue that the purpose of a business is to maximize shareholder value, on the one hand, and those who would argue that shareholder value is only a means to an end. For example, Milton Friedman raises the maximization of shareholder value to the level of a social responsibility – 'The social responsibility of business is to increase its profits' (Friedman, 1970, p. 32) – while Charles Handy looks for something beyond it: 'The purpose of a business ... is not to make a profit, full stop. It is to make a profit so that the business can do something more or better. That "something" becomes the real justification for the business' (Handy, 2002, p. 5). The intellectual debates aside, even scholars have told us that managers want to do something beyond maximizing shareholder profit.

For example, in 2003 Aspen BSP embarked upon a long-term project to explore the ways that corporate governance and accountability are understood and taught at leading graduate business schools in the United States. The project was launched with a set of in-depth interviews with faculty from finance, economics, accounting, business law and strategy, and they were invited to comment upon the shareholder value maximization model as a guiding framework for managerial action.

By and large, most interviewees taught and valued this model for its clarity and elegance, and although they acknowledged its limitations – the problems of incomplete and asymmetrical information, of externalities unaccounted for by either the market or government regulation, of competing short- and long-term time frames, of corruption and fraud, and so on – most of them pointed out that, in theory at least, the market would take such factors into account. These interview findings were not surprising, as it is in fact this model of shareholder value maximization that permeates the business education environment.

What was interesting, however, was the number of these scholars who also expressed their sense that neither they nor, in their view, business managers, really wanted to manage this way. One finance professor noted that managers were human beings, after all, and so they needed or wanted to look beyond the narrow maximization of shareholder value. Several others pointed out that, even from a narrow managerial effectiveness perspective, maximizing shareholder value was not very motivating as a focus for rallying employees. Others noted that there was something beyond narrow profit maximization that mattered, but the problem was that there were no rigorous or predictive decision guidelines that one might teach on how to make tradeoffs. In the face of such a messy calculus, the clarity of the single optimization model would always trump. Finally one interviewee noted that, in the recent market bubble, the appearance of a direct and almost immediate link between managerial action and market reaction fueled a sense that one could and even should 'manage the market' by acting in a manner that would always maximize share price. But this individual noted that such an attempt would be akin to the futility of trying to manage the scoreboard at a baseball game; the real focus should be on the playing field.

In their different ways, each of these interviewees was acknowledging the limitations, as well as the strengths, of business purpose narrowly defined as the maximization of shareholder value while regretting the lack of analytic and decision-making tools that would enable them to teach anything else. They felt their hands to be tied.

However, when this group of academics assembled in January 2004 to discuss the themes from their interviews, they began to search for ways out of this bind. Several of the legal scholars shared recent research demonstrating the latitude that executives and directors have under the law to consider stakeholders beyond investors in their decision making.[4] Some of the scholars talked about the diversity of objectives among shareholders themselves and the consequent lack of alignment around maximizing shareholder value: for example, there are short- and long-term investors; there are investors seeking consistent dividend returns and those looking to maximize share price in the short term and move on; there are those who hold certain social investment criteria; and so on. And others spoke about the need for a move away from the tyranny of single objective optimization models and the need to teach future business leaders to accept, even embrace, more complex and 'messy' decision making.

So, rather than a matter of free will – 'The devil made me do it' as Constance Bagley puts it, tongue firmly in cheek (Bagley and Page, 1999, p. 897) – perhaps the problem is a lack of tools, the surrender to the seduction of an elegant model, or even a failure of imagination? A quick look at some of the recent commentary from leading business thinkers on managerial practice suggests where some of the challenges lay. In response to current scandals and increased public scrutiny, Krishna Palepu and Paul Healy write in the *Harvard Business Review* about the failure of market intermediaries to maintain the system of checks and balances needed for the market to function, even as practitioners often lobby against strengthening them (Healy and Palepu, 2003). Max Bazerman writes of the power of individual managerial biases in judgment to obscure the consequences of their own actions and suggests structural changes in the public auditing process that may protect managers from their own blind spots (Bazerman *et al.*, 2002).

And even Michael Jensen writes of the need for executives to 'Just say no to Wall Street', arguing that a blind devotion to managing market signals at the expense of sound business practices is not optimal (Fuller and Jensen, 2002).

Whether advocating a structural, systemic 'fix' or an individual one, this sampling of commentators all identify the perverse incentives that make it difficult for managers to define their sense of purpose more capaciously than the maximization of shareholder value. Yet, even when their analysis suggests the ways in which managers' hands appear to be tied, these authors suggest that managerial will exists in the potential to support, or at least refrain from blocking, structural solutions to these incentive problems.

And this is exactly what an attention to Social Impact Management proposes: a commitment to ask the question beyond the status quo; to go to the space where alternatives emerge; to find ways to express one's will, just as those economists did when they gathered to discuss corporate governance and accountability. And, ironically, one of the lessons we have learned from both business leaders and scholars alike is that 'raising the stakes' (or perhaps more accurately seeing how high they have always been) can be the means to unleashing the will actually to go to this space of alternatives.

In 2000, 2001 and 2002, Aspen BSP gathered together groups of business executives and outstanding practitioners in leadership development to consider how to motivate business practitioners to move beyond a narrow definition of their purpose and to practice 'balanced leadership': that is, leadership attentive to the wider social impacts of management as well as economic performance; to both short- and long-term implications of decision; and to the concerns and voices of multiple stakeholders in the enterprise (Jusela *et al.*, 2002). In initial meetings when markets were soaring, there was a shared commitment to the need for such an expansion of the notion of leadership. Later, however, in the face of plummeting markets and hemorrhaging balance sheets, some participants wondered if this so-called 'balanced leadership' was merely a luxury.

The group explored this idea and concluded that, rather than relegating such leadership to the margins, times of crisis provided important lessons that made their efforts more effective. And perhaps the most important of these lessons had to do with purpose; that is, while times of crisis appear to 'raise the stakes' for management decision making, in reality they allow leaders to see the stakes that have been there all along. This recognition enables them to define their purpose as something worth their commitment and the commitment of their employees. As a business strategy scholar explained it, forcing oneself to confront the reality of what is at stake in a business decision creates a heightened awareness of the options that are actually available to decision makers. Choices, he argues, do exist.

One of the participants in these leadership dialogues, a senior executive in a once high flying tech firm reflected:

> In our firm's heyday, about a year and a half ago ... the object of the game here was to make money. Money had become a substitute for everything else we had learned about people, purpose and so on. And when the money went away, we now feel we have nothing to fall back upon. (Jusela *et al.*, 2002, p. 9)

A desire to define the firm's purpose in a deeper way grew out of such conversations, but such a desire led to another iteration of our original question, this time about the individual manager's degrees of freedom in defining and acting on his or her sense of personal purpose.

Individual purpose

Frequently the attempt to discuss a broader purpose for the corporation, whether among executives, directors or business students, begins and ends with a reference to the idea that, although shareholder profit must be maximized, one should do so *within constraints* (legal, ethical, social). This reference to 'constraints' is too often a kind of sleight of hand that smooths away the thorniest questions without actually putting any rigor or necessity or specifics around what this kind of management would really look like.

And often when we actually get to the point in the conversation where we have to talk about the specifics of Social Impact Management, we arrive at a discussion of the individual manager and his or her own personal sense of purpose. And this brings us flat up against another conflict between stated values and our belief (or disbelief) in free action.

In 2001 and 2002, Aspen BSP conducted a survey of MBA student attitudes about the role of business in wider society, and their findings raise many questions relevant to this discussion.[5] For one thing, when asked to assess how much consideration current business leaders give to shareholders, employees, consumers and social and environmental conditions when making business decisions, students consistently reported that shareholders received the lion's share of attention. But when asked what balance they would strike if they were the ones heading the firm, these students offered a different picture where attention to shareholders, while still receiving the largest share, was much more in balance with the attention they would give to other considerations.

Despite this reported commitment, when asked whether they expected they would have to make business decisions that conflict with their values during their careers, half the respondents in 2002 (and more than half in 2001) said they did. The vast majority of respondents in both years reported that it would be very likely or somewhat likely that they would experience this as stressful. And in 2001, more than half of respondents said their response to such a conflict would more than likely be to look for another job; in 2002, that number declined to 35 per cent, still a significant number. Other action alternatives such as advocating alternative approaches in the company increased, but one in five students reported that their business education was not preparing them at all to manage such conflicts.[6]

This survey, along with Aspen BSP faculty and student interviews and focus groups, the Beyond Grey Pinstripes[7] survey of global business school programs on social and environmental impact management, and my own consulting at leading business schools reinforce the observation that students fully expect that values conflicts will emerge for them in their careers. In fact one leading business school invited students to share situations where they had experienced such conflicts and the vast majority had no problem at all presenting such examples from their pre-MBA work experience. And student survey respondents acknowledge that these situations do not just roll off their backs; they experience them as stressful, so much so that a significant number of them say they will look for another job. These students do indeed have values and they want to act upon them.

But, as noted above, a significant number do not report being well prepared to handle such conflicts. Most often they request attention to these issues within the contexts where they will emerge: that is, they want to talk about how the conflict will play out in a marketing decision or a financial management assignment. And they want to hear real-world examples of how real-world managers dealt with such situations.

Recognizing this need among future business leaders, Aspen BSP has piloted a workshop called 'Moving Beyond Whistle-Blowing: Empowering Managers to Make Positive Change in the Workplace'. Its purpose is to provide participants with the capacity and tools to be able to respond effectively when faced with decisions in their business careers that conflict with their values. The workshop was inspired, not only by the need revealed in Aspen BSP's student attitudes survey, but also by the sense that, if our choices in such situations do indeed come down to 'exit, voice or loyalty' (Hirschman, 1990), someone needs to prepare future leaders for voice.

Rather than using such a platform to debate whether or not to act in accordance with one's values, this workshop focuses on how to do so. The emphasis is upon pre-scripting oneself, as research shows that those who anticipate and state what they would do if confronted with a values conflict are more likely to be able to live up to their own expectations (London, 1970; Huneke, 1985). The hypothesis here, supported by this research, is that, given a belief that they actually have a choice, more managers would behave as if they did, making free will a self-fulfilling prophecy.

Social context: adversarial systems

Some of the stickiest protestations of a lack of free choice surface when business leaders, business scholars and business students consider the wider societal context of business. That is, even if they allow for a business purpose that is broader than the maximization of shareholder profit, an attempt to consider other so-called 'stakeholders' in their decision making is rife with all sorts of procedural constraints rooted in role identities.

Thus at the heart of Aspen BSP's work is a fundamental commitment to the value of cross-sector dialogue as a tool for identifying and resolving challenges at the intersection of business needs and wider societal concerns. This commitment has led to the Aspen BSP Business Leader Dialogue, an annual convening of leaders from business, the public sector and wider civil society, who gather for three days to address complex issues of mutual interest, such as globalization and the role of the corporation, the wealth gap, trust, global employment sourcing, and so on. At these convenings, we see many illustrations of a belief in the limitations of free choice across societal sectors, but we also see the beginnings of an attempt to deconstruct those self-limiting beliefs through dialogue.

For example, leaders of major multinational corporations have shared their personal and organizational frustration when confronted with the decisions to relocate their corporate headquarters in order to limit the firm's tax burden. On the one hand, they identify themselves as citizens – both personal and corporate – and experience an obligation to pay their fair share, but, on the other, they feel compelled to minimize the firm's tax burden to enhance their competitiveness. They recognize the long-term problems with this thinking, as they are starving the societal infrastructures upon which they and their firms rely, but they feel stuck.

An interesting counterpoint came from the head of a major technology firm based in the developing world who shared his conflicts over a supportive tax policy in his country that has enabled his industry to gain a global foothold. Now, however, he wonders how to identify when it is time to start sharing more of their gains with the public sector, but he gets stuck on the notion that, by doing so, his firm may be seen as (and he may be) limiting the opportunities of his in-country competition. How can he balance his firm's needs with those of his industry and his nation?

A public health expert painted a vivid and disturbing portrait of the impacts of global corporations on the social and family lives of poor women in developing economies who take employment with those firms, while business executives, visibly moved, wondered how to address these challenges while maintaining their competitive advantages.

And this belief that action choices are limited is not restricted to the business leaders. The head of a government agency shared stories of extensive, laborious outreach to the private sector concerning employment practices, only to discover that their hard-won agreements were regularly disregarded by those corporations with whom they had forged relationships. And with her trust violated, she wondered whether she had any choice but to abandon cooperative efforts.

At the same time that we hear such stories of constrained choices from the participants in Aspen BSP cross-sector dialogues, we encounter similar barriers in our work with business educators. Faculty regularly acknowledge that concepts like the discussion of economic externalities, those 'spillover' costs and benefits to society of public or private actions that are not captured in the traditional accounting balance, are frequently crowded out of the core business curriculum because they are not 'relevant' to an individual business manager's decision making. If they do not affect the balance sheet, the manager is not required (or perhaps is even unable) to consider them. And yet, for an individual manager to truly understand the impacts of his or her decision on both the firm and its stakeholders, would not such externalities need to be part of the calculus?

Similarly discussions of the kinds of tax policy issues raised by our troubled executives at the Aspen BSP dialogues are often viewed as extraneous to the business classroom because they are deemed public policy concerns. And discussions of the latitude to be enjoyed by internal auditors are conducted without an understanding of the ways in which those latitudes only function effectively when the system of checks and balances comprised by the board audit committee and the public auditor relationship is not compromised.

Without an understanding and respect for the interlocking map of private, public and civil society (NGOs, consumer advocacy groups, and so on), a discussion of managers' relevant spheres of action and the degrees of freedom that they enjoy is meaningless. How can one exclude a discussion of tax policy from a macroeconomics course on the grounds that it is not the sphere of business when businesses regularly exercise their policy voices (and their funding) to influence those very issues? Here we see that free will is indeed being exercised. What appears to be needed is the chance to bring these different conversations – the conversation about the manager's lack of choices, the conversation about the relevancy of public sector and civil society perspectives for managerial decision making and the conversation about corporate attempts to influence policy – into the same room.

Aspen BSP has had some success in attempting to encourage such conversations. Their Business Leader Dialogues are one example and there are numerous stories of individuals who partnered across sectors to address a particular issue as a result of hearing each other's points of view at these dialogues. But this attempt to encourage a recognition of the ways in which business leaders not only have free will, but are already exercising it, often works at cross-purposes with the logic of adversarial systems.

The logic of adversarial systems is the underlying structural paradigm for many of the most important societal institutions in the United States. The legal system, the political system with its 'two-party' structure and the free market system are all explicitly or implicitly assumed to function according to a model of survival of the fittest.

The appeal of these systems is mixed. On the one hand, we are drawn to such systems because there appears to be a kind of impersonal mechanism at their heart. We are only too aware that no one individual has all the information necessary to make a wise and prudent and just decision about the complex questions we face, so we try to design a process than can take the decision out of our hands. We spread the decision around to include more parties or voices (elections, juries, peer review panels, the stock market, and so on) and this inclusion of many voices seems a good thing. However, ironically, this process can also depersonalize a decision, allowing us to feel less personally responsible for any one choice. And then we design a role for ourselves, narrowly defining our function so that we can find some clear sense of mastery and moral focus: an attorney defends or prosecutes to the best of her or his ability, regardless of a defendant's guilt or innocence and regardless of the attorney's own point of view; a firm operates with an eye to maximizing the indicators valued by the stock market, abdicating moral culpability to the impersonal market's dictates; the politician plays to the polls and the voter plays down the significance of her or his individual choice because it is balanced out (best case) or cancelled out (worst case) by other voters. And the press sees itself as 'objectively' reporting information, trusting to the impersonal (or multipersonal) mechanism of popular taste and judgment to sort, weigh and assess that information in the war of words and images.

All of this emphasis upon seeming objectivity, distance, process and impersonal adversarialism functions, at best, as protection from partiality and manipulation, but, at worst, as protection from personal responsibility and a sense of free choice. Where is the balance? Can there be a process that uses the best of this system of impartial and procedural justice, without the adversarial aspects that shift our focus from the true goal in each case toward a more narrowly defined objective? Can we be loyal to the process and the greater purpose, not the narrow manifestation of it; to justice, not a particular client; to statespersonship, not to a particular party or candidate; to long-term value, not to a short-term market indicator?

Such a refinement of the adversarial paradigm is only possible when it is based upon a sophisticated understanding of the interdependent map of societal responsibility, between the public, private and civil sectors, and a comprehension that this interdependency only functions when each party is allowed to play its part. Robert Reich has argued that this understanding of the interplay of sectors means that

> The meta-social responsibility of the corporation ... is to respect the political process by staying out of it .... [yet] just the opposite is occurring. Even as institutional investors impose ever greater pressure on management to maximize returns, causing corporations to loudly eschew broader social responsibilities, corporations are becoming more openly and aggressively involved in the making of social policy. (Reich, 1998, p. 16)

That is, he is identifying the contradiction in the aforementioned protestations of constraints on free action. He points out that businesses do in fact act freely and often to influence public policy, but he is counseling restraint so that the elegant system of checks and balances between public and private interests can function as intended. In effect, he is arguing that, for this system to work, it is necessary to respect and operate within the limits imposed by its structure.

However this perspective is still premised on a dichotomous view of business as somehow opposed to the public and civil sectors. Appealing as this logic may be, it is still the logic of adversarial systems described above: a logic of seeming objectivity, distance, process and impersonal action; a logic that absolves the individual actor from choice and responsibility. But the world is more complex than that. To define it otherwise is to reinforce a false dichotomy that premises business as somehow apart from the wider community; workers and consumers as distinct from citizens; industrial resources as distinct from the environment in which we live; shareholders as distinct from stakeholders; industrialized countries as independent of developing countries; and individual nations as independent of the wider world.

While Reich is correct that we cannot have it both ways – that is, protesting that competitive forces preclude us from considering social responsibility in management decisions while simultaneously working to prevent policies that would level the field by making such considerations *de rigueur* – it is also true that we cannot close our eyes to any business impacts that are not addressed within the law. Business practitioners can and should play a role in policy debates, but not a role that is privileged over that of other constituencies. They should have a voice, but that voice should come from their full identities, not simply their role as managers. As one participant in the Aspen BSP 2001 Business Leaders Dialogue phrased it: 'We are not just business executives, but also family members and citizens. The best case for social innovation through business is that we're all part of the whole.'

Judith Samuelson, founder and executive director of The Aspen Institute Business and Society Program, based the organization on a belief in the potential and the reach and even the necessity of the private sector to address the most critical social and environmental challenges of our day. That potential is achieved through many cross-sector conversations; through a willingness to define shared goals across sectors, that are broader than any one sector's narrow self-interest. Samuelson argues:

> in my view, it is ultimately business – big, audacious, profit-hungry, globe trotting business that will unlock the solutions to our most complex problems as a society. It won't happen alone – it will happen in partnership with government or at the prodding of the third sector, who function as advocates, watchdogs and increasingly as partners – but more frequently in important cases I expect that change will be business-led because it is business in the U.S. and round the globe, that has the resources, the talent, the problem-solving skill, the distribution systems and, increasingly, the motivation to act. (Samuelson, 2003, p. 3)

An illustration of this different stance, this non-adversarial, cross-sector stance, surfaced in 2003 at the Walter V. Shipley Business Leadership Case Competition. Each year J.P. Morgan Chase Bank partners with Aspen BSP and sponsors this event, where MBA student teams from leading US business schools compete for the most creative and promising solution to complex business problems with compelling social and ethical dimensions. In 2003, the students were asked to place themselves in the role of CEO of a leading multinational pharmaceutical company and to respond to the following questions.

- What stance can/should you take to address the human and ethical challenge of an accelerating HIV/AIDS crisis while maintaining incentives for costly innovation and research on this disease?
- What is at stake? Is this a tradeoff between the lives of millions of people with HIV/AIDS versus the global intellectual property rights (IPR) system – and your profitability? Can there be a viable compromise around IPR principles? Is there another way to position and resolve this struggle?

Student teams rose to the challenge and, because they were asked to figure out how to address this seemingly insoluble dilemma, rather than whether they could do so, they did in fact propose creative answers: another example of free will in business decision making.

What is of particular interest here, however, is that, of the six finalists, only one student team stood outside their own firm's boundaries to discuss, not only the ways in which the needs of persons with HIV/AIDS could be served while preserving the future profitability of their own multinational company and the incentives for research and development, but also the ways in which developing world pharmaceutical firms could gain and maintain an important role on the global competitive stage. Rather than viewing these smaller producers as adversaries only, this team saw a way in which they could play a constructive role in addressing the particular needs of their local consumers, without threatening the profitability of the existing, major MNCs. Ultimately this strategy was designed to serve consumers better, but it required a broader angled view, a commitment to the wider goal of value creation as opposed to the narrower one of firm-specific, short-term profit maximization. And this is the kind of different view that a commitment to cross-sector conversation is designed to foster.

Metrics: what and why do we count?
Finally we turn to the third lens for considering the question of free will in business: metrics, or how performance and profitability are measured. Much has been made of the familiar maxim: 'we manage what we measure' and, for that reason, many of those committed to improving the capacity and the willingness of business to manage its social impacts have focused their attention on identifying or developing new measures of performance that take into account the so-called 'triple bottom line': economic, social and environmental performance. This is important work, but it seems that metrics are a necessary but not sufficient factor for social impact management and freedom of choice.

Yes, of course, a large part of the seductiveness of 'managing to the market' and of the adversarial system described above lies in the clarity of focusing on a single optimization (share price) and a single target audience in Wall Street. Put aside the fact that this single audience is more complex than it seems (that is, investors are a diverse lot with diverse goals, as we noted above) and put aside the fact that share price is a complex number in itself, achieved in a not entirely predictable fashion (efforts at earnings management notwithstanding). Despite these caveats, there is an appeal and an elegance in this model, but the fact is, managers have always been required to consider multiple optimizations and multiple audiences.

The models that managers construct to guide their decision making routinely involve creating measurable factors to serve as proxies for various economic impacts. The same approach can and has been applied to social and environmental impacts. Product life cycle accounting has been important in efforts to measure the environmental costs and benefits of product policy decisions, and models of accounting for intangibles have proved useful in efforts to measure intellectual and human capital, particularly in research-based industries. So what are some of the factors that have discouraged attempts to utilize and extend the metrics of performance to include social and environmental impacts?

For one thing, generally speaking, extending these metrics may suggest that one is opening the door to possibly accepting responsibility for what one is measuring. For example, there is a whole raft of societal issues where arguably business is one of many players who bear some responsibility – not total responsibility, but some. For example, what is the role of business in the dramatic 'epidemic' of obesity we see in the United States and increasingly around the globe? Obviously consumers bear personal responsibility for their diet choices, but, on the other hand, the proliferation of less healthy product offerings, heavily marketed to children, often in schools as an explicit payback for educational funding, is surely a relevant factor in this debate. The role of government subsidies for particular food crops plays into this equation as well. And so does the pace of modern living, where time to prepare healthy meals at home is at a premium and so families turn to low-cost, fast-food alternatives. Certainly corporations are not solely responsible for this problem, but then again, it is interesting to review the role of corporations and their trade associations and the government agencies they lobby in actively resisting World Health Organization efforts to create more informational packaging and eating guidelines for consumers. When this topic was proposed as a business education case topic, executives consulted were skeptical, asking: 'but what is the cost to shareholders?'

It would be difficult to measure this cost, but not impossible to develop some interesting proposals. A review of increasing numbers of consumer lawsuits could yield some probabilities concerning the number of such likely suits, and the average cost of responding to them, even when they are ultimately unsuccessful, as they have been thus far. Some predictions of the prevalence of media coverage for this issue could yield estimates of the cost of image repair and reputation management. Economists have already begun to calculate the tax burden of rising health costs associated with obesity and their impacts upon corporations and consumers could be estimated. Lessons could be learned from the experiences of other target industries, such as the tobacco industry or even the pharmaceutical industry. The point is that looking beyond the usual boundaries of the balance sheet might allow managers to see a bit further and understand the future costs they may bear, both financial and reputational, if they do not join a public dialogue around such an issue. And, surely, some of these costs would even affect the shareholders?

Once again, the mechanism that seems most suited to such an expanded vision of one's role and goals is a conversation across sectors: in this case, corporations, government, health advocacy and research organizations, consumer representatives and so on. And by sharing the conversation, one is also sharing the responsibility for what one is measuring, possibly both a comforting and a troubling proposition.

Another possible explanation for why we do not more often see expanded metrics within corporations may have to do with the seeming contradiction between short- and long-term time horizons. Aspen BSP recently co-sponsored a CEO/Investor Forum with the Conference Board on the short-term/long-term paradox in the market, attempting to consider the market factors that encouraged a short-term orientation among executives, and what the costs of that orientation were for sustainable value creation and the management of social impacts. Not surprisingly participants discussed factors such as the decline of 'owners' and the rise of short-term investors and even hedge funds, the explosion of executive compensation, particularly its reliance upon stock options, the failure of market intermediaries to provide checks on the system, and so on.

One of the interesting meta-issues to emerge, however, was the acknowledgment that a fundamental conflict between short- and long-term orientations was built into human experience and the calculus we use to measure our risks and benefits. Participants pointed out that day-to-day living invariably involved such tradeoffs between pleasure and security, now or later. Given this fundamental reality, what is the optimal time frame for measurement?

Although participants did not offer a solution to this tradeoff, interestingly its very acknowledgment does suggest that neither an entirely short-term, nor an entirely long-term orientation is optimal. Framing the question in this way moves us beyond the false dichotomy of short term versus long term and opens the path to a set of multiple criteria to be considered in making, and particularly in communicating to the market, managerial decisions. Such a reframing of the metrics and their time horizon opens the door to more degrees of freedom in managerial choice, much as Jensen and Fuller argue in their article on CEOs who forgo short-term pressures to be more transparent with Wall Street (Fuller and Jensen, 2002).

Free will: individual or collective?
By now it is clear that free will is a matter of free will: that is, managers and anyone else have choices all the time. If the system constrains us, we can choose to comply; we can work to change it for our narrow ends; or we can collaborate to change it in ways that serve broader yet still shared objectives. Considerations of purpose, social context and metrics provide a set of lenses through which to view this challenge and a set of questions to raise in efforts to address it. And at the heart of this question of free will in business is the question of leadership. Leaders who want to integrate a conscious and constructive attention to Social Impact Management into their organization will need, first and foremost, to help employees recognize

and believe in their own freedom of choice. These leaders will be most effective when they help their employees to do what they think they cannot, as opposed to focusing on preventing them from doing what they know they should not. And this kind of effort is most effective, perhaps only possible, when it involves looking across boundaries and collaborating across sectors, developing and exercising a truly collective free will.

Notes

1. See Appendix I for a description of The Aspen Institute Business and Society Program and its mission.
2. This discussion of 'Social Impact Management' as well as many of the other examples used throughout this chapter are drawn from or based upon Aspen Institute Business and Society Program discussion papers and speeches, written by Mary C. Gentile and available in full at www.aspenbsp.org.
3. See Appendix II for examples of Social Impact Management topics.
4. In the second phase of this corporate governance project, we will be assembling teaching modules on these topics for distribution at Aspen BSP's interactive teaching resource website: www.CasePlace.org.
5. The report on this study, 'Where Will They Lead? MBA Student Attitudes About Business & Society', is available at www.aspenbsp.org.
6. Only 23 per cent said that their business education was preparing them 'a lot', while the majority (58 per cent) reported that their business education was preparing them 'somewhat' to manage such values conflicts.
7. See www.beyondgreypinstripes.org for the results of this global survey of MBA programs conducted by Aspen BSP and the World Resources Institute every two years.

References

Bagley, C. and K. Page (1999), 'The devil made me do it: replacing corporate directors' veil of secrecy with the mantle of stewardship', *San Diego Law Review*, **36** (4), 897.

Bazerman, M., G. Loewenstein and D. Moore (2002), 'Why good accountants do bad audits', *Harvard Business Review*, **80** (11), 96–102.

Friedman, M. (1970), 'The social responsibility of business is to increase its profits', *The New York Times Magazine*, 13 September, 32–3.

Fuller, J. and M.C. Jensen (2002), 'Just say no to Wall Street: courageous CEOs are putting a stop to the earnings game and we will all be better off for it', *Journal of Applied Corporate Finance*, **14** (4), 41–6.

Handy, C. (2002), 'What's a business for?', *Harvard Business Review*, **80** (12), 49–55.

Healy, P.M. and K.G. Palepu (2003), 'How the quest for efficiency undermined the market', *Harvard Business Review*, **81** (7), 76–85.

Hirschman, A.O. (1990), *Exit, Voice and Loyalty: Responses to Decline in Firms, Organizations and States*, Cambridge, MA: Harvard University Press.

Huneke, D.H. (1985), *The Moses of Rovno*, New York: Dodd, Mead.

Jusela, G.E., W. Wiggenhorn and M.C. Gentile (2002), 'Raising the stakes, or finally seeing them clearly? Balanced leadership in times of economic crisis', *New Academy Review*, **1** (1), 37–47.

London, P. (1970), 'The rescuers: motivational hypotheses about Christians who saved Jews from the Nazis', in J. Macaulay and L. Berkowitz (eds), *Altruism and Helping Behavior: Social Psychological Studies of Some Antecedents and Consequences*, New York: Academic Press, pp. 241–50.

Reich, R.B. (1998), 'The new meaning of corporate social responsibility', *California Management Review*, **40** (2), 8–17.

Samuelson, J. (2003), 'Leadership and values: moving beyond the ethics debate', speech presented to the Corporate Contributions Council of the Conference Board, p. 3.

Appendix I   The Aspen Institute Business and Society Program

The mission of the Aspen Institute's Business and Society Program is to help business executives integrate financial success and social and environmental progress. Our vision is one of businesses committed to addressing complex global problems – led by executives who possess the skills, values and long-term view required to consider the social impact of business decisions and who employ social innovation as a key element of business strategy.

We work with educators to develop a more effective response to issues at the intersection of business needs and wider societal concerns (social impact management) through classroom discussion and research. We convene faculty and business leaders, invest in innovation in MBA programs and conduct research to understand and track change in business education and student attitudes.

www.aspenbsp.org

Appendix II   Examples of social impact management topics by discipline

Accounting	Full cost accounting
	Differential accounting standards
	Integrity and accountability in reporting systems
	Potential conflicts of reporting standards in global businesses
	Social auditing
Business/ government relations	Social impacts of regulation, deregulation and privatization
	Technology transfer and its impact on economic opportunities
	Jurisdictional disputes
	Negotiating responsibility for 'externalities' with host country
	Public/private partnerships
Economics	Distribution of wealth within and between countries: business influence/impacts
	Family/community impacts of employee time use
	Fiscal incentives or disincentives; e.g., tax policy
	Causes and impacts of wage and income gap
	Social impacts of key economic concepts; e.g. market power, consumer power, market externalities, property rights, etc.
Finance	Impacts of individual and institutional investor incentives
	Impacts of capital flows across international borders
	Differential access to capital
	Examination of the changing nature and role of shareholders
	Discussion of social venture capital and social investing
Information technology	Digital divide
	Social impacts of technology transfer
	Confidentiality and information ownership
	Workforce impact of IT enhancements
Marketing	Impacts of product development, design and pricing on consumers
	Niche marketing impact on business strategy and target markets
	Cultural impacts of advertising messages
	Social and cause-related marketing
Operations management	Impacts of labor standards: risk and safety, child labor, hours, etc.

	Accountability and risk management in supplier relationships
	Plant siting decisions and stakeholders
	Differential safety and labor standards
Organizational behavior/HR	Employee rights and participation
	Work/life balance issues
	Workplace equity and diversity issues
	Labor relations and union strategies
Strategy	Corporate reputation/image
	Executive compensation strategies
	Competitive analysis of employee ownership models
	Operating in economically disadvantaged areas and emerging markets
	Standards for 'fair' competition in a global context
	Downsizing, plant closings and re-engineering strategies
	Trends and critiques of corporate governance

Source: Reprinted from 'Social Impact Management: A Definition' by Mary C. Gentile, The Aspen Institute Business and Society Program, www.aspenbsp.org.

PART IV

RESPONSIBLE GOVERNANCE IN CORPORATIONS AND PROFESSIONAL SERVICES FIRMS

13 Management, governance and corporate responsibility

Shawn D. Howton, Shelly W. Howton and Victoria B. McWilliams

Introduction

Corporate governance is currently one of the hottest topics of discussion in business. Studies of corporate governance and its impact on both an organization and a society appear regularly in top academic journals across all business disciplines. Articles appear almost daily in the popular press reporting accusations of scandals and fraud perpetrated by managers and members of a firm's board of directors. The government is also becoming more involved in corporate governance as evidenced by the passage of the Sarbanes–Oxley Act of 2002, the purpose of which is 'To protect investors by improving the accuracy and reliability of corporate disclosures made pursuant to the securities laws, and for other purposes' (Sarbanes-Oxley Act of 2002, 1).

Although the increased publicity of corporate scandals in the late 1990s and early 2000s has brought new attention to corporate governance, its importance to the firm has been widely studied across the business disciplines. An early theoretical paper by Jensen and Meckling (1976) on agency theory is a common starting point for examining the issues surrounding corporate governance. Jensen and Meckling (ibid., p. 308) describe an agency relationship as 'a contract under which one or more persons (the principal(s)) engage another person (the agent) to perform some service on their behalf which involves delegating some decision-making authority to the agent'. Agency theory is used to examine corporate governance issues by focusing on the shareholders of the firm as principals and managers as agents and then discussing the likelihood of the interests of these two parties to conflict.

The separation of ownership and control in organizations results in many of the conflicts that arise in the agency relationship discussed in Jensen and Meckling (1976). Shareholders are the owners of the firm but do not have explicit control over its day-to-day operations. Instead shareholders empower the board of directors with control over the firm's top management team. The board controls and monitors existing policies, proposes and adopts new policies and plays a crucial role in hiring and firing managers. The firm's managers are in a position to suggest actions and make decisions that affect the firm's ability to succeed (Fama and Jensen, 1983a). Managers have incentives to make decisions that are in their own best interests and these decisions are often not in the best interests of shareholders. As shareholders can be hurt by poor managerial decisions, they have incentives to use tools or put structures in place to protect their interests. John and Senbet (1998) define corporate governance as the devices used by shareholders against managers to protect these interests. Additionally Fama and Jensen (1983b) argue that agency conflicts are decreased because the board's function, which is one of control, is dissimilar from the management function.

A portion of the academic literature on governance issues looks at specific areas of conflict that might arise and then offers potential resolutions to these conflicts. Much of the literature then empirically examines these conflicts and avenues of resolution to determine the effectiveness of various governance mechanisms. In this chapter we discuss corporate governance and responsibility within the current climate of corporate accountability.

The literature

It does not matter whether you are an academic or a practitioner, corporate governance, social responsibility and corporate accountability are extensively discussed topics. Government, industry and the academy all are concerned with the issue of appropriately structuring the organization and putting into place governance mechanisms that will provide for the most effective decision making on the part of the board in the role of overseers, and on the part of top managers, particularly CEOs. Actions to make firms more effective with respect to governance and social responsibility have been discussed by various constituents and stakeholders. These discussions have been followed by a great deal of hypothesizing (for example, Barkema and Gomez-Mejia, 1998) and empirical study (for example, Dalton *et al.*, 1998) on the part of academics in areas as diverse as accounting, economics, finance, law and management.

The focus of this chapter is to summarize the various mechanisms of corporate governance and the empirical efficacy. We begin by discussing external governance mechanisms and provide an explanation of why they have been generally ineffective in recent years. We then turn our attention to internal mechanisms of control. Internal control mechanisms include a strong board of directors and alignment of board, manager and shareholder interests. The board of directors is meant to be the ultimate monitor of shareholders, but the ability of boards to fulfill this role has been brought into question. Practitioners, academics and government agencies have all weighed in on what constitutes a strong board. We will discuss the aspects of the theoretical determinants of board monitoring ability and whether or not each is supported empirically. Following the discussion of board leadership and structure, methods to align managerial and shareholder interests through incentives and their effectiveness are reviewed and, finally, other methods of corporate governance and future issues surrounding corporate governance are discussed.

External and internal governance mechanisms

One of the strongest mechanisms in place to control management behavior is the threat of firing. Internally the board of directors is responsible for managers that are not making optimal decisions for the shareholders. The ability of the board to fulfill this role is an open question that will be discussed in the next section. In cases where the board does not remove underperforming managers, external market forces can, and do, act to provide discipline. The market for corporate control can be broadly defined as actions taken through the market to remove current management and restructure the firm. Takeovers are the most obvious and extreme form of control, but other forms of restructuring such as leveraged and management buyouts, stock repurchases and divisional sales can also be used to change or remove management.

Jensen (1993) addressed the effects of external control mechanisms in his 1993 presidential address to the American Finance Association. The focus of his address was 'the Modern Industrial Revolution' that we are currently experiencing. He argues that the massive improvements in information technologies, computing power and the world political landscape have made the current times very reflective of the late 1800s and the first industrial revolution. Overall the productivity improvements associated with this revolution will benefit society, but they are also a problem in that they lead to overcapacity and vast shifts in factor and product markets. The focus of the address is on governance structures and whether they will allow for the efficient transformation of the economy. Jensen argues that, through the early 1990s, internal control mechanisms were not effective in inducing the required changes needed to meet the needs of the new economy.

While internal control mechanisms were not functioning effectively, external market mechanisms were working. Jensen provides evidence of the effectiveness of the market for corporate control from two industries, the tire and oil industries (Jensen, 1986, 1988). Both of these industries had overcapacity and a large number of inefficient high-cost producers. The market for corporate control allowed for a large reduction in capacity and an elimination of high-cost producers in both industries. While the market for corporate control has proved to be an effective tool in limiting the inefficient use of capital and assets, it is a blunt instrument. Generally the market for corporate control involves layoffs, displacement and strong feelings of resentment in many constituencies. Owing to the nature of corporate takeovers and cases of fraud and insider trading by market participants, the market for corporate control was virtually closed in the early 1990s. Comment and Schwert (1995) described the breakdown of the market for corporate control and discussed the implications of this process.

Since the market for corporate control was effectively shut down, Jensen (1993) argues that the focus on internal control mechanisms must increase. The question of what makes boards effective and how companies align shareholder and decision maker interests is more important than ever. Jensen proved to be prophetic, as the late 1990s showed. Overbuilding in industries such as telecommunications led to vast destruction of capital in firms like WorldCom and Global Crossing. The energy industry also had problems, most notably with Enron. Could a well functioning market for corporate control have prevented these problems? That is not clear. External governance is generally not effective in cases of fraud and deception. What is clear is that these industries did not have strong internal control mechanisms in place, and the groups hurt by the lack of these control mechanisms were shareholders, the economy and society. The next section focuses on internal governance measures and the empirical effectiveness of each.

Internal governance refers to the systems in place that ensure that managers make optimal decisions for shareholders. The major forces of internal control are the board of directors and all systems that align manager and shareholder interests. Ultimately the board of directors is responsible for managerial oversight. The debate about what constitutes effective boards has been going on for decades. The evidence suggests that, historically, the majority of boards have not been effective in overseeing managers. The question with the current framework is how firms and society can restructure boards to ensure that they are effective in their role of monitors of managers. Issues in this area include the optimal composition, leadership structure, ownership stake and size of the board. One of the serious issues facing policy makers is a complete lack of agreement on what constitutes an effective board. The following sections will attempt to make sense of what has become a very controversial topic.

Board leadership and composition
A number of studies suggest that the firm's leadership structure and board composition are two important aspects of the firm's structure (for example, Bhagat and Black, 1999, 2002; Coles *et al.*, 2001; Johnson *et al.*, 1996; Pearce and Zahra, 1991, 1992; Rechner and Dalton, 1991; Morck *et al.*, 1989). In general, the leadership structure of the firm and the composition of the board of directors are the subjects of continuing debate.

By and large, the monitoring function is the responsibility of the board of directors. The critical charge of the firm's board is to ensure that the firm's top management team is taking action that creates value for the firm's stakeholders. The firm's leadership structure, defined by whether the CEO is also the board's chair, is one structural mechanism about which there is controversy. For example, Jensen (1993) views a combined structure, which is the situation where the CEO is also board chair, as an unsuitable way to design one of the most vital control relationships in the firm. The rationale for this argument is that combining the CEO and board chair positions leads to a single individual having a concentrated power base that will allow the CEO to make decisions in his or her own self-interest, which ultimately are at the expense of the firm's stakeholders. This argument supports a separate leadership structure in which the CEO and board chair are two individuals. In this way, power is not concentrated in one individual but broadened in a way that permits boards to achieve their fiduciary duty more fully.

Others (for example, Coles *et al.*, 2001; Boyd, 1995; Harrison *et al.*, 1988) suggest that having the CEO also act as the board chair provides benefits for several reasons. Since there is a single individual assuming both roles, the direction for the firm is more unambiguous than it would be with two individuals occupying these top-level positions. Additionally, the CEO–board chair has more complete knowledge of the firm than an outsider (that is, an independent board chair) has. Furthermore, as an insider for the firm, the CEO has greater commitment to the firm than an outside board chair.

There is considerable empirical work that has been done to provide insight into the relation of leadership structure and firm performance. These studies include Baliga *et al.*, (1996), Daily and Schwenk (1996), Lublin (1992), Rechner and Dalton (1989, 1991) and Berg and Smith (1978). In spite of the large volume of study, the evidence is inconclusive. For example, Rechner and Dalton (1989) examined shareholder returns from 1978 to 1983 and found no significant distinction between the performance of firms when the CEO was the board chair and that of firms where the CEO and board chair positions were separate. However, in a later study, Rechner and Dalton (1991) examined accounting-based measures of return and profitability and found that firms in which the CEO is not chair of the board outperformed firms with both positions held by one individual. In addition, several studies (for example, Mallette and Fowler, 1992; Zahra and Pearce, 1989; Dalton and Kesner, 1987) suggest that governance structures are more effective when the CEO and board chair positions are separate.

Arguments to the contrary appear in Baliga *et al.* (1996) who found little evidence to support a performance difference between the two types of firms when using market value added (MVA) and economic value added (EVA) as measures of performance. Consistent with Baliga *et al.*'s conclusions, other studies (for example, Baysinger *et al.*, 1991; Baysinger and Hoskisson, 1990; Hill and Snell, 1988) concur that there are arguments and evidence that support combining the roles of CEO and board chair. Evidence suggests that the CEO/chairman configuration is slanted towards duality. Empirical evidence taken from Coles *et al.* (2001) and Rechner and Dalton (1991) indicates that between 70 and 80 per cent of large US firms combine the roles of CEO and board chair. This suggests that managerial monitoring concerns described above have not resulted in separating the positions of firm CEO and board chair, which is consistent with the varied data also described above.

Logic suggests that the firm's leadership configuration may be closely associated with other control mechanisms, in particular the composition of the board of directors. A frequent explanation of why combining the positions of CEO and board chair does not lead to major agency problems is that independent board members, those unaffiliated with the firm, serve on auditing, compensation and nominating committees. The importance of an independent board has been the recent focus of academic theory, practitioner rhetoric and regulatory practice. Zahra and Pearce (1989) summarize the theoretical arguments of the benefits of an independent board. Practitioners including the National Association of Corporate Directors and the Business Roundtable have endorsed boards that include a 'substantial majority' of independent outside directors. Large institutional investors, including CalPERS, have specifically identified board independence as a desirable governance characteristic (Bryant, 1997). In fact board independence has recently become the focus of federal lawmakers. One recognized motivation for the Sarbanes-Oxley Act of 2002 is to provide independence to firm boards. Such outside representation is ostensibly an effective monitoring device over management actions. In the situation where the CEO is the board chair but the majority of the board members are unaffiliated with the firm, the firm seemingly has the best of both worlds. That is, the outside directors monitor managerial actions and limit opportunism, and the firm receives the benefit of having a focused direction since the CEO is also the board chair.

As with most issues related to corporate governance, there is an opposing view. The supposition that board composition minimizes or perhaps resolves agency problems is countered by the managerial hegemony theory, which views boards as passive players who are loyal to the managers who chose them, who lack information about the firm and who rely on top-level managers to provide the information that they lack (Kosnik, 1987). Evidence suggests that outside directors are not always effective monitors of managers (for example, Bathala and Rao, 1995; Baysinger *et al.*, 1991; Baysinger and Hoskisson, 1990; Hill and Snell, 1988). Nevertheless outside forces have driven directors, particularly unaffiliated directors, to consider gravely their monitoring responsibilities. The public awareness of organizational malfeasance, the progressively more active role of large shareholders and the greater than ever incidences of shareholder lawsuits are forcing directors to recognize the importance of their fiduciary accountability to the firm's stakeholders.

Support for board independence is provided by Bathala and Rao (1995) who conclude that board structure is a function of whether alternative monitoring mechanisms exist. For firms with few monitoring alternatives, Bathala and Rao conclude that board independence is essential. Empirical evidence also supports the conclusion that outside directors are effective in monitoring managers and protecting the interests of the firm's stakeholders. Firms with boards dominated by outside directors are more likely to fire poorly performing CEOs (Weisbach, 1988), have a lower probability of paying greenmail in a control contest (Kosnik, 1990), have a lower probability of adopting a poison pill (Mallette and Fowler, 1992) and have a lower probability of being sued for not fulfilling their fiduciary responsibilities (Kesner and Johnson, 1990). Coles and Hesterly (2000) find that the presence of these apparently impartial directors allows the board to carry out a monitoring function when there is vast power vested in a single person, as would be the case when the CEO is also the board chair. Finkelstein and D'Aveni (1994) also support the belief that vigilant boards are positively related to a single individual acting as both CEO and chair.

In addition to specific instances of improved monitoring, there is evidence that the market views outside directors as superior monitors. Schellenger *et al.* (1989) find that the presence of outside directors is related to higher risk-adjusted performance. Brickley *et al.* (1994) find that both the market's reaction to adoption of a poison pill and the probability the pill is used to create value for shareholders in a control contest are positively related to the share of board seats held by unaffiliated directors. Rosenstein and Wyatt (1990) find significant positive, though economically small, shareholder wealth effects associated with the appointment of outside directors.

Some authors have offered arguments against the effectiveness of outside directors. Baysinger and Hoskisson (1990) suggest inside directors may be better monitors thanks to the superior amount and quality of information they have about the operations of the firm. There is evidence of a positive relation between inside board representation and R&D spending (Baysinger *et al.*, 1991), corporate diversification (Hill and Snell, 1988) and CEO pay (Boyd, 1995).

In response to the lack of coherent empirical support for the role of board structure in corporate performance, several large-scale studies have recently addressed this issue. Bhagat and Black (1999, 2002), Coles *et al.* (2001), Rhoades *et al.* (2000) and Dalton, Daily, Ellestrand and Johnson (1998) use different methods including longitudinal studies and large-scale Meta-Analysis to draw conclusions on the relation between performance and board structure. Each of these studies reports no relation between independent boards and firm performance. Bhagat and Black (1999, 2002) specifically question the rush to adopt independent boards and suggest further study is required to determine the optimal mix of directors for different types of companies.

In summary, the relation between outside directors and overall firm performance is unclear. Outside directors have been proved to be effective monitors of managers in certain situations, especially when other forms of corporate governance are weak and in the context of specific firm decisions. In certain situations, the market responds favorably to firms with independent boards. However recent large-scale studies find little to no relation between performance and board independence and question the current view that board independence is optimal.

Several authors have provided potential reasons for the inability to establish empirically an independence–performance link. Daily and Dalton (1994) question whether the distinction between inside and independent outside directors is able to capture the actual level of independence of the outside directors. The level of director independence or lack thereof relates to researchers' ability to reflect director independence accurately in their measures (Johnson *et al.*, 1996; Bainbridge, 1993). Traditional algorithms for categorizing directors as inside, affiliated and outside (that is, independent) may not account for various factors that could influence board member effectiveness. Examples of traditional board categorization methods appear in Buchholtz and Ribbens (1994), Johnson *et al.* (1993) and Byrd and Hickman (1992). The role of board independence is thus an open issue with several important questions as yet unanswered.

Mechanisms to align agent incentives
In addition to the composition of the board, the incentive structure of the board and the managers of the firm can be an important variable when attempting to align shareholder and manager interests. One frequently presented method to lower the agency costs and make board members better monitors is share ownership. As board members increase their ownership stake in the firm, their personal wealth will be negatively affected if they shirk their duties. In other words, by monitoring activities of top-level management and thereby ensuring that value is created, board members will benefit as well. Bhagat *et al.* (1999) argue that ownership is a simple way to improve the monitoring function of boards. They test

this hypothesis and find a weak relation between performance and board ownership. They also find evidence that boards do increase their monitoring when ownership stakes are higher. Specifically they find that boards with higher ownership percentages have higher levels of CEO turnover when performance is poor. Brickley *et al.* (1988) find that directors owning shares in the firm have increased incentives to monitor managers. Rosenstein and Wyatt (1997) demonstrate the importance of ownership in the market's perception of the monitoring effectiveness of inside board members. They find that the market's reaction to the appointment of new inside directors is directly related to the ownership stake of those directors. The market reacts negatively to appointments of insiders with ownership levels below 5 per cent and positively to appointments of insiders with ownership levels between 5 per cent and 25 per cent. Howton *et al.* (2001) find that firms with high levels of inside board ownership significantly outperform firms with low levels of inside board ownership in the three years following an initial public offering.

Ownership can serve another role in the lowering of agency costs. Managerial ownership of stock increases the likelihood of effective managerial decisions as owner's and manager's interests are aligned through high levels of managerial ownership. Top-level management that has a large ownership stake in the firm experiences an increase in their wealth when they make day-to-day operating decisions that increase firm value. Himmelberg *et al.* (1999) and Zhara *et al.* (2000) argue that directors and managers with low ownership levels are more likely to take opportunistic actions by supporting projects that advance their own interests instead of creating value for the firm's stakeholders. Furthermore Jensen and Murphy (1990b) observe that share ownership results in executives' wealth varying directly with firm performance. Morck *et al.* (1988) demonstrate the relation between firm performance and officer and director shareholdings, which is consistent with Jensen and Meckling's (1976) arguments that agency costs arise as a result of the separation of ownership and control.

While the positive aspects of ownership have been demonstrated, there are costs of increased ownership. The most significant cost of ownership, especially at high levels, is management entrenchment. As managers and inside board members increase their percentage of shares owned, the likelihood of removing these agents owing to poor decision making is greatly reduced. Not surprisingly, the existence of the costs and benefits of share ownership led some studies (for example, Dalton *et al.*, 2003; Rediker and Seth, 1995; Short, 1994) to conclude that empirical results linking board and/or top-level management share ownership with firm performance are, at best, mixed. Morck *et al.* (1988) model this non-linear relation and find support for the theory that performance and ownership are directly related at low levels of ownership but inversely related at higher levels of ownership. Short and Keasey (1999), Holderness *et al.* (1999) and Chen *et al.* (1993) all find support for a non-linear relation between performance and ownership consistent with the theory of Morck *et al.* (1988).

In addition to director and managerial share ownership, the share ownership of large blockholders can also have an important role in firm governance. It is argued (for example, Frye, 2001; Shleifer and Vishny, 1997; Admati *et al.*, 1994; Huddart, 1993) that large shareholders, including activist institutional investors, have the resources to monitor their investments and can have an effect on managerial behavior because of the scale of their investments. The threat that large shareholders will sell some or all of their shareholdings if the firm fails to provide a suitable return, or is not quick to respond to governance issues that investors view as significant, is becoming a more important factor for top-level managers. Barclay and Holderness (1991), McConnell and Servaes (1995) and Denis and Serrano (1996) all find evidence supporting the value of large blockholders as monitors. Barclay and Holderness (1991) find a positive shareholder wealth effect when a large block of shares is purchased by an outsider. McConnell and Servaes (1995) find that blockholder presence and Tobin's Q are directly related. Denis and Serrano (1996) find that blockholders increase shareholder wealth by acting as monitors following a failed takeover.

Incentive contracting with the CEO is another tool available to the firm. Incentive contracting works in the same way that share ownership does, in that owner and manager interests are aligned owing to the relation between compensation and performance. Jensen and Meckling (1976) argue that performance-contingent pay is an effective way to deal with agency problems. Jensen and Murphy (1990a, 1990b) demonstrate a weak relationship between executive compensation and firm performance. They suggest that the performance–pay relation has been declining through time. Mehran (1995) provides evidence that suggests a positive relation between firm performance and the level of equity-based managerial compensation. Core *et al.* (1999) find that the relation between pay and performance is a function of other governance variables. Firms with poor internal governance structures had higher CEO compensation and an inverse relation between pay and performance. The results suggest that, while compensation systems theoretically lower agency costs, other control mechanisms are necessary to ensure that CEO pay and performance are closely tied.

Another important influence on director and managerial behavior is firm size and the relation that exists between the firm's industry and the firm's performance. For example, Powell (1996), Rumelt (1991), Wernerfelt and Montgomery (1988) and Schmalansee (1985) examine the relation between a firm's industry membership and performance, and conclude that industry effects normally predict between 17 and 20 per cent of financial performance. These results suggest that firms are inhibited to a certain extent by opportunities available to the firm's industry.

Other internal governance variables
In addition to types of governance mechanisms described above, several others have been suggested as influencing corporate governance and responsibility. There exists controversy about whether larger boards are better monitors. For example, Ocasio (1994), Pearce and Zahra (1992) and Zahra and Pearce (1989) argue that larger boards are less vulnerable to top-level management dominance than are smaller boards. Ocasio (1994) and Pearce and Zahra (1992) report evidence to support this argument. Alternatively Lipton and Lorsch (1992) argue that smaller boards are more effective. Jensen (1993) agrees with the argument in favor of smaller boards, and Yermack (1996) empirically determines that there is a negative relation between board size and market valuation. In a Meta-Analysis of the relation between board size and performance, Dalton *et al.* (1999) find an unambiguously positive relation. This relation is stronger in small firms than in big firms.

Stewardship theory (Davis *et al.*, 1997) also provides insight into governance mechanisms. Coles *et al.* (2001) argue that one way to assess the stewardship of top management would be to establish how long top-level management has been with the firm in their existing positions. The underlying logic of this argument is based on the premise that top managers who are excellent stewards will maintain their positions longer than managers that are not good stewards for the firm. However Miller (1991) argues that, the longer the tenure, the more likely top management is to become out of date.

In addition to individual variables affecting governance, academics argue that mechanisms substitute for each other (for example, Sundaramurthy *et al.*, 1997; Rediker and Seth, 1995; Beatty and Zajac, 1994) and that there are interaction effects between or among the governance variables (for example, Coles *et al.*, 2001). Bathala and Rao (1995) demonstrate a substitute relation between outside directors and inside shareholdings. Jensen, Solberg and Zorn (1992) find that firms with high levels of inside ownership choose lower levels of debt. Coles *et al.* (2001) provide preliminary substantiation that governance mechanisms may be important in terms of the capability of firms to develop governance configurations, instead of simply focusing on their choice of individual mechanisms.

Future issues

It is clear from our discussion that there is virtually no consensus regarding the best way for firms to maximize stakeholder wellbeing through corporate governance and accountability. This conclusion leads to obvious areas that need resolution. We suggest that the way to begin is by looking at interactions among various governance mechanisms. Agrawal and Knoeber (1996) present a model that allows for substitute and/or complementary relations between various governance mechanisms. John and Senbet (1998) discuss substitution effects between external and internal governance devices with the intent of benefiting all of the firm's stakeholders, not just shareholders.

Another area of future interest is the effectiveness of policy maker decisions on governance. Sarbanes–Oxley has required the restructuring of boards for the largest corporations. It is important to determine whether these changes have the intended impact or lead to large deadweight costs with no associated improvements in board effectiveness.

Another area that we believe is important for future study to address relates to the independence of board members. One of the key measures in the Sarbanes–Oxley Act is to increase the independence of directors to the point of requiring supermajority status for these outsiders. Independent outsiders are also required to hold leadership positions on the audit and nominating committees. The efficacy of independent directors in these roles has yet to be empirically established, however legislators are making laws that place increased responsibility for monitoring managers with these directors. These functions deserve a closer look from researchers so that we can more conclusively say that a focus on independence of the board will lead to improved oversight of managers.

Finally a more positive approach to studying corporate governance needs to be established. What types of firms do a good job in the area of corporate governance and what do they look like? The focus has generally been on firms that do not handle governance well; however many firms do a great job of meeting the objectives of stakeholders. Future research should focus on the organizational structure of these high-quality firms in a search for effective governance tools. We believe that true accountability will be fostered once we have a better understanding of how governance mechanisms work together to provide an optimal setting for the board and top-level managers to perform their functions.

We also believe that there quite likely are differences across industries that may affect the governance configuration chosen by the firm. At this time, we have no clear view of how these issues will be resolved by practitioners, government officials and academicians. We do know that the extant literature does not focus on governance structure for the firm as a complete unit. Nor does it focus on interrelations between and among mechanisms.

All of this discussion is missing one vital component and that is the role of individual morals and ethics. No governance configuration or government legislation will completely resolve the issues that have become the focus of our society. We are speaking, for example, of actions discovered at Enron, WorldCom, HealthSouth and Parmalat. We are speaking of corporate activity that, by and large, led to the Sarbanes–Oxley Act of 2002. Commissioner Paul Atkins, US Securities and Exchange Commission, summarizes the situation very well in his 25 March 2003 speech to International Financial Law Review:

> we need to be mindful of the fact that morality and ethics cannot be legislated into existence. Government controls alone – too often paternalistic – will never be a solution if individuals and individual firms are not upholding their own end of simple business ethics through their own effective compliance. Internal controls and the culture of an organization are basic structural aspects to reinforce the inherent nature of most people to do the right thing.

We could not have stated it better.

References

Admati, A.R., P. Pfleiderer and J. Zechner (1994), 'Large shareholder activism, risk sharing, and financial market equilibrium', *Journal of Political Economy*, **102** (6), 1097–1130.

Agrawal, A. and C.R. Knoeber (1996), 'Firm performance and mechanisms to control agency problems between managers and shareholders', *Journal of Financial and Quantitative Analysis*, **31** (3), 377–97.

Bainbridge, S.M. (1993), 'Independent directors and the ALI corporate governance project', *George Washington Law Review*, **61**, 1034–83.

Baliga, B.R., R.C. Moyer and R.S Rao (1996), 'CEO duality and firm performance: what's the fuss?', *Strategic Management Journal*, **17** (1), 41–3.

Barclay, M.J. and C.G. Holderness (1991), 'Negotiated block trades and corporate control', *Journal of Finance*, **46** (3), 861–78.

Barkema, H.G. and L.R. Gomez-Mejia (1998), 'Managerial compensation and firm performance: a general research framework', *Academy of Management Journal*, **41** (2), 135–45.

Bathala, C.T. and R.P. Rao (1995), 'The determinants of board composition: an agency theory perspective', *Managerial and Decision Economics*, **16** (1), 59–60.

Baysinger, B.D. and R.E. Hoskisson (1990), 'The composition of boards of directors and strategic control: effects on corporate strategy', *Academy of Management Review*, **15** (1), 72–87.

Baysinger, B.D., R.D. Kosnik and T.A. Turk (1991), 'Effects of board and ownership structure on corporate R&D strategy', *Academy of Management Journal*, **34** (1), 205–14.

Beatty, R.P. and E.J. Zajac (1994), 'Managerial incentives, monitoring and risk bearing: a study of executive compensation, ownership, and board structure in initial public offerings', *Administrative Science Quarterly*, **39** (2), 313–35.

Berg, S.V. and S.K. Smith (1978), 'CEO and board chairman: a quantitative study of dual vs. unitary board leadership', *Directors & Boards*, 34–9.

Bhagat, S. and B. Black (1999), 'The uncertain relationship between board composition and firm performance', *The Business Lawyer*, **54** (3), 921–63.

Bhagat, S. and B. Black (2002), 'The non-correlation between board independence and long-term firm performance', *Journal of Corporation Law*, **27** (2), 231–43.

Bhagat, S., D.C. Carey and C.M. Nelson (1999), 'Director ownership, corporate performance, and management turnover', *The Business Lawyer*, **54** (3), 885–919.

Boyd, B.K. (1995), 'CEO duality and firm performance: a contingency model', *Strategic Management Journal*, **16** (4), 301–12.

Brickley, J.A., J.L. Coles and R.L. Terry (1994), 'Outside directors and the adoption of poison pills', *Journal of Financial Economics*, **35** (3), 371–90.

Brickley, J.A., R.D. Lease, and C.W. Smith (1988), 'Ownership structure and voting on antitakeover amendments', *Journal of Financial Economics*, **20** (1,2), 267–91.

Bryant, A. (1997), 'CalPERS draws a blueprint for its concept of an ideal board', *New York Times*, 17 June, p. D5.

Buchholtz, A.K. and B.A. Ribbens (1994), 'Role of chief executive officers in takeover resistance: effects of CEO incentives and individual characteristics', *Academy of Management Journal*, **37** (3), 554–79.

Byrd, J.W. and K.A. Hickman (1992), 'Do outside directors monitor managers? Evidence from tender offer bids', *Journal of Financial Economics*, **32** (2), 195–222.

Chen, H., J.L. Hexter and M.Y. Hu (1993), 'Management ownership and corporate value', *Managerial and Decision Economics*, **14** (4), 335–46.

Coles, J.W. and W.S. Hesterly (2000), 'Independence of the chairman and board composition: firm choices and shareholder value', *Journal of Management*, **26** (2), 195–214.

Coles, J.W., V.B. McWilliams and N. Sen (2001), 'An examination of the relationship of governance mechanisms to performance', *Journal of Management*, **27** (1), 23–50.

Comment, R. and G.W. Schwert (1995), 'Poison or placebo? Evidence on the deterrent and wealth effects of modern antitakeover measures', *Journal of Financial Economics*, **39** (1), 3–43.

Core, J. E., R.W. Holthausen and D.F. Larcker (1999), 'Corporate governance, chief executive officer compensation, and firm performance', *Journal of Financial Economics*, **51** (3), 371–407.

Daily, C.M. and D.R. Dalton (1994), 'Corporate governance and the bankrupt firm: an empirical assessment', *Strategic Management Journal*, **15** (8), 643–54.

Daily, C.M. and C. Schwenk (1996), 'Chief executive officers, top management teams and boards of directors: congruent or countervailing forces?', *Journal of Management*, **22** (2), 185–214.

Dalton, D.R. and I.F. Kesner (1987), 'Composition and CEO duality in boards of directors: an international perspective', *Journal of International Business Studies*, **18** (3), 33–42.

Dalton, D.R., S.T. Certo and R. Roengpitya (2003), 'Meta-analyses of financial performance and equity: fusion or confusion?', *Academy of Management Journal*, **46** (1), 13–26.

Dalton, D.R., C.M. Daily, A.E. Ellstrand and J.L. Johnson (1998), 'Meta-analytic reviews of board composition, leadership structure, and financial performance', *Strategic Management Journal*, **19** (3), 269–90.

Dalton, D.R., C.M. Daily, J.L. Johnson and A.E. Ellstrand (1999), 'Number of directors and financial performance: a meta-analysis', *Academy of Management Journal*, **42** (6), 674–87.

Davis, J.H., F.D. Schoorman and L. Donaldson (1997), 'Toward a stewardship theory of management', *Academy of Management Review*, **22** (1), 20–47.

Denis, D.J. and J.M. Serrano (1996), 'Active investors and management turnover following unsuccessful control contests', *Journal of Financial Economics*, **40** (2), 239–66.

Fama, E.F. and M.C. Jensen (1983a), 'Separation of ownership and control', *Journal of Law and Economics*, **26** (2), 301–26.

Fama, E.F. and M.C. Jensen (1983b), 'Agency problems and residual claims', *Journal of Law and Economics*, **26** (2), 327–49.

Finkelstein, S. and R.A. D'Aveni (1994), 'CEO duality as a double-edged sword: how boards of directors balance entrenchment avoidance and unity of command', *Academy of Management Journal*, **37** (5), 1079–1108.

Frye, M.B. (2001), 'The evolution of corporate governance: evidence from initial public offerings', working paper, University of Central Florida.

Harrison, J.R., D.L. Torres and S. Kukalis (1988), 'The changing of the guard: turnover and structural change in the top-management positions', *Administrative Science Quarterly*, **33** (2), 211–32.

Hill, C.W.L. and S.A. Snell (1988), 'External control, corporate strategy and firm performance in research intensive industries', *Strategic Management Journal*, **9** (6), 577–90.

Himmelberg, C.P., R.G. Hubbard and D. Palia (1999), 'Understanding the determinants of managerial ownership and the link between ownership and performance', *Journal of Financial Economics*, **53** (3), 353–84.

Holderness, C., R.S. Kroszner and D. Sheehan (1999), 'Were the good old days that good? Changes in managerial stock ownership since the great depression', *Journal of Finance*, **54** (2), 435–69.

Howton, S.D., S.W. Howton and G. Olson (2001), 'Board ownership and IPO returns', *Journal of Economics and Finance*, **25** (1), 100–114.

Huddart, S. (1993), 'The effect of a large shareholder on corporate value', *Management Science*, **39** (11), 1407–21.

Jensen, G.R., D.P. Solberg and T.S. Zorn (1992), 'Simultaneous determination of insider ownership, debt and dividend policies', *Journal of Financial and Quantitative Analysis*, **27** (2), 247–63.

Jensen, M.C. (1986), 'The takeover controversy: analysis and evidence', *Midland Corporate Finance Journal*, **4** (2), 6–32.

Jensen, M.C. (1988), 'Takeovers: their causes and consequences', *Journal of Economic Perspectives*, **2** (1), 21–48.

Jensen, M.C. (1993), 'The modern industrial revolution, exit, and the failure of internal control systems', *Journal of Finance*, **48**, 831–80.

Jensen, M.C. and W. Meckling (1976), 'Theory of the firm: managerial behavior, agency costs and ownership structure', *Journal of Financial Economics*, **3** (4), 305–60.

Jensen, M.C. and K.J. Murphy (1990a), 'CEO incentives – It's not how much you pay, but how', *Harvard Business Review*, **68** (3), 138–50.

Jensen, M.C. and K.J. Murphy (1990b), 'Performance pay and top-management incentives', *The Journal of Political Economy*, **98** (2), 225–63.

John, K. and L.W. Senbet (1998), 'Corporate governance and board effectiveness', *Journal of Banking and Finance*, **22** (4), 371–403.

Johnson, J.L., C.M. Daily and A.E. Ellstrand (1996), 'Boards of directors: a review and research agenda', *Journal of Management*, **22** (3), 409–38.

Johnson, R.A., R.E. Hoskisson and M.A. Hitt (1993), 'Board of director involvement in restructuring: the effects of board versus managerial controls and characteristics', *Strategic Management Journal*, **14** (special issue), 33–50.

Kesner, I.F. and R.B. Johnson (1990), 'An investigation of the relationship between board composition and stockholder suits', *Strategic Management Journal*, **11** (4), 327–36.

Kosnik, R.D. (1987), 'Greenmail: a study of board performance in corporate governance', *Administrative Science Quarterly*, **32** (2), 163–85.

Kosnik, R.D. (1990), 'Effects of board demography and directors' incentives on corporate greenmail decisions', *Academy of Management Journal*, **33** (1), 129–50.

Lipton, M. and J.W. Lorsch (1992), 'A modest proposal for improved corporate governance', *The Business Lawyer*, **48** (1), 59–77.

Lublin, J.S. (1992), 'Other concerns are likely to follow GM in splitting posts of chairman and CEO', *Wall Street Journal*, 4 November, B1.

Mallette, P. and K.L. Fowler (1992), 'Effects of board composition and stock ownership on the adoption of "poison pills"', *Academy of Management Journal*, **35** (5), 1010–35.

McConnell, J.J. and H. Serveas (1995), 'Equity ownership and the two faces of debt', *Journal of Financial Economics*, **39** (1), 131–57.

Mehran, H. (1995), 'Executive compensation structure, ownership and firm performance', *Journal of Financial Economics*, **38** (2), 163–84.

Miller, D. (1991), 'Stale in the saddle: CEO tenure and the match between organization and environment', *Management Science*, **37** (1), 34–52.

Morck, R., A. Shleifer and R. Vishny (1988), 'Management ownership and market valuation: an empirical analysis', *Journal of Financial Economics*, **20** (1,2), 293–317.

Morck, R., A. Shleifer and R.W. Vishny (1989), 'Alternative mechanisms for corporate control', *The American Economic Review*, **79** (4), 842–52.

Ocasio, W. (1994), 'Political dynamics and the circulation of power: CEO succession in US industrial corporations', *Administrative Science Quarterly*, **39** (2), 285–312.

Pearce, J.A. and S.A. Zahra (1991), 'The relative power of CEOs and boards of directors: associations with corporate performance', *Strategic Management Journal*, **12** (2), 135–53.

Pearce, J.A. and S.A. Zahra (1992), 'Board composition from a strategic contingency perspective', *Journal of Management Studies*, **29** (4), 411–38.

Powell, T.C. (1996), 'How much does industry matter? An alternative empirical test', *Strategic Management Journal*, **17** (4), 323–34.

Rechner, P.L. and D.R. Dalton (1989), 'The impact of CEO as board chairperson on corporate performance: evidence vs. rhetoric', *Academy of Management Executive*, **3** (2), 141–3.

Rechner, P.L. and D.R. Dalton (1991), 'CEO duality and organizational performance: a longitudinal analysis', *Strategic Management Journal*, 12 (2), 155–60.

Rediker, K.J. and A. Seth (1995), 'Boards of directors and substitution effects of alternative governance mechanisms', *Strategic Management Journal*, **16** (2), 85–99.

Rhoades, D.L., P.L. Rechner, and C. Sundaramurthy (2000), 'Board composition and financial performance: a meta-analysis of the influence of outside directors', *Journal of Managerial Issues*, **12** (1), 76–91

Rosenstein, S. and J.G. Wyatt (1990), 'Outside directors, board independence and shareholder wealth', *Journal of Financial Economics*, **26** (2), 175–92.

Rosenstein, S. and J.G. Wyatt (1997), 'Inside directors, board effectiveness and shareholder wealth', *Journal of Financial Economics*, **44** (2), 229–51.

Rumelt, R. (1991), 'How much does industry matter?', *Strategic Management Journal*, **12** (3), 167–85.

Sarbanes–Oxley Act (2002). H.R. 3763, United States of America.

Schellenger, M.H., D.D. Wood and A. Tashakori (1989), 'Board of director composition, shareholder wealth and dividend policy', *Journal of Management*, **15** (3), 457–67.

Schmalansee, R. (1985), 'Do markets differ much?', *American Economic Review*, **75** (3), 341–51.

Shleifer, A. and R.W. Vishny (1997), 'A survey of corporate governance', *Journal of Finance*, **52** (2), 737–83.

Short, H. (1994), 'Ownership, control, financial structure and the performance of firms', *Journal of Economic Surveys*, **8**, 203–49.

Short, H. and K. Keasey (1999), 'Managerial ownership and the performance of firms: evidence from the UK', *Journal of Corporate Finance*, **5**, 79–101.

Sundaramurthy, C., J.M. Mahoney and J.T Mahoney (1997), 'Board structure, antitakeover provisions, and stockholder wealth', *Strategic Management Journal*, **18** (3), 231–45.

Weisbach, M.S. (1988), 'Outside directors and CEO turnover', *Journal of Financial Economics*, **20** (1,2), 431–60.

Wernerfelt, B. and C. Montgomery (1988), 'Tobin's q and the importance of focus in firm performance', *American Economic Review*, **78** (1), 246–51.

Yermack, D. (1996), 'Higher market valuation of companies with a small board of directors', *Journal of Financial Economics*, **40** (3), 185–211.

Zahra, S.A. and J.A. Pearce (1989), 'Boards of directors and corporate financial performance: a review and integrative model', *Journal of Management*, **15** (2), 291–334.

Zahra, S.A., D.O. Neubaum and M. Huse (2000), 'Entrepreneurship in medium size companies: explaining the effects of ownership and governance systems', *Journal of Management*, **26** (5), 947–76.

14 Corporate governance reform: global, North American and European trends
Christine Mallin

Introduction

Corporate governance is increasingly high on the agenda for directors, investors and governments alike in the wake of financial collapses and corporate scandals in recent years. These collapses and scandals have not been limited to a single country, or even a single continent, but have been a global phenomenon. They have not been confined to a particular industry, nor to a particular business form, and, whilst it has been the large firms that have hit the headlines, there have doubtless been similar events in smaller firms which have not been caught in the glare of media headlines but which nonetheless will have had a significant impact on the lives of those affected, whether they be employees who have lost their jobs, or providers of equity or debt finance.

Many financial scandals stem from problems rooted in the separation of ownership and control. As long ago as 1838, Adam Smith identified this problem: 'the directors of such companies however being the managers rather of other people's money than of their own, it cannot well be expected that they should watch over it with the same anxious vigilance' (Smith, 1838, p. 586).

In this chapter the concept of corporate governance and its growth as a global phenomenon are examined. The impact of differing legal systems and ownership structures and how these may affect corporate governance developments are discussed. The influence of institutional investors is examined and it is shown how, with the internationalization of cross-border portfolios, they are one of the key drivers for the growth in corporate governance. Increasingly firms are under pressure, from a variety of groups, to have regard to the interests of, not just shareholders, but the wider stakeholder groups on whom their activities may have an impact. Such stakeholder groups may encompass employees, customers, suppliers, local communities and governments. In other words, firms are expected to exhibit more corporate social responsibility and to have regard to the ethical, social and environmental impact of their operations.

Concepts of corporate governance

Shleifer and Vishny (1997) defined corporate governance as follows: 'corporate governance deals with the ways in which suppliers of finance to corporations assure themselves of getting a return on their investment'. A wider definition is favoured by many, for example, the Organisation for Economic Co-operation and Development (OECD) (1999, p. 11) which defined corporate governance as 'a set of relationships between a company's management, its board, its shareholders and other stakeholders. [It] also provides the structure through which the objectives of the company are set, and the means of attaining those objectives, and monitoring performance, are determined'. The latter definition hints at the broader more encompassing nature of corporate governance, and such a definition was also given by Millstein (1998):

> the term 'corporate governance' has many definitions. It can broadly encompass all of the corporation's relationships: relationships among capital, product, service and human resource providers, customers and even society at large. It can encompass all the laws designed to hold the corporation accountable to shareholders and the public, as well as the workings of the market for corporate control.

From these definitions, we can see why corporate governance has become such an important feature of everyday life in the business world: its all-encompassing nature means that it is essential for helping to ensure that firms operate to their best ability, that they are run by competent boards in an efficient manner, that they have appropriate internal controls in place and that, whilst the firm is generally run with the objective of maximizing shareholder value, there should also be consideration of the wider stakeholder interests too. In the words of Sir Adrian Cadbury (2002, p. 160), 'the essence of the contract between society and business is that companies shall not pursue their immediate profit objectives at the expense of the longer-term interests of the community'.

The impact of legal system and ownership structure on the development of corporate governance

Much has been written about the development of corporate governance in the last decade in both individual countries and comparative international studies by academics and practitioners. There have been a number of seminal papers analysing the impact of legal system and ownership structure on the type of corporate governance system adopted in particular countries.

Denis and McConnell (2003) have written an excellent paper surveying two generations of research on corporate governance systems internationally. They find that earlier studies of corporate governance tend to concentrate on 'individual governance mechanisms – particularly board composition and equity ownership – in individual countries' whilst the second generation of research 'considers the possible impact of differing legal systems on the structure and effectiveness of corporate governance and compares systems across countries' (ibid., p. 1).

Corporate governance systems
Figure 14.1 illustrates the various influences on the development of corporate governance globally. These influences include the legal system, ownership structure, regulatory structure and cultural influences.

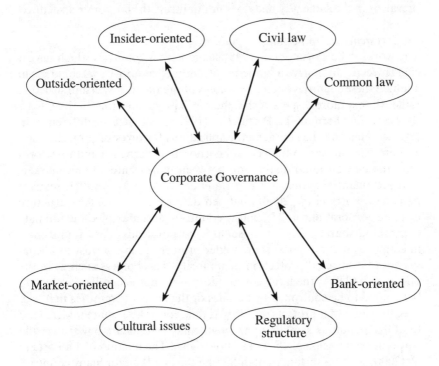

Figure 14.1   Key influences on the development of corporate governance

Franks and Mayer (1995) used the terms 'insider' and 'outsider' systems to differentiate between two types of ownership and control structures. In the outsider system there is dispersed ownership of corporate equity amongst a large number of outside investors (as in both the UK and the USA) whereby institutional investor ownership is predominant although the institutional investors do not tend to hold large shareholdings in any given company; hence they have little direct control. In contrast, in an insider system, such as in many Continental European countries, ownership tends to be much more concentrated, with shares often being owned either by holding companies or by families.

Sometimes a corporate governance system may also be termed 'bank-oriented' or 'market-oriented'. A bank-oriented system implies that banks play a key role in the funding of companies and so may well be able to exercise some control via the board structure (for example, bank representatives may have seats on the supervisory board in German companies); on the other hand, a market-oriented system is one where banks' influence is not prevalent in the same way and does not infiltrate the corporate structure.

Legal systems and ownership structure
The work of La Porta *et al.* (1998) suggests that countries which have a civil law/code often have a limited protection of minority shareholders; in addition these countries often have a concentrated share ownership structure rather than a more dispersed shareholder base such as that in the UK or the USA. Furthermore La Porta *et al.* (1999) argue that the differences in legal systems and the consequent implications for investor protection are a 'more fruitful way to understand corporate governance and its reform than the conventional distinction between bank-centered and market-centered financial systems' (La Porta *et al.*, 2000, p. 3). Another seminal paper (La Porta *et al.*, 2000) analysed data on the ownership structure of large corporations in 27 wealthy countries, and identified the ultimate controlling shareholders in those large corporations. They found that, in countries without good shareholder protection, in contrast to a legal system that fostered protection of minority shareholders such as in the UK and the USA, the large corporations were not generally widely held but tended to be controlled by families or the state. In countries that lack a legal system that protects minority rights, controlling shareholders tend to utilize pyramids as a device through which to exercise power over the corporation in excess of their cash flow rights. The findings of La Porta *et al.* (2000) were important in highlighting the fact that, for many countries around the world, preventing the expropriation of minority shareholders' rights by the controlling shareholders is the fundamental problem.

In the context of the Asian countries with weak institutions and poor property rights (including protection of minority shareholders' rights), Claessens and Fan (2002, p. 73) state 'resulting forms of crony capitalism, i.e., combinations of weak corporate governance and government interference, not only lead to poor performance and risky financing patterns, but also are conducive to macro-economic crises'. In a study of nine Asian countries, Claessens *et al.* (2000, p. 81) find that 'in all countries, voting rights frequently exceed cash flow rights via pyramid structures and cross-holdings'. This is indicative of the power that the dominant shareholders are able to build up. However most Asian countries seem set on improving their corporate governance by enhancing transparency and reinforcing minority shareholders' rights, and this will likely lead to more parity between voting rights and cash flow rights in the future.

Klapper and Love (2003) undertook a study of firm-level governance in fourteen emerging market countries including South Africa, India and Brazil. They state that one interpretation of their results is that 'firm-level corporate governance matters more in countries with weak shareholder protection and poor judicial efficiency' (ibid., p. 1). Therefore adopting good governance practices can help to mitigate poor legal protection for investors.

Recent developments in corporate governance

Mallin (2004) noted that increasingly the corporate governance practices of individual countries need to satisfy certain core principles of accepted good practice. This is largely attributable to the reduction of barriers between different countries' capital markets, the internationalization of cross-border portfolios and technological advances.

This section reviews some of the recent developments in North America, the UK, Europe and globally, and highlights the fact that there are key areas where corporate governance thought and practice are coming together across the world. The recommendations contained in the Cadbury Report (1992) and the OECD Principles (1999) have been influential in the determination of these core principles.

The Cadbury Report (1992) contained a Code of Best Practice recommendations, applicable to all listed companies in the UK, and covered the operation of the main board (including essentially the separation of the roles of chair and CEO); the establishment, composition and operation of key board committees (audit, remuneration and nomination); the importance of, and contribution that can be made by, non-executive directors (the majority of whom should be independent); remuneration of executive directors to be recommended by the remuneration committee, with full and clear disclosure of directors' total remuneration; and the reporting and control mechanisms of a business. The Cadbury Report utilized a 'comply or explain' mechanism whereby a company should comply with the Code or else state why it has been unable to do so.

The OECD Principles (1999) covered the rights of shareholders, the equitable treatment of shareholders, the role of stakeholders in corporate governance, disclosure and transparency and the responsibilities of the board. The Principles are discussed in more detail below.

North America

The USA is characterized by a well-developed capital market with widespread share ownership, an important aspect of which is the influence of institutional investors including pension funds, such as the California Public Employees' Retirement System (CalPERS). However, although US institutional investors often play an active role as shareowners and not just as shareholders, there have still been a number of high-profile corporate collapses and scandals. Following corporate scandals of huge proportions including Enron, Tyco, Worldcom and Global Crossing, there has been tremendous pressure on the US government to instigate a review of corporate accountability and corporate governance. There followed the publication of the Sarbanes–Oxley Act (2002).

The Sarbanes–Oxley Act seeks to strengthen (external) auditor independence and also to strengthen the company's audit committee. Listed companies, for example, must have an audit committee comprising only independent members, and must also disclose whether they have at least one 'audit committee financial expert' on their audit committee. The 'audit committee financial expert' should be named and the company should state whether the expert is independent of management (as stated earlier, for listed companies, the audit committee should comprise only independent members).

The Act establishes a new regulatory body for auditors of US listed firms, the Public Company Accounting Oversight Board (PCAOB) with which all auditors of US listed companies have to register, including non-US audit firms. Correspondingly the Securities Exchange Commission (SEC) has issued separate rules which encompass the prohibition of some non-audit services to audit clients, mandatory rotation of audit partners and auditors' reports on the effectiveness of internal controls. The SEC implementation of the Sarbanes–Oxley Act prohibits nine non-audit services that might impair auditor independence. In many cases these effectively prohibit the audit firm from either auditing accounting services provided by the audit firm's staff or providing help with systems which will then be audited by the audit firm. These nine areas include book-keeping or other services related to the accounting records or financial statements of the audited company; financial information systems design and implementation; appraisal or valuation services, fairness opinions or contribution-in-kind reports (where the firm provides its opinion on the adequacy of consideration in a transaction); actuarial services; internal audit outsourcing services; management functions/human resources (an auditor should not be a director, officer or employee of an audit client nor perform any executive role for the audit client such as supervisory, decision making or monitoring); broker or dealer, investment adviser or investment banking services; legal services or expert services unrelated to the audit; any other service that the PCAOB decides is not permitted.

There are also requirements relating to the rotation of audit partners such that the lead audit partner should rotate every five years, and is then subject to a five-year period when he or she cannot be the audit partner for that company. Similarly other partners involved with the audit, but not acting as the lead partner, are subject to a seven-year rotation followed by a two-year bar. Any member of the audit team is barred for one year from accepting employment in certain specified positions in a company that they have audited. The auditor is required to report to the audit committee various information which includes all critical accounting policies and practices, and alternative accounting treatments. The Sarbanes–Oxley Act provides for far-reaching reform and has caused much disquiet outside the USA as the Act applies equally to US and non-US firms with a US listing.

The Commission on Public Trust and Private Enterprise was formed by the Conference Board, an influential US-based non-profit-making organization, to look at the circumstances which gave rise to corporate scandals which resulted in a loss of confidence in the US markets. The Commission's work focused on three main areas: executive compensation, corporate governance and auditing and accounting. The Commission issued its first report on executive compensation in 2002 and the second report, on corporate governance, and auditing and accounting, was issued in early 2003.

In its first report, the Commission listed seven principles relating to the compensation (remuneration) committee and its responsibilities, the importance of performance-based compensation, the role of equity-based incentives, creating a long-term focus, accounting neutrality, shareholders' rights and transparency and disclosure. It recommended, inter alia, that the compensation committee should comprise directors who are free of any relationships with the company and its management; performance-based remuneration incentives should be linked to the firm's long-term strategic goals as set by the board; and there should be disclosure of any costs to shareholders associated with equity-based compensation (for example, dilution of earnings per share).

In its second report, the Commission listed nine principles relating to corporate governance which cover the following areas: relationship of the board and management, fulfilling the board's responsibilities, director qualifications, role of the nominating/governance committee, board evaluation, ethics oversight, hiring special investigative counsel, shareowner involvement and long-term share ownership.

Recommendations of particular interest include the separation of the roles of chairman and CEO (which would mirror the predominant situation in UK firms); an emphasis on the importance of a substantial majority of independent directors nominated by a nominating/governance committee; encouragement of long-term share ownership and activism as shareowners; an audit committee comprising independent members, rotation of outside audit firms, and the development of an ethical culture at board level to be applied across the company (this is viewed as essential for the firm's long-term viability).

In June 2003, the SEC approved a proposal by the New York Stock Exchange (NYSE) that there should be shareholder approval of equity compensation plans and, in November 2003, the NYSE's new corporate governance standards for listed companies were approved by the SEC. The new standards have been designed to improve corporate governance, transparency and disclosure in companies listed in the USA, and to help restore and maintain investor confidence after the corporate financial scandals of recent years. The NYSE's Corporate Governance Rules (2003) include the following:

- listed companies must have a majority of independent directors;
- the board of directors has to 'determine affirmatively' the independence of directors who are deemed to be independent directors;
- non-management directors should meet regularly at scheduled executive sessions without management being present;
- there should be a nominating/corporate governance committee, a compensation (remuneration) committee and an audit committee, each of which should comprise wholly independent directors;
- the audit committee should have a minimum of three members;
- the nominating, compensation and audit committees should each have a written charter addressing the purpose and responsibilities of the respective committees;
- there should be an annual performance evaluation of each of the nominating, compensation and audit committees;
- companies must disclose their corporate governance guidelines and charters of their committees on their websites and make the information available upon request to any shareholder who asks for it;
- there should be adoption and disclosure of a code of business conduct and ethics for directors, officers and employees, with prompt disclosure of any exceptions made for directors or executive officers;
- foreign companies listed in the USA should disclose any significant differences in the corporate governance practices of their home country and the NYSE corporate governance listing standards;
- each CEO should certify to the NYSE annually that he or she is not aware of any violation of the NYSE corporate governance listing standards by the company.

The means of enforcement of the above requirements is interesting as the NYSE recognizes that it would be damaging to shareholders to suspend or delist the shares of a company that had violated the standards. Therefore the NYSE states that it 'may issue a public reprimand letter to any listed company, regardless of type of security listed or country of incorporation, that it determines has violated a NYSE listing standard' (NYSE, 2003, p. 17).

The NYSE corporate governance listing standards represent an important landmark in the development of corporate governance in the USA, and include a number of innovative requirements that should help ensure that US corporate governance standards maintain confidence in the stock market.

The UK

As mentioned earlier the UK's Cadbury Report (1992) influenced the development of corporate governance in many countries around the world, Russia and India to mention but two. The Cadbury Committee was established following corporate collapses and scandals in the UK and since the early 1990s there have been a number of corporate governance committees and reviews which have reported on directors' remuneration, internal controls, audit committees, institutional investment and the role and influence of non-executive directors. The Combined Code (2003) incorporates the substance of the recommendations of many of the earlier committees and reviews.

The Combined Code has two main parts: one on companies and one on institutional shareholders. The part on companies contains sections on directors, remuneration, accountability and audit, and relations with shareholders. In relation to directors, the Combined Code states that there should be an effective board, which is collectively responsible for the success of the company and a clear division of responsibilities at the head of the company (separation of the roles of chair and CEO).

The inclusion of a balance of executive and non-executive directors (and in particular independent non-executive directors) on the board will help prevent an individual becoming too dominant, and a formal, rigorous and transparent procedure for the appointment of new directors to the board should help ensure that the most appropriate people are appointed as directors. Information should be provided to the board in a timely manner to enable it to make informed decisions, and all directors should regularly update their skills and knowledge. A formal and rigorous evaluation should be carried out annually of the board's performance and that of the committees and individual directors. Finally all directors should be put forward at regular intervals for re-election (as long as their performance remains satisfactory).

In relation to remuneration, the Combined Code states that 'levels of remuneration should be sufficient to attract, retain and motivate directors of the quality required to run the company successfully' (Combined Code 2003, para. B1, 12). Executive directors' remuneration should also be largely linked to company and individual director performance, and should be set through a formal and transparent procedure. It is recommended that a remuneration committee comprising independent non-executive directors should be established.

Regarding accountability and audit, the board should give a balanced and comprehensible assessment of the company's position, and should maintain a sound system of internal controls. The board should establish an audit committee of independent non-executive directors. Appertaining to relations with shareholders, there should be 'a dialogue based on the mutual understanding of objectives' (ibid., para. D1, 18). Whilst there should be continuing dialogue between the companies' directors and its major shareholders, the annual general meeting is seen as a means of communicating with investors generally and encouraging their participation.

Institutional investors are seen as having a particularly important role to play in helping to ensure that corporate governance best practice is followed. This is because, in the UK, there has been a sea change in the level of share ownership by individuals and institutional investors. Whilst share ownership by individuals has decreased over the last 40 years, ownership by institutional investors has increased. The Office of National Statistics (2003) shows that, in 1963, individual investors owned 54 per cent of shares in the UK. The proportion of shares owned by this group fell steadily, until by 1989 it had dropped to just under 21 per cent. Since 1989 there have been a few factors that should have encouraged individual share ownership. Firstly there were the large privatization issues which occurred in the UK in the early 1990s and, in more recent years, the demutualization of some of the large building societies. Nonetheless, by the end of 2002, the share ownership by individuals had dropped to just under 14 per cent.

In contrast to the individual investors' level of share ownership, the ownership of shares by the institutional investors (largely insurance companies and pension funds) has increased dramatically over the same period. Ownership by insurance companies increased from 10 per cent in 1963 to 20 per cent in 2002, whilst that of pension funds saw an increase to 16 per cent. There has also been a notable increase in the overseas level of ownership from 7 per cent in 1963 to 32 per cent in 2002. Many of the overseas shareholders are US investors, with European Union countries also holding significant amounts. US institutional investors are used to being more proactive in certain areas of corporate governance. For example, private pension funds in the USA are mandated by the Employee Retirement

Income Security Act (ERISA) (1974) to vote their shares and this has meant that public pension funds tend to vote their shares, too, as there is more of a culture and expectation that they should vote and exercise this valuable asset. In the UK, there has been increasing pressure in recent years for institutional investors to exercise their votes and more and more are doing so, although there remains a somewhat mysterious reluctance on the part of fund managers to publish information about the number of votes cast on various companies' resolutions.

Given the size of their shareholdings, the power of the institutional investors cannot be doubted. In his seminal work, Hirschman (1970) identified the exercise of institutional power within an 'exit and voice' framework, arguing that 'dissatisfaction [may be expressed] directly to management', the *voice* option, or by selling the shareholding, the *exit* option. The latter choice is not viable for many institutional investors, given the size of their holdings or a policy of holding a balanced portfolio.

The Combined Code (2003) recommends that institutional investors should have a dialogue with companies based, as previously mentioned, on the 'mutual understanding of objectives'. Institutional investors are encouraged to take all factors into account when assessing a company's corporate governance (for example, smaller companies often have fewer independent non-executive directors). As with earlier UK corporate governance codes, institutional investors are exhorted to make considered use of their votes.

Some interesting parallels can be seen between developments in the NYSE corporate governance listing standards and the UK's Combined Code, especially in terms of board structure (key board committees: audit, remuneration, nomination), evaluation of board performance and emphasis on the importance of independent directors.

Increasingly institutional investors have become aware of the benefits of socially responsible investment (SRI). These are on a number of fronts: client demand, corporate citizenship and potential economic benefits. The OECD (1998, p. 73) corporate governance report stated:

> in the global economy, sensitivity to the many societies in which an individual corporation may operate can pose a challenge. Increasingly, however, investors in international capital markets expect corporations to forego certain activities – such as use of child or prison labour, bribery, support of oppressive regimes, and environmental disruption – even when those activities may not be expressly prohibited in a particular jurisdiction in which the corporation operates.

It is key to the development of SRI that the large institutional investors in both the UK and the US have become more involved and willing to screen potential investments as appropriate. In terms of socially responsible investment, an important development in the UK was that, from 3 July 2000, pension fund trustees have had to take account of SRI in their Statement of Investment Principles. This change means that pension fund trustees must state the extent to which social, environmental or ethical considerations are taken into account in the selection, retention, and realisation of investments.

Recognition of the growing importance of SRI was also evidenced by the Association of British Insurers (ABI) (2003) with the publication of its disclosure guidelines on SRI. The ABI is an influential voice in institutional investors' involvement in corporate governance issues. The main focus of the guidelines is the identification and management of risks arising from social, environmental and ethical issues that may affect either short-term or long-term business value. The flip side of this is that appropriate management of these risks may mean opportunities to enhance value.

European corporate governance
There have been a number of developments aimed at 'harmonizing' regulation and governance at a European level. The EU High Level Group of Company Law Experts, comprising a group of lawyers, was established in late 2001 by the EU to provide independent advice for modernizing company law in Europe. The Group, headed by Jaap Winter, issued the Winter report (2002), which made the following recommendations for listed companies in relation to corporate governance issues.

- EU law should require companies to publish an annual corporate governance statement in their accounts and on their website. Companies would need to state their compliance with their national corporate governance code, on a 'comply or explain' basis.
- The nomination and remuneration of directors, and the audit of accounts, should be decided upon by non-executive, or supervisory, directors, the majority of whom are independent.
- Companies should disclose in their annual corporate governance statement who their independent directors are, why they are independent, what their qualifications are to serve on the board, and their other directorships.
- The remuneration of individual directors should be disclosed in detail.
- Share option schemes would require the prior approval of the shareholders.
- In relation to (annual) general meetings, companies should be required to publish all relevant material on their website, and offer facilities for electronic voting.

- Companies should inform shareholders as to the procedure for asking questions at general meetings, and also the process for submitting shareholder resolutions (proposals).

Frits Bolkestein, the EU internal markets commissioner, promised action to take forward the recommendations of the Group, and in May 2003 an Action Plan on 'Modernising Company Law and Enhancing Corporate Governance in the EU' was published. It was open to consultation for three months, and a final version was published in November 2003. The corporate governance initiatives that are seen as the most important are the introduction of an annual corporate governance statement; the development of a legislative framework aimed at helping shareholders to exercise various rights (with specific problems relating to cross-border voting being given urgent attention); promoting the role of (independent) non-executive or supervisory directors and establishing minimum standards on the creation, composition and role of audit, remuneration and nomination committees; more transparency regarding directors' remuneration including detailed disclosure of individual directors' remuneration and greater shareholder influence in this area; and creation of a European Corporate Governance Forum to encourage coordination and convergence of national codes.

The aim is not to create a European Corporate Governance Code as such as it is felt that this would simply complicate the matter by adding an extra layer to existing national and international codes/principles. However, given the increasing integration of European markets, the idea is to lay down some common ground rules. There are clear implications for all members of the EU. As far as the UK is concerned, the Group's recommendations are generally similar to those of the UK Company Law Review and should not pose any problems. Indeed the UK is generally ahead of the game and is the only country in Europe where the remuneration report is put to the vote at the company's annual general meeting.

Global developments
The World Bank, the Global Corporate Governance Forum, the International Corporate Governance Network and the OECD have all influenced the development of corporate governance globally.

The International Corporate Governance Network (ICGN) was founded in 1995. Its membership encompasses major institutional investors, investor representative groups, companies, financial intermediaries, academics and others with an interest in the development of global corporate governance practices. Its objective is to facilitate international dialogue on corporate governance issues. In 1999, the ICGN issued its Statement on Global Corporate Governance Principles which endorsed the OECD (1999) Principles, describing them as 'a remarkable convergence on corporate governance common ground among diverse interests, practices, and cultures' (ICGN, 1999, p. 1). The ICGN also amplified the OECD Principles, expanding on, and interpreting, each one.

Notably the OECD Principles of Corporate Governance (1999) have underpinned the development of many corporate governance codes and guidelines, both of individual country codes (for example, Greece and China) and of broader initiatives such as the World Bank/International Monetary Fund Reports on Standards and Codes. The Principles cover the rights of shareholders, the equitable treatment of shareholders, the role of stakeholders in corporate governance, disclosure and transparency, and the responsibilities of the board.

The Principles are currently under review and a draft of the revised Principles was issued for comment with responses due in early 2004. The draft revised text states at the start that 'the corporate governance framework should be developed with a view to its impact on overall economic performance and the incentives it creates for market participants and the promotion of transparent and efficient markets. The legal and regulatory requirements that affect corporate governance practices in a jurisdiction should be transparent and enforceable' (OECD, 2004, p. 5). The detailed annotations relating to the existing five principles are expanded upon, and made more encompassing. For example, investors should have the right to nominate company directors and play a more proactive role in electing them; institutional investors should disclose their voting policies and also state how they manage conflicts of interest that may have an impact on, inter alia, voting; 'whistle blowers' should receive more protection; and there should be better protection of the rights of creditors. After extensive consultation the OECD published its revised Principles in 2004.

Moving towards a global consensus?

The review in the previous section of international developments in corporate governance has shown how, in general, the rights and responsibilities of shareholders, directors' remuneration, directors' accountability and responsibility, improved transparency, the role of key board committees (especially audit and risk management) and the role of independent non-executive directors all feature prominently in the corporate governance codes/principles. In this sense there is a convergence on perceived corporate governance best practice which countries around the world aim to incorporate into their own country's corporate governance. These core principles are evident whether the legal system is based on civil law or common law, and whether the ownership structure comprises a diversified shareholder base (for example, institutional investors in the UK and the USA), family-owned firms (as in many continental European countries) or firms where the state remains dominant (as in China).

However no corporate governance system will ever be perfect in the sense of totally preventing fraud and misappropriation or misuse of corporate assets. Good corporate governance can, however, help to limit the incidence of such abuse, and good corporate governance may also increase shareholder value; and, although the jury is out for debate on this aspect, an increasing body of evidence points towards a link between good corporate governance and the maintenance or increase in shareholder value in the longer term. Indeed we come full circle to the idea that corporate social responsibility is integral to good corporate governance and that a company cannot operate in isolation from the wider society in which it operates. Good corporate governance, incorporating a socially responsible attitude, should therefore help ensure the company's long-term viability and prosperity by taking into account the views of the wider stakeholder groups. The recognition of this by influential institutional investors should help ensure that, in the future, corporate social responsibility becomes a globally recognized core principle of corporate governance best practice.

References

Association of British Insurers (2003), *Disclosure Guidelines on Socially Responsible Investment*, London: ABI.

Cadbury, A. (1992), 'Report of the committee on the financial aspects of corporate governance', London: Gee & Co. Ltd.

Cadbury, A. (2002), *Corporate Governance and Chairmanship, A Personal View*, Oxford: Oxford University Press.

Claessens, S. and J.P.H. Fan (2002), 'Corporate governance in Asia: A survey', *International Review of Finance*, **3** (2), 71–103.

Claessens, S., S. Djankov and L.H.P. Lang (2000), 'The separation of ownership and control in East Asian corporations', *Journal of Financial Economics*, **58** (1,2), 81–112.

Combined Code (2003), 'The combined code on corporate governance', The Financial Reporting Council, London.

Conference Board (2002), 'Commission on public trust and private enterprise findings and recommendations Part 1: Executive compensation', posted at http://www.conference-board.org/PDF_free/756.pdf.

Conference Board (2003), 'Commission on public trust and private enterprise findings and recommendations Part 2: Corporate governance; Part 3: Audit and accounting', posted at http://www.conference-board.org/pdf_free/758.pdf.

Denis, D.K. and J.J. McConnell (2003), 'International corporate governance', *Journal of Financial and Quantitative Analysis*, **38** (1), 1–36.

Franks, J. and C. Mayer (1995), 'Ownership and control', in H. Siebert (eds), *Trends in Business Organization: Do Participation and Co-operation Increase Competitiveness?*, Tübingen: Mohr (Siebeck).

Hirschman, A.O. (1970), *Exit, Voice and Loyalty*, Cambridge, MA: Harvard University Press.

International Corporate Governance Network (1999), 'Statement on global corporate governance principles', International Corporate Governance Network, London.

Klapper, L.F. and I. Love (2003), 'Corporate governance, investor protection, and performance in emerging markets', *Journal of Corporate Finance*, **195**, 1–26.

La Porta F., F. Lopez de Silvanes, A.Shleifer and R.Vishny (1998), 'Law and finance', *Journal of Political Economy*, **106** (6), 1113–55.

La Porta R., F. Lopez-de-Silanes, A.Shleifer and R.Vishny (1999), 'Corporate ownership around the world', *Journal of Finance*, **54** (2), 471–517.
La Porta R., F. Lopez-de-Silanes, A. Shleifer and R. Vishny (2000), 'Investor protection and corporate governance', *Journal of Financial Economics*, **58** (1,2), 3–27.
Mallin C.A. (2004), *Corporate Governance*, Oxford: Oxford University Press.
Millstein, I.M. (1998), 'The evolution of corporate governance in the United States', remarks to the World Economic Forum, Davos, Switzerland, 2 February.
New York Stock Exchange (2003), 'Corporate governance listing standards', NYSE, New York.
OECD (1998), 'Corporate governance: improving competitiveness and access to capital in a global market', A Report to the OECD by the Business Sector Advisory Group on Corporate Governance, OECD, Paris.
OECD (1999), *Principles of Corporate Governance*, Paris: OECD.
OECD (2004), *Principles of Corporate Governance*, draft revised text, January, Paris: OECD.
Office of National Statistics (2003), 'Share ownership: a report on ownership of shares as at 31 December 2002', HMSO, Norwich.
Sarbanes–Oxley Act (2002), US Legislature.
Shleifer, A. and R. Vishny (1997), 'A survey of corporate governance', *Journal of Finance*, **52** (2), 737–83.
Smith, A. (1838) *The Wealth of Nations*, London: Ward Lock.
Winter, J. (2002), 'Report of the high level group of company law experts on a modern regulatory framework for company law in Europe', EU Commission, Brussels.

15 Management and governance of professional services firms

Kevin D. Clark, Jonathan P. Doh and
Stephen A. Stumpf

Introduction

In this chapter, we uncover the particular features and challenges associated with the management and governance of professional services firms.[1] We begin with a discussion of the enormous global growth of professional services firms (PSF) in the areas of management consulting, information technology (IT) consulting, public accounting, investment banking, law and advertising/public relations. Problems associated with PSF service, particularly for large management consultancies, have been documented (for example, see O'Shea and Madigan, 1997; Pinault, 2000; Schaffer, 1997). Recent ethical and legal questions raised with respect to public accounting have highlighted the need to reassess the management and governance structures of PSFs.

We assert that there are inherent differences in the structure of ownership and the resulting management in PSFs as compared to traditional organizations, and that research in management and governance as it is currently conceived fails to account satisfactorily for these differences. We review the research on PSFs that is suggestive of the issues we highlight. We observe, however, that this research fails to address the core incentive and alignment issues in PSFs that have contributed to the recent high-profile cases. These cases, and the paucity of research to draw upon to address them, provide both a scholarly and a practical justification for the critical importance of aggressively incorporating PSFs into the organizational theory research agenda.

We will focus on one mechanism that has been identified as a main agent for internal corporate control in the modern corporation, that of the top management team (TMT). We observe that PSFs have historically been organized as partnerships or quasi-partnerships, and that they lack top management teams of the sort studied in the TMT literature. We compare PSFs and traditional industrial corporations along a number of dimensions central to the TMT literature.

We then review the assumptions about governance structures in modern corporations, such as the existence of an external and independent board of directors that oversees the CEO and TMT, large block shareholders who can exert significant influence, and a vibrant market for corporate control that provides discipline on managers and constrains their tendencies to behave opportunistically. We observe significant derogations to these structures in the case of PSFs and suggest critical exceptions and adaptations to these assumptions in the governance literature that must be made when studying governance in this increasingly important sector of the economy. We punctuate our observations with researchable propositions that summarize the substantial exceptions to these widespread and long-held assumptions in governance research. For example, in PSFs, officers are members of an exclusive private class – a peer group that has voting rights, has the right to obligate the firm legally and financially, and requires one to be elected into it by the exclusive votes of existing members.[2] Top management in PSFs comprise officers elected by the officer core and serve at the pleasure of their constituency rather than through appointment by an independent board of directors. Moreover decision-making and control mechanisms are distributed and shared among the officer class (Maister, 1993; Stumpf, 2002).

Having identified key differences in the governance structures of PSFs, we examine a fundamental approach to top management control and oversight in corporations for possible insight: agency theory. Inherent in our analysis is the clear observation that most PSFs do not demonstrate the traditional separation of officers (which make up most if not all leadership roles) and owners that is a critical assumption of research into the motivations of and incentives systems directed toward top management. The agency problem as traditionally articulated is absent in PSFs because officers (senior partners and managing directors) and owners are one and the same. We identify an agency-like problem that emanates from the temporal and geographic separation of short and long-term interests of the individuals who constitute the owners and leaders of professional services firms.

A practical approach to facilitate our quest for theoretical framing to address the problems we identify is to use established theories of management and governance to instruct our thinking with regard to PSFs. We take advantage of the literature in corporate governance and agency theory to draw conclusions as to the origins of some of the issues facing PSFs and to offer possible solutions. We suggest, however, that in applying these perspectives to PSFs, some core assumptions of the theories must be relaxed. Although we argue that agency in its *classic* formulation is not applicable to the study of PSFs, there are important elements of the structure of employment and ownership within PSFs that make agency principles a useful theoretical tool.

A key outcome of the work in governance and agency has been the recommendation for firms to tie executive compensation to firm performance directly through ownership (Jensen and Meckling, 1976). This notion is supported by the contention that manager-owners are more likely to act in ways that benefit all owners of the firm. Hence we argue that, in the case of PSFs, this argument must be adapted to account for the three tiers of employees present in PSFs: non-owner staff, non-leader partners who have an ownership stake and officer-leaders (managing partners) who have an ownership stake and leadership responsibilities for the firm.

Following our discussion of agency theory applicability to PSFs, we examine how changes in the organizational strategy and form of PSFs will affect their governance. Changes have resulted from pressures for growth in institution size for a more global footprint, from clients to satisfy more of their demands, from shareholders over questionable auditing/advising practices and from the general turbulence in the external environment. These developments are exerting pressures on the historically loosely connected, often decentralized organizations to improve accountability and organizational effectiveness. We note that, as PSFs take on some of the characteristics of traditional corporations through their growth, merger with non-PSFs and sale of equity to non-partners, governance theories that recognize intermediate forms will need to be developed.

Management and governance in professional services firms

The emergence of the professional services sector
Services industries account for a large and growing share of overall employment and economic output. In 2000, services accounted for 65 per cent of GDP in higher income countries, up from about 40 per cent in 1947 (Arkell, 2001). By comparison, manufacturing has declined from about 27 per cent of GDP in 1947 to 16 per cent in developed economies in 2000 (ibid.).[3] Professional services firms, especially accounting, advertising and public relations/public affairs consulting, insurance, law, and securities, have grown concomitantly with overall growth in services employment and output. Thus, the professional services sector constitutes a large and growing share of overall economic output and employment, and as such, commands the attention of managerial research. Moreover, the recently highlighted problems of governance and management control at Andersen and other professional auditing firms suggest a need to do more research geared toward dealing with the challenges facing PSFs.

Characteristics of professional services firms
Professional services firms possess a number of characteristics that differentiate them from traditional corporations (Maister, 1993, 1997;

Maister *et al.*, 2000; Stumpf, 1999; Stumpf and Longman, 2000). In particular, the structure and organizational design of PSFs, as well as the associated incentive systems, differ greatly from traditional corporate forms (see Table 15.1). These differences hold important implications for the effective management and governance of PSFs. In the remainder of this section, we review extant research on PSFs to see how these differences have been addressed in the literature. We discuss differences in the top management structure of PSFs referred to in Table 15.1, and introduce a structure we term the 'top management strata' (TMS). We discuss traditional management and governance mechanisms to assess if they have been effective in explaining basic differences between PSFs and traditional corporations. Finally we detail an agency-like problem particular to PSFs, and offer possible remedies for that problem drawing from agency and governance theory.

Managerial research on professional services
Although the marketing literature has long considered services marketing issues, the general management literature is only beginning to focus on leadership questions generated by the emergence of large, global PSFs (Maister *et al.*, 2000; Rackham *et al.*, 1996; Stumpf and Longman, 2000). One explanation for the limited research is that existing managerial theories, such as those derived from analysis of management of industrial corporations, are not directly applicable to PSFs. They must be adapted or modified before they can become useful. Although Freidson (1970, 1983, 1984) provided much of the foundation for current research on PSFs, his perspective, rooted in sociology and an historic conceptualization of the role of the 'professions' in society, has less relevance for the large, sophisticated, globally integrated PSFs that have emerged in the contemporary environment and that are the focus of our discussion.

Lowendahl (1998) offers a simple but compelling argument that professional services firms are different from manufacturing firms and that the tools and techniques put forward in traditional strategic management offer little help in the management of PSFs. Using the resource-based view perspective, Lowendahl suggests that, in PSFs, outputs are intangible, idiosyncratic and innovative, so perceptions of high service quality depend on client expectations. The core resource base of the firm lies in professional expertise and individual judgment, which is controlled by the individual rather than the firm (Maister, 1993, 1997). Hallowell (1999) argues that increasing consolidation in services is driven by pressure for economies of scope. Although Hallowell does not discuss professional services explicitly, we believe consolidation between IT and/or management consulting firms with traditional industrial companies may be motivated, in part, by such

Table 15.1   Comparison of professional service firm and corporation
organizational governance attributes

Corporations	Professional service firms (PSFs)
Many levels of hierarchy, and many differences in job duties at each level	Few levels of hierarchy, few differences in job duties by level
Many non-revenue producing employees and support staff to handle key functions such as recruiting, training and employee relations	Few non-revenue producing employees, few support staff; support functions such as recruiting and professional development are often done by client staff during non-billable moments
Selection to officer level is by the unit managers and/or an organizational committee	Election to officer level is by existing officers
Equity ownership optional at senior executive levels, and often share incentives restricted to TMT	Equity ownership is required at officer level
Many external equity owners: generally the firm has publicly traded shares	Few or no external equity owners: rarely are the firm's shares publicly traded
Officers are expected to be managers, leaders and administrators	Officers are frequently expected to continue their client services, 'producer' (revenue-generating) role while taking on managerial responsibilities
Senior management roles are held until one leaves, or is advanced, retired or fired	Senior management roles are often rotated among officers
Succession planning is common, new leaders are selected	Succession planning is rare; new leaders are elected
Pretax income is defined post officer bonuses and used to determine dividends for shareholders, taxes and other disbursement, including capita reinvestment	Pretax income is distributed among the officer-owners at the end of each fiscal year; little or no earnings are retained, little or no corporate income tax is paid
Work involves a broad array of skills and competencies with few clear 'end of job' points known well in advance	Work involves knowledge-based projects and programs, often competitively bid, with hourly/daily rates and duration used to determine costs
Few employees directly serve external customers or clients face to face	Most employees directly serve external clients or customers face to face
Promotions occur if and when someone is ready and an opening exists	'Up or out' promotion system is common, coupled with an alumni network
Productivity is defined by overall corporate returns, as evaluated by shareholders, and a commensurate internal performance review system	Productivity is defined in rates times billable hours and/or fees earned

considerations. Lee and Pennings (2002) examine the emergence and diffusion of the PSF governance structure (the so-called 'partner–associate' structure) among a population of Dutch professional services firms during the period 1925–90. They suggest that institutional change emerged out of an interaction between selection at the level of sector and imitative adoption at the firm level. Market feedback regarding this structure fostered its legitimacy. Diffusion as a legitimatization processes unfolds, therefore, at both the sectoral and the firm levels of analysis.

A growing practitioner literature has provided advice to professionals and leaders in PSFs on how to attract, manage and motivate talent, including advice on how senior partners can take a more active mentoring role in helping junior professionals create a 'partner persona' (Ibarra, 2000; Stumpf, 1999; Stumpf and Tymon, 2001). Other efforts have centered on demonstrating the importance of knowledge production and application in PSFs, showing how explicit efforts to share and disseminate knowledge can promote efficiency and result in more innovative and value-added services (Weiss, 1999). To accomplish this, however, PSFs must recognize the difference between 'rationalized' and 'embedded' knowledge. Variables such as reciprocity, trust, power, politics and rewards are influential in determining whether professionals are effective in sharing what they know (Maister, 1997; Maister *et al.*, 2000; Stumpf and Longman, 2000).

One modern theoretical lens, stewardship theory, would appear to provide a useful vehicle for examination of some of the motivations and incentives present in PSFs that lack the traditional principal/owner–agent/manager relationship. Indeed the 'professions' as historically conceived suggest that members of these quasi-guilds exhibit a custodial-type protection of the name and reputation of both the profession and the specific firm (Freidson, 1970, 1983). Stewardship theory, which suggests that there are situations in which executives as stewards are motivated to act in the best interests of their organization, would appear to be an apt theoretical framework for examination of PSFs principals (Davis *et al.*, 1997; Fox and Hamilton, 1994). In particular, the assumption that collectivistic behaviors have higher utility than individualistic, self-serving behaviors would appear to track the partnership organization of PSFs in which individuals have a collective motivation to advance that role of the firm and the profession (Davis *et al.*, 1997). Yet the very motivation for our critique is that perverse incentives exist in PSFs that result from the absence of agency-like contracts (O'Shea and Madigan, 1997; Pinault, 2000). While these distortions may have at one time been mitigated by a stewardship-like custodial desire to protect 'the profession' or 'the firm', increasingly PSF officers view themselves as independent, entrepreneurial agents with little allegiance to their firm (but great – perhaps too great – allegiance to the client). Indeed some officers and their clients opportunistically move from firm to firm to seek more hospitable or favorable conditions.

Sharma (1997) provides a comprehensive and pertinent theoretical discussion of the inapplicability of traditional agency concepts to PSFs. He uses an agency approach to evaluate the relationship between corporations and the outside PSFs they employ, arguing that principal–professional exchanges are intrinsically distinct from others types of agency exchanges such as owner–manager agency. Sharma questions key assumptions in agency theory, notably those that presume power asymmetry; that is, that principals have the power to discipline agents. In the case of the principal–professional relationship, the professionals wield power by virtue of their technical expertise (ibid.). The agency concept of oversight in PSFs is more effectively provided by peers, internal boards and professional associations. This limits the oversight potential for principals, but affords another potential route for monitoring. Finally, in the business exchanges between principals and professionals, the service is coproduced by the principal and the agent, generating social exchanges and ties that may provide a different type of oversight opportunity. Sharma concludes by describing four categories of restraints on potential opportunistic behavior by professional agents that are somewhat distinct from such constraints in the traditional, owner–manager context of corporate control: (1) self-control, (2) community control, (3) bureaucratic control and (4) client control. He shows how idiosyncratic features of the principal–professional relationship determine the way each of these controls will be most effective in constraining professionals' self-interested behaviors.

Although Sharma's theoretical discussion provides a useful contribution in evaluating the failings of agency theory to explain fully, in its traditionally conceived form, the important relationships between a firm and a professional organization with which it contracts, this perspective is limited to one kind of agency relationship: that between the firm and the PSF. Our goal is to demonstrate that there is a wider range of circumstances in which managerial and governance theories fall short in explaining the main motivations, incentives and failings of management of PSFs. We highlight the managerial and governance challenges *within* PSFs, some of which are newly generated by recent changes in nature of professional services work and the pressures on PSFs. In our theoretical critique, we also propose that there is a distinct category of agency-like failings not anticipated by extant literature, including Sharma's analysis. These agency-like problems are generated by the temporal gulf between the perspectives and incentives of junior partners and senior officers in PSFs, and these misaligned incentives are not sufficiently addressed through other theoretical perspectives such as stewardship theory.

Top management team strata in professional services firms

One critical element of corporate governance and control implied by governance research is the existence of top-level managers who act as agents for boards or other shareholders or, at least, to advocate their own individual or institutional preferences for the organization's future. There is a long tradition of top management team research beginning with the early research focused on dominant coalitions (Cyert and March, 1963), managerial theories and analyses (Mintzberg, 1973; Kotter, 1982; Luthans *et al.*, 1988) and demography (Dearborn and Simon, 1958; Pfeffer, 1983; Hambrick and Mason, 1984). More recently, TMT research has focused attention on process and decision making (Eisenhardt, 1989a; Smith *et al.*, 1994; Wally and Baum, 1994; Lawrence, 1997; Clark and Collins, 2002). Throughout most of this work, the composition, purpose and tasks of the top management team have been defined similarly, and in relation to the organizational forms found within the large publicly traded corporation. Thus much of what we know about TMTs is driven by a research model that may have little relevance for executive teams in other organizational forms.

Recently there have been calls for improved methods of investigation (Smith *et al.*, 1994; West and Schwenk, 1996; Lawrence, 1997), incorporation of additional explanatory variables (Finkelstein and Hambrick, 1996) and investigation of additional outcomes of TMTs (Clark, 2001). In this section, we compare the traditional TMT form with that found in the professional services firm, which we term the 'top management strata' (TMS). Table 15.2 compares the traditional TMT with the TMS of the professional services firm (Maister, 1993; Stumpf, 2002).

The top management team is generally conceived in the literature (Hambrick and Mason, 1984; Finkelstein and Hambrick, 1996) as a small group of senior-level managers who, with the CEO, formulate the strategy of the firm. The CEO is appointed by the board of directors of the firm, and then selects the members of the team, hence the CEO and TMT members act as agents of the board. Although TMT members may hold small ownership positions in the firm, this is not always the case. Top managers may be selected from within the firm or, particularly if large-scale strategic change is desired, may be selected via an external search process (Finkelstein and Hambrick, 1996).

TMTs often comprise senior-level executives representing the various functional areas within the firm (marketing, finance, operations), although there may be a greater proportion of managers from a specific area considered critical to competitive advantage, or boards may select (or remove) TMT members with specific functional specializations depending upon the competitive circumstances faced by the firm (Ancona and Nadler, 1989; Bantel and Jackson, 1989; Janis, 1972; Murray, 1989). Implicit in most of the research on top management teams is a focus on the strategic decision-making role. Although much of the ethnographic research on TMTs reports significant time spent by executives on non-decision activities (such as networking), research continues to explore strategy-making activities almost exclusively (Mintzberg, 1973; Kotter, 1982; Luthans *et al.*, 1988).

PSFs often operate as partnerships or confederations of senior-level service providers, so they do possess some of the characteristics of executive managerial control (Maister, 1993). Even here, however, the 'team' within PSFs is actually more of a 'stratum'. The members of the 'stratum' are more numerous in PSFs than in traditionally governed corporations, they are not as functionally diverse, they hold their internal leadership positions for relatively short periods of time and they continue to focus on their 'line' responsibilities (selling business and managing client projects) while leading their practice or the firm (Stumpf, 1999). Importantly these officers assume responsibilities traditionally associated with both boards of directors and top management teams of traditionally structured organizations. They perform a critical top management role that is complex, overlapping, multidimensional and matrix in structure, but which combines some of the characteristics of both the board (principal) and management (agent) of traditional corporations.

As shown in Table 15.2, the top management responsibilities of PSFs differ from those of the conventional TMT. The structure of the TMS can be described as a loose confederation of senior officers who serve a term as key planners for the PSF. Such officers are not appointed by an external body, but rather serve at the pleasure of the other officers of the PSF. In contrast to the TMT, officers of the PSF are *required* to be owners. Planning and strategy are not considered the main priorities of the TMS to achieve success in leading the firm. Rather the primary task of the officer-leaders of the PSF remains revenue production, as many of these officers maintain their client portfolio while serving 'part time' as members of the TMS. Indeed planning and strategy tasks are viewed as necessary tasks that should take place as time away from clients and client development allows.

One officer–leader of a PSF we studied, for example, coordinated the global energy and utilities practice of a Big 5 accounting/consulting firm on a part-time basis while continuing to serve (and bill hours) as the lead client services partner for one of the firm's largest utility clients. In part because there are fewer external performance metrics available (for example, no market-driven stock price or analyst reports), officer performance is measured largely by the amount of business they service or bring to the firm, or both. Moreover, because sales performance is the single most important task in the PSF, officers are similar in terms of their 'functional' background (though industry knowledge and technical skills may vary). As

Table 15.2   Comparison of the traditional top management team with the top management strata (TMS) of professional services firms

Traditional TMT	Professional services firm TMS
Typically three to 10 senior-level managers	A loose federation of 30 or more senior officers (for larger firms)
Appointed by the board of directors, or hired by board-appointed CEO	Selected by existing officer core for rotating terms
May be recruited from outside the organization	Almost exclusively an internal selection process
May hold some equity in the firm, but this is not a requirement	All TMS members hold equity in the firm
Upon exit from organization, may continue to hold equity in firm	Upon exit from organization, must relinquish ownership stake through a buyout process
Typically reflects broad representation by functional area	TMS members are similar in primary role as revenue producers via client service
Primary task is strategic decision-making, and setting organizational direction, rarely involved in implementation tasks.	Primary task is revenue production; only secondarily concerned with planning and strategy formulation
TMT members compensated on the basis of a variety of goals, some of which may be long-term in nature	TMS members paid an annual 'cut' of pre-tax earnings of the partnership, thus current sales is key objective
TMT accountable to external owners	TMS accountable only to internal owner-managers.

a consequence, the skills required to be successful (and thus to become an officer) in a PSF are not necessarily those needed to lead an organization and develop organizational strategy (Stumpf, 1999). Because the structure and task orientation of the TMS is so different from that of the traditional TMT, the research to date offers little assistance to professional services firms as they attempt to design the TMS as an effective governance mechanism.

Although the TMT is responsible for management and control of the organization, governance is fundamentally concerned with protecting the interests of the owners of the firm. Below, we demonstrate that many of the governance protections that are effective in traditional corporations do not apply to the PSF.

Traditional governance mechanisms and the professional services firm

In the traditional corporate form, managers are hired as agents of the shareholders (principals) to run the business and to make important strategic choices that affect the future viability of the business. For many reasons the motivations and subsequent actions of managers may not perfectly match those of the owners (Alchian and Demsetz, 1972; Eisenhardt, 1989a; Jensen and Meckling, 1976). While small and temporary deviations are expected and tolerated, owners have sought to build in assurances against significant departure from their interests. Such governance mechanisms have fallen primarily into three categories: (1) establishment of an independent board of directors that oversees the activities of top management (Dalton *et al.*, 1998; Pfeffer, 1972); (2) the presence of large block shareholders who take an active interest in the activities of top management (Fields and Mais, 1994); and (3) a market for corporate control that serves to discipline managers for poor performance (Eisenhardt, 1989a; Jensen and Meckling, 1976; Zahra and Pearce, 1989). Each of these governance mechanisms is either absent or severely compromised in the professional services firm.

The board of directors is an oversight structure developed to ensure that top managers act in the best interest of the owners. In order to safeguard owners' interests effectively, the board of directors must be independent from management. However the empirical evidence regarding the performance implications of board independence is mixed (Harris and Helfat, 1998). While some studies have reported weak positive performance outcomes for captive boards (Cannella and Lubatkin, 1993; Mallette and Fowler, 1992), others have reported either negative impacts or no relationship (Chaganti *et al.*, 1985; Dalton *et al.*, 1998). Generally cooptation of the board by the TMT through overlapping membership or through CEO–board duality is seen as a failure of governance (Dalton and Kesner, 1987; Fama and Jensen, 1983; Morck *et al.*, 1989; Patton and Baker, 1987), though the increased autonomy and discretion afforded management may be functional in some circumstances.

Assuming an independent functioning board, there are two main mechanisms of control that can be used to discipline top management. First, the board of directors is responsible for the hiring, evaluation and firing of top managers (Zahra, 1996; Zahra and Pearce, 1989). The threat of potential job loss (and the concomitant blow to reputation) is the ultimate discipline mechanism available to the board (Fama and Jensen, 1983). Second, the compensation committee of the board is responsible for developing and adjusting compensation for top-level managers (Tosi and Gomez-Mejia, 1994). The focus of much of the governance literature has been on the structuring of executive compensation systems to align manager and owner interests better through the use of long-term stock options (Gomez-Mejia *et al.*, 1987; Halpern, 1983; Roll, 1987). With the exception of TMT–board duality, the board of directors has proved an effective mechanism for disciplining top management in the traditional corporation (Tosi *et al.*, 1997).

PSFs differ from traditional corporate forms in that their leaders are elected to officer level by the existing cadre of officers, not an external and independent board of directors. The selection of the CEO is either based on an aristocratic process (in smaller, first or second generation firms) or a democratic process (in larger, older, more global firms) (Maister 1993). Senior management roles are often rotated among officers rather than through a selection procedure overseen by an independent external body. The means by which an officer in a PSF becomes part of the senior management strata is often a peer election that must be approved by the CEO. Moreover officer–leaders in PSFs may be only marginally more powerful than high producing officers, and the managerial tasks associated with being an officer–leader are often devalued (Maister, 1993; Stumpf, 1999). The discipline effected by a board of directors' governance mechanism is absent. The position of officer–leader is not nearly as desirable as CEO, and the rotating nature of the position alleviates the necessity to avoid being 'fired'. Hence the behavior of PSF officer-leaders is not subject to the same oversight experienced by members of a TMT.

Whereas traditional large and global corporations are often publicly traded, ownership of large, global PSFs is distributed among the officer and non-officer partner classes. Some owners (such as officers) are also the leaders of the enterprise and there are rarely any external equity owners. This difference between PSFs and traditional corporations contributes to a further weakening of governance. In a traditional corporation, large block shareholders often act as vigilant commentators on top management behaviors (Fama and Jensen, 1983; Jensen and Meckling, 1976), with the effect being to moderate any deviations from the interests of owners.[4] In the PSF, it is unusual for any single officer to hold more than a minimal (1–2 per cent) share of the stock – stock that must be sold back to the firm upon retirement or separation from the firm. Thus, although internally distributed, ownership of PSFs is dispersed, with no owners controlling a sufficiently large block of shares to effectively control management.[5] A second cornerstone of governance in traditional firms is therefore absent in PSFs.

A final governance mechanism available to protect the interests of owners is what has come to be known as the 'market for corporate control' (Fama and Jensen, 1983; Manne, 1965). Assuming that owners are economically rational, managers should seek to serve the interests of owners by increasing the value of their capital investment in the business. In the context of the modern corporation, this equates to behaviors on the part of management that increase common stock price. Under the market for corporate control rationale, management behaviors at odds with the interests of owners will precipitate a decrease in stock price, causing the shareholders to exert pressure on management to reform, or, if necessary, organizing a takeover in order to undertake more radical changes.[6] Because top managers tend to lose their jobs when the firm is acquired, the threat of takeover serves to discipline their behavior (Fama and Jensen, 1983).

In the PSF, there are few, if any, external shareholders. When officers leave, they are required to relinquish ownership interests in the firm through a process of stock buyback at a fixed internally controlled price. Because PSFs are privately held by officers and non-officer partners of the firm, there is no threat of takeover. Thus a final factor in the governance of traditional firms is absent PSFs. Many of the traditional assumptions about governance in the modern corporations do not apply in the context of the PSF.

Professional services firms and the agency problem
Since Berle and Means (1932) introduced the notion that conflicts of interest occur when ownership and control are separated and that the resultant moral hazard problem creates a demand for monitoring and control mechanisms (Jensen and Meckling, 1976), much of management research has been concerned with various aspects of the agency problem. Cyert and March (1963) introduced the concept of 'dominant coalitions' of upper echelon managers as the principal internal control mechanism of differentiated corporations. Since that time, the study of top management teams (TMT) has gained currency in management research and practice (Finkelstein and Hambrick, 1996; Hambrick and Mason, 1984; Lawrence, 1997), and agency and its various applications have dominated research in corporate governance (for example, Daily, 1994; Daily and Dalton, 1992; Eisenhardt, 1989a; Jensen and Meckling, 1976; Zahra, 1996; Zahra and Pearce, 1989). Yet the emergence of multi-billion dollar, highly profitable, decentralized, officer-owned professional services firms (PSFs) poses questions as to the applicability of these constructs that have constituted much of the core reference points in corporate governance and managerial control.[7]

Berle and Means (1932) first described the agency problem that arises from the separation of ownership from the management of the firm. The classic agency problem as summarized by Eisenhardt (1989a) stems from differences in the motivations and abilities of principals and their agents. Specifically agents are thought to exhibit a moral hazard, such that they may behave in a self-interested manner (perhaps with guile) and that such behavior may injure the interests of the principals. Though the risk of malfeasant behavior is real enough, the focus of much of the governance literature has been on the differing risk preferences of principals and their agents. Agents are thought to be risk-averse, that is, they seek to protect their jobs through conservative action (Eisenhardt, 1989a; Fama and Jensen, 1983). In the PSF, there is no separation of ownership from management, thus the agency problem as originally formulated appears absent. Upon direct examination, however, an agency-like problem emerges in the context of the PSF. The key components of the classic agency problem are moral hazard (for example, that agents may act in a self-interested manner), that agents are risk-averse and that agents may not be competent. In the PSF, officers are required to purchase equity in the partnership and receive a proportional share of the pretax earnings. Power and status are earned by producing more business than other officers, and thus contributing more to the pot of earnings. Given the relatively direct and measurable contributions of officers, and the relatively direct compensation for such efforts through the end of year payout, there would seem to be no moral hazard problem in the PSF. Indeed it is precisely because the compensation of TMTs has not traditionally been directly tied to earnings that the moral hazard problem arises.[8] To combat this, the executive compensation literature advocates tying compensation directly to earnings by making managers shareholders of the corporation (Jensen and Meckling, 1976).

In the PSF, the analogy to the moral hazard problem has less to do with job protection behavior than with a strong predisposition to ensure short-term earnings (and payout), particularly those of the individual officer's portfolio, even at the expense of the longer-term profit maximization of the firm. PSFs have notoriously short time horizons: their 'book of business' is often less than one year (Maister, 1993). This is accentuated by the peculiar way in which officers receive their compensation. At the end of each fiscal year the partnership determines the pretax earnings, and a distribution of most (but not all) of pretax earnings is made to each officer, based on their contribution to the PSF. Under this arrangement, there is considerable emphasis placed by officers on efforts that are likely to yield a payout in the current year. This pressure would be no different from the widely observed quarterly earnings obsession of CEOs of American firms (Jacobs, 1991; Zahra, 1996), except that officers of PSFs are *required* to relinquish their ownership position in the partnership should they leave. This distinguishing characteristic of PSFs makes any longer-term investment in the firm (for example, where the payoff is likely to be more than a year away, and certainly if payoffs from an investment are anticipated to occur after an officer's separation date) appear risky and not in their self-interest. Consequently, a PSF officer–leader may not be motivated to invest human and social capital in efforts requiring long incubation or development periods – unless they define their leadership role to be that of a trustee (Maister, 1997; Stumpf,

2002). However officer–leaders risk a loss of earnings and status through the switching of effort from revenue production/client service to investments in furthering the interests of the firm long-term. This issue resembles the tragedy of the commons problem in several ways, as officer-owners have an incentive to free-ride with regard to longer-term investments of time and resources. We have chosen to adopt an agency approach because the governance failure observed in PSFs also includes elements of risk aversion and task-specific competence.

The primary governance failure is that there are few mechanisms in place to discipline the TMS to do work necessary for the long-term continuity and survival of the firm. The compensation system in PSFs creates temporal risk aversion that is dysfunctional for the partnership over the longer term and does not serve the interests of longer-term owners, typically the non-officer partners. In a sense, older, more established officers act as agents for the entire firm and, even though they are owners (like executive owners of public corporations), the character of ownership in a PSF creates a moral hazard similar to the internal agency problem described by Eisenhardt (1989a). Somewhat ironically, senior officers' time horizons may be much shorter than those of non-officer partners whose interests are more oriented toward the firm's growth, its future and its viability. Whereas executive compensation systems in publicly traded firms have partially solved this problem through the use of long-term stock options (Jones and Butler, 1992), there is no similar remedy available to the PSF in its current form.

In summary, structural characteristics and incentive systems of PSFs create a situation in which the interests of some owners (for example, shorter tenure partners or new officers) may not be protected. A compensation system based exclusively on present year performance and the requirement that former employees not participate in future earning through continued ownership places a large burden on the officer-leaders of the partnership to forgo near-term incentives for longer-term initiatives. Though this is not strictly an agency problem as traditionally defined, an investigation of governance remedies to principal–agent misalignment in the modern corporation is instructive.

In the next section, we review recent changes in PSFs in response to the pressures in both the external and internal environment. We note that some of the largest PSFs and traditional organizational forms appear to be converging.

Professional services firms in transition
Several trends are under way that call attention to the importance of management and governance issues in PSFs. Previously dispersed and fractured practices of PSFs are being integrated into very large global

firms. Many PSFs have merged with other PSFs (and some have merged with client-like organizations) creating large conglomerates (such as in advertising and public accounting) or mid-sized organizations.[9] PSFs have gone global, not just via the traditional loose coalition of independently run, autonomous offices around the globe, but with increasingly standardized products, services and processes (offerings) that are intended to appeal to different clients, clients in different countries and multinational clients in their operations across countries.[10] The pressures of globalization and integration have caused PSFs of all sizes and scopes to seek managerial structures and organizational designs that allow them to coordinate and control their much more complex organizations effectively.

The expansion of size and complexity of PSFs has also raised issues of managerial control and oversight. Over the past decade, the percentage of overall revenue generated by the largest accounting firms from their consulting and business advisory practices has grown, as have questions about possible conflicts of interests, confusion of roles, and competencies at these firms. Specifically the SEC issued rules in late 2000 that place restrictions and disclosure requirements on accounting firms that also engage in consulting work for their audit clients (SEC, 2001).[11] At the same time, consulting partners at the Big 5 have become increasingly aggressive in pushing for independence from both the operational practices and culture and the regulatory restrictions of their accounting parents. Such pressures, and related forces suggesting that the consulting practices of accounting firms share more synergies with other strategy and IT consulting organizations, have resulted in a number of consulting arms becoming fully independent of their accounting parents (for example, Accenture, KPMG), some being sold to or receiving strategic investments from consulting or technology firms (for example, Cap Gemini's purchase of Ernst & Young's consulting arm; Cisco's investment in KPMG; Hewlett Packard's efforts to acquire KPMG). Related trends have been under way in investment banking and advertising firms for more than a decade. In particular, many of these financial and advertising firms had been organized as independent partnerships, but are now either publicly traded corporations (such as Goldman Sachs) and/or divisions of larger integrated financial services firms (as with, for example, Citigroup's purchase of Salomon Smith Barney in the case of investment banking) or larger media firms (in the case of advertising).

As PSFs pursue growth and globalization to enhance owner wealth, they have become larger and more integrated in their outlook and structure. In addition, they have found it desirable (or perhaps necessary) to capitalize investments by distributing shares to the public through initial public offerings (IPOs) (for example, KPMG, Accenture) or merge with traditional corporations (for example, EDS' investment in AT Kearney, Cisco's in

KPMG Consulting, and H-P's in Cap Gemini). The resulting more closely held, publicly traded PSFs or subsidiary-like PSFs create a new type of organization for governance research. The emerging organizational and control structures appear to be less hierarchical and more decentralized than traditional corporations, but sharing some of their structural features, governance mechanisms and decision-making practices. These hybrid organizational forms combine characteristics of the traditional corporation and the pure form PSFs discussed above. While the assumptions inherent in existing governance theories may need to be modified if these theories are to generalize to these new organizational forms, so might our newer perspectives need to be tempered to account for these intermediate organizational forms that straddle the two extremes and combine features of both.

As we consider some of the changes in professional services described above, institutional theory, with its focus on institutionalized pressure groups and their impact on firm structures (Meyer and Rowan, 1977; Oliver, 1991), may offer insight for understanding both the antecedents and consequences of these trends. According to some institutional perspectives, firms are rewarded for developing internal structures that are adaptive to external institutional pressures. These rewards include increased legitimacy, resources and survival capabilities (DiMaggio and Powell, 1983; Meyer and Rowan, 1977).

PSFs have perceived institutional pressures for reform on a number of fronts. The controversies and conflicts described above between audit and consulting practices and officers are one. Specifically the SEC has urged further separation of these two aspects of the largest of PSFs. Without audit practices to feed consulting work, the consulting arms of the accounting firms have initiated other strategic responses, including going public, allying with larger IT firms and developing relationships with hardware and software providers. Globalization, and the need to follow domestic clients abroad and provide a standard, consistent level of services, have pressured firms to sew together what had been a loose coalition of independent firms into a single, integrated, global unit. Chandler's (1962) pioneering work on the strategy and structure of industrial enterprise, and the influence of legal, political, and institutional environments in defining firm structure, appears to be as telling for PSFs as other firms.

As PSFs transition from their pure type to more hybrid organizational forms, we suggest that some of the assumptions of traditional corporate governance will re-emerge. In particular, as PSFs grow in size and complexity, experience continuing pressures to globalize (or integrate geographically and culturally dispersed units) and merge with non-PSF organizations, structural and other organizational changes will ensue. First, because size and scale places natural demands on organizations to develop administrative policies and procedures to oversee activities (Chandler, 1990), we suggest that, as PSFs become larger, they will become more likely to assume some of the governance characteristics of traditional corporations.

Within the mergers and acquisitions literature, 'strategic fit' refers to the anticipated benefits of merger to the strategy of the acquirer, based on the congruence or complementarity of the assets and operations of the merging firms (Jemison and Sitkin, 1986; Lubatkin, 1983; Salter and Weinhold, 1979). Often these benefits result from synergies between the merging firms' resources and capabilities. For potential synergies to be realized and value to be created, the target and the acquirer must integrate. Because mergers and acquisitions naturally result in some resource exchange and integration between acquiring and acquired firms, we suggest that PSFs that combine in part or in whole with traditional corporations are more likely to exhibit some of the traditional governance characteristics of corporations. Moreover, as PSFs are acquired by traditional corporations, they will experience pressures from various stakeholders to become isomorphic with the structures and practices of the acquirer. Stakeholders of publicly traded firms are unlikely to value a system of private partnerships having few oversight provisions. For example, it is unlikely that the board of directors of the acquiring firm would tolerate a significant portion of the merged enterprise remaining outside its control. Investors would likely require assurances against agency abuses as well. Thus, as PSFs pursue various arrangements with traditional organizations, incorporation of some elements of traditional governance mechanisms will be needed to gain legitimacy.

Because the integration of wholly owned subsidiaries into globally assimilated organizations naturally requires transnational policies and frameworks (Bartlett and Ghoshal, 1989), we suggest that PSFs that expand their global reach or combine national practices into globally integrated organizations are more likely to exhibit some of the governance characteristics of corporations.

Top management strata and the transitional PSF
On a managerial level, as the literature on top management teams suggests, we would expect similar changes to characteristics of the top management stratum resulting from these trends. As PSFs increase in size and complexity, the role of the TMS will be expanded to include more of the tasks and responsibilities traditionally associated with TMTs. Strategic planning will take on greater importance as the firm expands, requiring the TMS to develop more advanced decision-making capabilities (Andrews, 1971; Mintzberg, 1973). The loose federation structure of the TMS is not equipped to handle the strategy formulation task (Finkelstein and Hambrick, 1996). First, the large size and geographic dispersion of the group presents a

severe logistical challenge to be overcome. Second, the ability of the TMS to achieve consensus in a timely fashion is in question (Bourgeois, 1980; Dess, 1987). Finally, the lack of functional specialization and the insular nature of the TMS present a significant impediment to comprehensiveness in decision making (Jemison, 1984; Fredrickson, 1986) and flexibility in response to changing environmental conditions (Bantel and Jackson, 1989). Hence we would expect the emergence of a top management structure that has characteristics of the large, diffuse strata of PSFs with some of the hierarchical and functional specialization of traditional corporate management teams.

As PSFs seek capital and other resources in order to increase their geographic reach and practice depth, they are increasingly joining traditional firms in adjacent industries through merger or by being acquired. As described above, stakeholders of traditional firms are unlikely to invest in organizations which have no recognizable (legitimate) governance mechanisms. Coercive and normative isomorphic pressures on PSFs will ensue to develop and exhibit governance safeguards (DiMaggio and Powell, 1983).

In contrast to regional or domestic PSFs, those that have expanded globally, or that seek to integrate geographically and culturally dispersed units, face a much more complex and changing environment. As the complexity of the environment increases, top management structures need to perform a buffering function for their organizations (Thompson, 1967). TMTs endeavor to buffer the organizational core by providing a consistent and overarching layer through which inputs and information are filtered, thus protecting the core from turbulence and uncertainty in the environment. Because of its loose structure, the TMS is poorly configured for this task. In addition to the need for increased decision-making effectiveness due to reduced capacity to analyze and process elements of the external environment (Scott, 1991), a more coordinated and structured TMS is needed to provide the necessary buffering function.

Conclusion and implications

We have identified a significant gap in extant research in and theoretical perspectives on managerial control and governance as applied to PSFs. Specifically we have isolated important exceptions to many of the assumptions and presuppositions to existing governance theory. We have drawn from principal–agency theory to inform possible problems with top management control in PSFs. We have argued that professional services firms appear to operate under a set of incentives and challenges that differ from those of the traditional corporation.

Implications for policy and practice

There are a number of important implications of our research for managerial practices and public policy, especially our observations regarding the changing theoretical assumptions associated with hybrid or transitional forms of PSFs.

Regarding efforts to respond to some of the challenges inherent in PSFs as a result of the absence of many of the governance and control mechanisms associated with traditional corporations, we have suggested that compensation systems may be one area for better aligning the incentives of more senior, short-term focused officer-leaders with more junior non-officer partners. Compensation systems may need to be developed that reward officers for organizational, reputational and structural improvements to the firm beyond their year-end payout. A critical difference between PSFs and traditional corporations is the forced buyout provision for PSF employees that retire or leave the partnership. In conjunction with the PSF compensation system, this provision exacts a significant financial toll on senior officers who choose to act as stewards of the long-term success of the firm. Although many PSF officers choose to absorb this price, others may be tempted to 'cash out' by investing human and social capital only in activities that promise to pay off during their tenure in the firm. Moreover, even if stewardship principles were fully adhered to, is it fair for officers who engage in ethically and morally responsible behavior to suffer financial costs for such actions?

Whereas corporate governance theorists have suggested changes in the compensation of executives (such as long-term stock options) as an effective way to temper the tendency to trade longer-term prosperity for short-term results, the forced buyout provision favors the opposite behavior. Thus we suggest that PSFs eliminate or severely adapt this provision so as to reward officer-leaders for the results of their efforts even after they leave the firm. There is no particular reason why former officers could not retain some level of ownership for a period of time, perhaps five years. To protect the ability of PSFs to retain managerial discretion (an advantage of looser governance touted by stewardship scholars) these former partners would retain modest ownership positions but not be involved in PSF strategy. Thus officers who leave the PSF are able to capture more fully the longer-term outcomes of their firm-building efforts.

As mentioned in our discussion of the potential conflicts inherent in multi-practice accounting and consulting firms, government regulators play a major role because of their ability to influence and define roles and relationships among various stakeholder groups, implement incentives and disincentives, and establish some of the boundaries of the organization through rules and regulation. From the perspective of public policy makers interested in contributing to the goal of better aligning short- and long-term interests in the absence of formal oversight, alternative tax schemes that would allow for the carry-over of retained earnings without tax penalty (if such earnings were reinvested) could further these goals.

Practical consequences of transitional PSFs
From the perspective of a formerly pure PSF having publicly traded shares or being owned by a non-PSF parent organization, new owners will want a share of annual operating profits. While a pure PSF can distribute all pretax profits to the owners at year end (and have minimal corporate income tax obligation), non-partner shareholders or the parent organization will want a return on their investment. Whether this outlay is a dividend to shareholders or a contribution to corporate income, it decreases the cash take by officers. The partner–producer model that seems to drive most PSFs (of doing more and getting more without having to share it with non-partners) is threatened. Higher dividends or contributions made to non-partners may lower a partner's motivation to produce more and thereby lower annual growth in billability and billings.

A potential benefit of this new organizational form lies in the PSF's obligation to its non-partner (and non-officer partner class) owners to plan beyond the current year and to take a multi-year view of business development and investments. Pure PSFs struggle to justify activities or investments that do not provide a return within the near term, often defined by individual officers as something that will yield them a higher cash share of the business profits by fiscal year end. To the extent that such longer-term investing materializes, one would hypothesize that the co-owned PSFs would enter and remain in new markets, new geographies and new lines of business more successfully over a longer period of time than pure PSFs. This arrangement and incentive system begins to resolve the unique agency problem we described above but, again, may create or aggravate the traditional agency dilemma.

Another implication for subsidiary PSFs relates to the likely dilution of the brand equity of the pure PSF relative to that of the parent company. Clients often select a PSF in the belief that they are getting 'untainted expert advice', where the advice giver has no motive other than to provide the best advice for a fee (Maister *et al.*, 2000; Stumpf and Longman, 2000). When there are additional owners and influencers (principals) of the PSF, there is an increased likelihood of some form of bias being introduced into the advice being given. To the extent that this general perception is held by senior client buyers, we would hypothesize that co-owned PSFs would have less client revenue from organizations that would traditionally not hold their parent organization in high esteem; and vice versa.

Future research directions

Our research has demonstrated that the application of traditional corporate governance assumptions to research directed toward the professional services firms is inappropriate. Specifically we have noted that several core assumptions of corporate governance (establishment of an independent board of directors that oversees the activities of top management, the presence of large block shareholders who take an active interest in the activities of top management, a market for corporate control that serves to discipline managers for poor performance) are not present in PSFs. Although we find that a form of the top management team *is* present in PSFs, many of the characteristics of that team are quite different from a traditional team as conceived by TMT researchers; notably that group is a loose confederation of senior officers who serve a term as key planners for the PSF, are not appointed by an external body, and are very similar in terms of their 'functional' service background, causing us to term the group the top management strata. Hence the concept of and research regarding top management teams may be less relevant for PSFs because they lack the hierarchical design and control structures of industrial organizations. At the least, the TMT concept requires adaptation to be useful in the study of PSFs and other organizational forms that rely on diffuse, horizontally decentralized, practice-focused structures.

We have shown that PSFs face unique agency-like problems that stem from temporal discontinuities that result from asymmetries in the personal incentives and objectives of the individual members of the top management stratum (officer–leader class), the non-officer partner core and the organizational objectives of the firm. As PSFs move from their archetype to a more hybrid organizational form, additional research will be required to understand the sequential evolution of these firms, how different PSF subsectors respond differently to these pressures, what sort of governance mechanisms emerge during different stages of the transition and how these governance arrangements affect the management of PSFs, their strategies and performance. Empirical tests of our model would be the next step in further refining what is so far a preliminary view of governance in PSFs.

In addition to presenting observations related to the pure form PSF, we have also explored how existing governance perspectives would apply to hybrid, transitional organizations. Comparisons of different types of professional services firms that we would expect to fall on different places on our continuum would be most interesting. We have shown that PSFs face unique agency-like problems somewhat unrelated to separation of management and ownership. The intensity of this problem might be mitigated as PSFs respond to some of the environmental and organizational pressures mentioned above. However we might also expect the re-emergence of the traditional agency problem as organizational complexity increases, outside owners emerge, and management and ownership become separated.

As PSFs become larger and more complex, the ability of officers to discern the payoff horizons of various investments of human and social capital decreases. Moreover the contribution of any individual officer to the overall pot of profits becomes less important to the payout amount at year's end. Instead the health and growth of the overall partnership becomes of prime importance. Although free-rider problems are possible under such a scenario, it is equally likely that the interdependence of officers and the need for formalized planning will be highlighted. Thus traditional governance mechanisms will begin to emerge to combat the free-rider issue, while the identification by officers of a longer-term strategy occurs.

Moreover, because traditional organizations have governance mechanisms in place to discipline managers, PSFs that become absorbed into such organizations will likely be held to similar standards of accountability (whether through formal governance or normative isomorphism). Although there is a well documented preoccupation of TMTs of US firms with short-term performance, markets are also quick to discipline those having no well articulated longer-term strategy. PSFs will face increasing pressures to plan beyond the end of the fiscal year, setting aside to some extent individual preferences for short-term efforts.

As PSFs take on governance characteristics that are equivalent or analogous to those of traditional corporations, so are historically hierarchical organizations developing practices and approaches to their management that are more akin to those of the pure PSF. Specifically pressures for cost cutting, downsizing, streamlining, outsourcing and calls for greater employee empowerment, organizational decentralization, and corporate entrepreneurship all appear to contribute to more flexible, adaptable and responsive organizations that may not possess all of the governance characteristics of traditionally organized corporations. A growing literature on executive leaders as stewards of the corporation makes a strong case for the advantages of managerial decision making unfettered by corporate governance and monitoring. In addition employees at all levels are increasingly becoming owners, calling into question long-standing ideas regarding agency. As such, our research may contribute, not only to future insights regarding services firms, but also to an expanding research agenda relating to all organizations and the challenges they face in balancing the interests of managers, owners and stakeholders.

As researchers begin to contemplate governance in new organizational forms, like the PSF, additional theoretical lenses may prove helpful. Resource dependence theory has suggested that organizations are constrained by, and depend on, other organizations (Pfeffer and Salancik,

1978). Organizations attempt to manage these constraints in order to secure greater autonomy and to exercise independence. Individuals and coalitions within organizations differ in their ability to attain this control. Some positions or levels within the organization carry high levels of discretion in determining organizational goals and resource allocation, yet individuals in those positions are considerably interdependent, and their actual exercise of discretion must take this interdependence into account. Research has shown that resource dependence between organizations triggers cooptive ties, such as interlocking directorates, vertical integration and business alliances between the organizations (Burt, 1982; Pfeffer and Salancik, 1978).

As a complement to resource dependence perspectives, social network analysis centers, not on the resources, but on the exchange of resources and the structures or frameworks of interaction themselves (Wasserman and Galaskiewicz, 1994; Nohria and Eccles, 1992). Network theory views organizations, not as individual bounded entities, but as a set of organic relationships that are dynamic and fluid over time (Wasserman and Faust, 1994; Wasserman and Galaskiewicz, 1994; Wellman and Berkowitz, 1988). Unlike agency or stakeholder theory that focus on specific actors and their activities, network theory centers on relationships (Granovetter, 1985) and examines such relationships as systems that can be investigated and modeled. Within such networks, resources can be shared among network participants (Thorelli, 1986).

As noted above, members of the top management strata of professional services firms are rewarded as much for their ability to develop network relationships, especially those directed toward clients external to the firm, as they are for their organizational or managerial skills. Partners in professional services firms face a range of incentives and disincentives both to cooperate with and to coopt each other. To the extent that individual economic gains are somewhat dependent on the firm's overall survival and success, individual incentives are congruent with cooperative behavior. To the extent that managers view their economic return as a variable share of a fixed pool, their approach will be one of cooptation. Hence moves to 'corporatize' professional services firms by selling shares to the public or to a larger parent owner, establishing a more permanent managerial class and hierarchy, and adopting other characteristics of corporations, may begin to resolve this problem.

In some ways, our contribution revisits the traditional conceptions of Cyert and March (1963) related to dominant coalitions. Since this pioneering work, researchers have tended to lose track of the interdependencies and implied contracts between and among a range of coalitions, not just between top management, boards and employees. In fact organizations are developing into fluid networks, and the separation between agents and principals, and more broadly between individuals, groups and organizations, is blurring. By studying PSFs in their pure and transitional forms, we gain insight into a number of governance issues and challenges that may face an increasing range of organizations as they confront continuous changes, progressions and evolutions.

Notes

1. Research supporting some of the views put forth herein was conducted by the Global Professional Development Forum (GPDF), a forum of professional service firm senior human resource professionals who met quarterly during 1998–2000 to 'share ideas in order to develop the best professional workforce possible'. Member companies include A.D. Little International, A.T. Kearney, Bain & Company, Booz Allen & Hamilton, The Boston Consulting Group, Deloitte Consulting, Ernst & Young/Cap Gemini, Korn Ferry, KPMG Consulting and Mercer Consulting. Stephen Stumpf, the third author of this chapter, was a founding member of GPDF and attended all meetings. The authors express their appreciation to the many PSF professionals who shared their ideas and concerns, and particularly to John Helding, Mark Nevins and John Savage as thought leaders in this regard.
2. While some PSFs use the term 'officer' for the elite equity owners of firm, others use the terms 'managing director' or 'partner'. To avoid misinterpretation of the latter two terms, we use the term 'officer' throughout. An officer is someone who is considered by non-officers as a leader of the firm, who typically has equity in the firm, and who is legally able to obligate the firm to perform duties on a client's behalf. Employees who provide direct service to clients, sometimes called client staff, managers, associates and so on are referred to herein as 'professional service providers' (PSPs).
3. In the USA, total nonfarm payroll reached 132 482 000 in October of 2001 of which just 25 310 000 was in the goods-producing sectors (6 866 000 of which was in construction and 17 882 000 in manufacturing) while 107 173 00 was in services-producing industries, of which 23 546 000 was in retail trade, 41 052 000 was in services proper, and 20 782 000 was in government (US Census Bureau, 2001). From 1980–1990, the percentage of US employees in services has grown from approximately 70 per cent to 75 per cent of total employment.
4. Two current examples demonstrate this effect. The Hewlett family has been an increasingly vocal critic of Hewlett-Packard (HP)'s proposed acquisition of Compaq, believing that entry into the low-margin hardware segment will hurt HP shareholders. Similarly shareholders have radically affected the management of Ford Motor Company, most recently resulting in the ouster of CEO Jacques Nassar by the still influential Ford family.
5. While it can be argued that owner-managers may be more vigilant than the typical shareholder of a widely held corporation, the fact that many incentive plans reward failure nearly as generously as success suggests that these plans are often unsuccessful in properly aligning interests.
6. Recent scandals involving improper corporate reporting practices, and the resulting market reaction to the exposure of these practices, demonstrate the continued viability of shareholder activism, and the long-term disciplines exerted by shareholders on corporate governance and management.
7. Many terms are used to capture the leadership roles in PSFs. Most PSFs distinguish the equity owner roles from the employee roles with terms such as 'officer' for owner and staff member or 'employee' for everyone else. For the purposes of this chapter, we use the term 'partner' to signify the officer, managing director, vice president and other roles in PSFs that (1) are required to provide personal funds to the organization to finance operations, (2) own voting shares in the organization (or subsidiary if the PSF is part of a non-PSF organization), and (3) are members of the group (TMT) that is responsible

300 Responsible leadership and governance in global business

and empowered to make strategy decisions for the organization. It should be noted, however, that some firms have a non-equity partner level below that of 'full' equity-bearing partner.

8. For example, the 'managerial motives' literature demonstrates that CEOs sometimes acquire unrelated businesses, even when doing so is unlikely to increase profits, in the belief that running a larger and more complex organization will drive up their compensation, and their reputation in the market for CEOs.

9. The trend toward mergers of the largest accounting firms has reduced their number from ten to five in less than a decade. The Big 5 (KPMG Peat Marwick, Deloitte Touche Tohmatsu, PricewaterhouseCoopers, Arthur Andersen, and Ernst & Young) together employ more than 500 000 worldwide, with several individual firms employing more than 100 000 (PricewaterhouseCoopers, KPMG Peat Marwick). Consulting firms have grown in size and scope as well. Accenture, the newly named Andersen consulting unit, employs more than 75 000 worldwide, while EDS and its consulting arm, A.T. Kearney, employs more than 130 000.

10. In accounting, this trend has been characterized by mergers between and among the Big 10 accounting firms, reducing them to the Big 8, then Big 6 and now Big 5. Similarly, law firms, even those under the different legal codes and traditions of the USA and Europe, are developing formal alliances or completely merging their operations.

11. After heavy lobbying by some accounting firms, the SEC backed away from more aggressive rules. In the end, then-SEC chairman Arthur Levitt, Jr compromised, settling for a rule requiring corporations to disclose the fees they pay their auditors for audits and other services. The first round of such disclosures has now been reported and shows that, on average, for every dollar a company paid its independent audit firm for auditing last year, it paid $2.69 for other services. Audit firms were paid an average of $2.2 million for each corporate audit, and $5.9 million for selling other services to the audit client (ibid.).

References

Alchian, A. and H. Demsetz (1972), 'Production, information costs, and economic organization', *American Economic Review*, **62**, 777–95.

Ancona, D. and D. Nadler (1989), 'Teamwork at the top: creating high performing executive teams', *Sloan Management Review*, **19**, 41–53.

Andrews, K.R. (1971), *The Concept of Corporate Strategy*, Homewood, IL: Dow Jones Irwin.

Arkell, J. (2001), 'Services: trends, consequences and the effects of a new WTO round', paper presented at the 2001 Roundtable of the Committee for Trade, Industry and Enterprise Development. UN Economic Commission for Europe.

Bantel, K. and S. Jackson (1989), 'Top management and innovations in banking: does the demography of the team make a difference?', *Strategic Management Journal*, **10**,107–24.

Bartlett, C. and S. Ghoshal (1989), *Managing across Borders: the Transnational Solution*, Boston: Harvard Business School Press.

Berle, A.A. and G.C. Means (1932), *The Modern Corporation and Private Property*, New York: The Macmillan Company; reprint 1991, New Brunswick, NJ: Transaction Publishers.

Bourgeois, L.J. (1980), 'Performance and consensus', *Strategic Management Journal*, **1** (2), 227–48.

Burt, R.S. (1982), *Toward a Structural Theory of Action: Network Models of Social Structure, Perception and Action*, New York: Academic Press.

Cannella, A. and M. Lubatkin (1993), 'Succession as a sociopolitical process: internal impediments to outsider succession', *Academy of Management Journal*, **36**, 763–93.

Chaganti, R., V. Mahajan and S. Sharma (1985), 'Corporate board size, composition and corporate failures in the retailing industry', *Journal of Management Studies*, **22**, 400–17.

Chandler, A.D. (1962), *Strategy and Structure: Chapters in the History of the American Industrial Enterprise*, Cambridge, MA: MIT Press.

Chandler, A.D. (1990), *Scale and Scope: the Dynamics of Industrial Capitalism*, Cambridge, MA: Harvard University Press.

Clark, K.D. (2001), 'A relational approach to top management groups: social capital, information processing, co-optation, and efficiency', unpublished doctoral dissertation, University of Maryland.

Clark, K.D. and C.J. Collins (2002), 'Strategic decision-making in high velocity environments: a theory revisited and a test', in M.A. Hitt, R. Amit, C.E. Lucier and R.D. Nixon (eds), *Creating Value: Winners in the New Business Environment*, Oxford: Blackwell.

Cyert, R.M. and J.G. March (1963), *A Behavioral Theory of the Firm*, Englewood Cliffs, NJ: Prentice-Hall.

Daily, C.M. and D.R. Dalton (1994), 'Bankruptcy and corporate governance: the impact of board composition', *Academy of Management Journal*, **37** (6), 1603–18.

Daily, C.M., and D.R. Dalton (1992), 'The relationship between governance structure and corporate performance in entrepreneurial firms', *Journal of Business Venturing*, **7**, 375–86.

Dalton, D. and I. Kesner (1987), 'Composition and CEO duality in boards of directors: an international perspective', *International Business Studies*, **18**, 33–42.

Dalton, D.R., C.M. Daily, A.E. Ellstrand and J.J. Johnson (1998), 'Meta-analytic reviews of board composition, leadership structure, and financial performance', *Strategic Management Journal*, **19**, 269–90.

Davis, J.D., F.D. Schoorman and L. Donaldson (1997), 'Toward a stewardship theory of management', *Academy of Management Review*, **22**, 20–47.

Dearborn, D.C. and H.A. Simon (1958), 'Selective perception: a note on the departmental identification of executives', *Sociometry*, **21**, 140–44.

Dess, G.G. (1987), 'Consensus on strategy formulation and performance: competitors in a fragmented industry', *Strategic Management Journal*, **8**, 259–77.

DiMaggio, P. and W. Powell (1983), 'The iron cage revisited: institutional isomorphism and collective rationality in organization fields', *American Sociological Review*, **48**, 147–60.

Eisenhardt, K. (1989a), 'Agency theory: an assessment and review', *Academy of Management Review*, **14**, 57–74.

Eisenhardt, K. (1989b), 'Making fast strategic decisions in high velocity environments', *Academy of Management Journal*, **32**(3), 543–76.

Fama, E.F. and M.C. Jensen (1983), 'Separation of ownership and control', *Journal of Law and Economics*, **26**, 301–25.

Fields, L.P. and E.L. Mais (1994), 'Managerial voting rights and seasoned public equity Issues', *Journal of Financial and Quantitative Analysis*, **29**, 445–58.

Finkelstein, S. and D. Hambrick (1996), *Strategic Leadership: Top Executives and their Effects on Organizations*, St Paul, MN: West.

Fox, M.A., and R.T. Hamilton (1994), 'Ownership and diversification: agency theory or stewardship theory', *Journal of Management Studies*, **31**, 69–81.

Fredrickson, J.W. (1986), 'The strategic decision process and organizational outcomes: the moderating role of managerial discretion', *Academy of Management Review*, **11**(2), 280–87.

Freidson, E. (1970), *Professional Dominance*, Chicago: Aldine.

Freidson, E. (1983), 'The theory of the professions', in R. Dingwall and P. Lewis (eds), *The Sociology of the Professions*, New York: St Martin's Press, pp. 19–37.

Freidson, E. (1984), 'The changing nature of professional control', *Annual Review of Sociology*, **10**, 1–20.

Gomez-Mejia, L.H. Tosi and T. Hinkin (1987), 'Managerial control, performance, and executive compensation', *Academy of Management Journal*, **30**, 51–70.

Granovetter, M. (1985), 'Economic action and social structure: the problem of embeddedness', *American Journal of Sociology*, **91**, 481–510.

Hallowell, R. (1999), 'Exploratory research: consolidations and economies of scope', *International Journal of Service Industry Management*, **10** (4), 359–68.

Halpern, P. (1983), 'Corporate acquisitions: a theory of special cases? A review of event studies applied to acquisitions', *Journal of Finance*, **38**, 297–317.

Hambrick, D. and P. Mason (1984), 'Upper echelons: the organization as a reflection of its top managers', *Academy of Management Review*, **9**(2), 193–206.

Harris, D. and C. Helfat (1998), 'CEO duality, succession, capabilities and agency theory: commentary and research agenda', *Strategic Management Journal*, **19**, 901–4.

Ibarra, H. (2000), 'Making partner: a mentor's guide to the psychological journey', *Harvard Business Review*, **78** (2), 146–55.

Jacobs, M. (1991), *Short-term America: The Causes and Cures of our Business Myopia*, Cambridge, MA: Harvard Business School Press.

Janis, I. (1972), *Victims of Groupthink*, Boston: Houghton Mifflin.

Jemison, D.B. (1984), 'The importance of boundary-spanning roles in strategic decisionmaking', *Journal of Management Studies*, **21**, 131–52.

Jemison, D.B. and S.B. Sitkin (1986), 'Corporate acquisitions: a process perspective', *Academy of Management Review*, **11**, 145–63.

Jensen, M.C. and W.H. Meckling (1976), 'Theory of the firm: managerial behavior, agency costs and ownership structure', *Journal of Financial Economics*, **3**, 305–60.

Jones, G. and J. Butler (1992), 'Managing internal corporate entrepreneurship: an agency theory perspective', *Journal of Management*, **18**, 733–49.

Kotter, J. (1982), *The General Managers*, New York: Free Press.

Lawrence, B. (1997), 'The black box of organizational demography', *Organization Science*, **8**(1), 1–22.

Lee, K. and J.M. Pennings (2002), 'Mimicry and the market: adoption of a new organizational form', *Academy of Management Journal*, **45**, 144–62.

Lowendahl, B.R. (1998), *Strategic Management of Professional Service Firms*, London: Carfax.

Lubatkin, M. (1983), 'Mergers and the performance of the acquiring firm', *Academy of Management Review*, **8**, 218–25.

Luthans, F., R.M. Hodgetts and S.A. Rosenkrantz (1988), *Real Manager*, Cambridge, MA: Harper and Row.

Maister, D.H. (1993), *Managing the Professional Services Firm*, New York: Free Press

Maister, D.H. (1997), *True Professionalism*, New York: Free Press.

Maister, D.H., C.H. Green and R.M. Galford (2000), *The Trusted Advisor*, New York: Free Press.

Mallette, P. and K. Fowler (1992), 'Effects of board composition and stock ownership on the adoption of "poison pills"', *Academy of Management Journal*, **35**, 1010–35.

Manne, H. (1965), 'Mergers and the market for corporate control', *Journal of Political Economy*, **73**(2), 110–20.

Meyer, J. and B. Rowan (1977), 'Institutionalized organizations: formal structure as myth and ceremony', *American Journal of Sociology*, **83**, 340–63.

Mintzberg, H. (1973), *The Nature of Managerial Work*, New York: Harper and Row.

Morck, R., A. Schleifer and R.Vishny (1989), 'Alternative mechanisms for corporate control', *American Economic Review*, **79**, 842–52.

Murray, A. (1989), 'Top management group heterogeneity and firm performance', *Strategic Management Journal*, Special Issue, 125–42.

Nohria, N. and R.C. Eccles (1992), *Networks and Organizations: Structure, Form and Action*, Boston: Harvard Business School Press.

Oliver, C. (1991), 'Strategic responses to institutional processes', *Academy of Management Review*, **16**, 145–79.

O'Shea, J. and C. Madigan (1997), *Dangerous Company*, New York: Times Business, Random House.

Patton, A. and J. Baker (1987), 'Why won't directors rock the boat?', *Harvard Business Review*, **65**(6), 10–18.

Pfeffer, J. (1972), 'Size and composition of corporate boards of directors: the organization and its environment', *Administrative Science Quarterly*, **17**, 218–28.

Pfeffer, J. (1983), 'Organizational demography', in L.L. Cummings and B.M. Staw (eds), *Research in Organizational Behavior*, vol. 5, Greenwich, CT: JAI Press, pp. 299–357.

Pfeffer, J. and G. Salancik (1978), *The External Control of Organizations: a Resource Dependence Perspective*, New York: Harper and Row.

Pinault, L. (2000), *Consulting Demons*, New York: HarperCollins.

Rackham, N., L. Friedman and R. Ruff (1996), *Getting Partnering Right*, New York: McGraw-Hill.

Roll, R. (1987), 'Empirical evidence on takeover activity and shareholder wealth', in T.E. Copeland (ed.), *Modern Finance and Industrial Economics*, New York: Blackwell, pp. 287–325.

Salter, M.S., and W.A. Weinhold (1979). *Diversification through Acquisition: Strategies for Creating Economic Value*, New York: Free Press.

Schaffer, R. (1997), *High Impact Consulting*, San Francisco, CA: Jossey-Bass.

Scott, J. (1991), *Social Network Analysis: a Handbook*, London: Sage.

SEC (2001), Final Rule: Revision of the Commission's Auditor Independence Requirements, 17 CFR Parts 210 and 240. [Release nos. 33–7919; 34–43602; 35–27279; IC-24744; IA-1911; FR-56; File no. S7-13–00]. RIN 3235-AH91.Revision of the Commission's Auditor Independence Requirements. 12/01/2000 (http://www.sec.gov/rules/final/33–7919.htm Retrieved 13 October 2001).

Sharma, A. (1997), 'Professional as agent: knowledge asymmetry in agency exchange', *Academy of Management Review*, **22**, 758–99.

Smith, K.G., K.A. Smith, J.D. Olian, H.P. Sims Jr, and D.P. O'Bannon, J.A. Scully (1994), 'Top management team demography and process: the role of social integration and communication', *Administrative Science Quarterly*, **39**, 412–38.

Stumpf, S.A. (1999), 'Phases of professional development in consulting', *Career Development International*, **4** (7), 392–9.

Stumpf, S.A. (2002), 'Becoming a partner in a professional services firm', *Career Development International*, **7** (2), 115–21.

Stumpf, S.A. and R. Longman (2000), 'The ultimate consultant: building long term, exceptional value client relationships', *Career Development International*, **5** (3), 124–34.

Stumpf, S.A. and W. Tymon (2001), 'Consultant or entrepreneur?: Demystifying the "War for Talent"', *Career Development International*, **6** (1), 48–55.

Thompson, J.D. (1967), *Organizations in Action*, New York: McGraw-Hill.

Thorelli, H.B. (1986), 'Networks between markets and hierarchies', *Strategic Management Journal*, **7**, 37–51.

Tosi, H.L. and L.R. Gomez-Mejia (1994), 'Compensation monitoring and firm performance', *Academy of Management Journal*, **37**, 1002–16.

Tosi, H.L., J.P. Katz and L.R. Gomez-Mejia (1997), 'Disaggregating the agency contract: the effects of monitoring, incentive alignment and term in office on agent decisionmaking', *Academy of Management Journal*, **40**, 584–602.

Wally, S. and R. Baum (1994), 'Personal and structural determinants of the pace of strategic decision-making', *Academy of Management Journal*, **37**, 932–56.

Wasserman, S. and K. Faust (1994), *Social Network Analysis: Methods and Applications*, New York: Cambridge University Press.

Wasserman, S. and J. Galaskiewicz (1994), *Advances in Social Network Analysis: Research in the Social and Behavioral Sciences*, Thousand Oaks, CA: Sage.

Weiss, L. (1999), 'Collection and connection: the anatomy of knowledge sharing in professional service firms', *Organization Development Journal*, **17** (4), 61–78.

Wellman, B. and S.D. Berkowitz (eds) (1988), *Social Structures. A Network Approach*, Cambridge: Cambridge University Press.

West, C.T. and C.R. Schwenk (1996), 'Top management team strategic consensus, demographic homogeneity and firm performance: a report of resounding non-findings', *Strategic Management Journal*, **17**, 571–6.

Zahra, S.A. (1996), 'Governance, ownership, and corporate entrepreneurship: the moderating impact of industry technological opportunities', *Academy of Management Journal*, **39**, 1713–35.

Zahra, S.A. and J. Pearce (1989), 'Boards of directors and corporate financial performance: a review and integrative model', *Journal of Management*, **15**, 291–344.

PART V

RESPONSIBLE LEADERSHIP AND GOVERNANCE: INTERNATIONAL, CROSS-CULTURAL AND GLOBAL PERSPECTIVES

16 Responsible leadership: a cross-cultural perspective

Sonja A. Sackmann[1]

Introduction

The cases of Enron, Tyco and WorldCom in the US, Barings Bank in the UK, Ahold in The Netherlands and Parmalat in Italy have shaken up not only the business world but society at large on a worldwide scale. What happened so that well respected companies all of a sudden had to declare bankruptcy, turning from reported success to huge failure? How could some of them deceive and betray the investment community, employees, shareholders, customers, suppliers and even auditors in such magnitude? Why did existing governance structures fail? How could well respected and accomplished CEOs and business leaders behave in such a way that – in hindsight – can only be characterized as irresponsible and/or fraudulent? These events raise questions that are still searching for explanations.

One approach in trying to find answers is to question and scrutinize existing corporate governance. Is the US governance structure, in which CEO and chairman can be the same person, the major problem, as opposed to governance structures in which these positions have to be filled by different people? Is it the composition of boards, their working style, their members' time pressure, or their exposure to limited information? Or is it the kind of leadership in a firm that allows cases like Enron to happen? These issues, as well as the Sarbanes-Oxley Act of 2002, suggest that institutional, organizational, personal and interpersonal issues may play a role in the conduct of organizations and their leaders.

Consequently, *corporate governance structures*, *corporate citizenship* and *corporate ethics* have become the focus of attention during the past few years. In a statement released in 2002, 36 CEOs from all over the world emphasized that, first and foremost, corporate citizenship involves the way CEOs run their business and that relationships with key stakeholders are fundamental for success both inside and outside their companies (World Economic Forum (WEF) and The Prince of Wales International Business Leaders Forum (IBLF) 2002).

How can leadership in organizations be more responsible and be conducted in more responsible ways so that events like the ones that occurred in the above-mentioned companies will be significantly reduced or even eliminated in the future? Which perspectives need to be considered for a comprehensive perspective of responsible leadership? What can we learn from leadership research on the issue of responsibility? And is responsibility treated the same way in different cultures? These questions will be addressed in this chapter.

The following sections will first define culture and cross-cultural perspective, then address the issue of responsibility in leadership with its potentially different interpretations from a cross-cultural perspective. Given the scope of the chapter, the focus will be on comparative research investigating cross-cultural differences with relevance to responsible leadership. Finally, a model of responsible leadership is proposed that may guide future research from a cross-cultural perspective.

Culture and a cross-cultural perspective
In the context of this chapter, a cross-cultural perspective implies two aspects: culturally influenced conceptions of responsible leadership and the enactment of responsible leadership in different cultural contexts. Even though the former convergence hypothesis of cultures (for example, Farmer and Richman, 1965) has received some impetus from globalization debates, there is growing evidence that culture matters (for example, Hofstede, 1980a, 2003; Harrison and Huntington, 2000) and that it may have an influence on individuals, organizations and institutions. Culture influences the orientation of institutional frameworks at the macro level, of organizational frameworks at the mesa level and of organizational members' actions at the micro level. Hence the concept of responsible leadership needs to address the framework in which responsible leadership happens as well as the enactment of responsible leadership within a specific organization.

Culture can be defined as a set of basic understandings commonly held by a group of people. This set is distinctive of the group and the understandings serve as guides to acceptable and unacceptable perceptions, thoughts, feelings and behaviors. They are learned and passed on to new members of the group through social interaction and may change over time (Phillips, 1994; Sackmann, 1992). This definition has several implications. One is that the important aspect of culture is cognitive and, hence, invisible. The second is that culture may develop whenever a group of people interacts over an extended period of time. Finally, people may be simultaneously members and potential carriers of several cultures. Hence culture is not restricted to the national level. Instead cultural groupings may form around nation, region, industry, organization, department, function or discipline, workgroup, profession, gender, religion, ideology, ethnicity or critical issues allowing different kinds of cross-cultural perspectives to emerge. These potential subcultures may interact with each other, be independent of each other or even counter-active. As a consequence, the conception of responsible leadership, its enactment and its control may vary across different kinds of cultures at the national, industry, organizational and group level. In addition, leaders may be confronted in their daily work with multiple cultures and a dynamic interplay of different cultures (Phillips and Sackmann, 2002).

At present, a cross-cultural perspective in the area of leadership research has primarily focused on international and cross-national differences addressing interpersonal leadership. Two major frameworks and associated databases exist that suggest cultural differences across nations in regard to human problem solving with relevance for responsible leadership (Hofstede, 1980a, 2003; Trompenaars, 1993). In his reanalysis of IBM survey data from 116 000 employees, Hofstede (1980a; 2003) extracted four universal and independent dimensions of culture around which 'mental programming' occurs and with which every society has to cope. He labeled these dimensions individualism–collectivism, power–distance, uncertainty avoidance and femininity–masculinity. In a later study, the time-oriented dimension Confucian dynamism was added (Chinese Culture Connection, 1987). These dimensions allow culture to be measured and have stimulated a vast body of research (for example, Kirkman *et al.*, 2000).

Trompenaars (1993) offers an alternative set of dimensions to describe and analyze similarities and differences across nations. In comparison to Hofstede's empirically derived dimensions that are conceptualized as bipolar and independent of each other, Trompenaars' dimensions are theoretically derived, interdependent and applied in practice. He employs a critical incidence technique that asks respondents to make a choice in ambiguous situations. He also considers that these dimensions characterize universal problems of human beings across cultures: universalism v. particularism, individualism and collectivism, affective v. neutral, specific v. diffuse, ascription v. achievement, and the conception of time. These dimensions help us to understand differences in legal systems between nations, in governance systems and in understandings of responsible leadership and its enactment.

The dimension *universalism v. particularism* describes the extent to which laws, ethics, morals, leadership styles and behavior or rules are seen to apply universally across different cultures. Universal cultures try to create laws, systems, rules and regulations that are universally valid (for example, Anglo-Saxon countries). A particularistic orientation suggests that existing rules, norms and laws need specific interpretation and enactment in a given cultural context (for example, Latin countries).

Affective v. neutral orientation describes the extent to which emotions can be readily expressed and are expected to be expressed (affective) or retained (neutral). Cultures with a neutral orientation expect responsible leaders to be objective and restrain emotions.

The dimension *specific v. diffuse* refers to the domain of action. In a specific orientation, responsibilities may be compartmentalized and specified for certain functions, roles, levels or situations. A responsible leader is expected to take care and charge of his or her area of responsibility, but not intrude into other areas or go beyond this to include a broader range of issues (for example, the USA). Conversely, in cultures with a preference for diffuse orientation, responsibilities of a leader may reach beyond the immediate job and show concern for a wider range of issues including subordinates' family life (for example, Japan).

The dimension *individualism and collectivism* may give some indication in regard to the expected reach of responsible leadership. To what extent is it acceptable, expected and likely that leadership is exerted by one person who is given power to act (for example, a CEO in the USA) as opposed to a collective that needs to be involved and consulted, such as the *keiretsu* system in Japan?

Ascription v. achievement refers to the extent to which status (ascription) or personal achievement is considered important. In ascription-oriented cultures, responsibility is ascribed and may be almost inherently associated with a certain position or social status in society or business without being questioned, regardless of actual conduct. In cultures with a predominant achievement orientation, such as Anglo-Saxon countries, responsibility needs to be earned. Leaders have to prove that they are worthy of the trust of their subordinates who then will attribute their action as responsible on the basis of personal accomplishments.

Time can be differentiated into a past, present and future orientation. In cultures with a past orientation, responsible leaders are expected to honor history, past accomplishments and the elderly, who are considered guardians of oral history with wisdom – activities and expertise which may be considered unnecessary, old-fashioned or even a waste of time and outdated in cultures with a present time orientation – and even more so in cultures with a future orientation. A culture orientation with a focus on the present may consider leadership responsible if actions are taken to deal with immediate problems. Individuals influenced by a future time orientation are likely to expect strategic and long-term planning from responsible leaders.

Cultural differences at the national level that can be described with these dimensions influence the institutional and organizational context of responsible leadership as well as its enactment.

The institutional context of responsible leadership

Decades of research on interpersonal leadership have contributed to a vast amount of data and various leadership theories such as the trait, behavioral and contingency theories and 'new leadership', most of them developed in the USA (for example, Bass, 1990). None of these theories, however, is an explicit theory of responsible leadership. One may argue that responsibility is and has always been an integral part of the concept of leadership in the Western world. People who were entrusted with a position of leadership were expected to be responsible, act in responsible ways and take responsibility, in regard both to taking actions and for the results of those actions. Hence one can assume that a leadership position was only given to a person who had a reputation for responsible leadership and who was expected to act responsibly. The recent increase in irresponsible behavior in business by business leaders suggests, however, that the formerly implicit contract and assumption that leadership is automatically coupled with legally and morally appropriate and responsible action may no longer be taken for granted. Responsibility associated with leadership needs explicit attention and explication from different perspectives.

In this endeavor, three critical questions need to be addressed at an institutional level. Who is a leader? To whom and for what is that leader responsible? Answers to these questions are culturally influenced and require inclusion of different fields.

Who is a leader?

Giving direction, moving toward a new direction and taking people along are the most general characteristics of leadership as defined in the Anglo-Saxon world (for example, Bass, 1990). These leadership activities may occur in the context of a formal, legitimized position such as a specified managerial or executive function. However they may also happen without such a formal position, as witnessed by the history of societies, nations and companies. Informal leaders may emerge despite the existence of formal, legitimized leaders and may be given power to influence and to lead by their followers, even without a formal relationship. In ascription-oriented cultural settings, leaders may be legitimized by their family background (for example, a king or sheikh) or by religion. If we focus on legitimized leadership in the context of a Western conception of organizations that operate within a specified legal framework, legitimized leaders are chosen and appointed as specified in the organizations' statutes. In the case of a senior manager, the official choice is usually made by the top executive group. In the case of a top executive, the official choice is made by the board of the company which is partially elected by the shareholders. Depending on the specific cultural context at both the national and the organizational level, these official choices may be more or less influenced by informal networks of power. A major shareholder of a company is likely to have a stronger influence in such a decision process than a board member who represents, for example, the workforce in a German company. Hence an exploration and conception of responsible leadership needs to include and consider the person of the leader, the organization and the institutional context in which leadership happens.

To whom and for what is a leader responsible?
These two questions address the issue of accountability and corporate governance. In the tradition of Kantian philosophy, individuals are first and foremost responsible to themselves (Immanuel Kant [1787] 1998). In this philosophical tradition, leaders have to justify their behavior and its consequences before their own conscience. This differs, for example, for religious leaders. In their role as a member of an organization or corporation, organizational or corporate leaders are responsible *for* the resources that are entrusted to them. They are accountable for their actions *to* those people who have entrusted them with these resources and delegated certain tasks and associated responsibilities to them within the formal lines of authority. In the case of a CEO or members of the top executive group, the jurisdiction of the particular country, the corporate governance system and the lines of authority as defined in a particular organization specify to whom leaders are responsible and accountable.

Jurisdictions determine required governance systems and both are culturally influenced. Lorsch and Graff (1997) describe the different governance systems in the USA, UK, Japan and Germany according to their decision-making methods (checks and balances versus networks), their ownership patterns (dispersed versus concentrated) and their chief goals (shareholder primacy versus stakeholder welfare). The USA has adopted a checks and balances approach that is enforced through litigation with a focus on individual and shareholder wealth creation and dispersed ownership. Germany and Japan are more concerned about collective welfare, employ a stakeholder perspective and have more concentrated ownership through banks (Germany) or the *keiretsu* in Japan.

Board structures and practices also vary across countries even though the functions of boards in Germany, the USA, and the UK are the same: to oversee the selection and succession of managers and directors; to review financial performance, approve corporate strategy and monitor activities of management; and to ensure that legal and ethical standards are met. Japanese boards have more of a symbolic function.

One- or two-tier board systems can be differentiated. Whereas the one-tier system that most Anglo-Saxton countries have adopted allows a CEO in the USA to act as his or her own control in the role of the chairman of the board, the two-tier system of Germany requires by law different people in the positions of CEO and chairman. Whether this formal division between governance and execution creates more responsibility in leadership depends, however, on the specific composition of the board and, most importantly, on the working culture of the board (for example, Schilling, 2001, 2002).

Boards vary in size, number of outside directors, and working style (for example, Pic, 1995; Lorsch and Graff, 1997; Schilling, 2002) even though several changes have been introduced over the past few years. Boards of Anglo-Saxon companies average eight to 12 members who meet six to eight times a year. Depending on the size and the industry, the number of board members of German companies is defined by law and may vary between 12 and 22 members. Half of them are elected by the shareholders and the other half by employees. In Japan, the *keiretsu* presents yet another governance structure that reflects the relational nature of the enveloping culture and its intricate network of relationships.

Jurisdictions as well as formal governance structures can, however, only provide frameworks for responsible leadership. They leave room for different kinds of understandings and enactments of responsibility. They also leave room for variations in monitoring behavior by the respective control agents, as business cases have shown in the past. These may be influenced by culture at the national, industry and corporate level, as well as by (board) group culture.

At the organizational level, understandings of responsibility are influenced by the (culturally) preferred model of corporate responsibility, regardless of national culture. Does the top executive group adopt a shareholder or a stakeholder model of responsibility? Or does the top executive group try to act in 'the best interests of the company' (Malik, 2002)? Within a shareholder perspective, leaders are considered responsible for acting in the best interest of the company's owners, investors or shareholders. With a stakeholder perspective (for example, Andriof *et al.*, 2002), the 'allocation' of responsibility depends on the definition of who are considered the most important stakeholders. This, again, is shaped by the organization's culture, as are the interpretation and focus placed in regard to corporate social responsibility. Both perspectives contain inherent conflicts of interest that may diffuse actual perceptions and enactments of responsibility. Depending on the situation, a certain shareholder or stakeholder group may be favored or (mis-)used as justification for a leader's action. For these reason, Malik

(2002) proposes with reference to Drucker (1992) to place the organization and its customers as the focus of attention – to act in their best interest and feel responsibly toward them. Return on investments will ultimately follow. This perspective, however, also leaves room for culturally specific interpretation that may differ across departments, divisions, hierarchical levels, companies and industries and requires specification of the subject of responsibility.

At the organizational level, work contracts further specify responsibilities in terms of duties. They may be complemented by job descriptions and goal agreements. Some of them may also specify the legitimate means to reach those goals. Members of low-context cultures (for example, the USA, Canada and the UK) are specific in defining what they mean and are more likely to create long and specific contracts whereas high-context cultures such as Japan imply tacit knowledge that guides interpretations of broad assignments. In the case of a foreign work assignment, 'go over there and work hard' may be considered sufficient, whereas a Western employee would expect and need more specific and explicit directions.

The recent cases of irresponsible leadership have demonstrated that the mere existence of institutional arrangements such as laws, corporate governance structures, work contracts and job descriptions may not suffice if leaders are too creative in their interpretation, bypass or even violate them and, hence, do not behave in responsible and ethical ways. For this reason, ethics, ethical behavior and codes of conduct have received increased attention in business, with a focus on the person of the leader and his or her personal make-up. This leads us to the enactment and process of leadership and the person of the leader.

Responsible leadership in action: leaders and their behavior
Business ethics, moral philosophy and research on ethical leadership have indirectly addressed issues of responsibility. Each of the different moral philosophies provides a basis for ethical decisions (for example, Ferrell *et al.*, 2000; Robertson and Crittenden, 2003). Three different perspectives can be differentiated: a focus on virtues or morals, a focus on ethical conduct in terms of the Golden Rule and a focus on legitimate actions based on dialogue (see also Kuhn and Weibler, 2003). While the first two perspectives locate responsibility in the person of the leader with a normative appeal, responsibility is considered the outcome of a communication process between leader and followers in the last perspective.

Responsibility as personal virtue
Traditional ethics go back to Aristotle's and Stoa's appeal to personal virtues such as justice, integrity, honesty and discipline. The assumption is

that responsible leaders have the right morals based on their virtues and they adhere to principles that guide their behavior. This ethical position can be found both in normative appeals of the business world and in many leadership theories. Several business initiatives have formulated principles for business conduct that also include responsible leadership. One prominent organization is the International Business Leaders Forum (IBLF), a not-for-profit organization that promotes international leadership in responsible business practices to benefit business and society. In collaboration with the World Economic Forum, IBLF conducted a survey on the major challenges that companies will face in the future. One of the results points to the responsibility of leaders to communicate the right values within their organizations (WEF and IBLF, 2002).

Several interpersonal leadership theories (for example, trait theories, behavioral approaches and 'new' leadership theories) focus on the person of the leader: his or her personal attributes and behavior. In terms of responsible leadership, the leader's values, morals and ethical conduct are therefore of utmost interest. The Great Man theory as well as 'new leadership' theories such as charismatic and transformational leadership (for example, Bass, 1985, 1990; Burns, 1978; Shamir *et al.*, 1993; Yukl, 2002), include personality traits and values that are related to responsible behavior of a leader. From their perspective, responsibility is first and foremost a property of the leader and an obligation of the leader. Responsibility-related traits such as integrity, honesty, trustworthiness and being just are personality traits that can be found in the attribute lists of trait theories, in business ethics and as core elements of effective leaders according to transformational and value-based leadership. Transformational (as opposed to transactional) leadership includes

> broadening and elevating the interests of followers, generating awareness and acceptance among the followers of the purposes and mission of the group, and motivating followers to go beyond their self-interests for the good of the group and/or the organization .... Charismatic or transformational leaders articulate a realistic vision of the future that can be shared, stimulate subordinates intellectually, and pay attention to the differences among the subordinates. (Den Hartog *et al.*, 1999, p. 223)

This kind of leadership is seen to be grounded in a specific set of personal values of the leader and was found to have transforming effects both on individuals and on organizations (Tichy and DeVanna, 1997). The positive effects of transformational leadership are summarized by Fiol *et al.* (1999) in their review of over one hundred empirical studies. Results include better organizational performance (effects ranging from 0.35 to 0.50), higher employee commitment, satisfaction and identification (effects ranging from

0.40 to 0.80) and a high corrected correlation (0.81) between charisma and employees' ratings of perceived leadership effectiveness (Lowe *et al.*, 1996). This positive transformational effect on individuals can be achieved by raising the awareness of the value and importance of desired outcomes, getting followers to transcend their own self-interests, and altering or expanding their needs (Bass, 1985).

Despite these positive results, a charismatic or transformational leader's values and morals are not necessarily virtuous and ethical. The critical aspects or the potentially 'dark side' of charisma-based leadership as evidenced in history as well as business are addressed by several authors (for example, Conger, 1989; Den Hartog *et al.*, 1999; Yukl, 2002). From the perspective of the traditional virtue-based ethics perspective, careful selection and a screening of the potential leader's values becomes a critical issue to ensure responsible leadership. It needs, however, to be complemented by governance practices that take their monitoring responsibilities seriously.

Responsibility as responsible decision making

This perspective on responsibility is based on Kant's philosophy that ultimately all responsibility rests within the individual and his or her assessment of right and wrong and of responsible and irresponsible behavior, based on a set of general principles. This implies that leaders who want to act responsibly need to evaluate potential actions in a process of an inner dialogue and apply reason that allows them to be able to justify their final decision before their own conscience.

Zimmerman's (1996) concept of personal responsibility is based on this perspective. Personal responsibility may include a moral, legal or professional obligation and may be assessed by moral, legal or professional standards in terms of adherence to their norms. Responsibility works retrospectively, in the here and now as well as prospectively. Responsible leadership includes the consequences of actions that were taken or omitted in the past, of current actions and of the consequences that these actions may have in the future. Thus a leader can be held accountable for not having taken an action in time, for the kind of actions he or she takes at present as well as for the consequences of actions taken.

Some authors have combined both perspectives of responsibility. Chester Barnard ([1938] 1968) framed executive responsibility in terms of conforming to a complex code of morals as well as creating moral codes for others. This idea is further developed by Treviño *et al.* (2000) into ethical leadership that is based on two pillars: the moral person and the moral manager. The moral (= ethical) person is characterized by three attributes that have the quality of values. These are integrity, honesty and trustworthiness. Moral individuals show four types of behaviors: they do the right thing, they have concern for people, they are open and they show personal morality. Moral people also follow four guidelines in decision making: they hold to values, they are objective/fair, they are concerned for society and they follow ethical decision rules. In addition, the role of the moral manager and leader includes role modeling through visible action, rewards and discipline, and communication about ethics and values – all based on the right (= ethical) values. Both perspectives of responsibility, alone or in combination, still rest exclusively with the person of the leader.

Responsibility as legitimized action
This perspective is based on intersubjective ethics grounded in dialogue (for example, Habermas, 1984). Kant's intrapersonal dialogue is placed in the context of interpersonal interaction and communication. Actions are considered responsible if underlying reasons have been discussed, if these reasons are understood and if the final choice of action is evaluated as the most responsible under given circumstances. Hence leadership is ultimately considered responsible if those who are concerned understand why the leader had to decide and behave the way he or she did and approve of actions taken even if they might have made a different choice.

In contrast to the other two person-based perspectives of responsibility, this perspective is capable of addressing responsibility in leadership when facing leadership dilemmas that may include conflicting issues or values. Even if a leader has to lay off people, he or she may act responsibly when considering the entire organization and the consequences of alternative courses of action.

The above discussion shows that the concept of responsibility can be tied to different ethical perspectives. The majority of leadership theories with relevance for responsible leadership focus on a person-centered perspective of responsibility with a universal appeal to virtues and morals. Given that these leadership theories mentioned above are US-based theories, the question arises whether they are applicable across cultures and – despite the claim for universals – differences exist across cultures in regard to the conception of responsible leadership. We first address cross-national differences and their potential impact on responsible leadership and then review relevant research on leadership theories that have been tested across nations, regions and hierarchies.

Cross-national differences relevant to responsible leadership
Research on cultural differences at the national level has implicitly assumed that effective leadership is expected to be value-congruent. The study by Newman and Nollen (1996) of 176 workers in 18 countries supports the notion that business performance is better when management practices are

congruent with national culture. That is, societal preferences are expected to be matched by the respectively fitting leadership behavior.

Hofstede's dimensions

According to Hofstede (1980b), leadership issues are predominantly related to the dimension of power distance. High (versus low) power distance scores imply that nations accept hierarchical differences, inequalities among people and, hence, an unequal treatment of people including salary differences, the use of privileges and status symbols that demonstrate the differences. Leaders are expected to make decisions without consulting and to make use of their status and position power. Hence a patriarchic type of leadership with the leader making decisions and taking responsibility may therefore be more readily accepted and even expected in countries with high power distance scores. Being and acting responsible rests with the leader who is expected to take charge, give directions, set goals, motivate employees and make decisions with little involvement from subordinates. The leader's positional power base tends to be accepted without much questioning. Countries with high power distance scores are, for example, the Philippines, Mexico, Venezuela, India and Singapore.

Low scores in power distance refer to the opposite and imply that responsible leaders are expected to consult their employees before making a decision, that they should rely on expert power rather than position power and that they do not demonstrate hierarchical differences in status and privileges. In countries with low power distance, the responsibility of leadership is more likely to be shared. Even though designated superiors exist, they are less likely to refer to or insist on their position power in order to accomplish goals. Countries with low power distance scores are, for example, Austria, Israel, New Zealand, Ireland, Switzerland and the Scandinavian countries (Hofstede, 1997) with the USA being close to the middle (40 out of 100), scoring higher than Germany (35).

The dimension of uncertainty avoidance may also have some implications for what is considered responsible leadership and what is expected from a responsible leader. Strong uncertainty avoidance refers to a subjective feeling of anxiety, a desire for and reliance on rules and regulations that are observed in order to reduce uncertainty and related stress. Responsible leadership can be expected to take care of this need for uncertainty avoidance by providing clear structures, processes and transparent rules, and by explicating expectations. Countries with high scores in uncertainty avoidance are Greece, Portugal, Belgium, Japan, Peru, France, Chile, Spain, Argentina, Turkey, Mexico, Israel and Columbia, whereas Singapore, Denmark, Sweden, Hong Kong, Ireland and Great Britain have the lowest scores in uncertainty avoidance.

Trompenaars' dimensions

Trompenaars' (1993) cultural dimensions give additional insight into cross-cultural differences in regard to responsible leadership. In universalistic-oriented cultures, responsible leadership is likely to be associated with traditional ethics with a reference to universally applicable virtues and morals that characterize a responsible leader. The institutional context defines the range of authority and accountability of a leader. In more particularistic-oriented cultures, responsibility in leadership and its respective institutional context are more likely to be contextually interpreted.

Cultures with a stronger affective orientation may expect responsible leaders to express their feelings openly, to be open to their feelings and expressions of emotion. Speeches of leaders considered to be responsible appeal to pathos which is considered inappropriate in neutral-oriented cultures. These expect logos, logical reasoning supported by facts and figures.

A responsible leader in a diffuse culture may ask for a personal favor from his subordinate, such as helping him at home on a weekend (for example, Trompenaars, 1993, pp. 86–8) – a behavior that may be considered unacceptable and even unethical or irresponsible in a culture with a specific orientation. In countries that score high on both power distance and collectivism, for example, Turkey or Japan, the responsibility of a leader goes even beyond the workplace and extends to the family. A responsible leader is expected to take care of the employee's entire family, to include hiring family members. Resulting firms are clans that are likely to influence public and political life.

Even though Trompenaars' work and Hofstede's dimensions have not been without criticism (see, for example, Dorfman and Howell, 1988; Smith *et al.*, 1996), associated research indicates that expectations in regard to responsible leadership may differ from country to country and that responsible leadership may be interpreted differently across countries.

We now review leadership research relevant to responsible leadership from a cross-cultural perspective including international and cross-national, cross-regional, cross-societal and cross-hierarchical perspectives as well as research on cross-organizational, professional and gender-based differences.

Cross-cultural leadership research relevant to responsible leadership

Comprehensive and recent reviews exist on the topic of international and so-called 'cross-cultural' leadership (Dorfman, 2004; Smith and Peterson, 2002) that will not be repeated here. Both reviews stress the importance of the topic for today's increasingly internationalizing and globalizing business and the impact that culture may have on leadership. Both review empirical research that tested US-based leadership theories in other countries. They also describe findings from two non-US based leadership theories that were developed in Japan and in India and both reviews report findings from the current GLOBE project – a comparative research project investigating leadership preferences, primarily across regions.

In general, most studies show differences in leadership across countries that are attributed to culture without further exploration. Most of these studies are also difficult to compare since they tend to use different kinds of operationalizations. In regard to responsible leadership, research on charismatic or transformational leaders (Bass, 1985, 1997) and value-based leadership (House *et al.*, 2004) is of particular interest.

Transformational leadership across nations

Transformational leadership as defined above (Bass, 1985) with a focus on the person of the leader and a shared vision between leader and subordinates was investigated in more than 20 nations, with a focus on effectiveness. Researchers used translations of the Multifactor Leadership Questionnaire (MLQ) that asks subordinates to characterize the leader's transformational style in a relatively general manner. The results of these studies support the effectiveness of transformational leadership across cultures. One may hypothesize that this type of leadership and its implicit notion of responsible leadership in terms of leader characteristics such as integrity and trustworthiness as well as the ability to articulate a vision that can be shared may apply across nations and is therefore universalistic. The statements in the MLQ are general enough for respondents to be able to fill in country specifics. Bass (1997) acknowledges that leaders may need to vary their transformational style across different cultures in order to be perceived as transformational. In Indonesia, inspirational leaders need to persuade their followers of the leader's own competence, a behavior that would appear inappropriate in other countries. Shamir *et al.* (1993) suggest that, despite its universal applicability, charismatic leadership may be culturally contingent. This implies that what is considered responsible leadership may be different across cultures at different levels.

Indigenous non-Western leadership theories support the notion that leadership and concepts of leadership differ across nations. Based on the Western notion of leadership functions, Misumi's (1985) performance-maintenance (PM) theory of leadership differs in its enactment from one setting to another. Effective leaders score high on both dimensions that are considered to be complementary rather than independent of each other. In addition, Misumi argues that effective leadership varies in different settings and that different instruments need to be developed and used for investigating substantially different settings. Researchers using his PM theory had to add, for example, the additional leadership factor 'C' for assessing character and morals in order to characterize adequately Chinese leadership.

A study of effective leadership styles comparing US managers with managers from Jordan and Saudi Arabia revealed large differences (Scandura *et al.*, 1999). In the US sample, the people-oriented leadership style was related to job satisfaction and leadership effectiveness, the task-oriented style was not. The opposite results were found for the sample from Jordan and Saudi Arabia whose representatives expected 'strong and decisive' leadership. Hence a people-oriented style is probably interpreted as being weak in these countries.

Value-based leadership across nations and regions
The GLOBE project is a current research project on leadership prototypes across cultures with a prominent focus on regional cultures. A network of 170 social scientists from 62 cultures throughout the world investigates culture's influence on value-based leadership and variables that relate to organizational effectiveness (House *et al.*, 1999). Combining etic and emic research approaches, the GLOBE researchers developed nine one-dimensional scales to assess culture (Dickson *et al.*, 2000). They define leadership as the ability to influence, motivate and enable others to contribute to the success of their organization (House *et al.*, 2004). The leadership prototype is approached from an attribution perspective (Lord and Maher, 1991) and refers to people's endorsement of leadership. Respondents are asked for their perceptions of what they consider to enhance or impede outstanding leadership in terms of both leader attributes and leader behaviors. The behaviors that are rated most facilitative define the leadership prototype.

The 21 basic leadership factors identified from 112 leadership items were grouped into six global leadership dimensions by conducting first- and second-order factor analysis:

- charismatic/value based (visionary, inspirational; self-sacrifice, integrity, decisive, performance oriented);
- self protective (self-centered, status conscious, conflict inducer, face saver, procedural);
- humane (modest, humane orientation);
- team-oriented (including collaborative team orientation, team integrator; diplomatic, malevolent, administratively competent);
- participative (including autocratic, non-participative; delegate);
- autonomous (individualistic, independent, autonomous, unique).

GLOBE researchers Den Hartog *et al.* (1999) investigated the issue of culture-specific and universal aspects of endorsed transformational leadership in 60 countries. At least three countries are represented in the geographic regions of Africa, Asia, Europe (central, eastern and northern),

Latin America, North America, the Middle East and the Pacific Rim. Across countries and cultures several universal attributes of outstanding leadership as well as negative leadership could be identified. Outstanding leadership was most importantly characterized by integrity, including attributes such as being trustworthy, just and honest. Outstanding leaders are also described as charismatic, inspirational and visionary, including attributes such as encouraging, positive, motivational, confidence building, dynamic and with foresight. They are team-oriented (effective in team building, communicating and coordinating), excellence-oriented, decisive, intelligent and win–win problem solvers. Attributes such as being loners, being non-cooperative, ruthless, non-explicit, irritable and dictatorial were considered ineffective and impediments to outstanding leadership.

Several attributes associated with charismatic/transformational leadership were, however, found to be culturally contingent. Some attributes showed high variations in country means. Their item means range, for example, from 2.14 to 5.96 for risk taking or from 3.72 to 6.44 for enthusiasm. Den Hartog *et al.* (1999, p. 242) suggest that 'shared preference for transformational/ charismatic leadership does not mean transformational/charismatic attributes will be enacted in exactly the same manner across cultures or that similar meaning would be attached to all exhibited behavior across all cultures'. Qualitative data analysis revealed that the term 'charisma' invoked ambivalence in several countries. In Mexico it is, for example, considered dangerous (Martinez and Dorfman, 1998) as it may be in countries with histories of dictatorships. Different interpretations of vision are reported for India, The Netherlands, Australia and Austria, as well as for the way the vision is communicated.

At present, the GLOBE project can be considered the most comprehensive research project on leadership (prototypes) from a cross-cultural perspective with relevance to responsible leadership. Even though the chosen leadership theory is still US-based, the project tried to incorporate cross-cultural perspectives when developing their instruments. GLOBE researchers have also addressed cultural differences in regard to hierarchy, which will be reported below.

Cross-cultural leadership differences at the organizational and suborganizational level
Several studies indicate that culture at the organizational level influences the kind of leadership in that organization (for example, Sackmann, 1991, 2002; Schein, 1997; Schumacher, 1997; Ybema, 1997) and that the kind of leadership and culture may differ from organization to organization.

A GLOBE follow-up study in The Netherlands tested the hypothesis that the perception of an effective leader may differ according to the hierarchical level (Den Hartog *et al.*, 1999). A total of 2161 respondents of 19 years and older who held at least a part-time job were asked to characterize both an outstanding lower-level manager and a top manager using the same 22 leadership characteristics. The results revealed significant differences. Effective top managers were characterized as being innovative, visionary, persuasive, long term-oriented, diplomatic and courageous, whereas lower-level managers scored higher in regard to attention to subordinates, team building and a participative style. No significant differences were found for the attributes 'trustworthy', 'communicative' and 'calm'.

The 18-country study by Zander (1997) on the relationship between employees' preferences regarding interpersonal leadership and national culture found not only country differences but also significant differences between departments/functions within the two organizations studied regarding rewards or positive feedback, incentives and control mechanisms as well as differences across work positions. In addition, the degree of preference in different departments varied across items. The author concludes that employees have different preferences for interpersonal leadership regarding participation, control, feedback and concern in kind and in degree. Even though a normative ideal could be found across countries, actual preferences and preferred frequencies of leadership behavior varied substantially across countries, departments and even work positions.

These findings suggest that a truly cross-cultural perspective of responsible leadership needs more refinement in conceptualization and research that go beyond national differences. A truly cross-cultural perspective of responsible leadership also includes cultural differences at the organizational and group level.

Current state and future directions
Responsible leadership has been indirectly addressed by some interpersonal leadership theories that have been tested across cultures. Cross-national culture research indicates that leadership is culturally contingent. In addition, the fields of business ethics, organizational culture, corporate governance and corporate social responsibility have relevance for what is considered responsibility in leadership.

Research on interpersonal leadership has clearly established that effective leadership varies across culture at the national (and to some extent at the regional, hierarchical and departmental) level in terms of both the perception of effective leadership and the leader's enactment of leadership. Leader attributes that are associated with responsibility, such as integrity and being honest, trustworthy and just, have been shown to be considered as enhancing effective leadership universally, but their specific enactment needs differ across cultures. A focus on attributes, however, is not sufficient for characterizing the entire phenomenon of responsible leadership. Attributes refer to a few personal characteristics of responsible leaders, with no consideration of the institutional and organizational context, the perceived domain of responsibility, the way responsibility is enacted in different contexts or the outcomes of actions taken and their evaluation in terms of responsibility. Consequently existing knowledge is predominantly based on the virtue perspective described above, with little or no information on the personal decision being taken, with no consideration of the interaction between leader and followers and no consideration of the organizational and institutional contexts.

In addition, insights from cross-cultural research have predominantly focused on national differences that have been attributed to culture at this level. Research indicates, however, that organizational culture may influence leadership effectiveness (for example, Schein, 1997), hierarchical differences may exist in regard to leadership expectations and effectiveness (Den Hartog *et al.*, 1999), gender differences may exist in regard to leadership style (for example, Carless, 1998; Druskat, 1994; Eagly *et al.*, 2003) and ethics (Forte, 2004), all of which may influence the perception of what is considered responsible leadership.

The study by Forte (2004) also suggests that managers' moral reasoning may be less influenced by personality traits than previously assumed. The author investigated the degree to which differences exist in the moral reasoning ability of top, middle and first-line managers in different industries. She included three different independent variables: reported organizational ethical climate, locus of control, and selected demographic and institutional variables. In all, 400 questionnaires were analyzed from a stratified random sample of managers from a random sample of Fortune 500 firms in the USA. The results reveal that the personality variable locus of control had no significant influence on moral reasoning, while gender did. Furthermore age and management levels influenced the perception of perceived organizational climate types.

Recent research on value congruency between personal and business values conducted from a dynamic perspective suggests that business values may be less stable across situations than previously assumed and that context matters (Watson *et al.*, 2004). In Watson *et al.*'s laboratory study, layoff decisions were justified and legitimized to maintain self-concepts in situations where personal values contradicted business-related decisions. The researchers conclude that those values are contextually influenced and that organizational context plays a more important role than previously assumed. This observation had already been made by Zimbardo ([1972] 2001) who concluded from his observations that people's behavior is largely contextually determined and values may be situationally suspended.

A model of responsible leadership from a cross-cultural perspective
The various streams of research reviewed above indicate that a conception of responsible leadership needs to go beyond the focus of the person of the leader and include interactive as well as contextual aspects. Hence we propose a dynamic model of responsible leadership from a cross-cultural cross-disciplinary perspective that may be tested in subsequent research.

The model in Figure 16.1 differentiates two perspectives within a common context of interaction: that of the leader and that of the perceiver who may be not only a 'follower' but an interaction partner in general. Existing research has shown that, in regard to responsible leadership, the leader's integrity in terms of being honest, just and trustworthy is important since these personal predispositions are assumed to influence choices of actions. In addition, the leader's perceived range of responsibility has been added. Do leaders consider themselves only responsible for a narrowly defined function or do they consider themselves responsible for a larger entity and a set of different stakeholders? The actual behavior that leaders show is an enactment of their perception of the range of responsibility on the basis of their intrapersonal dialogue as well as dialogues with their interaction partners. The actual performance is also influenced by skills, knowledge and experience that are not specifically listed in Figure 16.1. The result of enacted responsibility leads to consequences that leaders compare to the potential results of alternative courses of actions and related consequences. A leader's behavior may thus be considered relatively responsible in a given situation and under a given set of circumstances. A layoff may still be considered responsible leadership behavior if that decision will protect the majority of jobs and if it is conducted in a way that is – despite all hardship involved – acceptable to those involved under the given circumstances. The kind of behavior as well as the evaluation of consequences will enhance the leaders' own perception of their integrity in the case of positive evaluations or diminish it in the case of negative evaluations. In the entire process, the leaders' thoughts, perceptions, actions and evaluations are influenced by their socialization into different cultures. Depending on the issues at hand, different cultural perspectives may become salient, such as culture at the societal and national level (for example, economic ideology or societal values), aspects of regional, industrial, organizational or professional cultures, as well as cultural perspectives due to hierarchy, function, workgroup or gender.

While acting, leaders are being perceived by their interaction partners and attributed with a certain degree of integrity in terms of being honest, just, trustworthy and credible, and they are seen to take a certain range of responsibility into consideration. Their actions are evaluated and comparisons are made to other leaders and to other potential courses of

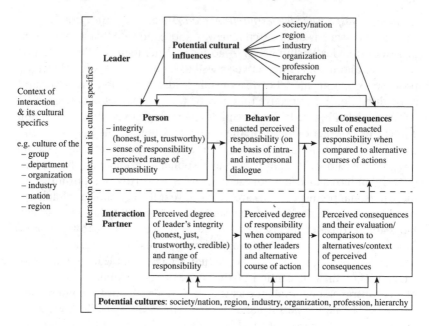

Figure 16.1   A dynamic model of responsible leadership from a cross-cultural perspective

action. The consequences of their actions are evaluated and also compared to alternatives within the context of perceived consequences. In this process, co-occurrences may either enhance or diminish leaders' perceived integrity even though they may have no direct influence on them or the situation. In addition, the consequences of their actions and their evaluation within the given context will sustain and reinforce, enhance or diminish a leader's perceived responsibility. Responsibility is therefore a quality that is attributed to the leader on the basis of a combination of perceived personal attributes, leadership behavior and experience from interactions and consequences of behavioral outcomes. In the entire process, the interaction partners are also influenced in their perceptions, behaviors and evaluations by their learnings from socialization into different kinds of cultures at different levels. These will most likely not be the same set as for the leader and therefore bear some inherent risk of misinterpretation, misunderstanding and a misfit in expectations and actual observations.

In addition, leader and interaction partners act within a common context that may add other culture perspectives and influence the interaction process. To give an example, a leader born and raised in Northern California with 20 years of experience in the computer industry may interact with a fellow worker born and raised in Paris, who has worked in the aerospace industry. They work together in a software development project in Bangalore. Both people bring with them different (culturally influenced) perspectives and experiences that they use in making decisions about responsible leadership and in evaluating leadership actions in terms of responsibility. They interact in a context that differs from their personal and professional culture background, creating and negotiating a new cultural context. Hence what they consider responsible leadership may differ somewhat and may differ from what is expected in the particular work context in Bangalore. Awareness of these potential differences (as well as similarities) may help in negotiating contextually meaningful responsible leadership.

Finally the institutional framework and issues of corporate governance need to be part of a model of responsible leadership. These include not only legal requirements and structural aspects such as the number of board members but also the degree of personal independence of selected board members to speak their minds as well as the working culture of the board. The latter refers to expectations in regard to the kind of contribution made by board members, time expected to dedicate to board work and the rules that guide board work. Is it considered a working board or a symbolic board? At Hilti AG, only those are selected as board members who are considered to make a contribution to Hilti AG and they are expected to dedicate 20 days to board work. Another critical issue is the culture of the board. Are critical issues being raised, or is the board an 'exclusive club' that acts polite without addressing critical issues (Schilling, 2002)? If critical issues can be raised, how informed, open and deep are subsequent discussions? Malik (2002) suggests that the board should observe and follow the same principles and guidelines that it uses in monitoring and evaluating management.

Directions for future research
The field of responsible leadership, institutional and organizational context and its enactment and interpretation offers a broad field for research. The model proposed in Figure 16.1 can guide future research that investigates indicated issues in different cultural contexts. Studies may focus on same leaders with different interaction partners in the same cultural context; same leaders with same interaction partners in different contexts; and different leaders with different interaction partners in the same as well as in different cultural contexts. Issues that will test the perceived and enacted kind of responsibility need systematic variation. In this endeavor, the cultural context needs to be defined, characterized and observed and also to be varied systematically. Research questions of interest are also how different kinds of approaches to corporate governance, and how different board working cultures and different organizational cultures, may influence

leadership behavior in terms of perceived and enacted responsibility and related results. These research efforts may eventually refine or modify the proposed model and add to a growing body of knowledge about responsible leadership from an interdisciplinary perspective in different kinds of cultural contexts.

Note
1. I would like to thank Jeanne McNett and Thomas Eberle for their helpful comments on an earlier version of this paper.

References
Andriof, J., S. Waddock, B. Husted and S. Rahman (eds) (2002), *Unfolding Stakeholder Thinking: Theory, Responsibility and Engagement*, Sheffield: Greenleaf.

Barnard, C.I. (1938), *The Function of the Executive*, 30th anniversary edn 1968, Cambridge: Harvard University Press.

Bass, B.M. (1985), *Leadership and Performance Beyond Expectations*, New York: Free Press.

Bass, B.M. (1990), *Bass and Stogdill's Handbook of Leadership: Theory, Research and Managerial Application*, 3rd ed, New York: Free Press.

Bass, B.M. (1997), 'Does the transactional–transformational leadership paradigm transcend national boundaries?', *American Psychologist*, **52** (2), 130–39.

Burns, J.M. (1978), *Leadership*, New York: Harper & Row.

Carless, S.A. (1998), 'Gender differences in transformational leadership: an examination of superior, leader, and subordinate perspectives', *Sex Roles*, **39** (11–12), 887–902.

Chinese Culture Connection (1987), 'Chinese values and the search for culture-free dimensions of culture', *Journal of Cross-cultural Psychology*, **18** (2), 143–64.

Conger, J.A. (1989), *The Charismatic Leader: Behind the Mystique of Exceptional Leadership*, San Francisco: Jossey-Bass.

Den Hartog, D.N., R.J. House, P.J. Hanges, S.A. Ruiz-Quintanilla, P.W. Dorfman and 170 co-authors (1999), 'Culture specific and cross-culturally generalizable implicit leadership theories: are attributes of charismatic/transformational leadership universally endorsed?', *Leadership Quarterly*, **10** (2), 219–56.

Dickson, M.W., R.N. Aditya and J.S. Chhokar (2000), 'Definition and interpretation in cross-cultural organizational culture research: some pointers from the GLOBE research program', in N.M. Ashkanasy, C.P.M. Wilderom and M.F. Peterson (eds), *Handbook of Organizational Culture and Climate*, London, UK and Thousand Oaks, USA: Sage, pp. 447–64.

Dorfman, P.W. (2004), 'International and cross-cultural leadership research', in B.J. Punnett and O. Shenkar (eds), *Handbook for International Management Research*, 2nd edn, Ann Arbor: University of Michigan Press, pp. 256–355.

Dorfman, P.W. and J.P. Howell (1988), 'Dimensions of national culture and effective leadership patterns: Hofstede revisited', in R.N. Farmer, E.G. McGoun, R.B. Peterson and P. Marer (eds), *Advances in International Comparative Management*, vol. 3, Greenwich: JAI Press, pp. 127–50.

Drucker, P.F. (1992), *Managing for the Future: The 1990s and Beyond*, New York: Truman Talley/Dutton.

Druskat, V.U. (1994), 'Gender and leadership style: transformational and transactional leadership in the Roman Catholic Church', *Leadership Quarterly*, **5** (2), 99–119.

Eagly, A.H., M.C. Johannesen-Schmidt and M.L. van Engen (2003), 'Transformational, transactional, and laissez-faire leadership styles: a meta-analysis comparing women and men', *Psychological Bulletin*, **129** (4), 569–91.

Farmer, R.N. and B.R. Richman (1965), *Comparative Management and Economic Progress*, Homewood: Richard D. Irwin.

Ferrell, O.C., J.P. Fraedrich and L. Ferrell (2000), *Business Ethics: Ethical Decision Making and Cases*, 4th edn, Boston: Houghton Mifflin.

Fiol, C.M., D. Harris and R.J. House (1999), 'Charismatic leadership: strategies for effecting social change', *Leadership Quarterly*, **10** (3), 449–82.

Forte, A. (2004), 'Antecedents of managers' moral reasoning', *Journal of Business Ethics*, **51** (4), 313–47.

Habermas, J. (1984), *The Theory of Communicative Action: Reason and the Rationalization of Society*, vol. 1, trans. Thomas McCarthy (original text in German, 1st edn 1981), Boston: Beacon Press.

Harrison, L.E. and S.P. Huntington (eds) (2000), *Culture Matters: How Values Shape Human Progress*, New York: Basic Books.

Hofstede, G.H. (1980a), *Culture's Consequences: International Differences in Work-related Values*, London, UK and Newbury Park, USA: Sage.

Hofstede, G.H. (1980b), 'Motivation, leadership, and organization: do American theories apply abroad?', *Organizational Dynamics*, **9** (1), 42–63.

Hofstede, G.H. (1983), 'The cultural relativity of organizational practices and theories', *Journal of International Business Studies*, **14** (2), 75–90.

Hofstede, G.H. (1997), *Cultures and Organizations: Software of the Mind: Intercultural Cooperation and Its Importance for Survival*, rev. edn, London, UK and New York, USA: McGraw-Hill.

Hofstede, G.H. (2003), *Culture's Consequences, Comparing Values, Behaviors, Institutions and Organizations across Nations*, London, UK and Newbury Park, USA: Sage.

House, R.J., P.J. Hanges, M. Javidan and P.W. Dorfman (2004), *Leadership, Culture and Organizations: The Globe Study of 62 Societies*, London, UK and Thousand Oaks, USA: Sage.

House, R.J., P.J. Hanges, S.A. Ruiz-Quintanilla, P.W. Dorfman, M. Javidan, M. Dickson, V. Gupta and 170 co-authors (1999), 'Cultural Influences on leadership and organizations: project GLOBE', in W.H. Mobley, M.J. Gessner and V. Arnold (eds), *Advances in Global Leadership*, vol. 1, Stamford: JAI Press, pp. 171–233.

Kant, I. (1787), *Kritik der reinen Vernunft*, 2nd edn, trans. Paul Guyer and Allen W. Wood (eds) (1998), *Critique of Pure Reason*, New York: Cambridge University Press.

Kirkman, B.L., K.B. Lowe and C.B. Gibson (2000), 'Twenty Years of Culture's Consequences: A Review of the Empirical Research on Hofstede's Cultural Value Dimensions', working paper, University of North Carolina at Greensboro.

Kuhn, T. and J. Weibler (2003), 'Führungsethik: Notwendigkeit, Ansätze und Vorbedingungen ethikbewusster Mitarbeiterführung', *Die Unternehmung*, **57** (5), 375–92.

Lord, R.G. and K.J. Maher (1991), *Leadership and Information Processing: Linking Perceptions and Performance*, Boston: Unwin-Hyman.

Lorsch, J. and S.K. Graff (1997), 'Corporate governance', in A. Sorge and M. Warner (eds), *The IEBM Handbook of Organizational Behavior*, London: International Thomson Business Press, pp. 252–61.

Lowe, K.B., K.G. Kroeck and N. Sivasubramaniam (1996), 'Effectiveness correlates of transformational and transactional leadership: a meta-analytical review of the MLQ literature', *Leadership Quarterly*, **7** (3), 385–425.

Malik, F. (2002), *Die Neue Corporate Governance: Richtiges Top-Management, wirksame Unternehmensaufsicht*, 3rd enlarged edn, Frankfurt am Main: Frankfurter Allgemeine Buch.

Martínez, S.M. and P.W. Dorfman (1998), 'The Mexican entrepreneur: an ethnographic study of the Mexican empresario?', *International Studies of Management and Organizations*, **28** (2) 97–123.

Misumi, J. (1985), *The Behavioral Science of Leadership: An Interdisciplinary Japanese Research Program*, Ann Arbor: University of Michigan Press.

Newman, K.L. and S.D. Nollen (1996), 'Culture and congruence: the fit between management practices and national culture', *Journal of International Business Studies*, **27** (4), 753–79.

Phillips, M.E. (1994), 'Industry mindsets: exploring the cultures of two macro-organizational settings', *Organization Science*, **5** (3), 384–402.

Phillips, M.E. and S.A. Sackmann (2002), 'Managing in an era of multiple cultures: finding synergies instead of conflict', *The Graziadio Business Report*, vol. 5 (online journal). http://gbr.pepperdine.edu/024/multi-cultural.html (accessed 15 February 2005).

Pic, J.-J. (1995), *Europe's Diverse Corporate Boards – How they Differ from Each Other & The U.S.*, San Francisco, CA: Spencer Stuart Executive Search Consultants.

Robertson, C.J. and W.F. Crittenden (2003), 'Mapping moral philosophies: strategic implications for multinational firms', *Strategic Management Journal*, **24** (4), 385–92.

Sackmann, S.A. (1991), *Cultural Knowledge in Organizations: Exploring the Collective Mind*, Newbury Park: Sage Publications.

Sackmann, S.A. (1992), 'Cultures and subcultures: an analysis of organizational knowledge', *Administrative Science Quarterly*, **37** (1), 140–61.

Sackmann, S.A. (2002), *Unternehmenskultur: Erkennen, Entwickeln, Verändern*, Neuwied, Kriftel: Luchterhand.

Scandura, T.A., M.A. Von Glinow and K.B. Lowe (1999), 'When East meets West: leadership "best practices" in the United States and the Middle East', in W.H. Mobley, M.J. Gessner and V. Arnold (eds), *Advances in Global Leadership*, vol. 1, Stamford: JAI Press, pp. 235–48.

Schein, E.H. (1997), *Organizational Culture and Leadership*, 2nd rev. edn, San Francisco: Jossey-Bass.

Schilling, F. (2001), 'Mitbestimmung und Corporate Governance: Die deutsche Mitbestimmung auf dem Prüfstand', *Frankfurter Allgemeine Zeitung*, **25**, 26 November.

Schilling, F. (2002), 'Corporate Governance: Form oder Inhalt? Qualität der Corporate Governance als Investitionskriterium', *Frankfurter Allgemeine Zeitung*, 27 May, p. 25.

Schumacher, T. (1997), 'West Coast Camelot: the rise and fall of an organizational culture', in S.A. Sackmann (ed.), *Cultural Complexity in Organizations: Inherent Contrasts and Contradictions*, Thousand Oaks: Sage, pp. 107–32.

Shamir, B., R.J. House and M.B. Arthur (1993), 'The motivational effects of charismatic leadership: a self-concept based theory', *Organizational Science*, 4 (4), 577–95.

Smith, P.B. and M.F. Peterson (2002), 'Cross-cultural leadership', in M. J. Gannon and K. L. Newman (eds), *The Blackwell Handbook of Cross-Cultural Management*, Oxford, UK and Malden, USA: Blackwell, pp. 217–35.

Smith, P.B., S. Dugan and A. Trompenaars (1996), 'National cultures and values of organizational employees: a dimensional analysis across 43 nations', *Journal of Cross-cultural Psychology*, **27** (2), 231–64.

Tichy, N.M. and M.A. DeVanna (1997), *The Transformational Leader: The Key to Global Competitiveness*, 2nd edn, New York: John Wiley & Sons.

Treviño, L.K., L.P. Hartman and M. E. Brown (2000), 'Moral person and moral manager: how executives develop a reputation for ethical leadership', *California Management Review*, **42** (4), 128–42.

Trompenaars, A. (1993), *Riding the Waves of Culture: Understanding Cultural Diversity in Business*, London: Nicholas Brealey; 2nd rev. edn, with co-author C.M. Hampden-Turner (1998), *Riding the Waves of Culture: Understanding Cultural Diversity in Global Business*, New York: McGraw-Hill.

Watson, George W., Steven D. Papamarcos, Bruce T. Teague and Cindy Bean (2004), 'Exploring the dynamics of business values: a self-affirmation perspective', paper presented at the International Association for Business and Society (IABS) 2004 Annual Meeting, Jackson Hole, Wyoming, 3–7 March.

World Economic Forum (WEF) and The Prince of Wales International Business Leaders Forum (IBLF) (eds) (2002), *Global Corporate Citizenship: The Leadership Challenge for CEOs and Boards*, Geneva: WEF.www.weforum.org/pdf/GCCI/GCC_CEOstatement.pdf (15 February 2005).

Ybema, S.B. (1997), 'Telling tales: contrasts and commonalities within the organization of an amusement park: confronting and combining different perspectives', in S.A. Sackmann (ed.),

Cultural Complexity in Organizations: Inherent Contrasts and Contradictions, Thousand Oaks: Sage, pp. 160–86.

Yukl, G.A. (2002), *Leadership in Organizations*, 5th edn, Upper Saddle River: Prentice-Hall.

Zander, L. (1997), 'The license to lead: an 18 country study of the relationship between employees' preferences regarding interpersonal leadership and national culture', unpublished doctoral dissertation, Institute for International Business, Stockholm School of Economics, Sweden.

Zimbardo, P.G. (1972), 'The pathology of imprisonment', *Society*, **9** (6), 4–8, reprinted in J.M. Henslin (ed.) (2001), *Down to Earth Sociology*, 11th edn, New York: Free Press, pp. 272–7.

Zimmerman, M. J. (1996), *The Concept of Moral Obligation*, London: Cambridge University Press.

17 Comparative models of corporate governance: a sociocultural perspective

Andre A. Pekerti

Introduction

Two relevant questions that scholars in the area of corporate governance have posed are whether there is, and whether it is appropriate for firms to utilize, a universal corporate governance system. It is of interest that the two questions posed above actually suggest that there may be significant variations in the way corporations are governed across nations.

This chapter discusses different models of corporate governance that exist in business, and how culture has significantly constructed these governance systems by outlining how culture influences economic systems and ownership structures. The chapter highlights the area of managerial assessment to discuss the possible biases that may arise when firms adopt a universal corporate governance system. In particular, the chapter discusses how ownership structures and various corporate governance systems may influence the way corporate boards (firms) evaluate their managers. It illustrates how corporate governance practices are affected by macro cultures by providing an example from the field of social psychology and leadership studies. The example highlights how biases may disadvantage managers when factors in the environment are not accounted for during performance evaluation. The chapter concludes with a number of simple yet practical recommendations that can be applied to alleviate some of the biases that corporate governance boards may have during performance evaluation.

Corporate governance as a socially constructed concept

In recent years there has been a wealth of studies on corporate governance; however most have focused on the principal–agent paradigm. The literature also indicates that only a modest amount of systematic research has been done on the determinants of international differences in corporate governance (Gedajlovic and Shapiro, 1998; Groot, 1998; Pedersen and Thomsen, 1999). This chapter endeavors to contribute to the literature concerning the origins of variation in corporate governance from a sociocultural perspective, as well as the impact of these cultural differences on corporate governance practices. It aims to do so by adopting a business systems perspective and conceptually illustrating variations in corporate governance structures that stem from societal and cultural variables. Therefore the underlying premise of this chapter is that business systems are socially constructed; thus society constructs distinctive economic systems in which business systems and management practice are developed (Berger and Luckman, 1966; Bhagat *et al.*, 1990; Roe, 1993; Whitley, 1992b). The chapter also focuses on corporate ownership as a variable that causes variations in corporate governance practices.

The second goal of the chapter is to identify the linkages between societal variables such as cultural values and institutions and their impact on corporate governance. Thus it integrates social cognition into the equation of corporate governance to draw attention to the fact that information processing plays a significant part in the corporate governance process in international business. This information-processing view naturally poses the question of whether it is valid to have a ubiquitous model of corporate governance, or whether the context must be fundamentally incorporated into corporate governance structure. Although the chapter will not alleviate the lack of empirical research on the topic, as identified by several authors (Buhner *et al.*, 1998; Gedajlovic and Shapiro, 1998; Groot, 1998; Pedersen and Thomsen, 1999), it will provide some foundation on which future empirical research may be undertaken.

Comparative models of corporate governance

A number of authors have conceptualized corporate governance as the system by which companies are directed and controlled with the aim of ensuring sustained growth of the company, in addition to being accountable to shareholders and stakeholders (Charkham, 1992, 1995; Kuada and Gullestrup, 1998; Pedersen and Thomsen, 1999). It is important to note that the above conceptualization of corporate governance shared by a number of authors is virtually the same as Whitley's (1992a, 1994) view on the way business systems function and govern in various societies. Other authors have also agreed that the means of control by which companies govern may come from a number of sources, such as indirect and direct influences of financial markets, government, culture and ownership structure, which in turn leads to differences in corporate governance structures across countries (Buhner *et al.*, 1998; Charkham, 1992; Demirag, 1998; Lashgari, 2003; Li, 1994).

Theorists have further claimed that business systems also reflect the structures of a given society or are even 'isomorphic' to each other (Clegg and Redding, 1990; Orru *et al.*, 1997). It can be argued, therefore, that contextual variables such as key social institutions within nations and states, are important determinants of economic systems and corporate governance structures. The influence of key institutions has been documented by Roe

(1993), who argued that differences in corporate structure among countries are substantial, such that German and Japanese structures would be illegal in the United States. Moreover, existing corporate theories, which focus on economic factors and do not consider political forces, cannot adequately explain the differences.

In other words, there are factors apart from financial economy that explain differences in economic systems, namely, different histories, economic developments and cultures.

The key points of the business systems framework proposed by Whitley (1992a, 1994) are that national business systems differ as a function of key social institutions such as government regulations, financial systems and culture. It follows that the more differentiated the key social institutions, the greater the variations found in the business systems, and the greater tendency of each system to develop its own business structures in conducting business. In essence, this framework views culture as the foundation on which accepted rules of appropriate managerial behavior are built. Thus the cultural divide between nations, industries and companies can explain the diversities in corporate governance structures and processes in different countries.

International studies in corporate governance indicate that countries do differ significantly with regard to the institutional environment that corporate governance exists in, which in turn directly affects the structure of corporate ownership and corporate boards (Fukao, 1995; Charkham, 1995; Roe, 1993). This chapter also identifies corporate ownership as a variable that can significantly contribute to international differences in corporate governance. It acknowledges that, by focusing only on ownership structure, it runs the risk of oversimplifying the complexities that are associated with corporate governance systems in a global context. However it chooses to do so for two reasons. One is simply the fact that ownership is measurable (Demirag, 1998; Gedajlovic and Shapiro, 1998; Kuada and Gullestrup, 1998; Li, 1994; Pedersen and Thomsen, 1997, 1999). Second, the literature has extensively documented the fact that ownership, coupled with sociocultural forces, is a significant factor that determines corporate governance structures and practices in different nations (Demirag, 1998; Gedajlovic and Shapiro, 1998; Hamilton and Biggart, 1988; Kuada and Gullestrup, 1998; Li, 1994; Pedersen and Thomsen, 1999; Roe, 1993; Whitley, 1992a).

Culture and ownership structure as determinants of international differences in corporate governance

The fact that institutions reflect the underlying values of a society implies that corporate ownership preferences might also be a by-product of values of a particular culture. In some countries political institutions favor direct state ownership and corporate control as a way to ensure equitable distribution of wealth. In contrast, other nations encourage private ownership. To some extent, members of these nations perpetuate these differences because, in societies where private ownership of wealth is dominant, financial systems are designed to develop growth of this private wealth (Kuada and Gullestrup, 1998).

The literature indicates that there are two general categories of corporate governance system that characterize control and ownership structure. One is generally used to describe the system in the United States (USA) and the United Kingdom (UK), which is characterized by a dispersed ownership structure. The second is generally used to describe systems in East Asia, South East Asia, Continental Europe and Japan, and is characterized by concentrated ownership (Fukao, 1995; Groot, 1998; Orru *et al.*, 1997; Pedersen and Thomsen, 1997; Wilkinson, 1996). In general, the UK and USA have a dispersed market-oriented ownership structure, and have been described as 'outsider' corporate governance structures. In contrast, many Continental European nations, such as Germany, and East and South East Asian nations, such as Japan, South Korea and Indonesia, have a concentrated network-oriented ownership structure. Hence they have been described as 'insider' corporate governance structures (Buhner *et al.* 1998; Kuada and Gullestrup, 1998; Lashgari, 2003; Li, 1994; Pedersen and Thomsen, 1999; Pekerti, 2003; Whitley, 1992a, 1994).

The insider–outsider corporate governance distinction as a function of culture and ownership structure

The term 'insider–outsider' corporate boards is used to differentiate between corporate boards, which consist of board members that are also managers in the firm and those who are not, respectively (Demirag, 1998; Li, 1994). This implies that in many Continental European nations and East and South East Asian nations numerous corporate boards consist of board members that are also managers in the firm, as well as board members who are shareholders. Studies have also observed that in some Nordic European nations, East and South East Asian countries the firms are family-owned; thus one person or a family owns a (voting) majority of the company (Pedersen and Thomsen, 1997).

The sociocultural literature supports the above conclusion and indicates that East and South East Asian business systems and firms are very much a by-product of the values that are salient in these societies. Wilkinson (1996, p. 430) describes the East and South East Asian business systems as 'embedded in networks of institutionalized relationships'. He further elaborates and categorizes East Asian businesses as having an institutionalized ascription to a centralized consensual decision-making structure. Other authors such as Hamilton and Biggart (1988), Hamilton *et al.* (1990), as well as Whitley

(1991, 1994) express the same view. For example, Japan can be described as possessing a communitarian management practice, Korea as patrimonial, Taiwan as patrilineal, with Taiwan and Hong Kong having an economic familism management practice (Biggart, 1990; Hamilton and Cheng-Shu, 1990; Whitley, 1991, 1994), the point being that the management practices ascribed by East Asian businesses reflect the structures of these societies (Whitley, 1990), thus substantiating Clegg and Redding's (1990) claim that society and business cultures are essentially isomorphic.

Other studies also suggest that the institutionalized ascription to a centralized consensual decision making structure in East and South East Asia is due to the combination of values ascribed by people in these societies, namely, the complementary by-product of Confucian philosophy as well as collectivist and high-power distance orientation (Smith and Bond, 1994; Triandis *et al.*, 1993). In other words, these values contribute to developing and complementing the paternalistic business culture, as well as the network-oriented ownership structure found in East and South East Asia, the relevant issue being that the variations in corporate governance due to cultural factors affect the way in which corporate governance operates in each respective nation.

Implications of ownership structures for corporate governance control
A number of studies have also shown that regulations of financial institutions dictate whether countries such as the USA implement a market-based system that results in a dispersed ownership structure, while countries such as Germany and Japan adopt a bank-based system that results in a concentrated ownership structure (Roe, 1990, 1993). Li (1994) found that ownership structure is a significant element that influences corporate governance. Specifically firms that have concentrated ownership also tend to have smaller percentages of outside directors. Li suggested that that agency theory is useful in explaining differences in corporate governance under this institutional arrangement. In other words, in concentrated ownership situations large shareholders take a leadership role in monitoring management, as well as reducing the risk involved with managerial discretion.

It can be argued that Li's (1994) findings are consistent with one of the premises underlying agency theory; that is, the only legitimate stakeholders in firms are shareholders. It also supports the view that the primary aim of corporate governance is one of ensuring a return for investors and protecting the shareholder's interest (Demirag, 1998). The smaller percentages of outside directors found in a concentrated ownership structure, therefore, imply that large shareholders are looking after their own interest and investment. This instrumental view of corporate governance of course stems from the belief that managers may take actions that hurt shareholders (Tirole, 1999; Walsh and Seward, 1990). Again agency theory suggests that the smaller percentage of outside directors in concentrated ownership is logical since it serves the dual purpose of reducing the agency cost and potential conflict between shareholders and managers (Demirag, 1998).

Managerial discretion and control
Other studies have further fueled the notion that the participation of large shareholders in both the board and management is significant as regards the company's financial performance. Specifically discretion and control of firms by non-shareholders have been found to lower company's profits (Gedajlovic and Shapiro, 1998). Gedajlovic and Shapiro (ibid., p. 535) have gone as far as to summarize: 'where managerial discretion is present, firm profitability will be reduced'. This chapter therefore argues that it makes sense for firms to have an insider corporate board and concentrated ownership structure where the legal institutions allow it, since it reduces agency costs and potential conflict between shareholders and managers.

Other authors have suggested that this is the main reason why banks play a critical (insider) role in Germany and Japan, where they act as both investors and debt-holders (Buhner *et al.*, 1998; Demirag, 1998; Lashgari, 2003; Li, 1994). Effectively this allows the banks to have the comparative advantage of being able to obtain inside information about the firm.

Another inherent advantage for firms that use a concentrated, insider corporate structure is the fact that it can evaluate the firm's performance from a 'long-term' perspective. In other words, the fact that the bank (financier) and boards have good knowledge of the business (for example, its current and future strategy) helps to provide cheaper and safer capital for the business (Demirag, 1998; Shleifer and Vishny, 1986). Li (1994) has also documented that, in non-market systems where concentrated ownership is the norm, members of boards who are shareholders effectively have access to a considerable amount of privileged information. Again it is logical that knowledge of certain privileged information, such as current and future strategy, gives the boards the capability to review the firm's situation and performance from a *long-term* perspective. Thus, directors should be in a position to incorporate internal factors affecting the firm into their decisions (Demirag *et al.*, 1994; Demsetz and Lehn, 1985; Shleifer and Vishny, 1986). Demirag (1998) further suggests that a concentrated ownership is also advantageous for shareholders in that it can yield better returns, because it is a powerful constraint on managerial discretion.

It is of interest to note that the long-term perspective associated with concentrated ownership stems from the fact that the board embraces the goal of corporate wealth maximization as opposed to pure shareholder wealth maximization (Demirag, 1998; Demsetz and Lehn, 1985; Kuada and Gullestrup, 1998; Tirole, 1999). This is relevant to the discussion since it further suggests that, apart from structural variations between the concentrated and dispersed corporate ownership system, there is also an implicit difference in the managerial goals of the two systems. Specifically, in a dispersed ownership system where managers have discretion, their goal is to ensure the well-being of the firm: that is, ensuring that it grows and survives, which in turn safeguards the managers' jobs (Gedajlovic and Shapiro, 1998; Shleifer and Vishny, 1986). In contrast, in concentrated ownership systems, managers endeavor both to ensure the wellbeing of the firm and to maximize profits for shareholders, because the managers themselves are also shareholders. This explains why some authors have argued and documented that, in the USA, where diffused ownership is practiced, managers are partly motivated by the risk of losing their jobs, while in countries like Japan and Continental Europe, where concentrated ownership is practiced, managers view their positions as relatively stable (Tirole, 1999; Charkham, 1992; Monks and Nell, 1996).

Evaluation of management by corporate boards
One obvious conclusion that can be derived from the discussion above is that firm value maximization (long-termism) and shareholder value maximization (short-termism) are not always consistent objectives (Demirag, 1998; Demsetz and Lehn, 1985; Gedajlovic and Shapiro, 1998; Li, 1994; Tirole, 1999; Walsh and Seward, 1990). Therefore the literature suggests that there has been no set and established universal way to measure firm performance by international corporate boards. To complicate matters further, Monks and Nell (1996) argue that some failures in large companies can be partly attributed to the failure of their corporate governance structure.

The fact that there are implicit variations in managerial goals between the concentrated and dispersed ownership system indicates that there may also be differences in the way that corporate boards evaluate firm performance in various systems. Buhner and colleagues (1998), Charkham (1992) and Lashgari (2003) agree that significant differences in corporate governance practices that have been influenced by nations and cultures also imply differences in competitive outcomes depending on the nation where the firms are located. For example, Demirag (1998) believes that firm performance is very much linked to the way financial systems are structured in particular nations. In financial environments where there is great need to have high levels of current profits, short-termism may be the mode of operation. In other words, firms accept projects with either 'an excessive discount rate and/or a foreshortened time horizon' (ibid., p. 7).

This chapter argues that the relevant issue for international corporate governance is that short-term pressures tend to stem from within the firm; therefore evaluators (that is, corporate boards) will also have biases stemming from these internal firm goals (Demirag, 1998; Marsh, 1990). Other studies indicate that there are also other biases associated with short-termism and long-termism. Demirag and colleagues (1994) as well as Ittner and Larcker (1997) suggested that companies that rely too much on a financial control system have a tendency to emphasize short-term financial objectives. Furthermore it is believed that short-termism is practiced at the expense of reduced future investments, while long-termism considers future investments to be part of the firm's objectives (Demirag *et al.*, 1994; Demirag, 1998; Kuada and Gullestrup, 1998).

The obvious concern for corporate boards when evaluating a firm's performance is that they are under constant pressure to ensure that their companies are performing optimally in the stock market. Thus corporate boards are accountable and have to take action when their firms are performing poorly. In many cases, corporate boards attempt to determine the source of the firm's suboptimal performance, and in many situations implicitly assume that it is directly related to the actions of managers: suboptimal performance is blamed on management (Walsh and Seward, 1990).

This chapter argues that corporate boards cannot simply assume that suboptimal performance is directly related to the actions of managers. Tirole (1999) in fact argues that that there is a false assumption that management has formal control, when in essence it has not. Management often has to refer to higher authorities in its decision-making process. This chapter asserts that corporate boards must ask the question of whether the situation and environment caused the suboptimal performance, the rationale being that attributional processes are situationally bound (Dasborough and Ashkanasy, 2002).

Sternberg and Vroom (2002) suggests that, when evaluating people in a leadership position, we should also take account of the situations in a way that acknowledges the dimensions on which situations vary. Therefore, in measuring performance, we have to take account of both persons and situations. The problem, however, as Walsh and Seward (1990) pointed out, is that in many cases the board of directors simply do not have enough information to conduct a fair and accurate assessment. This chapter, therefore, also asserts that the lack of information to conduct a fair and accurate assessment may be an inherent limitation that exists in a dispersed corporate governance system, especially one that operates in the short-term mode.

Culture, ownership and performance evaluation

In theory it has been suggested that a good corporate governance structure should be one that is able to select the best managers and those who are then accountable to shareholders; and, in turn, the boards should then consider social interest in their actions (Cutting and Kouzmin, 2000; Tirole, 1999). It has been argued, therefore, that in general decisions made by a corporate board should also reflect the sociocultural environments where the firms exist (Biggart and Hamilton, 1987). The previous section highlighted the fact that performance criteria which corporate boards use to evaluate firm performance may differ according to the financial system and ownership structure in which firms operate. This chapter argues that evaluation of firm performance by corporate boards may also be influenced by cognitive and cultural biases associated with the ownership structure. Moreover it argues that there is indirect evidence to show that corporate boards evaluate firm performance on the basis of their sociocultural environments.

In general theorists working in the area of corporate governance suggest that managers should be rewarded as a function of the measurement variables that are within their control and/or that their behavior can affect (Buhner *et al.*, 1998; Charkham, 1992; Demirag, 1998; Lashgari, 2003; Tirole, 1999). Therefore performance measurement must be a flexible and changing concept that takes account of the context. Monks and Nell (1996) have advocated that someone other than management, that is, the board of directors, should also set the standard of performance. This chapter argues that, in many cases, especially in a dispersed ownership system, boards of directors do not have enough information to conduct a fair and accurate assessment of management's actions. Indirect evidence suggests that this problem may be limited to corporate boards that operate in a dispersed ownership system, that is, an outsider corporate board structure.

This chapter asserts that corporate governance systems which operate under a dispersed ownership structure may be subject to short-term mode biases that can lead to inaccurate performance evaluations. In contrast, in concentrated ownership situations where there are smaller percentages of outside directors, the boards are in effect also evaluating themselves as managers and thus are more likely to have a longer-term perspective. For example, in concentrated ownership systems shareholders play a direct and major part in corporate governance. Studies suggest that in many situations a self-evaluation process may prove to be more advantageous for management, as well as the corporate boards.

It is this chapter's observation that theorists have categorized nations which operate on the dispersed corporate ownership structure as operating on the short-term financial system (for example, the UK and USA), while nations that operate on the concentrated corporate ownership structure have been described as operating under a long-term financial system (for example, Japan; East Asia and South East Asia: Demirag, 1998; Demirag *et al.*, 1994; Ittner and Larcker, 1997; Kuada and Gullestrup, 1998; Marsh, 1990). The relevant point is that corporate boards that operate in a dispersed ownership system appear to be the ones that are most likely to have a short-term bias, while corporate boards that operate in a concentrated ownership system are most likely to have a long-term perspective. This claim is consistent with cultural studies which indicate that nations such as Japan, East Asia and South East Asia, where concentrated ownership is practiced, are most likely to have a long-term perspective, since members of these nations tend to favor long-term orientation (Hofstede, 1991; Kuada and Gullestrup, 1998; Whitley, 1990, 1994).

Monks and Nell (1996) noted that directors could never know as much about the operation as management and people who are in day-to-day charge of the firms. Therefore boards of directors are dependent on being supplied with necessary, accurate and timely information by management. Despite the view that management may not be fully in control of firm performance, Tirole (1999) believes that in many cases managers possess accurate and necessary information to make fundamental decisions concerning the firm, the relevant issue being that corporate boards in concentrated ownership systems have more information that in turn might lead to a more accurate evaluation of a company's performance.

Role of information in the evaluation process

Kuada and Gullestrup's (1998) work suggests that culture does affect organizational members in a corporate governance system. This chapter argues that corporate governance practices are influenced by culture at the 'macro culture' level.

Research in the area of leadership attribution indicates that the way people generate explanations for events and people's behavior can vary with the information that people have at the time (Lee and Hallahan, 2001; Lee and Tiedens, 2001; Lord *et al.*, 1999; Pekerti, in press). Research findings in attribution processes are relevant for corporate governance since the way in which corporate boards attribute performance has consequences for workers and managers in the company. For example, if a board decides to attribute suboptimal performance of a firm to management's actions as opposed to other factors (such as a downturn in the economy), this will affect the board's future decisions concerning the firm and/or management (for example, management will be held accountable).

Errors and biases due to lack of information

One of the most basic and pervasive tendencies uncovered by attribution research has been referred to as the 'fundamental attribution error' (Ross, 1977); that is, the tendency for perceivers not to take account of situational factors, thus overattributing causality to internal factors in the actor.[1] The error lies in the perception that the actor's actions are the foremost causal factor when the situation is, in fact, as much a contributing factor.

Another source of error that has been found in the attribution process is the actor–observer bias. Jones and Nisbett (1971) suggested that actors and observers are attuned to different sets of information that in turn lead to differences in causal attribution. Actors were described as having a propensity to overattribute causes to situational factors, while observers have a tendency to overattribute the same actions to dispositional factors. For example, an actor bias suggests that, when a firm underperforms, management will attribute this sub optimal performance to causes in the environment. In contrast, the corporate board, which is the observer evaluating management, will attribute this suboptimal performance to a lack of ability and/or effort on the part of management (observer bias).

Another bias that may affect the performance evaluation process is the self-serving bias, that is, the tendency for people to take more credit for their successes and blaming failure on other people or circumstances. For example, when a firm performs well, management will attribute this success internally, that is, as directly due to the actions of management. In contrast, when the firm underperforms, management will attribute this to external factors, such as poor economic conditions.

What the above discussion clearly indicates is that, when there is deficiency in information, coupled with our natural cognitive limitations and biases, the process of assigning causality to events is a less than optimal process. This chapter argues that all of the above biases that plague the cognitive process of evaluators during performance evaluation may also plague corporate boards when they are attempting to determine the source of the firm's optimal or suboptimal performance (Walsh and Seward, 1990).

Culture's influence on the corporate governance evaluation process
Of particular interest to this chapter's argument concerning ownership structure and its effect on corporate board evaluation is the self-serving bias and actor–observer bias, especially on boards that have high percentages of board members who are also managers in the firm. The work of Martinko and Douglas (1999), as well as Lord and colleagues (1999), suggested that leaders (at least in Western cultures) are prone to self-serving biases during performance evaluation processes. At the same time these authors have suggested that the way in which people perceive themselves may also affect their attributions (Lord *et al.*, 1999; Martinko and Douglas, 1999).

Differences in causal attributions have been explained with reference to the attention paid to particular types of information. For example, Morris and Peng (1994) found that writers and editors of American newspapers tended to make more internal attributions to social events and crimes. In contrast,

Chinese writers and editors provide more situational explanations for similar social events and crimes. Other studies have confirmed Morris and Peng's findings and provide other explanations for the way cultures affect information processing. Pekerti (2001) found that there were significant differences in culturally based communication styles between people from low- and high-context cultures.[2] It was suggested that variations in communication styles may be explained with reference to people's self-concept and preference for certain types of information. Specifically members of low-context cultures are socialized to be independent, and thus have a propensity to attune themselves to self-referent and task-relevant information. This in turn biases them to make internal types of attributions. In contrast, members of high-context cultures are socialized to be interdependent. As a result, they have a propensity to attune themselves to situational relevant information and this, in turn, biases them to make external types of attributions, one of the rationales being that their interdependent self-concept predisposes them to take account of the situational factors to ensure in-group harmony.

The relevance of the above studies to this chapter's discussion is that cultures described by Hall (1976) as being low- and high-context are very similar to the individualistic–collectivistic cultures described by Hofstede (1980): see (Gudykunst *et al.*, 1988). Moreover cultures that are described as being individualistic and low-context are also the ones that are more likely to operate under the dispersed, corporate ownership structure, such as the UK and USA, while cultures that are described as being collectivistic and high-context are the ones likely to operate under the concentrated ownership structure, such as Japan, East Asia and South East Asia (Demirag, 1998; Demirag *et al.*, 1994; Ittner and Larcker, 1997; Kuada and Gullestrup, 1998; Marsh, 1990). In other words, it is possible that corporate boards that operate under the dispersed ownership structure are prone not to take account of situational information. In contrast, because corporate boards in concentrated ownership structures have a large percentage of their members who are also part of the management team, they are more likely to take account of situational information since they act as both *actor* and *observer*. More importantly they are less likely to attribute a company's suboptimal performance to direct actions by management because they are partially evaluating their own performance.

Implications concerning board of directors under the insider and outsider corporate governance structure
In the context of firm performance evaluation by corporate boards, it is this chapter's contention that insider corporate boards are effectively also conducting a self-evaluation process. Stated in another way, in concentrated ownership corporate governance systems where there are large percentages

of corporate board members who are also managers in the firm, the board of directors are in essence conducting an evaluation of their own performance as managers. Consequently these boards of directors (as actors) are also more likely to take account of situational factors and less likely to attribute a company's suboptimal performance to direct actions by management.

Research in the area of leadership attributions, for example, indicates that attribution errors are reduced when evaluators know more about people they are to evaluate (Jones and Nisbett, 1971). There is also supporting evidence to suggest that closer monitoring of workers by their managers has increased external attributions. In the same way, this chapter suggests that corporate board members who are also managers (actors being observed) would tend to be self-serving, attuned to the environment and more likely to make external attributions for suboptimal performances of their firm.

This chapter also asserts that, along with the advantage of being able to conduct a self-evaluation process, corporate boards that operate under an insider corporate governance structure also have an advantage in that they have access to privileged information that outsider boards do not. In other words, insider corporate boards would have access to both internal and external information that reduces the likelihood of their making a fundamental attribution error. Furthermore they are also more likely to be able to make an accurate assessment of the company's performance because they have information concerning current and future strategy. In essence, corporate boards that operate under the insider corporate governance structure should take into account the range of internal factors of the firm, as well as the dimensions on which situations vary.

The major implication for corporate boards that operate in a dispersed market-oriented ownership structure and under an outsider corporate governance structure is that they may perform evaluations without adequate information (Monks and Nell, 1996; Tirole, 1999). In this case, there is a strong possibility that, when corporate boards are attempting to determine the source of the firm's optimal or suboptimal performance they may be prone to biases and make observer attributional errors; in turn, this may disadvantage management.

Despite the apparent additional information that is available for corporate boards in concentrated ownership structures, it is this chapter's contention that it may also be prone to other cognitive biases that can lead to suboptimal results for the firm. This chapter asserts that, in concentrated ownership structures where a high percentage of insider corporate board members are present, there is the potential for a hegemonic mind-set to exist. The risk of these types of limitations existing is high; for example, cognitive overload is likely to occur when the CEO and chairman of the board are the same person. In the same manner a social phenomenon, such as groupthink, is also likely to occur when there are high percentages of board members who are also managers in the firm (Cutting and Kouzmin, 2000). Likewise Tirole (1999), for example, has also observed that undivided control generally creates biased decision making.

Practical suggestions to reduce cultural and cognitive biases during performance evaluations

Cutting and Kouzmin (2000) suggest that one of the ways to ensure accuracy during performance evaluation by corporate boards is to include solutions to avoid cognitive errors in corporate governance structures (for example, devil's advocate role). This chapter argues that, again, works in the area of leadership are useful. For example, the work of Martinko and Douglas (1999) suggests that attributional training might be a valuable intervention to reduce attributional biases. In brief, attributional training involves making people aware of their own potential biases and how these can affect attribution processes.

Another bias this chapter has discussed that occurs during performance evaluation is caused by deficiency in information. It is of interest that Lee and Tiedens (2000) found attributional biases not only to be caused by lack of external information, but also to be due to people's lack of sensitivity and attention to situational information. This chapter asserts that that sensitivity to situational information can be increased through training and other interventions such as utilizing disconfirmatory strategies. Disconfirmatory strategies include evaluators being open to information that disconfirm expectations and should, therefore, include alternative sources of information. Causal explanations of performance from individuals who are being evaluated from the worker's perspective may also function as an alternative source of information in the evaluation process. Another simple but useful disconfirmatory strategy is to ask a colleague with no stake to examine the existing information and conduct the evaluation (Feldman, 1981). Eminent leadership scholars actually suggest that leaders should always consult with others if possible, since this is one of the ways that leaders can be informed about stakeholders' interests (Sternberg and Vroom, 2002).

Interestingly a commitment to being accurate and rigorous during decision making has been shown to reduce cognitive biases that occur during performance evaluation. The work of Kunda (1990) suggests that specific informational prompting can influence both behaviors and subsequent attributions. For example, Kunda found that subjects are less prone to making judgments based on internal factors when they are motivated to be accurate. Therefore prompts that remind evaluators to be accurate may reduce the occurrence of fundamental attribution error, or at least result in people taking account of situational conditions, which in turn may lead to evaluations that are more accurate.

As Jones and Nisbett (1971) found, attribution errors are reduced when evaluators know more about people they are to assess or when they decrease their 'psychological distance'. Therefore this chapter recommends that corporate boards serve shareholders and management well by becoming more familiar with management activities. This, in turn, may provide corporate boards with both an observer and a pseudo-actor perspective. In other words, Jones and Nisbett suggest that, when people make an attribution concerning behaviors of a familiar person, a similar process is activated to that used in a self-attribution process. Therefore, as an actor, one would be attuned to the environment and external information, which in turn would reduce fundamental attribution errors.

In general this chapter argues that attributional training, as well as a commitment to accuracy and rigor during performance evaluation, would be useful for all corporate boards regardless of culture and/or ownership structure. However, as Cutting and Kouzmin (2000) suggest, utilizing a disconfirmatory strategy and asking a third party to take on the role of devil's advocate may be most beneficial for corporate boards with a high percentage of board members who are also managers in the firm. In contrast, decreasing the psychological distance between corporate boards and management may be most beneficial for corporate boards operating under the dispersed ownership structure. In other words, familiarity with management and their activities may result in the board of directors taking account of both internal and situational conditions.

Conclusions and implications for future research
This chapter acknowledges that it comprises very much a theoretical discussion; therefore one major direction for the future in corporate governance research is empirical and multicultural validation of the assertions made in the chapter.

Future research directions
One major assertion discussed was the idea that corporate boards are cognitively biased according to their cultural environment. Specifically, corporate boards that operate in a low-context culture are more likely to make fundamental attribution errors when they evaluate management performance. In contrast, corporate boards that operate in a high-context culture are less likely to make fundamental attribution errors when they evaluate management performance. Apart from testing the validity of these propositions cross-culturally, there are also a number of possible research avenues associated with the above propositions.

First, it would be fascinating to test these propositions. Second, it would be of interest to test whether or not having corporate boards who are also managers in the firm (insider corporate boards) affect the board's evaluation of a firm's optimal and suboptimal performance. Third, it would be fascinating to vary the type and amount of information to which insider corporate boards can gain access, and how it affects the board's evaluation of a firm's optimal and suboptimal performance. Finally, it would also be useful to investigate whether corporate boards within concentrated ownership structures have a higher risk of suffering cognitive overload and/or are more vulnerable to social phenomena, such as, groupthink.

This chapter contends that the future directions for corporate governance research suggested above can make significant contributions to the field. Testing the propositions contained in this chapter within and across cultures as well as across populations may also provide corporate governance scholars and corporate boards with further insights concerning variables that may cause performance evaluation in various situations.

Summary

To summarize, this chapter has discussed different models of corporate governance that exist in business. The discussion suggests that, as socially constructed entities, business systems and corporations are subject to cultural, cognitive and political biases. The discussion has therefore, partially answered both questions posed at the beginning of the chapter. That is, there is evidence to suggest that there is no universal corporate governance system in international business. Furthermore the fact that the differences go beyond national boundaries distinction, and actually affect how people process information indicates that adopting a universal corporate governance system may be inappropriate.

The discussion highlighted the fact that corporate boards may be biased towards attributing the cause of suboptimal performance of their firms to the direct actions of management, when other factors may have contributed equally to such outcomes. It suggested that the error of not taking account of situational information might be more prevalent in low-context cultures and nations, as well as those that operate under the dispersed corporate ownership structure. In contrast, in high-context cultures, those that operate under the concentrated ownership structure are less prone to these errors, thanks to their interdependent self-concept and the fact that there are large percentages of corporate board members who are also managers in the firm. Therefore they are cognitively able to take on the roles of both actors and observers, which in turn attune them both to internal and to external information concerning the firm and environment, respectively.

There is also evidence that preferences for different types of corporate ownership structures are influenced by strong cultural values. For example, the concentrated ownership structure found in East Asian and South East Asian cultures may be attributed to the values that are salient in these societies, such as long-term network relationships (Hamilton and Biggart, 1988; Hamilton *et al.*, 1990; Whitley, 1991, 1994). Likewise the cognitive biases found in different cultures has been linked to differences in the way cultural members perceive themselves, which in turn predisposes them to be more attuned to certain types of information (Pekerti, 2001). The relevant point is that harmonizing or adopting a universal corporate governance system may not fit the cognitive preference, as well as culturally based preferences for ownership structures. Moreover the fact that financial institutions dictate whether countries implement a market-based system that results in a dispersed ownership structure or adopt a bank-based system that results in a concentrated ownership structure suggests these institutions will not accommodate a universal corporate governance system (Roe, 1990, 1993).

In closing, this chapter contends that the belief systems and cultural differences that have given rise to a concentrated ownership structure and dispersed ownership structure are still prevalent. For example, Demirag (1998) observed that, despite globalization, in Japan movement towards market corporate control is slow to non-existent, thus suggesting that the non-market structure of corporate governance will continue to exist. Therefore, adopting a universal corporate governance system in international business is inappropriate. Whitley (1992a) effectively made a similar argument, that business systems are different in different contexts; therefore 'recipes' for business success which are effective in one nation or region will not be successful in another region or over time.

In general, the consensus among theorists is that there are too many variables to consider in corporate governance to adopt a ubiquitous or harmonized approach to corporate governance. Many also agree that we should not have just one corporate governance system (Buhner *et al.*, 1998; Charkham, 1992; Demirag, 1998; Lashgari, 2003; Tirole, 1999).

Notes
1. Internal and/or dispositional factors are those perceived as coming from a person's character and/or temperament, while situational factors are factors perceived as coming from outside a person's character and/or temperament, for example the environment.
2. Low context: societies where people tend to have many connections of shorter duration or for specific reason. High context: societies or groups where people have close connections over a long period of time.

References
Berger, L.P. and T. Luckman, T. (1966), *The Social Construction of Reality*, New York: Anchor Books.
Bhagat, R.S., B.L. Kedia, S.E. Crawford and M.R. Kaplan (1990), 'Cross-cultural issues in organizational psychology: emergent trends and directions in the 1990s', in C.L. Cooper

and I.T. Robertson (eds), *International Review of Industrial and Organizational Psychology*, vol. 5, New York: Wiley, pp. 59–99.

Biggart, N.W. (1990), 'Institutionalized patrimonialism in Korean business', *Comparative Social Research*, **12**, 113–33.

Biggart, N.W. and G.G. Hamilton (1987), 'An institutional theory of leadership', *The Journal of Applied Behavioral Science*, **23**(4), 429–41.

Buhner, R., A. Rasheed, J. Rosenstein and T. Yoshikawa, T. (1998), 'Research on corporate governance: a comparison of Germany, Japan and United States', *Advances in International Comparative Management*, **12**, 121–55.

Charkham, J.P. (1992), 'Corporate governance: lessons from abroad', *European Business Journal*, **4**(2), 8–16.

Charkham, J.P. (1995), *Keeping Good Company: A Study of Corporate Governance in Five Countries*, Oxford: Oxford University Press.

Clegg, S.R. and G.S. Redding (1990), 'Introduction', in S.R. Clegg, G.S. Redding and M. Cartner (eds), *Capitalism in Contrasting Cultures*, New York: Walter de Gruyter, pp. 1–28.

Cutting, B. and A. Kouzmin (2000), 'The emerging patterns of power in corporate governance – Back to the future in improving corporate decision-making', *Journal of Managerial Psychology*, **15**(5), 477–511.

Dasborough, M.T. and N.M. Ashkanasy (2002), 'Emotion and attribution of intentionality in leader-member relationships', *The Leadership Quarterly*, **13**, 615–34.

Demirag, I.S. (1998), 'Short termism, financial systems, and corporate governance: a theoretical framework', in Istemi S. Demirag (ed.), *Corporate Governance, Accountability and Pressures to Perform: An International Study*, Stamford, CT: Jai Press, pp. 7–24.

Demirag, I.S., A. Tylecote and B. Morris (1994), 'Accounting for financial and managerial causes of short-term pressures in British corporations', *Journal of Business Finance & Accounting*, **21**(8), 1195–1213.

Demsetz, H. and K. Lehn (1985), 'The structure of corporate ownership: causes and consequences', *Journal of Political Economy*, **93**(6), 1155–77.

Feldman, J.M. (1981), 'Beyond attribution theory: cognitive processes in performance appraisal', *Journal of Applied Psychology*, **66**(2), 127–48.

Fukao, M. (1995), *Financial Integration, Corporate Governance and the Performance of Multinational Companies.*, Washington, DC: The Brookings Institution.

Gedajlovic, E.R. and D.M. Shapiro (1998), 'Management and ownership effects: evidence from five countries', *Strategic Management Journal*, **19**(6), 533–53.

Groot, T.L.C.M. (1998), 'Determinants of shareholder's short-term pressures: empirical evidence from Dutch companies', *The European Journal of Finance*, **4**, 212–32.

Gudykunst, W.B., S. Ting-Toomey and E. Chua (1988), *Culture and Interpersonal Communication*, Beverly Hills, CA: Sage.

Hall, E.T. (1976), *Beyond Culture*, New York: Doubleday.

Hamilton, G.G. and N.W. Biggart (1988), 'Market, culture and authority: a comparative analysis of management and organization in the Far East', *American Sociology*, **94** (Supplement), 52–94.

Hamilton, G.G. and K. Cheng-Shu (1990), 'The institutional foundations of Chinese business', *Comparative Social Research*, **12**, 135–51.

Hamilton, G.G., W. Zeile and W-J Kim (1990), 'The network structures of East-Asian Economies', in S.R. Clegg, G.S. Redding and M. Cartner (eds), *Capitalism in Contrasting Cultures*, New York: Walter de Gruyter, pp. 383–90.

Hofstede, G. (1980), *Culture's Consequences*, Beverly Hills, CA: Sage.

Hofstede, G. (1991), *Cultures and Organizations: Software of the Mind*, London: McGraw-Hill.

Ittner, C.D. and D.F. Larcker (1997), 'Quality strategy, strategic control systems, and organizational performance', *Accounting, Organizations and Society*, **22**(3/4), 293–314.

Jones, E.E. and R.E. Nisbett (1971), 'The actor and the observer. Divergent perceptions of the causes of behavior', in E.E. Jones, D.E. Kanouse, H.H. Kelley, R.E. Nisbett, S. Valins and

B. Weiner (eds), *Attribution: Perceiving the Causes of Behavior*, Morristown, NJ: General Learning Press, pp. 79–94.

Kuada, J. and H. Gullestrup (1998), 'The cultural context of corporate governance, performance pressures and accountability', in I.S. Demirag (ed.), *Corporate Governance, Accountability and Pressures to Perform: An International Study*, Stamford, CT: Jai Press, pp. 25–56.

Kunda, Z. (1990), 'The case for motivated reasoning', *Psychological Bulletin*, **108**(3), 480–98.

Lashgari, M. (2003), 'Corporate governance: a theoretical perspective', *Journal of American Academy of Business*, **2**(2), 415–17.

Lee, F. and M. Hallahan (2001), 'Do situational expectations produce situational inferences? The role of future expectations in directing inferential goals', *Journal of Personality and Social Psychology*, **80** (4), 545–56.

Lee, F. and L.Z. Tiedens (2001), 'Who's being served? "Self-serving" attributions in social hierarchies', *Organizational Behavior and Human Decision Processes*, **84**(2), 254–87.

Li, J. (1994), 'Ownership structure and board composition: a multi-country test of agency theory predictions', *Managerial and Decision Economics*, **15**(4), 359–68.

Lord, R.G., D.J. Brown and S.J. Freiberg (1999), 'Understanding the dynamics of leadership: the role of follower self-concepts in the leader/follower relationship', *Organizational Behavior and Human Decision Processes*, **78**(3), 167–203.

Marsh, P. (1990), *Short-termism on Trial*, London: Institutional Fund Managers Association.

Martinko, M.J. and S.C. Douglas (1999), 'Culture and expatriate failure: an attributional explication', *The International Journal of Organizational Analysis*, **7**(3), 265–93.

Martinko, M.J. and W.L. Gardner (1987), 'The leader/member attribution process', *Academy of Management Review*, **12**(2), 235–49.

Morris, M.W. and K. Peng (1994), 'Culture and cause: American and Chinese attributions for social and physical events', *Journal of Personality and Social Psychology*, **67**(6), 949–71.

Monks, R.A.G. and M. Nell (1996), *Watching the Watchers: Corporate Governance for the 21st Century*, Cambridge, MA: Blackwell.

Orru, M., N.W. Biggart and G.G. Hamilton (1997), 'Organizational isomorphism in East Asia', *The Economic Organization of East Asian Capitalism*, Thousand Oaks, CA: Sage, pp. 151–87.

Pedersen, T. and S. Thomsen (1999), 'Business systems and corporate governance', *International Studies of Management and Organization*, **29**(2), 43–59.

Pedersen, T. and S. Thomsen (1997), 'European patterns of corporate ownership: a twelve-country study', *Journal of International Business Studies*, **28**(4), 759–78.

Pekerti, A.A. (2001), 'Influence of culture on communication: an empirical test and theoretical refinement of the high- and low-context dimension', unpublished doctoral dissertation, The University of Auckland, New Zealand.

Pekerti, A.A. (2003), 'Indonesian corporate governance', *The Indonesian Institute for Corporate Directorship*, Jakarta: S.T. Manajemen Prasetya Mulya.

Pekerti, A.A. (in press), 'Cross-cultural perceptions in the leadership process: theoretical perspective on the influence of culture on self-concepts, and manager–worker attributions', *Thunderbird International Business Review*.

Roe, M.J. (1990), 'Political and legal restraints on ownership and control of public companies', *Journal of Financial Economics*, **27**, 7–41.

Roe, M.J. (1993), 'Some differences in corporate structure in Germany, Japan and the United States', *Yale Law Journal*, **102**(8), 1927–2003.

Ross, L. (1977), 'The intuitive psychologist and his shortcomings: distortions in the attribution process', in L. Berkowitz (ed.), *Advances in Experimental Social Psychology*, vol. 10, New York: Academic Press, pp. 173–220.

Shleifer, A. and R.W. Vishny (1986), 'Large shareholders and corporate control', *Journal of Political Economy*, **94**(33), 461–88.

Smith, P.B. and M.H. Bond (1994), *Social Psychology across Cultures*, Boston: Allyn & Bacon.

Sternberg, R.J. and V. Vroom (2002), 'Theoretical letters: the person versus the situation in leadership', *The Leadership Quarterly*, **13**, 301–23.

Tirole, J. (1999), 'Corporate governance', Centre for Economics Policy Research, discussion paper no. 2086, London.

Triandis, H.C., C. McCusker, H. Betancourt, S. Iwao, K. Leung, J.M. Salazar, B. Setiadi, J.B.P.B. Sinha, H. Touzard and Z. Zalesi (1993), 'An etic-emic analysis of individualism and collectivism', *Journal of Cross-Cultural Psychology*, **24** (3), 366–83.

Walsh, J.P. and J.K. Seward (1990), 'On the efficiency of internal and external corporate control mechanisms', *Academy of Management Review*, 15, 421–58.

Whitley, R.D. (1990), 'Eastern Asia enterprise structures and the comparative analysis of forms of business organization', *Organization Studies*, **11** (1), 47–74.

Whitley, R.D. (1991), 'The social construction of business systems in East Asia', *Organizational Studies*, **12**(1), 1–28.

Whitley, R.D. (1992a), *Business Systems in Asia: Firms, Markets and Societies*. London: Sage.

Whitley, R.D. (1992b), 'The social construction of organizations and markets: the comparative analysis of business recipes', in M. Reed and M. Hughes (eds), *Rethinking Organizations*, London: Sage, pp. 120–43.

Whitley, R.D. (1994), 'Dominant forms of economic organization in market economies', *Organization Studies*, **15**(2), 153–82.

Wilkinson, B. (1996), 'Culture, institutions and business in East Asia', *Organization Studies*, **17**(3), 421–47.

Yukl, G. (2002), *Leadership in Organizations, 5th edn*, Upper Saddle River, NJ: Prentice-Hall.

18 Responsible leadership and governance in a global context: insights from the GLOBE study

Narda R. Quigley, Mary Sully de Luque and Robert J. House

Introduction

The increasing trend toward globalization in business is undeniable. At the start of the 21st century, more than ever, multinational corporations control large portions of the market in different industries; domestic firms compete against increasing numbers of foreign competitors; and companies seek to place in leadership positions managers who have had international experience (Choate and Linger, 1988; Ehrlich, 2002; Gregersen *et al.*, 1998; McFarland *et al.*, 1993). With this increased emphasis on the international arena, cross-cultural issues have continued to become a major research agenda in management. Although a number of articles on this topic have begun to explore cross-cultural influences on business ethics (for example, Christie *et al.*, 2003; Blodgett *et al.*, 2001; Russ-Eft and Hatcher, 2003; Stajkovic and Luthans, 1997), the area of business ethics has yet to become a focal point for cross-cultural researchers.

The findings to date of the GLOBE (Global Leadership and Organizational Behavior Effectiveness) research program are uniquely positioned to illuminate some of the ethical conflicts and misunderstandings that arise as firms conduct business within and across societal borders. GLOBE is a ten-year, multi-method, multi-phase research program that examines the relationships among societal and organizational culture, societal and organizational effectiveness and leadership. A complete description of the program and its findings can be found in House *et al.* (2004). Briefly, the major purpose of Project GLOBE is to increase knowledge relevant to cross-cultural interactions. The results of this study are presented in the form of quantitative data based on responses of over 17000 managers from more than 900 organizations functioning in 62 societies throughout the world (House *et al.*, 2004, p. 3). The study also includes analyses of archival data concerning societal economic performance and the psychological and physical welfare of members of each society studied.

One important accomplishment of the GLOBE program is the identification of nine major dimensions of culture: uncertainty avoidance, power distance, institutional collectivism, in-group collectivism, gender egalitarianism, assertiveness, future orientation, performance orientation and humane orientation. In this chapter we will define each dimension and show how each influences societal, organizational and individual-level variables. We will also discuss the ranking of societies on these dimensions and suggest how this information may help aid our understanding of societal members' ideas about corporate responsibility, governance and responsible leadership.

A second major accomplishment of the GLOBE program is the identification of six global leadership behaviors. Through a qualitative and quantitative analysis of leadership, GLOBE scholars discovered that leadership behaviors can be summarized into six broad categories: charismatic/value-based, team-oriented, participative, humane-oriented, autonomous and self-protective leadership behaviors. In this chapter, we will discuss the GLOBE findings associating the nine dimensions of societal culture with the six global leadership behaviors. We suggest that, when certain leadership behaviors are viewed as effective in a society, it is likely that those behaviors will also be perceived as responsible leadership behaviors.

The purpose of this chapter, then, is to use the GLOBE findings to reflect on the unique aspects of societies that may have an influence on perceptions of corporate responsibility, governance and responsible leadership within those societies. We explore two primary questions. First, how do the cultural dimensions have an impact on the society, organization and individual-level variables that are most likely to influence individual perceptions of corporate responsibility, governance and responsible leadership? Second, how might the dimensions directly influence those perceptions? Ultimately cultural differences may result in different interpretations about the nature of corporate responsibility, governance and responsible leadership, possibly even leading to cross-cultural ethical conflict. It is our hope that this chapter will contribute to the body of knowledge that promotes greater cross-cultural understanding.

Before we begin our discussion, a few points must be made. First, as Donaldson and Dunfee (1994) noted, the field of business ethics can be divided into scholars who write empirically (that is, describing the way things actually are) and those who write normatively (that is, describing the way things should be). Our approach is empirical; we examine quantitative dimensions of culture and leadership and make conjectures, based on those findings, about how a society's perception of ethical behavior may be an outgrowth of its cultural context. One issue that can arise with an empirical approach that examines *perceptions* of ethical behavior is relativism. We attempt here to illuminate cultural differences without endorsing relativism. To that end, we acknowledge that there are arguably some universal ethical norms that should be followed worldwide, regardless of culture (for example, the nine principles of the UN Global Compact; Jackson, 1997). However, we are most interested in illuminating activities that may fall under what Donaldson and Dunfee (1999, p. 45) call 'the perplexing grey zone that arises when two cultures – and two sets of ethics – meet'.

Second, this chapter has several recurring themes. One theme is that of the multi-level layers of complexity that are inherently part of the discussion regarding culture and our consideration of multiple layers of influence on individuals within organizations. Individuals are nested within teams, teams are nested within organizations and organizations themselves are nested in industries and societies. As a result of this nested structure, higher-level variables (for example, society-level variables) will influence lower-level variables (such as organization-level variables). In this chapter we focus on societal culture and its impact on other variables that exist both at the same level of analysis (the societal level) and at lower levels of analysis (the organizational and individual levels). As Klein and Kozlowski (2000) discuss, there are many conceptual and methodological issues associated with crossing levels of analysis. The GLOBE study's design allowed for a number of cross-level hypothesis testing, as questionnaires were worded to capture both societal and organizational levels of analysis.

Another major theme in this chapter is the difference between a culture's practices and values and how that difference might be leveraged. As noted above, Project GLOBE identified nine cultural dimensions; two forms of questions were asked for each dimension. Each manager was asked to report on the actual cultural practices of his or her respective society and organization (society/organization 'as is'), in addition to reporting on the values of his or her respective society and organization (society/ organization 'should be'). Therefore culture scale items were written 'as "quartets" having isomorphic structures across the two levels of analysis (societal and organizational) and across the two culture manifestations (As Is and Should Be)' (House and Javidan, 2004, p. 21). As we will review, in many cases there is a negative correlation between the practices and values of a culture (at both the organizational or societal level). As we describe each of the dimensions, we will discuss how a potential gap in practices versus values may offer some leverage for change in that particular culture, and how that leverage may be used to help navigate the sometime murky waters of cross-cultural ethical issues.[1]

A final theme in this chapter is the relationship between leadership and culture. We consider both the influence of societal culture on leadership and the impact leadership can have on organizational culture. With respect to the first point, Project GLOBE found that certain attributes of leadership were universally endorsed, while others were viewed as effective only in certain cultures (Dorfman *et al.*, 2004). The following aspects of leadership were found to be effective worldwide: being trustworthy, just and honest (having integrity); having foresight and planning ahead; being positive, dynamic, encouraging, motivating and building confidence; and being communicative, informed, a coordinator and a team integrator (ibid.). Although we acknowledge that leaders across the globe who adopt these aspects will be perceived as responsible, we focus in this chapter on culturally contingent leader behaviors, as these behaviors are most likely to lead to cross-cultural ethical friction. With respect to the impact of leadership on organizational culture, organizational leaders are in a unique position to be agents to promote cross-cultural communication, understanding and positive change.

Theoretical model
As we begin discussing our theoretical model, a few terms need clarification. First, Project GLOBE scholars define culture as 'shared motives, values, beliefs, identities, and interpretations or meanings of significant events that result from common experiences of members of collectives that are transmitted across generations' (House and Javidan, 2004, p. 15). For the remainder of this chapter, culture will be discussed as being composed of the nine dimensions. Project GLOBE researchers also defined six global leadership behaviors. Charismatic/value-based leadership reflects the ability of leaders to inspire, motivate and encourage high performance outcomes from others, based on a foundation of core values. Team-oriented leadership places emphasis on effective team building and implementation of a common purpose among team members. Participative leadership involves the extent to which leaders involve others in decisions and their implementation. Humane-oriented leadership comprises supportive and considerate leadership. Autonomous leadership refers to independent and individualistic leadership behaviors, while self-protective leadership 'focuses on ensuring the safety and security of the individual and group through status-enhancement and face-saving' (ibid., p. 14).

The model presented in Figure 18.1 provides a broad overview of the connections between the differing levels of influence on individual perceptions of corporate responsibility, governance and responsible leadership in a given societal culture. The model integrates Stajkovic and Luthans's (1997) social cognitive model (see Bandura, 1997) of business ethics across cultures, Carroll's (1979) categorization of levels of corporate responsibility and Clarkson's (1995) stakeholder management approach. The part of the model that the majority of this chapter will examine is the white background that underlies all other variables in the model. This is the societal cultural context in which accepted perceptions of corporate responsibility, governance and responsible leadership evolve. Given that these variables are embedded within societal culture, they are all influenced by societal culture.

The left side of the model depicts the triadic reciprocal interaction between institutional constraints (such as ethics legislation within a society), organizational factors (such as organizational policies and codes of ethics) and personal factors (such as individual level variables) that serves as the foundation for individual thought and action regarding business ethics. The bidirectional arrows indicate that individuals are not simply influenced by larger forces around them, but rather act as an influence for institutional and organizational change. The right side of the model depicts the ideas regarding corporate responsibility, governance and responsible leadership that arise out of the interplay of the triadic reciprocal interaction. The interplay of these levels of influence will have an impact on whether individuals perceive that organizations have economic responsibilities only, or whether legal, ethical and discretionary/philanthropic responsibilities also come into play (Carroll, 1979). This interaction will also have an impact on perceptions of whether organizations should be responsible to shareholders or stakeholders (Clarkson, 1995). Finally these levels of influence will have an impact on perceptions of responsible leadership, which will in turn have an influence on, and be influenced by, perceptions of corporate responsibility and governance. Ultimately, however, since all of these variables exist in a given societal context, our discussion will focus on societal culture's potential impact.

We organize the following sections of this chapter by the cultural dimensions identified in Project GLOBE. We begin each section with a short review of the origin of each dimension. We then discuss how each dimension might be a contextual influence on institutional, organizational and individual factors within a society. In addition we discuss how each dimension might influence perceptions of corporate responsibility, governance and responsible leadership. Following each section, we offer ideas on how managers may leverage this knowledge the better to navigate potential cross-cultural ethical dilemmas.

Collectivism I (institutional collectivism)

Overview of dimension
This cultural dimension is defined as the degree to which organizational and societal institutional practices encourage and reward the collective distribution of resources and collective action. Not surprisingly, the GLOBE

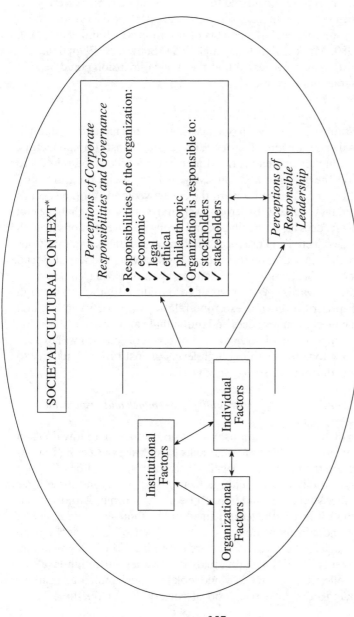

357

Note: * Societal cultural context comprises the following nine cultural dimensions: institutional collectivism, in-group collectivism, uncertainty avoidance, performance orientation, future orientation, humane orientation, power distance, gender egalitarianism and assertiveness.

Figure 18.1   Theorectical model: cultural influences on perceptions of corporate responsibilities, governance and leadership

findings suggest that Sweden is the top-ranked society out of a total of 62 societies in institutional collectivism practices. Sweden is known worldwide for its extensive social programs for all citizens.

Prior to the GLOBE study, collectivism I and collectivism II (discussed in the next section) were considered to be a single dimension reflecting the extent to which people within a given culture are perceived as autonomous individuals or interdependent members of in-groups (Gelfand *et al.*, 2004; Hofstede, 1980; Markus and Kitayama, 1991; Schwartz, 1994; Triandis, 1989). GLOBE analyses revealed that the single dimension could be split into two separate dimensions.

Collectivism I as a contextual influence

Societal institutional collectivism practices have an impact on institutional, organizational and individual factors. With respect to institutional factors, by definition, higher scores on the dimension will likely be related to more focus on the creation and longevity of laws, social programs and governmental agencies geared toward the collective good. With respect to organizational factors, GLOBE cross-level analyses[2] showed that societal collectivism I practices have a significant and strong positive relationship with organizational collectivism I practices (Gelfand *et al.*, 2004). Organizations in societies with high scores on institutional collectivist practices also tend to emphasize the collective good (for example, by emphasizing team rewards over individual rewards). With respect to individual factors, although the GLOBE program did not examine relationships between societal institutional collectivism practices and individual variables, it is likely that individuals from a society with high institutional collectivism will expect, value and work towards instilling high levels of institutional activity to promote the betterment of society as a whole.

Collectivism I and corporate responsibility, governance and responsible leadership

On the basis of the above relationships, we conjecture that individuals in societies with high levels of institutional collectivism will expect organizations to meet or exceed their economic, legal and ethical responsibilities. It is also likely that individuals will expect organizations to go beyond these three realms of responsibility and attempt to be philanthropic. Although this realm of responsibility is the least defined of the four – as Carroll (1979, p. 500) wrote, these 'responsibilities are those about which society has no clear-cut message for business ... they are left to individual judgment and choice' – it seems likely that individuals in societies with high levels of institutional collectivism practices would look favorably upon organizations that contribute to the collective good of society. As for the dimension's influence on corporate governance, we conjecture that societies high on institutional collectivism would expect to see organizations answering to stockholders and other stakeholders (that is, other actors who can affect or be affected by the organization's activities; see Maignan and Ferrell, 2003). This logic follows from the broader idea that the emphasis is placed on public good and collective interests when institutional collectivism practices are high. In support of this logic, Blodgett *et al.* (2001) found that individualism was negatively associated with ethical sensitivity toward stakeholders outside the company.

The GLOBE project, as noted in the introduction, also examined relationships between the cultural dimensions and six different dimensions of leadership. Gelfand *et al.* (2004) found that societies that value collectivism I are likely to view participative and self-protective leadership behaviors favorably ($p < 0.01$), while viewing autonomous leadership behaviors negatively ($p < 0.01$). Additionally GLOBE analyses found that societal collectivism I practices were negatively associated with participative and autonomous leadership behaviors ($p < 0.01$ for all relationships). It is likely that societies that value collectivism I will view participative and self-protective styles of leadership as responsible, while societies that practice collectivism I may view participative and autonomous leadership styles as either unrelated, or even negatively related, to perceptions of responsible leadership.

Leverage points for managers
This dimension's practices (as is) and values (should be) scores at the societal level were negatively correlated ($r = -0.61$, $p < 0.01$). The more a society emphasizes collective goals and interests, the less it values institutional collectivism. Managers operating in countries where practices for this dimension are low may be able to use the fact that individuals in that culture likely value institutional collectivism in order to help build strong teams within their organization and emphasize collective rewards and distribution of goods. Additionally it is likely that managers operating in countries where practices are high for this dimension should be aware that charismatic and team-oriented leadership behaviors will likely be well received. Also managers should remember that the societal cultures high in institutional collectivism may expect businesses to be 'good citizens', going beyond basic responsibilities and considering the broader good of all stakeholders.

Collectivism II (in-group collectivism)

Overview of dimension
This cultural dimension is defined as the degree to which individuals express pride, loyalty and cohesiveness in their organizations or families. The GLOBE findings suggest that the Philippines is the top-ranked society

on in-group collectivism practices, out of 62 societies; many other East Asian countries also rank in the highest grouping of scores on in-group collectivism practices.

As noted above, prior to the GLOBE study, collectivism I and II were discussed as a single dimension, reflecting the extent to which people within a given culture are autonomous individuals or embedded in their groups (House and Javidan, 2004). Most of the preceding work on individualism and collectivism has focused on the in-group aspect of the concept. As an example, the GLOBE measure of in-group collectivism correlated very highly and inversely with Hofstede's 1980 nation scores on individualism ($r = -0.82$, $p < 0.01$; Gelfand *et al.*, 2004), which has its roots in Triandis (1995).

Collectivism II as a contextual influence
Societal in-group collectivism practices have an impact on institutional, organizational and individual factors. With respect to institutional factors, it is likely that higher scores on the dimension will result in less emphasis on governmental policies and social programs. For example, in Iran, a country high on in-group collectivism, children are expected to care for their aging parents. As a result, there is less emphasis on social security programs. GLOBE analyses found in-group collectivism practices at the societal level to be positively correlated with passiveness towards government ($r = 0.66$, $p < 0.01$) and lack of voice ($r = 0.75$, $p < 0.01$). It is likely that the desire to protest governmental actions and have a voice in policy decisions is less important, 'given that the focus in these societies is on more immediate in-groups' (Gelfand *et al.*, 2004, p. 487). With respect to organizational factors, GLOBE cross-level analyses showed that societal in-group collectivism values have a significant and strong positive relationship with organizational in-group collectivism values ($p < 0.01$). Therefore organizations in societies with high scores on in-group collectivist values also value the expression of pride, loyalty and internal cohesion. With respect to individual factors, although the GLOBE program did not examine relationships between societal in-group collectivism practices and individual variables, by definition, it is likely that individuals from a society with high collectivism II will expect, value and work towards higher levels of loyalty, pride and cohesion within their family and group of peers.

Collectivism II and corporate responsibility, governance and responsible leadership
On the basis of the above relationships, we expect that individuals in societies with high levels of in-group collectivism practices will expect organizations to meet their economic, and perhaps legal, responsibilities. The fact that these societies tend to be somewhat passive and do not use voice with

respect to governance (Gelfand *et al.*, 2004) suggests that individuals in these societies may not monitor organizational activities closely; as a result, they may not be surprised when organizations are wholly concerned with above-average returns, regardless of whether the organization proceeded ethically. As for the dimension's influence on corporate governance, although the GLOBE program did not test these relationships specifically, it is likely that societies high on in-group collectivism practices will expect to see organizations answering to only those within the most immediate in-group – in this case, stockholders.

The GLOBE analyses found that in-group collectivism values and practices were each significantly positively related to charismatic/value-based leadership and team-oriented leadership ($p < 0.01$ for all relationships). Also in-group collectivism practices were positively related to humane-oriented leadership and self-protective leadership, while being negatively related to participative leadership ($p < 0.01$ for all relationships). On the other hand, in-group collectivism values were negatively related to self-protective leadership ($p < 0.01$). Therefore, in societies that practice high levels of collectivism II, charismatic/value-based, team-oriented, humane-oriented and self-protective behaviors will likely be perceived as responsible types of leadership, while participative leadership behaviors will likely be perceived as either unrelated or not particularly responsible.

Leverage points for managers
Unlike collectivism I, in-group collectivism values and practices at the societal level are not correlated ($r = 0.21$, NS; Gelfand *et al.*, 2004). Some countries most likely exhibit more parallel values and practices than others. In a high in-group collectivist society, it may be wise to assume that practices and values are concurrent; members of these societies both practice and value loyalty, pride and group cohesiveness. Potential ethical conflicts may arise when two cultures having different scores on this dimension interact. For example, individual expectations of the corporate responsibilities of organizations may be quite different in each culture. Also potential ethical conflicts may arise with the issue of nepotism. In societies that are high in in-group collectivism, it is expected that family members and close friends will be given preferential treatment. With respect to leadership, charismatic/value-based, team-oriented and humane-oriented leadership appear to be leader behaviors that are likely to be perceived as responsible.

Gender egalitarianism

Overview of dimension
This cultural dimension is defined as the degree to which a society minimizes gender role differences while promoting gender equality. Societies that are

high in gender egalitarianism practices, like Hungary, Russia and Poland, would likely have similar levels of education achieved and expected for both women and men within their societies, for example (Emrich *et al.*, 2004).

Prior to the GLOBE study, gender egalitarianism, performance orientation, humane orientation and assertiveness were in large part discussed as a single cultural dimension, entitled masculinity/femininity (Emrich *et al.*, 2004; Hofstede, 1980, 1998, 2001). GLOBE's gender egalitarianism dimension was created in order to reflect solely 'societies' beliefs about whether members' biological sex should determine the roles that they play in their homes, business organizations, and communities' (Emrich *et al.*, 2004, p. 347).

Gender egalitarianism as a contextual influence
Societal gender egalitarianism practices have an impact on institutional, organizational and individual factors. With respect to institutional factors, by definition, higher scores on the dimension will result in legislation to ensure that discrimination on the basis of gender does not occur. Additionally social and educational programs in high gender egalitarian societies will likely provide equal opportunities for males and females. GLOBE did examine the relationship between gender egalitarianism practices and various indicators of women's participation in key parts of society; not surprisingly, these correlations were positive and significant (cf. Emrich *et al.*, 2004). With respect to organizational factors, GLOBE cross-level analyses showed that societal gender egalitarianism practices and values have significant positive relationships with organizational gender egalitarianism practices and values ($p < 0.01$). With respect to individual factors, although the GLOBE program did not examine cross-level relationships between societal gender egalitarianism practices and individual variables, the societal level relationship between gender egalitarianism and average member longevity, knowledge and standard of living as measured by the Human Development Index ($r = 0.29$, $p < 0.05$), in addition to the relationships between the dimension and women's participation, suggest that both men and women may achieve benefits from more gender egalitarian societies.

Gender egalitarianism and corporate responsibility, governance and responsible leadership
No research to date has examined the relationship between gender egalitarianism and perceptions of corporate responsibility and, in our estimation, societies high and low in this dimension may differ with respect to perceptions of corporate responsibility. Societies high in gender egalitarianism, however, may be slightly more inclined to meet, not just economic and legal but also ethical and, perhaps, discretionary responsibilities, as these countries may place more of an emphasis on the

rights and freedoms of individuals. As for the relationship between gender egalitarianism and corporate governance, once again, it is likely that other dimensions may have more of an influence. However more gender egalitarian societies may be drawn toward a more inclusive stakeholder approach to corporate governance.

The GLOBE analyses indicate that societal gender egalitarian values were positively associated with participative and charismatic/value-based leader attributes, while they are negatively associated with self-protective leader attributes ($p < 0.01$ for all relationships: Emrich *et al.*, 2004). On the basis of these findings, participative and charismatic/value-based behaviors will likely be perceived as responsible, while self-protective leadership behaviors will likely be perceived as either unrelated or not particularly responsible. Also, by definition, leadership should take care to ensure that there is no discrimination and that women and men are afforded equal opportunities in organizations in high gender egalitarian societies.

Leverage points for managers
Gender egalitarianism values and practices at the societal level are positively correlated ($r = 0.32$, $p < 0.05$; Emrich *et al.*, 2004). Also, according to Emrich *et al.* (ibid., p. 364), '[m]anagers overall express a desire for their societies to be more gender egalitarian than they are currently'. In other words, gender egalitarian societies appreciate that aspect of their culture and are likely to strive toward even higher levels of gender egalitarianism. It will be important for managers who are from less gender egalitarian societies to be sensitive to this when dealing with more gender egalitarian societies. There is a point of leverage with the opposite situation, however: managers from societies that are more gender egalitarian should be aware that most countries value the dimension more than they practice it. As a result, managers may be in a good position to help the organization become more gender egalitarian, though caution should be exercised in order to avoid violating accepted practices. As for effective leadership that will likely be perceived as responsible, charismatic/value-based leadership and/or participative leadership appear to be good options; self-protective leadership in high gender egalitarian societies will likely not be perceived as favorably.

Performance orientation

Overview of dimension
This cultural dimension is defined as the degree to which an organization or society encourages and rewards members for performance improvement and excellence (House and Javidan, 2004). Societies high in performance

orientation practices, like Switzerland, Singapore and Hong Kong, expect and reward achievement (Javidan, 2004). On the other hand, societies that are low in performance orientation practices, like Greece and Venezuela, tend to value societal and family relationships, and have high respect for quality of life (ibid.).

Performance orientation was derived most directly from McClelland's (1961) work on need for achievement, although it traces roots back to Weber's (1904/1930, 1904/1998) work examining the history and doctrine of Catholicism, the Protestant work ethic and capitalism (House and Javidan, 2004; Javidan, 2004).

Performance orientation as a contextual influence
Societal performance orientation will have an impact on institutional, organizational and individual factors. With respect to institutional factors, GLOBE analyses found that societies that score high on performance orientation practices have governments that support economic prosperity, reflecting a preference for a strong role for private ownership of business (r = 0.50, p < 0.01; Javidan, 2004). As a result, institutions in these societies are focused on supporting the private sector, perhaps through tax legislation or deregulation of various industries. As an example, Hong Kong is known for its economic success, while China, another country high on performance orientation practices, places emphasis on the private sector even as it retains its communist government. With respect to organizational factors, GLOBE cross-level analyses showed that societal performance orientation practices and values have significant positive relationships with organizational performance orientation practices and values (p < 0.01; Javidan, 2004). With respect to individual factors, although the GLOBE program did not examine cross-level relationships between societal performance orientation practices and individual variables, the societal level relationship between performance orientation practices and average member general satisfaction is significant and positive (r = 0.51, p < 0.01). However, on average, members from societies that score higher in performance orientation practices do not enjoy healthier or longer lives (ibid.). The focus on achievement and performance may create more stress, resulting in a decline in health.

Performance orientation and corporate responsibility, governance and responsible leadership
In past research, more 'masculine' traits, such as competitiveness and aggressiveness, have been linked to unethical behavior (for example, Blodgett *et al.*, 2001; Chang and Ding, 1995; Vitell and Festervand, 1987; Modic, 1987). It may be that extremely high levels of performance orientation, when not balanced by ethical judgment, have a negative influence on corporate

responsibility. Some organizations may define achievement more broadly than simply economic achievement, of course (for example, socially responsible companies like Whole Foods and MBNA consider their philanthropic and environmental endeavors to be critical realms of achievement). However, for those high performance-oriented organizations that define achievement on exclusively fiscal and economic grounds, ethical judgment may be overridden by the need to perform (for example, Enron in 2001). As for the relationship between this dimension and corporate governance, the question of how organizations define achievement is critical. If organizations are solely concerned with short-term results in their performance orientation, it is likely that stockholders might be the only group to which those organizations would attend. If, on the other hand, achievement is defined as more long-range and broader than simply economic achievement, it is likely that organizations would adopt a stakeholder approach. Arguably the only truly performance-oriented companies are those that consider issues of longevity and impact, in which case high performance-oriented companies would be stakeholder-oriented.

The GLOBE analyses indicate that societal performance orientation values were positively associated with participative and charismatic/value-based leader attributes (p < 0.01; Javidan, 2004); societal performance orientation practices were positively associated with humane-oriented leadership (p < 0.01; Javidan, 2004). Using these findings, we may infer that these three sets of behaviors will likely be perceived as responsible types of leadership.

Leverage points for managers
Performance orientation values and practices at the societal level are modestly negatively correlated (r = –0.28, p < 0.05; Javidan, 2004). People's aspirations to achieve high levels of performance are not strongly related to their current assessments (ibid.). Interestingly, out of all the cultural dimensions, societal rankings on performance orientation values were the highest. As Javidan (ibid., p. 248) noted, 'People all over the world are seeking a society that strongly encourages and rewards innovation, challenging goals, and improvement.' The fact that performance orientation is valued highly is an important point of leverage for managers. Regardless of societal culture, individuals are likely to respond favorably when placed in situations where merit is fairly rewarded and ambitions can be achieved. If managers are careful to provide clear ethical guidelines and define success beyond simply economic targets, it is likely that high levels of performance and high ethical standards will produce a synergy of achievement. As for effective leadership behaviors that will likely be perceived as responsible, charismatic/value-based, participative and humane-oriented leadership

appear to be good options. Individuals in societal cultures that value performance orientation will likely respond favorably when any combination of tough expectations, core values, envisioned future, consideration and support, and empowerment are used.

Future orientation

Overview of dimension
Project GLOBE defines this cultural dimension as the degree to which individuals in organizations or societies engage in future-oriented behaviors such as planning, investing in the future and delaying individual or collective gratification (House and Javidan, 2004). In Singapore, for example, the top-ranking society studied in the GLOBE program in future orientation practices, 'The government always opts for what works for the country in the longer term rather than for what will please the people in the shorter term' (*Principles of Governance*, 2001).

Future orientation was derived most directly from Kluckholn and Strodtbeck's (1961) Past, Present, Future Orientation dimension, focusing on the temporal concerns of most people within a society (House and Javidan, 2004). The concept is also related to Hofstede and Bond's (1988) dimension, Confucian Work Dynamism, which eventually evolved into Hofstede's (2001) Long-Term Orientation. Seijts (1998) provides a more thorough review on the concept.

Future orientation as a contextual influence
Societal future orientation practices have an impact on institutional, organizational and individual factors. With respect to institutional factors, it is likely that the strong cultural emphasis on the future will probably mean that societies high in future orientation practices will have stable economies. GLOBE findings support this idea (Ashkanasy *et al.*, 2004). Also societies that exhibit higher levels of future orientation practices experience greater success in science (r = 0.54, p < 0.01; Ashkanasy *et al.*, 2004). These relationships suggest that institutions within societies high in future orientation practices are more likely to make decisions, policies and laws that consider the future. With respect to organizational factors, GLOBE cross-level analyses showed that societal future orientation practices and values have significant positive relationships with organizational future orientation practices and values (p < 0.01; Ashkanasy *et al.*, 2004). With respect to individual factors, although GLOBE analyses did not specifically examine societal future orientation's impact on individuals, at the societal level, future orientation practices were linked to higher levels of societal health, general satisfaction, gender equality and national savings (r = 0.70,

p < 0.01; r = 0.56, p < 0.01 ; r = 0.40, p < 0.05; and r = 0.42, p < 0.01, respectively; Ashkanasy *et al.*, 2004). This suggests that individuals in these societies are more likely to live longer, save for the future and consider men and women as equals.

Future orientation and corporate responsibility, governance and responsible leadership
Although the GLOBE program did not specifically examine these relationships, it is likely that societies high in future orientation practices would favor organizations that consider economic, legal, ethical and, probably, some discretionary/philanthropic responsibilities. In particular, we conjecture that undertaking discretionary responsibilities that ensure future success would be popular. As for the dimension's influence on corporate governance, societies high in future orientation practices would likely produce organizations that have long-term considerations. As a result, most of these organizations would be characterized by a stakeholder approach to governance.

The GLOBE analyses indicate that societal future orientation values were positively associated with self-protective and humane-oriented leader attributes (p < 0.01 for all relationships; Ashkanasy *et al.*, 2004). Therefore it is likely that these two types of leadership will be viewed as responsible in societies that value future orientation. The combined effect of self-protective and humane-oriented leader attributes may result in a paternalistic, yet benevolent, leadership style. Also GLOBE analyses found that team-oriented leadership is likely to be popular, and therefore likely also to be perceived as responsible, when societies reported low future orientation practices (p < 0.01; Ashkanasy *et al.*, 2004). Theoretically, charismatic/value-based leadership, with its emphasis on long-term vision, is most aligned with future orientation. We therefore conjecture that this type of leadership is also likely to be perceived as responsible in societies that value high levels of future orientation.

Leverage points for managers
Future orientation values and practices at the societal level were negatively correlated (r = –0.41, p < 0.01; Ashkanasy *et al.*, 2004). Ashkanasy *et al.* suggest that the negative correlation is driven by societies that are aware of their low use of future orientation practices. As a result, they have stronger aspirations for incorporating future orientation; as Ashkanasy *et al.* (ibid., p. 307) wrote, 'such societies are most conscious of the need for moving toward a more strategic and spiritually fulfilling perspective'. The fact that future orientation is so highly valued is an important point of leverage for managers. Regardless of societal culture, individuals understand the

368   Responsible leadership and governance in global business

value of decisions that are made with emphasis on the future. If managers
are careful to communicate this emphasis well, they will encounter less
resistance to change. And, if we are correct that higher levels of future
orientation practices will lead to more responsible organizations and
governance, managers may be in a good position to help the organization
become more future-oriented and ethically responsible simultaneously.
Theoretically charismatic/value-based leadership, with its emphasis on long-
term vision, is most aligned with future orientation. Additionally societies
that value future orientation highly will likely respond well to benevolent,
paternalistic leadership behaviors.

Uncertainty avoidance

Overview of dimension
This cultural dimension is defined as the extent to which members of a
society strive to avoid uncertainty by relying on established social norms,
rituals and bureaucratic practices (House and Javidan, 2004). Societies high
in uncertainty avoidance practices, like Germany, Denmark and China
(Sully de Luque and Javidan, 2004), 'actively seek to decrease the probability
of unpredictable future events that could adversely affect the operation of
... society' (House and Javidan, 2004, p. 12).
   Cyert and March (1963) originally used the term 'uncertainty avoidance'
to describe an organizational phenomenon. Hofstede (1980) used the term
to describe how people in societies accept uncertainty in everyday life
(Sully de Luque and Javidan, 2004); he also used the concept as one of his
dimensions of societal culture.

Uncertainty avoidance as a contextual influence
Societal uncertainty avoidance practices have an impact on institutional,
organizational and individual factors. With respect to institutional factors,
a strong cultural emphasis on avoiding uncertainty will mean that societies
high in uncertainty avoidance practices will develop a thorough legal system
that will be systematically implemented. GLOBE findings showed that
higher levels of uncertainty avoidance practices in a society were linked
to economic development ($r = 0.60$, $p < 0.01$; Sully de Luque and Javidan,
2004), in addition to government support for economic prosperity, which
reflects lower levels of unfair business practices, higher levels of economic
literacy and more positive industrial relations ($r = 0.74$, $p < 0.01$; Sully
de Luque and Javidan, 2004). Uncertainty avoidance practices were also
linked to democratic political ideology, greater participation and voice in
the political system, and a less active role of government (ibid.). Although
higher levels of uncertainty avoidance practices were associated with a

decrease in civil liberties (r = –0.36, p < 0.01; Sully de Luque and Javidan, 2004), overall, 'in societies characterized by a high degree of orderliness, consistency, and structure, there is a greater assurance of individual liberty' (ibid., p. 631). With respect to organizational factors, GLOBE cross-level analyses showed that societal uncertainty avoidance values have significant positive relationships with organizational uncertainty avoidance values (p < 0.01; Sully de Luque and Javidan, 2004). Contrary to GLOBE expectations, however, there was no relationship found between societal and organizational level uncertainty avoidance practices (ibid.). With respect to individual factors, although GLOBE analyses did not specifically examine societal uncertainty avoidance's impact on individuals, at the societal level, societies that exhibit higher levels of uncertainty avoidance practices enjoy a high quality of life, relative safety and security, a high life expectancy, and high levels of general satisfaction (r = 0.28, p < 0.05; r = 0.76, p < 0.01; r = 0.28, p < 0.05; and r = 0.63, p < 0.01, respectively; ibid.).

Uncertainty avoidance and corporate responsibility, governance, and responsible leadership
Although the GLOBE program did not specifically examine these relationships, the lack of a positive correlation between societal uncertainty avoidance practices and organizational uncertainty avoidance practices suggests that there may be little, if any, correlation between societal uncertainty avoidance practices and whether organizations are more or less responsible. Organization-level uncertainty avoidance practices will likely be a better predictor; organizations high in uncertainty avoidance practices can be expected to consider economic, legal, ethical and some philanthropic/discretionary responsibilities. As for uncertainty avoidance's impact on corporate governance, we conjecture that, if the organization exhibits a high level of uncertainty avoidance practices, all stakeholders will be considered important.

The GLOBE analyses indicate that societal uncertainty avoidance values were positively associated with team-oriented, humane-oriented and self-protective leader attributes (p < 0.01 for all relationships; Sully de Luque and Javidan, 2004). These values were negatively related to charismatic/value-based and participative leader behaviors (p < 0.01 for all relationships; ibid.). Therefore societies that value uncertainty avoidance will be likely to perceive team-oriented, humane-oriented and self-protective leader attributes as compatible with responsible leadership, while charismatic and participative leader behaviors are likely to be viewed negatively. Also uncertainty avoidance practices were positively associated with self-protective behaviors and negatively associated with team-oriented behaviors (p < 0.01 for all relationships; ibid.). Thus, for societies high in uncertainty avoidance practices, self-protective leadership is likely to be considered responsible, while team-oriented leadership may be viewed with suspicion.

Leverage points for managers
Uncertainty avoidance values and practices at the societal level were negatively correlated ($r = -0.61$, $p < 0.01$; Sully de Luque and Javidan, 2004). Like future orientation, the negative correlation may be driven by societies that are aware of their low use of practices reflecting uncertainty avoidance, yet have stronger aspirations for incorporating certainty-inducing parameters into daily life. This is an important point of leverage for managers as, regardless of societal culture, individuals understand the value of emphasis on rules, regulations and strong social norms. Moreover, if our conjectures are correct that higher levels of organizational uncertainty avoidance practices will lead to more responsible organizations and governance, managers may be in a good position to help organizations become more stable, predictable and ethically responsible concurrently. As for effective leadership behaviors that will likely be perceived as responsible in societies that practice uncertainty avoidance, self-protective leadership behaviors are widely accepted, while team-oriented leadership behaviors are not. In societies that value uncertainty avoidance, team-oriented, humane-oriented and self-protective leadership attributes are widely accepted and likely to be considered responsible.

Humane orientation

Overview of the dimension
This cultural dimension is defined as the degree to which members of a society encourage and reward individuals for being fair, altruistic, friendly, generous, caring and kind to others (House and Javidan, 2004). Societies that are high in humane orientation practices, such as Zambia, the Philippines and Ireland, tend to consider others as important, social support for others as fundamental, and paternalistic norms and patronage relationships as significant (Kabasakal and Bodur, 2004).

Humane orientation, according to House and Javidan (2004, p. 13), 'has its roots in Kluckholn and Strodtbeck (1961) dimension entitled Human Nature as Good versus Human Nature as Bad, as well as Putnam's (1993) work on civic society and McClelland's (1985) conceptualization of the affiliative motive'. In the cross-cultural literature, one of Hofstede's (1980, 2001) components of his masculinity–femininity dimension was a toughness–tenderness component; this aspect of his dimension is conceptually related to humane orientation.

Humane orientation as a contextual influence

Societal humane orientation practices have an impact on institutional, organizational and individual factors. With respect to institutional factors, in less-developed societies high in humane orientation practices, children are expected to give material support to their families by participating in the labor force; as a result, child labor practices are not considered to be an important issue by public policymakers (Kabasakal and Bodur, 2004). Also, the presence of paternalistic norms and patronage relationships results in less emphasis on formal welfare institutions in societies high in humane orientation practices (ibid.). With respect to organizational factors, GLOBE cross-level analyses showed that societal humane orientation practices are positively related to organizational humane orientation practices ($p < 0.01$; Kabasakal and Bodur, 2004). Humane societies seem to foster humane organizations. With respect to individual factors, although GLOBE analyses did not specifically examine societal humane orientation's impact on individuals, at the societal level, humane orientation practices were linked to lower life expectancy and general lower scores on the human development index, but were unrelated to psychological health ($r = -0.35$, $p < 0.01$; $r = -0.37$, $p < 0.01$; $p > 0.10$, respectively; ibid.). In addition societies scoring higher on humane orientation practices are less inclined to imprison people for long periods of time and largely oppose societal discrimination ($r = -0.56$, $p < 0.01$ and $r = 0.34$, $p < 05$, respectively; ibid.).

Humane orientation and corporate responsibility, governance and responsible leadership

Although GLOBE did not specifically examine these relationships, we expect that societies high in humane orientation will produce organizations that consider both economic and legal responsibilities. These organizations likely do not assume discretionary or philanthropic responsibilities formally, although employees would expect to receive help from their employers in the event of personal emergencies, thanks to the paternalistic nature of these societies. As for the relationship between humane orientation and corporate governance, as Kabasakal and Bodur wrote (2004, p. 585), 'In the more humane-oriented societies of the world, satisfying shareholders and making a profit is the primary focus of organizations ... Although ... some organizations apply the charity and stewardship principles and corporate social responsiveness.' Therefore we conjecture that most organizations operating in humane-oriented societies likely adopt a shareholder focus. In times of need, these organizations may be expected to support stakeholders within the organization (that is, employees); in general, however, these organizations do not institutionalize their support of all stakeholders.

The GLOBE analyses indicate that societal humane orientation values were positively associated with participative leader attributes and negatively related to self-protective leadership ($p < 0.01$ for all relationships; Kabasakal and Bodur, 2004). In contrast, societies high on humane orientation practices are more likely to perceive humane-oriented leadership as effective ($p < 0.01$; ibid.). Thus, for societies high in humane orientation practices, friendly, compassionate and supportive leadership is likely to be considered responsible, while for societies high in humane orientation values, participative leadership is likely to be considered responsible.

Leverage points for managers
Humane orientation values and practices at the societal level were modestly negatively correlated ($r = -0.32$, $p < 0.05$; Kabasakal and Bodur, 2004). Similar to both future orientation and uncertainty avoidance, the negative correlation may be driven by societies that are aware of their low use of humane orientation practices, yet have aspirations for incorporating it into daily life. This may also explain the increased emphasis on state institutions in many low humane orientation societies, as the need to take care of others must be addressed through formal means, rather than by social norms. Additionally individuals who appreciate the fundamental values associated with humane orientation – altruism, care for others and generosity – would likely embrace an organizational culture that incorporates these values (for example, Southwest Airlines). Regarding ethical conflicts, when managers from a society with a differing level of humane orientation enter another society, expectations regarding child labor and managerial paternalism may become points of conflict. As for effective leadership behaviors that will be perceived as responsible in societies that value humane orientation, leadership behaviors espousing participation and delegation are widely accepted and would likely be considered responsible. As for effective leadership behaviors that will likely be perceived as responsible in societies that practice humane orientation, not surprisingly, humane-oriented leadership behaviors are widely accepted and would likely be considered responsible.

Assertiveness

Overview of dimension
This cultural dimension is defined as the degree to which members of a society are assertive, confrontational or aggressive in social relationships (House and Javidan, 2004). Societies high in assertiveness practices, like the USA, Germany and Austria, tend to value competition, have a 'go-getting' attitude, and value assertive, dominant and tough behavior in the society (Den Hartog, 2004).

According to Den Hartog, the dimension originates in large part from Hofstede's (1980, 1998, 2001) masculinity–femininity dimension. As mentioned in the discussion of the origin of the gender egalitarianism dimension, Hofstede's masculinity–femininity dimension confounded several different dimensions. High masculinity in a society denotes, in part, high assertiveness or ambitiousness (Hofstede, 2001, p. 164). Prior to the GLOBE program, to our knowledge, no prior cross-cultural research had examined assertiveness as a separate cultural dimension.

Assertiveness as a contextual influence
Societal assertiveness practices have an impact on institutional, organizational and individual factors. With respect to institutional factors, because societies high in assertiveness by definition value competition, there will likely be emphasis on a free-market economy wherein organizations succeed on the basis of merit. Also GLOBE analyses revealed a negative relationship between assertiveness values and Schwartz's (1994) egalitarian values dimension, which indicates the transcendence of selfish interests to promote the welfare of others ($r = -0.53$, $p < 0.01$; Den Hartog, 2004). This may have two somewhat contradictory consequences. It may be that highly assertive societies create institutions to help level the playing field (welfare programs for those in need, and so on). On the other hand, it may be that highly assertive societies allow individuals to fend for themselves (thus less emphasis on social programs). With respect to organizational factors, GLOBE cross-level analyses showed that societal assertiveness values are positively related to organizational assertiveness values ($p < 0.01$; ibid.). However no relationship was found between societal practices and organizational practices (ibid.). With respect to individual factors, although GLOBE analyses did not specifically examine societal assertiveness's impact on individuals, at the societal level, assertiveness was not linked to many factors such as human development, economic stability, religion or political ideology. Societies that score higher on assertiveness values, however, tend to exhibit more respect for family and friends and greater success in science and technology ($r = 0.36$, $p < 0.01$ and $r = 0.34$, $p < 0.01$; ibid.).

Assertiveness and corporate responsibility, governance and responsible leadership
On the basis of past research, many 'masculine' traits, such as competitiveness and aggressiveness, have been linked to unethical behavior (for example, Blodgett *et al.*, 2001; Chang and Ding, 1995; Vitell and Festervand, 1987; Modic, 1987). These traits may be manifestations of assertiveness as well as being manifestations of high performance orientation. Left unchecked, high levels of assertiveness may therefore have a negative influence on corporate responsibility. Organizations may become so profit and competition

focused that they lose sight of all other responsibilities, focusing only on economic responsibilities. As for the relationship between the dimension and corporate governance, similar to performance orientation, to make reasonable conjectures about the influence of assertiveness on perceptions of corporate governance, the question of how organizations define merit and achievement is critical. If organizations are strictly concerned with short-term results in their desire to compete, it is likely that stockholders would be the only group to which organizations would be responsible. In contrast, if achievement is defined more broadly than simply economic achievement, it is likely that organizations with high assertiveness levels would adopt a stakeholder approach.

The GLOBE analyses indicated that the majority of the relationships between societal assertiveness practices and values and leadership behaviors were not significant. The relationship between societal assertiveness values and humane-oriented leadership, however, was significant ($p < 0.01$; Den Hartog, 2004). This finding is somewhat counterintuitive. One interpretation may be that societies that want to become more assertive also want to have humane-oriented leadership in order to provide a social support structure for the increased competition (ibid.). In any case, humane-oriented leadership is likely to be perceived as responsible in cultures that value assertiveness.

Leverage points for managers
Assertiveness values and practices at the societal level were modestly negatively correlated ($r = -0.26$, $p < 0.05$; Den Hartog, 2004). Also the pattern in most societies is that 'people see their country as having a fair amount of assertiveness and they want less of it ... perhaps reflecting the wish to belong to a relatively nonthreatening, nonaggressive society' (ibid., p. 409). Managers may be able to take this generalization and apply it to the organizational level, taking care to develop a non-threatening climate in the workplace. One possible point of conflict is that communication styles of cultures practicing high assertiveness are direct, expressive and explicit; less assertive societies communicate in more subtle, indirect and detached ways. It will be important to be cognizant of these differences, particularly when addressing sensitive issues. As for effective leadership behaviors that will be perceived as responsible in societies that value assertiveness, humane-oriented leadership behaviors are widely accepted and would likely be considered responsible.

Power distance

Overview of dimension
This cultural dimension is defined as the degree to which members of a society expect and agree that power should be stratified and concentrated at

higher levels of an organization or government (House and Javidan, 2004). Societies that are high in power distance practices, such as Morocco, Nigeria and Argentina, tend to accept and endorse authority, power differences and status privileges, in part because power is seen as providing social order, relational harmony and role stability (Carl *et al.*, 2004).

Power distance, according to House and Javidan (2004), was initially operationalized by Mulder (1971) as a measure of power differential between superiors and subordinates, though the dimension also had roots in McClelland's (1961, 1975) need for power construct. Mulder (1977) initially coined the term 'power distance' and Hofstede (1980, 2001) characterized it as a cultural dimension (Carl *et al.*, 2004).

Power distance as a contextual influence
Power distance practices have an impact on institutional, organizational and individual factors. With respect to institutional factors, by definition, institutions in high power distance societies tend to be stratified and somewhat bureaucratic. Also, in part because of the stratification, information tends to be localized, not shared. This may result in less emphasis on institutional transparency/checks and balances and relatively higher levels of public corruption (Carl *et al.*, 2004). Indeed GLOBE analyses revealed that higher GLOBE power distance societal values are related to greater corruption and lower civil liberties ($r = 0.36$, $p < 0.01$ and $r = 0.38$, $p < 0.01$, respectively; ibid.). These findings suggest that 'under conditions in which Power Distance is highly valued, corrupt behavior is legitimized as a privilege of position' (ibid., p. 558). With respect to organizational factors, GLOBE cross-level analyses showed that societal power distance practices and values are positively related to organizational power distance practices and values ($p < 0.01$). With respect to individual factors, although GLOBE analyses did not specifically examine societal power distance's impact on individuals, at the societal level, power distance practices and values were negatively related to economic prosperity, competitive success, societal health and human development ($r = -0.53$, $p < 0.01$; $r = -0.53$, $p < 0.01$; $r = -0.62$, $p < 0.01$; and $r = -0.36$, $p < 0.01$, respectively; Carl *et al.*, 2004). Thus societies with higher power distance practices 'might frustrate the ability of people to pursue their ambitions and dreams, and cause even the more powerful to worry about the protection of their status and prestige in the society. Under these conditions, the quality of life, organizations, and institutions will likely fail to adapt ... and would likely deteriorate' (ibid., p. 556).

Power distance and corporate responsibility, governance and responsible leadership
The link between power distance and perceptions of corporate responsibility may be complex. However the fact that societies high in power distance tend

to exhibit higher levels of corruption suggests that many organizations in those societies will likely be concerned with economic gains, whether or not the actions they take are legal or ethical. As an influence on perceptions of corporate governance, Blodgett *et al.* (2001) found that high levels of power distance negatively influenced ethical sensitivity to stakeholder interests. On this evidence, we conjecture that there will likely be more of an emphasis on shareholders in organizations that exhibit a high level of power distance.

Power distance values were positively correlated with self-protective and humane leadership, and negatively correlated with charismatic/value-based and participative leader attributes (p < 0.01 for all relationships; Carl *et al.*, 2004). Power distance practices scores were positively correlated with self-protective behaviors, while they were negatively correlated with participative leader behaviors (p < 0.01 for both relationships; ibid.).

Leverage points for managers
Power distance values and practices at the societal level were negatively correlated (r = –0.43, p < 0.01; Carl *et al.*, 2004). This inverse relationship suggests that societies with currently high power distance prefer a more equitable distribution of power (ibid.). Managers may be able to apply this to the organizational level, taking care to develop a more equitable distribution of power. However proper support, guidance and training must be provided in these situations, as prior unequal power distribution may mean that employees lack the knowledge and skills necessary to assume new responsibilities successfully. If the equitable distribution of power is indeed a goal, investments in human resources must be made, and the development of a supportive organizational culture that both incorporates and rewards the decrease in power distance is crucial. This focus on culture change at the organizational level is particularly important, as organizational structure would become less bureaucratic and members would increasingly rely on shared values and norms to guide behavior. Ethical conflicts will likely emerge when organizations from societies with differing levels of power distance work together, as the emphasis on accountability and transparency may be lower in societies with high levels of power distance. As for effective leadership behaviors that will likely be perceived as responsible in societies that value power distance, self-protective and humane-oriented leadership behaviors are widely accepted and would likely be considered responsible, while charismatic and participative leadership may be viewed negatively.

Conclusion
We have covered much ground in this chapter, but, as the discussion of societal cultural influences is extremely complex, we chose to examine each cultural dimension separately. The reality of the situation, of course, is that

there are many interrelationships among the dimensions themselves that will have an impact on perceptions of corporate responsibility, governance and responsible leadership. With this chapter, we intend to encourage the development of future cross-cultural ethical research. We hope to see future empirical work to test the many linkages we have suggested between societal dimensions and perceptions of corporate responsibility, governance and responsible leadership across cultures. We encourage further theoretical and empirical work examining combinations of cultural dimensions in tandem to understand better the complexity and reality of cross-cultural management.

Notes
1. GLOBE analyses examined the relationships between dimensions of societal culture and leadership. In this chapter we examine how both values and practices at the societal level influence perceptions of leadership. It should be noted, however, that on the whole societal values were more predictive of leadership than societal practices (Dorfman *et al.*, 2004)·
2. The statistical analyses for the GLOBE utilized hierarchical linear modeling (HLMs).

References
Ashkanasy, N., V. Gupta, M.S. Mayfield and E. Trevor-Roberts (2004), 'Future orientation', in Robert J. House, Paul J. Hanges, Mansour Javidan, Peter W. Dorfman and Vipin Gupta (eds), *Culture, Leadership and Organizations: The GLOBE Study of 62 Societies*, Thousand Oaks, CA: Sage, pp. 282–342.

Bandura, A. (1997), *Self-Efficacy: The Exercise of Control*, New York: W.H. Freeman.

Blodgett, J.G., L. Lu, G.M. Rose and S.J. Vitell (2001), 'Ethical sensitivity to stakeholder interests: a cross-cultural comparison', *Journal of the Academy of Marketing Science*, **29**(2), 190–202.

Carl, D., V. Gupta and M. Javidan (2004), 'Power distance', in Robert J. House, Paul J. Hanges, Mansour Javidan, Peter W. Dorfman and Vipin Gupta (eds), *Culture, Leadership and Organizations: The GLOBE Study of 62 Societies*, Thousand Oaks, CA: Sage, pp. 513–63.

Carroll, A.B. (1979), 'A three-dimensional conceptual model of corporate performance', *Academy of Management Review*, **4**(4), 497–505.

Chang, K. and C.G. Ding (1995), 'The influence of culture on industrial buying selection criteria in Taiwan and mainland China', *Industrial Marketing Management*, **24**, 277–84.

Choate, P. and J. Linger (1988), 'Tailored trade: dealing with the world as it is', *Harvard Business Review*, **66**(1), 87–8.

Christie, P.M.J., I.G. Kwon, P.A. Stoeberl and R. Baumhart (2003), 'A cross-cultural comparison of ethical attitudes of business managers: India, Korea and the United States', *Journal of Business Ethics*, **46**(3), 263–87.

Clarkson, M.B.E. (1995), 'A stakeholder framework for analyzing and evaluating corporate social performance', *Academy of Management Review*, **20**(1), 92–117.

Cyert, R.M. and J.G. March (1963), *A Behavioral Theory of the Firm*, Englewood Cliffs, NJ: Prentice-Hall.

Den Hartog, D.N. (2004), 'Assertiveness', in Robert J. House, Paul J. Hanges, Mansour Javidan, Peter W. Dorfman and Vipin Gupta (eds), *Culture, Leadership and Organizations: The GLOBE Study of 62 Societies*, Thousand Oaks, CA: Sage, pp. 395–436.

Donaldson, T. and T.W. Dunfee (1994), 'Toward a unified conception of business ethics: integrative social contracts theory', *Academy of Management Review*, **19**(2), 252–84.

Donaldson, T. and T.W. Dunfee (1999), 'When ethics travel: the promise and peril of global business ethics', *California Management Review*, **41**(4), 45–63.

Dorfman, P.W., P.J. Hanges and F.C. Brodbeck (2004), 'Leadership and cultural variation: the identification of culturally endorsed leadership profiles', in Robert J. House, Paul J. Hanges, Mansour Javidan, Peter W. Dorfman and Vipin Gupta (eds), *Culture, Leadership and Organizations: The GLOBE Study of 62 Societies*, Thousand Oaks, CA: Sage, pp. 669–720.

Ehrlich, H.J. (2002), *The Wiley Book of Business Quotations*, New York: John Wiley.

Emrich, C.G., F.L. Denmark and D.N. Den Hartog (2004), 'Cross-cultural differences in gender egalitarianism', in Robert J. House, Paul J. Hanges, Mansour Javidan, Peter W. Dorfman and Vipin Gupta (eds), *Culture, Leadership and Organizations: The GLOBE Study of 62 Societies*, Thousand Oaks, CA: Sage, pp. 343–94.

Gelfand, M.J., D.P.S. Bhawuk, L.H. Nishii and D.J. Bechtold (2004), 'Individualism and collectivism', in Robert J. House, Paul J. Hanges, Mansour Javidan, Peter W. Dorfman and Vipin Gupta (eds), *Culture, Leadership and Organizations: The GLOBE Study of 62 Societies*, Thousand Oaks, CA: Sage, pp. 437–512.

Gregersen, H.B., A.J. Morrison and J.S. Black (1998), 'Developing leaders for the global frontier', *Sloan Management Review*, **40**(1), 21–32.

Hofstede, G. (1980), *Culture's Consequences*, Beverly Hills, CA: Sage.

Hofstede, G. (1998), 'Cultural constraints in management theories', in R.P. Vecchio (ed.), *Leadership: Understanding the Dynamics of Power and Influence in Organizations*, Notre Dame, IN: University of Notre Dame Press, pp. 465–83.

Hofstede, G. (2001), *Culture's Consequences: Comparing Values, Behaviors, Institutions and Organizations across Nations*, Thousand Oaks, CA: Sage.

Hofstede, G. and M.H. Bond (1988), 'The Confucius connection: from cultural roots to economic growth', *Organizational Dynamics*, **16**(4), 4–21.

House, R.J. and M. Javidan (2004), 'Overview of GLOBE', in Robert J. House, Paul J. Hanges, Mansour Javidan, Peter W. Dorfman and Vipin Gupta (eds), *Culture, Leadership and Organizations: The GLOBE Study of 62 Societies*, Thousand Oaks, CA: Sage, pp. 9–28.

House, R.J., P.J. Hanges, M. Javidan, P.W. Dorfman and V. Gupta (eds) (2004), *Culture, Leadership and Organizations: The GLOBE Study of 62 Societies*, Thousand Oaks, CA: Sage.

Jackson, K.T. (1997), 'Globalizing corporate ethics programs: perils and prospects', *Journal of Business Ethics*, **16**, 1227–35.

Javidan, M. (2004), 'Performance orientation', in Robert J. House, Paul J. Hanges, Mansour Javidan *et al.* (eds), *Culture, Leadership and Organizations: The GLOBE Study of 62 Societies*, Thousand Oaks, CA: Sage, pp. 239–81.

Kabasakal, H. and M. Bodur (2004), 'Humane orientation in societies, organizations, and leader attributes', in Robert J. House, Paul J. Hanges, Mansour Javidan *et al.* (eds), *Culture, Leadership, and Organizations: The GLOBE Study of 62 Societies*, Thousand Oaks, CA: Sage, pp. 564–601.

Klein, K.J. and S.W.J. Kozlowski (2000), *Multilevel Theory, Research and Methods in Organizations*, San Francisco, CA: Jossey-Bass.

Kluckholn, F.R. and F.L. Strodtbeck (1961), *Variation in Value Orientations*, Evanston, IL: Row, Peterson.

Maignan, I. and O.C. Ferrell (2003), 'Nature of corporate responsibilities: perspectives from American, German and French consumers', *Journal of Business Research*, **56**, 55–67.

Markus, H. and S. Kitayama (1991), 'Culture and self: implications for cognition, emotion and motivation', *Psychological Review*, **98**, 224–53.

McClelland, D.C. (1961), *The Achieving Society*, Princeton, NJ: Van Nostrand.

McClelland, D.C. (1975), *Power: The Inner Experience*, New York: Free Press.

McClelland, D.C. (1985), *Human Motivation*, Glenview, IL: Scott, Foresman.

McFarland, L.J., S. Senen and J.R. Childress (1993), *Twenty-First Century Leadership*, New York: Leadership Press.

Modic, S.J. (1987), 'Forget ethics – and succeed?', *Industry Week*, **235**(2), 17–18.

Mulder, M. (1971), 'Power equalization through participation', *Administrative Science Quarterly*, **16**, 31–8.

Mulder, M. (1977), *The Daily Power Game*, Leyden, The Netherlands: Martinus Nijhoff.

Principles of Governance (2001), retrieved from the Singapore Government website, http://www1.moe.edu.sg/ne/About_NE/Governance/governance&-95;principles.htm.

Putnam, R.D. (1993), *Making Democracy Work*, Princeton, NJ: Princeton University Press.

Russ-Eft, D. and T. Hatcher (2003), 'The issue of international values and beliefs: the debate for a global HRD code of ethics', *Advances in Developing Human Resources*, **5**(3), 296–307.

Schwartz, S.H. (1994), 'Beyond individualism and collectivism: new cultural dimensions of values', in U. Kim, H.C. Triandis, C. Kagitcibasi, S.C. Choi and G. Yoon (eds), *Individualism and Collectivism: Theory, Method and Applications*, Newbury Park, CA: Sage, pp. 85–122.

Seijts, G.H. (1998), 'The importance of future time perspective in theories of work motivation', *The Journal of Psychology*, **132**, 154–68.

Stajkovic, A.D. and F. Luthans (1997), 'Business ethics across cultures: a social cognitive model', *Journal of World Business*, **32**(1), 17–34.

Sully de Luque, M. and M. Javidan (2004), 'Uncertainty avoidance', in Robert J. House, Paul J. Hanges, Mansour Javidan *et al.* (eds), *Culture, Leadership and Organizations: The GLOBE Study of 62 Societies*, Thousand Oaks, CA: Sage, pp. 602–54.

Triandis, H.C. (1989), 'The self and social behavior in differing cultural contexts', *Psychological Review*, **96**, 506–20.

Triandis, H.C. (1995), *Individualism and Collectivism*, Boulder, CO: Westview.

Vitell, S. and T.A. Festervand (1987), 'Business ethics: conflicts, practices and beliefs of industrial executives', *Journal of Business Ethics*, **6**, 111–22.

Weber, M. (1930), *The Protestant Ethic and the Spirit of Capitalism*, trans T. Parsons, New York: Scribner (original work published 1904).

Weber, M. (1998), *The Protestant Ethic and the Spirit of Capitalism*, 2nd edn, Los Angeles, CA: Roxbury (original work published 1904).

19 Responsible leadership and governance in global business: the role of business education

Ernest J. Scalberg

Introduction

Both the literature on global leadership and the contributors to this book underscore the growing importance of preparing responsible leaders for an increasingly global business environment. As the earlier chapters in this book will attest, there has long been attention paid in terms of theory and research, especially in the United States, as to what constitutes good leadership and to the approaches that can be employed to select and develop good leaders. In the last several decades, in recognition that a burgeoning amount of the world's commerce crosses national borders, growing attention has been paid in research and writing to the challenges presented to managers and leaders by global versus domestic business.

More recently, the research and writing on leadership is beginning to focus on 'responsible' global leaders. The increased attention is due to the broadening awareness of the need for leaders to be concerned about the social and environmental impact of their businesses as well as the highly visible cases of irresponsible leadership exercised by the executive teams of some major multinational corporations. As the spotlight of attention has focused on responsible leadership, business schools have shared some of the blame for the recent transgressions that have occurred in the business environment as well as shouldering some of the expectations for promoting positive change.

The contention in this chapter is that, although some business schools and select business postgraduate programs have been cognizant of the issues regarding responsible global leadership and have thus assumed the challenge of providing appropriate education, most have not fulfilled their potential to do so. Therefore the goals of this chapter will be (1), to review briefly the research and literature that defines responsible global leadership; (2) to identify some promising models that business schools might use to develop leaders; (3) to describe and critique the curriculum, programs and courses that are currently used in business schools; and (4) to propose a framework and delivery options that will enable business schools to contribute more significantly to the development of responsible global leaders and managers.

Models of responsible global leadership

In order to provide an education for responsible business leaders it is first necessary to have a grasp of what constitutes a responsible global leader. There are a variety of models that have been proposed in the literature that provide a framework for characterizing global leadership. Among those authors that provide comprehensive frameworks are Bird and Osland (2004), Black *et al.* (1999), Marquardt and Berger (2000), McCall and Hollenbeck (2002) and McCauley *et al.* (1998).

What becomes apparent in even a cursory review of the literature is that the capabilities that contribute to effective global leadership are developed throughout one's life and career. Van Velsor *et al.* (1998, p. 5) conclude that leadership capabilities, without doubt, can be attributed in part to genetics and childhood development as well as adult experience. McCall and Hollenbeck (2002, p. 50) also note that the background attributes developed prior to global job assignments, such as 'being open to experience; flexibility; being comfortable with moving; being open to other cultures; an honest, direct style; interest in other people; and eagerness to learn languages', play an important role in the development of global leaders.

The literature provides a solid foundation for the concept of the evolving stages of leadership. Not only does a leader's set of capabilities grow and evolve from early to late in life but there are also distinct stages of evolution that occur on the job. For example, Black *et al.* (1999, p. 214) describe the development of leadership skills during the early, middle and late stages of one's career. Bird and Osland (2004, pp. 58–9) distinguish five stages of global leader evolution that range from novice to expert. According to Bird and Osland, a leader achieves mastery, or the expert stage, through learning from experience, gaining more complex and sophisticated insights, and working to improve performance. McCall and Hollenbeck (2002, pp. 107–27) identify the evolution experienced by global leaders that is shaped by foundation assignments (such as early work experiences or the first managerial assignment), by major line assignments, by shorter-term experiences (such as consulting roles, rotational assignments or educational programs) and lastly by perspective-changing experiences such as career shifts that tend to occur during latter phases of career development.

It is apparent that much of the learning by and maturation of global leaders occurs during the formative years of their lives. Of equal importance is the development that occurs on the job, long after a traditional business education has been completed. Van Velsor *et al.* (1998, p. 17), along with most authors who write on leadership development, assume that individuals and teams can expand their capabilities as leaders throughout their careers. However not every human attribute, such as IQ or general personality, can be changed by education or development activities.

Which stages in the evolution of leadership development should be the focal point for business schools? Some business schools play a role in pre-college leadership development. For example, Shinn (2003, p. 35) reports that the business school at Virginia Tech is involved in a community program where their undergraduate students teach leadership to high school students (also providing an opportunity for the undergraduate business students to practice their own leadership skills). It can be argued with some validity that business schools have a lifelong impact on leadership development because their faculties conduct much of the research and produce many of the books and articles published on leadership topics. Use of this research by parents, teachers, managers and trainers is an indirect way that business schools develop leaders.

Even though it may be argued that business schools can affect leadership development throughout a leader's life and career cycle, this chapter will focus on the capacities that can be addressed through traditional undergraduate and graduate degree and executive training programs provided by business schools. One of the important answers to obtain from existing research and writing, then, is which leadership capacities can be and should be addressed by business schools.

Since business schools cannot directly influence traits that are innate or that develop before the beginning of the college experience, it is important to identify the leadership capabilities or competencies that can be learned during the college experience. Bird and Osland (2004, p. 58) report that both university researchers and corporate HR professionals have developed leadership models that propose from as few as a dozen or so competencies to as many as 250 different competencies that might contribute to effective global leadership. Bird and Osland lump the various terms used to define leadership characteristics, such as traits, attitudes, skills and abilities, under the term 'global competencies'. Because of the huge number of competencies that have been identified, as well as the overlap of concepts and terms from the many different aggregations that have emerged from research and practice, many of the leadership models cluster leadership competencies under a smaller number of more conceptually manageable 'categories'.

Using a survey of 130 senior line and human resource executives, Black *et al.* (1999, p. xiii) conclude that there is a foundation of fundamental capabilities that every leader must possess, but many of the attributes that will lead to success in global managerial roles will depend on the specific assignment and the context for it. Similarly McCall and Hollenbeck (2002, pp. 11–12) observe, following their interviews with 101 'exemplary global executives', that not only are all global executives not the same, but their jobs are not the same and their development needs are not the same. These findings suggest that business school educational programs should assess the backgrounds of their students and the types of global leadership roles they desire to pursue before enrolling them in a pre-established educational program or set of activities.

Researchers provide various descriptions of the fundamental competencies necessary for effective global leadership. For example, Van Velsor *et al.* (1998, p. 17), identify the following six capacities: self-awareness, self-confidence, ability to take a broad systemic view, ability to work effectively in social systems, ability to think creatively and ability to learn from experience. Dalton (1998, p. 386), after synthesizing the work of numerous researchers, identifies four basic capacities needed by global leaders, as follows: high level of cognitive complexity, excellent interpersonal skills, ability to learn from experience, and advanced moral reasoning.

Several of Dalton's categories overlap with those of Van Velsor *et al.* but the fact that not all do is fairly representative of the literature. For example, among the eight studies reviewed for this chapter that present comprehensive frameworks for describing global leaders, only eight competencies were listed in common by three or more of the studies out of more than 70 competencies identified. Another three competencies were common to two of the eight studies. No single competency was listed as important by more than half of the studies. The competencies that are common to three or more studies reviewed here are the following:

1. core business knowledge (Dalton, 1998; Dalton *et al.* 2002)/international business knowledge (Dalton *et al.*, 2002)/ value added technical skills (McCall and Hollenbeck, 2002)/foundation of global knowledge (Bird and Osland, 2004);
2. global mind-set (Bird and Osland, 2004; Marquardt and Berger, 2000; McCall and Hollenbeck, 2002);
3. cultural interest and sensitivity (Bird and Osland, 2004; Dalton, 1998; McCall and Hollenbeck, 2002;)/ cultural adaptability (Dalton *et al.*, 2002);
4. honesty and integrity (Bird and Osland, 2004; McCall and Hollenbeck, 2002)/ advanced moral reasoning (Dalton, 1998)/concern for ethics (Bird and Osland, 2004; Dalton *et al.*, 2002; Marquardt and Berger, 2000)/ character (Black *et al.*, 1999);
5. ability to think creatively (Guthrie and Kelly-Radford, 1998; Van Velsor *et al.*, 1998)/ ability to play the role of innovator (Dalton *et al.*, 2002; Marquardt and Berger, 2000);

6. ability to take a broad systemic view (Marquardt and Berger, 2000; McDonald-Mann, 1998; Van Velsor *et al.*, 1998);
7. ability to work effectively in social systems (McDonald-Mann, 1998; Van Velsor *et al.*, 1998)/interpersonal skills (Bird and Osland, 2004; Dalton, 1998);
8. empowerment of others (McDonald-Mann, 1998)/brings out the best in people (Dalton, 1998)/ability to manage people (Dalton *et al.*, 2002)/ teacher, coach, mentor and model learner (Marquardt and Berger, 2000).

The competencies that are common to two of the eight studies are the following:

1. cognitive complexity (Bird and Osland, 2004; Dalton, 1998),
2. self-awareness (Bird and Osland, 2004; Van Velsor *et al.*, 1998),
3. ability to learn from experience (Dalton, 1998; Van Velsor *et al.*, 1998).

Of the above competencies, all would be deemed desirable for most domestic leaders and managers. Only the first two, global business knowledge and global mind-set, will be uniformly needed by global business leaders. Nevertheless the literature that explores global leadership uniformly indicates that the circumstances of global leadership roles are significantly more complex than domestic ones. Bird and Osland (2004, p. 58) list seven reasons why the global leader's job is more challenging than the jobs of their domestic counterparts. These special challenges range from the continuing need for cross-cultural understanding and communication abilities, to the greater need for broad knowledge that spans functions and nations, to the more challenging ethical dilemmas relating to globalization. They conclude that, 'Put simply, the transition from purely domestic to global is a quantum leap.'

Another concept that is relatively rarely mentioned in the leadership literature is corporate social responsibility. Marquardt and Berger (2000) place significant importance on this competency through two of their key global leader attributes labeled 'servant and steward' and 'spirituality and concern for ethics'. Four of the 12 global leaders profiled in his book emphasize the importance of ethics and corporate social and environmental responsibility. Marquardt and Berger (2000) and Dalton *et al.* (2002) both refer to the Caux Roundtable code of international business ethics as the ethical framework for responsible global executives. The seven Caux principles include specific reference to corporate social and environmental responsibilities.

Although unanimous agreement on the competencies of responsible global leaders does not emerge from the literature, the studies available provide a rich foundation for university education and training programs. Since the literature points out that every person's developmental needs are somewhat different, one can conclude that it should be up to each educational program to draw from the excellent educational frameworks that exist, and then to match the desired competencies with the level of development of its students and the international careers to which they aspire.

The focus of this chapter will now turn to the literature that describes the ways in which responsible global leaders can be developed, in order to identify approaches that are congruent with the leadership frameworks that have been described up to this point in the chapter.

Developing responsible global leaders

Most of the literature on leadership development assumes that the process of learning to be a leader is on-going. For example, Van Velsor *et al.* (1998, p. 25) state that 'Leaders learn as they gain experience over time. It is facilitated by interventions woven into experiences and connected in meaningful ways.' Since the literature further underscores the point that some of the most fruitful learning environments will occur on the job, one can conclude that business schools will be an appropriate alternative for some of a leader's current learning and development, but a less effective option for other types that might best be learned on the job.

There are excellent resources available in the literature and in practice that suggest various career stages and learning venues for developing leaders. For example, the Center for Creative Leadership in Greensboro, North Carolina has conducted extensive research on leadership, and has designed and delivered global leadership training programs. The Center has published a variety of materials that can be useful in discerning appropriate roles for business schools to play in the development of global leaders (see, for example, Dalton *et al.* 2002; McCauley *et al.* 1998).

Dalton (1998) provides a particularly useful model as a departure for business schools. Dalton (1998, p. 379) cautions that her model is based upon cultural assumptions typical of those found in the United States, such as the following: 'that adults can learn; that individuals can and should take responsibility for their own destiny; that performance rather than age, family, connections, or education is the key to advancement; and that career success is central to identity'. Her caution is an important consideration for business schools where many of the students in educational and training programs are from outside the United States. Also the assumptions which underscore Dalton's model or other models like it will be used to produce graduates for assignments in countries where these cultural assumptions are not the norm.

The model that Dalton (1998, pp. 390–95) describes is heavily intertwined with job assignments. She identifies three elements that should be incorporated when developing global leaders. First, high potential global leaders should be identified early in their careers. Second, they should be provided with a set of developmental goals. Lastly, they should be assessed on their progress towards meeting the goals, and then the goals should be reset to continue the development process.

Examples of high potential global leaders according to Dalton include those who like travel, novelty and international work; those who speak multiple languages; and those who have worked or lived in other cultures or worked with foreign cultures. These attributes can be easily identified in the business school admission process, whether at the undergraduate, graduate or executive training level. Many of these attributes, such as travel and language training, may also be gained during the student's educational experience.

Clear developmental goals should be assigned in coordination with any activities undertaken. Early developmental assignments may include opportunities to host foreign guests, to be exposed to cultural differences (including those within one's own country) and to broaden one's global horizons in general. Then goal achievement (including identification of strengths and weaknesses) should be assessed after the completion of the assignment. Dalton cautions that the kind of intensive 360 degree feedback program typically provided at the Center for Creative Leadership, although successful with a large number of US corporate executives, might not be the most appropriate approach to assess and support the development process across all cultures. A thorough discussion of the Feedback-Intensive Model may be found in Chappelow (1998, pp. 29–65) and Guthrie and Kelly-Radford (1998, pp. 66–105).

The second element of the development process is the provision of a variety of challenging assignments. Examples of assignments include business and long-distance multi-country projects, working as a member of a cross-cultural team, an expatriate assignment, managing a multi-country project, and responsibility for a global project.

The third element is integrating the assessment process and the goal assignment process as part of an ever-increasing scope of responsibility. Each assignment should be new and challenging while building on the learning from the previous assignments.

In reviewing the long lists of leadership competencies such as those identified in the previous section of this chapter, Dalton concludes that there are two competencies that differentiate domestic and global assignments.

The first difference is the ability and willingness to learn across cultures. To develop leaders for global responsibilities requires that they understand

- How learning from experience occurs (a general principle)
- How the principle is put into operation within their own culture (a specific tactic)
- How it is operationalized in each of the cultures in which they work (learning how to learn globally). (Dalton et al., 2002, p. 399)

The second qualitatively different competency for global leaders is the development of moral reasoning. Dalton argues that the most difficult tasks encountered in global assignments are the moral and ethical dilemmas which inevitably arise. Concerns about the forces of globalization, the economic inequities and the impact of a business on scarce resources are piled on top of the differences in attitudes, behaviors and expectations. To prepare for these responsibilities, leaders need to be provided with assignments that address the skill of complex moral reasoning. Dalton (1998, p. 401) identifies three kinds of assignments in addition to the broader learning activities that will aid in developing a moral/ethical compass: (1) serving on a cross-cultural task force to design a company-specific business ethical code, (2) taking the code to corporate operations abroad to test the precepts and modify them according to the feedback received, and (3) serving as a member of a multinational business council that addresses and resolves moral and ethical issues.

Black *et al.* (1999, p. xiv) provide additional educational methodology based upon the reports of 130 senior line and human resource executives. Their sample of executives described the experiences that most helped them develop into capable global leaders. These four development options were labeled by the authors as the four Ts: travel, teams, training and transfers. Of these development options, 80 per cent of the executives sampled indicated that living and working in a foreign country was the single most influential cross-cultural learning experience of their lives. However the authors conclude that taking advantage of all four options during the course of one's career is the most effective approach to acquire the complete set of global leadership competencies.

McDonald-Mann (1998, pp. 113–17) identifies five training methods typically used in seminars and workshops: lecture, case study, role play, behavioral role modeling and simulation. These methodologies are arrayed in order of the degree of interactivity between the trainer and the students, from least (lecture) to most (simulation). She further provides examples of the types of skills that may be learned through each method. For example, the case study method can be effective in developing complex skills such as the ability to see alternative solutions, question assumptions, think analytically and detect and solve problems. Of particular importance to this chapter is that these methodologies are widely and frequently used in business school courses and training seminars.

As was concluded in a review of the frameworks for describing global leadership in the first section of this chapter, the literature and research on developing global leaders provides excellent conceptual models and training tools that have been successfully employed in corporations and training centers. The focus of this chapter will now turn to the business school environment to survey the extent to which the knowledge, skills and abilities needed by responsible global leaders are being provided through business education programs.

Contributions of business schools to responsible leadership

Over the last several decades there has been increasing attention paid in business schools to providing educational activities that help prepare graduates for international business, to assume leadership roles and to be committed to responsible social and environmental stewardship. It is only recently, however, that business schools have begun to integrate these three disciplines into programs and curricula that show promise in satisfying the world's growing need for responsible global leaders.

Most business schools now prepare students to understand better the forces of international competition and how to cope with it. A much smaller number of schools provide programs with a comprehensive curriculum to prepare graduates for international careers. A representative example is the current state of business education in the United States. Thanks to pressure in the late 1980s from both the corporate sector and educational accrediting agencies, nearly every business school has been forced to 'internationalize' their curricula and out of class activities to address better the growing challenge of global competition. Yet only a few schools have gone beyond requiring a course in international business or assigning one chapter at the end of the textbook for each core course. The schools that are fully committed to graduating students who can be successful in international business have elected to launch programs where cohorts of students are provided with an international business curriculum with multiple language and overseas experience requirements. Only a handful of schools are principally devoted to preparing true international business professionals. This observation is underscored by the *Financial Times* ranking of the top 100 international MBA programs, where only one business school in the entire US sample (the Monterey Institute of International Studies) required every student to have proficiency in more than one language (*Financial Times*, 2004).

Similarly there has been growing attention paid to the topic of leadership education in business schools. For example, *BizEd*, the magazine produced for business school leaders and stakeholders by AACSB International, published three feature articles on the topic over the course of one year, from 2002 to 2003 (Bisoux, 2002; Lorange, 2003; Shinn, 2003). The article by Bisoux (2002, p. 26) stems from the perception that the concept of leadership in today's organization has changed, and as a result business schools have been called upon to reinvent their programs to educate students who are 'equipped to work in groups, make decisions collaboratively, and delegate power to others' rather than to command and control subordinates. A few schools have recently identified the topic of leadership as a separate discipline; they include the Jepson School for Leadership at the University of Richmond in the USA (offering an undergraduate liberal arts program) and the newly created Thierry Graduate School of Leadership in Belgium. They are examples of programs that emphasize ethics and 'the moral responsibility of leadership, to see leadership as a service to society' (ibid., p. 29). These schools represent a small number of programs that are in the vanguard of preparing college students for responsible leadership.

The article on leaders by Shinn (2003) describes in more detail the ways in which some exemplary schools are teaching business students about leadership and how to lead. According to Shinn (2003, p. 30), 'business educators are trying to break leadership skills into a variety of teachable chunks, some of them experiential and some of them observational'. Approaches include studying both good and bad role models in the literature and daily news; experiential approaches such as the mentor program at the University of Missouri-Kansas City where students learn from an executive in the work environment; developing self-awareness through classroom cases and simulations, or pushing one's limits such as at the Wharton School's day-long session at a Marine Corps training center; and field projects with companies such as the Multidisciplinary Actions Projects and the Global Business Partnership at the University of Michigan.

The third area of importance in the education of responsible global leaders is the area of social and environmental stewardship. To be a responsible leader in the international community requires an attention to business sustainability, or the interrelationship of social, environmental and financial factors (sometimes referred to as 'the triple bottom line'). Although there is a growing focus in business schools on a variety of educational activities related to the triple bottom line, only a few business schools offer comprehensive educational programs.

The growth and evolution of such programs has been monitored through a current study conducted by the Aspen Institute and the World Resources Institute (2003) on how well schools prepare MBA graduates for social and environmental stewardship. A review of the data from the report leads to the conclusion that only a handful of schools worldwide provide the breadth and depth of coursework and extracurricular activities that would even begin to prepare responsible global leaders.

The report, entitled *Beyond Grey Pinstripes 2003: Preparing MBAs for Social and Environmental Stewardship*, is the fourth in a series of publications that was begun in 1998. The authors report that, although more business schools are addressing social and environmental issues than in the past, and that some of these schools have been broadening their coverage across educational programs, there still remains very limited in-depth coverage in the core of the curriculum. The *Beyond Grey Pinstripes 2003* report includes extensive information on 100 business schools from around the world. The schools are respondents from a survey sample of nearly 600 schools that are accredited by either the Association to Advance Collegiate Schools of Business International (AACSB) or the European Foundation for Management Development (EFMD), or are listed among more than 100 other leading MBA programs around the globe. The responding schools represent 20 different countries.

Although one cannot definitively conclude that the non-responding schools were bereft of social/environmental responsibility programs, it is very likely that most of the non-respondents do not offer such programs. Some corroboration for this assumption is provided by several studies on business schools in China (for example, Bunch and Powers, 2003; Hulme, 2004). In reviewing the study results, only a handful of business schools emerge in all of China that offer a focus in ethics, or social or environmental responsibility. In most cases, the offering is only a single elective course rather than a core course or a designated program.

There are thousands of business schools worldwide that could and should be offering a comprehensive program in social and environmental stewardship, but a review of the available data suggests that, despite the current spotlight of attention focused on these issues, relatively few business schools are even attempting to prepare responsible global leaders.

To provide a perspective on the relatively small number of business schools who address responsibility issues in their programs and curricula, one can again use the business school environment in the United States as an example. The *Beyond Grey Pinstripes 2003* report included information on only 68 out of more than 750 MBA programs that exist in the United States. There are an additional 500 or so US Business Schools that offer education at the undergraduate level only, and who consequently do not offer the MBA degree. It may well be then that less than 10 per cent of business schools in the USA pay any significant attention to developing graduates with a perspective and skill set in social/environmental responsibility.

The number of schools that provide any significant educational experiences aimed specifically at developing global leaders reduces the figures even further. Of the 100 schools included in *Beyond Grey Pinstripes 2003* only 38 offer elective courses on responsible leadership and only 22 require such a course in the core curriculum. A significant number of these courses have a domestic rather than a global focus, and consequently do not prepare students adequately for the complex challenges of cross-border business.

Despite the findings that most of the world's business schools do not have comprehensive programs to prepare responsible global leaders, the results of this research have identified a small group of schools from different parts of the world that provide curricula and activities that may be considered exemplary. The programs at these schools will be explored in the next section of this chapter, where a framework for preparing responsible global leaders will also be provided.

A new educational framework
Peter Lorange (2003, p. 24), president of IMD International in Switzerland, observes that business schools have traditionally prepared leaders for a regional or national assignment. But now, because of the growth of international competition, it is necessary to prepare global leaders. It is still important, however, to consider and include the cultural differences from region to region that may lead to different or better solutions to business problems and opportunities. According to Lorange (ibid.), 'As management educators, our central challenge is to design a multifaceted, comprehensive approach to global business education, while encompassing the different cultural perspectives of our students. Business schools must offer executive programs that focus on the issues of globalization, without teaching any one prescribed approach to those issues.'

A useful source in planning business programs and curricula to address leadership approaches for cultural diversity is Deresky (1997, pp. 391–420). Her text provides a very useful description of leadership differences across cultures. Deresky advocates a contingency approach to manage across different cultures, so that the approach to successful leadership will depend upon the attributes of the person, the attributes of the job, the characteristics of the task and the characteristics of the company and the business environment. Bartlett and Ghoshal (2003) further elaborate the concept of educating for different leadership roles. They conclude from their research on transnational organizations that there is no single model for the global manager. Most global business leaders will play a more specialized leadership role which utilizes a subset of skills depending upon each individual's opportunities, strengths and interests. Bartlett and Ghoshal (2003, p. 101) contradict much of the literature, and therefore many of the management theory courses in business schools, by observing that there is no such thing as a 'universal' global manager.

As was discussed in the first section of this chapter, leadership capabilities grow and evolve throughout one's life and career, and successful leaders start with different capabilities and evolve differently. Also to be considered are the different roles which leaders will confront in their careers. Given the preceding caveats about the variation in leadership roles, the first consideration for business schools in preparation of global leaders is the identification of high potential candidates. Such candidates may include the following:

- students who have lived in different countries, enjoyed moving or enjoyed their international travel or work experiences;
- students who speak multiple languages or desire to learn foreign languages;
- students open to experience and who can learn and grow from it;
- students who are flexible, with an honest, direct style; and
- students interested in other people and who are open to other cultures.

Some of the attributes of high potential leaders, such as overseas experience or multiple language proficiency, may be identified during the business school admissions process, while other attributes such as flexibility or the ability to learn from experience may be better identified in classes or experiential assignments.

Once the level of leadership capability is assessed, it is necessary to identify the knowledge, skills and abilities that need to be developed, keeping in mind that development needs may vary from individual to individual. Once the attributes that require development are identified, it is possible to design a plan to achieve the development goals of the student and to provide feedback on progress.

An important consideration in the design and delivery of a business program for responsible global leaders is to determine which competencies are considered important to address. As was noted in the first section of this chapter, there are many frameworks and lists of competencies that may serve as a foundation for a curriculum or program. No matter which list of competencies is selected from the literature as a basis for developing global business leaders, among the foundation competencies that are widely accepted as a prerequisite for success as a global leader is core business knowledge with value added technical skills. Providing this kind of knowledge and skill development is one of the principal functions of business schools, and therefore is an important role that schools can play in developing leaders for the world's corporations, governments and organizations.

Most BBA and MBA programs require courses across a broad range of business functions, such as accounting, finance, economics, marketing and strategy. What is required for the development of responsible global leaders is that a significant amount of the course content in the core courses or in electives address international business, leadership and social and environmental responsibility issues so that a foundation of global knowledge can be built.

An example program that provides the types of educational options suggested above is the Certificate in Global Management in the MBA Program at the University of California, Berkeley. In addition to functional core and elective courses such as International Finance, Global Marketing Strategy, International Trade and Competition in High Technology, Global Management, Business Strategies for Emerging Markets, and Global Strategy and Multinational Enterprise, the program also has a regional focus. Toward this end, courses focusing on China and Asia are provided. Another course, International Business Development, is a student consulting project conducted in small teams on projects with overseas clients. Further requirements include an overseas experience such as semester study abroad, summer internship abroad, a one-year work experience abroad or an independent study with overseas field work. Lastly, there is a requirement for proficiency in a second language. The program provides participants with alternative choices so that an individual student can craft a program that is responsive to his or her personal development needs (refer to www. haas.berkeley.edu).

In addition to a solid foundation of international business skills, another set of competencies that business students should develop includes cultural interest and sensitivity, self-awareness and a global mind-set. The development of these competencies can be initiated through foundation courses that focus on cross-cultural management issues and skills. But, in addition, business schools should incorporate a variety of experiential assignments that address not only cross-cultural sensitivity but self-awareness. Shinn (2003, p. 33) describes some of the activities that are offered at business schools to address these needs. For example, Wharton School students may participate in out-of-class experiences such as treks in the Himalayas or Patagonia that develop skills in decision making under stress as well as exposure to different countries and cultures at the same time. The University of Missouri-Kansas City offers in-class simulations to practice leadership and also assigns a leadership autobiography to develop self-awareness.

Another useful resource on developing self-awareness is provided by Whetten and Cameron (2002). The authors provide diagnostic surveys, learning objectives, cases, practice exercises and experiential activities to enhance self-awareness. They also provide similar tools for other skills important to global leaders, such as managing personal stress, problem solving, coaching and counseling, motivating, managing conflict, empowering and delegating, and building effective teams.

In order to develop cultural sensitivity, Lorange (2003, p. 27) advocates creating a 'global meeting place' in the business program, where students can come to work with colleagues who have different approaches and experiences in order to hone their international business skills. This environment should be multicultural, so that the diversity of cultures, languages and experiences can be shared among the participants. The global meeting place that Lorange describes can be promoted in business schools through programs which increase the proportion of international students, incorporate exchange programs or structure partnerships with schools in other countries so that students can study and work on projects in a multicultural environment.

According to McCall and Hollenbeck (2002, p. 105) the development of a global mind-set (the ability to develop new perspectives and to hold multiple and competing perspectives) requires fluency in at least two languages and the experience of living and working in multiple cultures. Methods that business schools commonly use to forge a global mind-set include courses that incorporate foreign travel and company visits; courses that are offered on campus that are team taught by faculty from business schools in different countries using videoconference or on-line technologies; study or consulting projects that team students with students from schools in other countries; exchange programs with foreign business or language schools; overseas internships; and the development of multicultural environments on the home campus.

In addition to the preceding examples, business school curricula can benefit from the inclusion of specific country or area studies (ideally, courses taught on business topics pertinent to the country in the language of the country) and various out-of-class activities such as speakers, events and competitions that address culture and leadership.

Another set of competencies that are important in developing responsible global leaders are honesty and integrity, ethics and social and environmental stewardship. A good example of functional course offerings that address these issues is the MBA curriculum of the Asian Institute of Management in the Philippines. According to their website (www.aim.edu.ph), the curriculum is designed to produce socially responsible leaders who are experts in Asian culture and management styles. The content of each course offered in the curriculum reflects these underlying values.

Another exemplary curriculum, as noted in the *Beyond Grey Pinstripes 2003* database, is provided by the Schulich School of Business at York

University in Toronto, Canada. A course in their curriculum entitled 'Skills for Leadership and Governance' is described in part as follows:

> Every MBA student in the Schulich program is required, as a part of the core leadership and management skill development, to confront, explore, challenge and potentially change the perspectives and assumptions they bring to the course and their future careers. There is an explicit focus on the strengths and limitations of globalization; the relationship between business and environment; respect for the 'triple bottom line' stakeholder model; social and organizational diversity; the impact of power and politics on decision-making; and how business decisions need to be approached within a broad social/cultural framework, not just with a narrow business-oriented bottom line.

Another exemplary program described in the *Beyond Grey Pinstripes 2003* website is the Management Practice core at Boston College (Carroll School). For example, the course on managing in a changing world is described as 'strategic management of the enterprise in the broadest possible context, that of the social, political, ecological and ethical environments'. The Carroll School offers specializations in Business Ethics/ Social Responsibility and Leadership for Change. Also the business school at ITESM in Monterrey, Mexico, offers a Global Leadership Program that provides coursework in environmental management, social impact management and leadership skills that include a focus on ethics and organizational values, and stakeholder balance among shareholders, employees, the community, government and clients.

There are other competencies that should be considered for inclusion in business school programs for responsible global leadership, including the ability to think creatively and to lead innovation, the ability to take broad systemic views, the ability to learn from experience, the ability to empower others and the ability to work successfully in social systems. If these competencies are selected as goals for the curriculum or the individual student they should be further defined so that progress in reaching them can be measured.

One excellent resource for competency definitions is McDonald-Mann (1998, p. 110). The author identifies a list of leadership competencies including the ability to interact socially, creativity, critical evaluation and systemic thinking, and empowerment. She further breaks down the competencies into skills. So, for example, the skills for working in social systems include conflict management, negotiation, influencing, team building, active listening, ability to give feedback, communication and adaptation. The breakdown that McDonald-Mann provides can be used, first, to structure courses and activities that develop student competencies, and then to help measure outcomes from the courses and activities. The skills assessment, learning, analysis, practice and application framework provided by Whetten and Cameron (2002), described earlier is also a good resource for this purpose.

In the preceding section, a variety of development activities used by corporations to develop global leaders were identified, such as hosting foreign guests, being exposed to cultural differences in one's own country, becoming knowledgable about broad global problems and opportunities, and so on. Each of these has a counterpart in the business school environment. For example, students can help host or guide visiting foreign dignitaries or business executives when they visit the business school as guest speakers or project clients. Students can be assigned business projects that involve them with different cultures in the local community.

Black *et al.* (1999) also provide an excellent resource for developing leaders. They provide a framework (ibid., p. 215) that breaks down their 'Four Ts' (travel, teams, training and transfers) into career development stages (early, mid-career, late) and specifies the development goals for each stage. For example, early global training activities should provide perspective, awareness and functional skills, while late career training should incorporate senior executive skills, networking and action learning. Although the fourth T, transfers, is used in their framework to refer to transfer to a new work assignment or job location, business students can gain a similar development experience by conducting an internship or project in another country or taking courses or language instruction at a foreign business campus.

Although the curricula, programs and activities described in this section may address many common student needs, the selection of activities and their timing and sequencing will need to be adapted to some extent to meet the individual development needs of a specific student. It should be recognized that the development goals for a young undergraduate business student who has never traveled outside the country will be different from goals set for an experienced executive MBA student or a senior executive in a training program.

Once the development goals have been set for each student, it is possible to design a plan to achieve the goals that have been specified and to provide feedback on progress. Then new goals should be established and the development cycle begun again.

This section of the chapter has provided a framework and specific examples of ways in which business school programs can be structured to develop responsible global leaders. Although designing such programs and training and educating individuals for these roles is challenging and time-consuming, there are valuable resources available from existing practice to assist the educator and student alike. Nonetheless a diligent effort from both will be necessary to produce the array of responsible global leaders that the world's companies and organizations will require in the years ahead.

Conclusions

The goals of this chapter were (1) to gain a working definition of responsible global leadership from the literature; (2) to identify leadership development models that may be suitable for business schools; (3) to provide an overview of the curriculum, programs and courses related to global leadership that are currently used in business schools; and (4) to provide an approach for business schools to assist in the development of responsible global leaders and managers.

A review of the literature on the topic of this chapter suggests that an enormous amount has been written over the years about leadership. As the business world has become more international there has been an increasing focus on global leaders and how their roles are more influential and complicated than their domestic counterparts. Much more recently there has been significant attention paid to defining responsible or balanced leadership for global companies and organizations. The review of current practice undertaken here leads to the conclusion that most corporate training programs and business schools have not yet developed curricula and activities that will provide comprehensive preparation for such roles.

It has been argued in this chapter that some of the attributes of successful leaders are innate or shaped early in life. The preponderance of research suggests that future leaders continue to grow throughout their lives and careers in different ways and toward different ends. Although much of the growth and development of a leader occurs on the job, there is a substantial and important development role that can be played by business schools, from the traditional college years to late in an executive's career.

The preponderance of models and frameworks for developing global leaders has been spawned by corporations, and the training approaches currently in use are largely oriented toward job assignments. Nonetheless most of the concepts from the corporate world transfer well to the business school environment where job experience can be simulated or replicated in numerous ways.

One can simply conclude from the literature that the basic attributes of successful global leaders are a solid international management foundation, multiple language capability and significant cross-cultural experience. Further review suggests that these attributes may be necessary but are not sufficient to ensure success.

Exemplary education and training programs for preparing responsible global leaders exist now and the numbers of them will no doubt continue to grow. This chapter was structured to provide a foundation for that development, but, as the global business world changes and new technologies for business and for learning and education emerge, this foundation will soon prove unsatisfactory. It will be important for business schools to continue to evolve in front of or at least in parallel with the changes ahead. The future of global business is even more likely than the present to require responsible leadership.

References

Aspen Institute and World Resources Institute (2003), *Beyond Grey Pinstripes 2003: Preparing MBAs for Social and Environmental Stewardship*, October (http://beyondgreypinstripes. org).

Bartlett, C.A. and S. Ghoshal (2003), 'What is a global manager?', *Harvard Business Review*, **81**(8), 101–8.

Bird, A. and J.S. Osland (2004), 'Global competencies: an introduction', in H.W. Lane, M.L. Maznevski, M.E. Mendenhall and J. McNett (eds), *Handbook of Global Management: A Guide to Managing Complexity*, Oxford: Blackwell, pp. 57–80.

Bisoux, T. (2002), 'The mind of a leader', *BizEd* (September/October), 26–31.

Black, J. S., A.J. Morrison and H.B. Gregersen (1999), *Global Explorers: The Next Generation of Leaders*, New York and London: Routledge.

Bunch, R. and N. Powers (2003), 'The greening of China's b-schools', *BizEd* (May/June), 34–7.

Chappelow, C.T. (1998), '360-degree feedback', in C.D. McCauley, R.S. Moxley and E.V. Velsor (eds), *The Center for Creative Leadership Handbook of Leadership Development*, San Francisco: Jossey-Bass, pp. 29–65.

Dalton, M.A. (1998), 'Developing leaders for global roles', in C.D. McCauley, R.S. Moxley and E.V. Velsor (eds), *The Center for Creative Leadership Handbook of Leadership Development*, San Francisco: Jossey-Bass, pp. 379–402.

Dalton, M., C. Ernst, J. Deal and J. Leslie (2002), *Success for the New Global Manager: What You Need to Know to Work Across Distances, Countries, and Cultures*, San Francisco: Jossey-Bass.

Deresky, H. (1997), *International Management: Managing Across Borders and Cultures*, Reading, MA: Addison-Wesley.

Financial Times Ltd (2004), *Financial Times Ranking of the Top 100 Full-time Global MBA Programs 2004*, London: FT.com.

Guthrie, V.A. and L. Kelly-Radford (1998), 'Feedback-Intensive Programs', in C.D. McCauley, R.S. Moxley and E.V. Velsor (eds), *The Center for Creative Leadership Handbook of Leadership Development*, San Francisco: Jossey-Bass, pp. 66–105.

Hulme, V.A. (2004), 'The MBA boom', *The China Business Review* (January/February), 24–36.

Irland, R.D. and M.A. Hitt (1999), 'Achieving and maintaining strategic competitiveness in the 21st century: the role of strategic leadership', *Academy of Management Executive*, **13** (1), 43–57.

Lorange, P. (2003), 'Developing global leaders', *BizEd* (September/October), 24–7.

Marquardt, M.J. and N.O. Berger (2000), *Global Leaders for the 21st Century*, Albany, NY: State University of New York Press.

McCall Jr, M.W. and G.P. Hollenbeck (2002), *Developing Global Executives: The Lessons of Global Experience*, Boston, MA: Harvard Business School Press.

McCauley, C.D., R.S. Moxley and E. Van Velsor (eds) (1998), *The Center for Creative Leadership Handbook of Leadership Development*, San Francisco: Jossey-Bass.

McDonald-Mann, Dana G. (1998), 'Skill-based training', in C.D. McCauley, R.S. Moxley and E. Van Velsor (eds), *The Center for Creative Leadership Handbook of Leadership Development*, San Francisco: Jossey-Bass, pp. 106–26.

Shinn, S. (2003), 'The leader', *BizEd* (November/December), 30–35.

Van Velsor, E., C.D. McCauley and R.S. Moxley (1998), 'Our view of leadership development', in C.D. McCauley, R.S. Moxley and E.V. Velsor (eds), *The Center for Creative Leadership Handbook of Leadership Development*, San Francisco: Jossey-Bass, pp. 1–25.

Whetten, D.A. and K.S. Cameron (2002), *Developing Management Skills*, Upper Saddle River, NJ: Prentice-Hall.

Index

internal
    attributions 342–3
    governance mechanisms 244–6, 253,
        254
    information 344
    responsibility management 182–3
    social capital 29
    succession 120, 121, 124–5, 126
internalization 91
International Business Leaders Forum
    (IBLF) 315
International Corporate Governance
    Network (ICGN) 271
International Financial Law Review
    255
International Monetary Fund 272
interpersonal leadership theories 315,
    323–4
intrinsic motivational factors 92, 209
Intuition at Work (2003) 71
investments, return on 295
investor confidence 55, 56–7, 64–5
Iran 360
Iraq, US attack on (2003) 77
Iraqi Governing Council 77
Ireland 318, 370
Islamic world 112
International Organization for
    Standardization (ISO) 183
isolationism 9–10
Israel 100, 318
Italy 59, 66

Japan
    corporate governance 312, 313, 334,
        335, 336, 337, 338, 340, 341,
        348
    corporate ownership structure 343
    culture 314
    leadership theories 320
    medicines 172
    uncertainty avoidance 318, 319
Jepson School for Leadership,
    University of Richmond, US 389
job
    challenges 149–50
    descriptions 314
    involvement/enrichment 92
    satisfaction and performance 91–2
John Paul II 112

Johnson & Johnson 15, 30, 47–8, 59,
    62–3, 161
Jordan, corporate governance 321
*Judgment in Managerial Decision
    Making* (2002) 71
Judgments under Stress (2000) 71

Kant, Immanuel 165, 172, 173, 312,
    316, 317
keiretsu 310, 312, 313
Kennedy, George 128
Kinder, Lydenburg and Domini
    (KLD) 211–12, 213, 215
King, Martin Luther 168
knowledge production 280
Korea 336
KPMG Consulting 290–91

labor standards 25–6, 28–9, 181, 182,
    185–8, 191
Larsen, Ralph 47–8
Latin America 322
    see also Argentina; Brazil; Chile;
        Peru; Venezuela
Latin countries 310
Lauder, Jane 175
Lay, Kenneth 72–3
layoffs *see* redundancies
leadership 4–8
    altruism as a component of 141–2
    behaviour 314–17
    boards of directors 246–50
    characteristics 123–4, 311–12, 320
    choice of 151–2
    classifications 3–4
    competencies 382–5, 392–6
    and culture 354–5
    definitions of 5, 7, 160–61
    dilemmas 317
    effectiveness 324
    integrity as a component of 140
    qualities 196
    responsibilities of 312–14
    sociological approaches to 113–18
    theory 197–8, 322
    types 7–8
    see also business education;
        succession
leadership development 137–8
    altruism 150–54